WEYERHAEUSER ENVIRONMENTAL BOOKS

WILLIAM CRONON, EDITOR

Weyerhaeuser Environmental Books explore human relationships
with natural environments in all their variety and complexity.
They seek to cast new light on the ways that natural systems affect
human communities, the ways that people affect the environments of
which they are a part, and the ways that different cultural conceptions
of nature profoundly shape our sense of the world around us.
A complete list of the books in the series appears at the end of this book.

A Storied Wilderness

REWILDING THE APOSTLE ISLANDS

JAMES W. FELDMAN

Foreword by William Cronon

UNIVERSITY OF WASHINGTON PRESS Seattle & London

A Storied Wilderness is published with the assistance of a grant from the Weyerhaeuser Environmental Books Endowment, established by the Weyerhaeuser Company Foundation, members of the Weyerhaeuser family, and Janet and Jack Creighton.

UNIVERSITY OF WASHINGTON PRESS
PO Box 50096, Seattle, WA 98145, USA
www.washington.edu/uwpress

Printed and bound in the United States of America
Designed by Ashley Saleeba
Composed in Minion and Gotham

LIBRARY OF CONGRESS CATALOGING-IN-PUBLICATION DATA
Feldman, James W.
A storied wilderness : rewilding the Apostle Islands / James W. Feldman ;
foreword by William Cronon.
p. cm. — (Weyerhaeuser environmental books)
Includes bibliographical references and index.
ISBN 978-0-295-99292-1 (pbk. : alk. paper)
1. Restoration ecology—United States—History.
2. National parks and reserves—United States—History.
3. National parks and reserves—United States—Management.
4. Restoration ecology—Wisconsin—Apostle Islands National Lakeshore.
5. Apostle Islands National Lakeshore (Wis.)—Management.
6. Apostle Islands National Lakeshore (Wis.)—Environmental conditions.
I. Title.
QH541.15.R45F45 2011
333.73'15—dc22   2011010289

The paper used in this publication meets the minimum requirements of American National Standard for Information Sciences— Permanence of Paper for Printed Library Materials, ANSI Z39.48-1984. ∞

FOR SAM AND BEN

Contents

Foreword

IRREVOCABLE LESSONS OF VANISHING FIELDS

WILLIAM CRONON

ON DECEMBER 8, 2004, PRESIDENT GEORGE W. BUSH SIGNED congressional legislation creating the Gaylord Nelson Wilderness Area in the Apostle Islands National Lakeshore of Lake Superior. Named for the Wisconsin senator who is best known as the founder of Earth Day, the new wilderness area represented the fulfillment of a decades-old dream. Although Nelson had been responsible for setting aside the Apostles as a national lakeshore in 1970, their statutory designation as "wilderness" more than three decades later brought the islands the highest form of land protection available in the United States. In the words of the 1964 Wilderness Act, the Apostles were now to be recognized as places "where the earth and its community of life are untrammeled by man, where man himself is a visitor who does not remain." Like most of its midwestern counterparts, Wisconsin had precious little federal wilderness before 2004, making all the more remarkable this formal declaration that within the state's boundaries was (again quoting the 1964 Act) "an area of undeveloped Federal land retaining its primeval character and influence, without permanent improvements or human habitation . . . with the imprint of man's work substantially unnoticeable."

But there was something more remarkable still about the new Apostle Islands wilderness area. In 1930, the landscape architect Harlan Kelsey had visited the area at the invitation of local boosters to determine whether the islands might be suitable for designation as a national park. As he toured the islands looking for the pristine conditions that his National Park Service employers expected of units in their system, Kelsey saw the marks of human habitation and activity everywhere: dwellings, agricultural fields and pastures, fishing camps, abandoned quarries, and cutover forests scarred by decades of logging. He pulled no punches in his final report. "The hand of man," he wrote, "has mercilessly and in a measure irrevocably destroyed [the islands'] virgin beauty." Far from being a wilderness, the Apostle Islands simply did "not meet National Park Service standards." Reading his report, one gets the sense that he couldn't believe he had been asked to make such a pointless trip.

How could Kelsey's "irrevocably destroyed" islands of 1930, so self-evidently unworthy of national park status, become Gaylord Nelson's national lakeshore by 1970 and a congressionally designated wilderness area by 2004? That is the intriguing question that the environmental historian James Feldman explores in his important new book, *A Storied Wilderness: Rewilding the Apostle Islands*. Feldman brings to this subject a lifelong engagement with wilderness in general and with Lake Superior in particular. Having spent boyhood summers attending and serving as a youth counselor for a camp on the lake's southern shore, he returned as a seasonal ranger for the National Park Service in the 1990s, guiding visitors through one of the many nineteenth-century lighthouses that are now among the most popular tourist attractions in the Apostles. As he did so, he became ever more intrigued by the ways in which the modern tourist experience of wild nature in the islands related to the long history of human habitation still visible—if only one knew where to look. Feldman embarked on his research for this book just as discussions of wilderness designation for the park were reaching their climax, and the arguments he offers in *A Storied Wilderness* played a significant role in shaping the outcome of those discussions. Because his insights have implications far beyond the Apostle Islands, this book has much to offer to anyone who cares about parks and wilderness areas in the United States.

In the stories Feldman tells, we learn of the Ojibwe peoples who made their homes in the Apostles, hunting, trapping, fishing, and participating in far-flung trade networks centering on that place. The Ojibwe were eventually joined by French, British, and American missionaries and fur traders who congregated on the largest of the islands and created the town of La Pointe that for a time was among the most populous settlements on the Upper Great Lakes. As the fur trade declined, commercial fisheries took its place in the local economy, along with the small immigrant farms that began to appear on the islands and the nearby Wisconsin mainland. The popularity of Lake Superior brownstone in the late nineteenth century led to large shoreline quarries, where the heavy stone blocks could be loaded directly onto ships for delivery to urban construction companies. The same was true of white pine and other timber that was gradually logged from the islands in large industrial operations that produced the deforested conditions Harlan Kelsey observed in 1930. And amid all these other activities, tourist camps and cottages began to appear, adding a recreational element to the regional economy that would become increasingly important over time.

Each of these activities left its marks, though by the mid twentieth century the economic life of the islands had come to rely most heavily on tourism and the remaining fisheries. Quarrying had ended by 1900, and logging and farming were largely gone from all but Madeline Island by the end of World War II. Because north woods vegetation is quick to reclaim any land whose human caretakers stop clearing, the cutover forests and old pastures and orchards soon began to disappear beneath the brush and early successional trees of the returning forest. By the time Gaylord Nelson began promoting a national lakeshore for the islands in the 1960s, the "merciless" human imprints that had seemed so irrevocable to Harlan Kelsey in 1930 required a trained eye even to notice — and most of the people who recognized them no longer regarded them as ugly. Covered with moss and filled with greenery, the brownstone quarries now presented themselves as romantic ruins, far more charming than repellant. The birches that are typically among the first trees to reclaim cutover land in the north woods proved to be favorites for tourists, making them icons of wild nature even though their relative abundance was itself a marker of past human modifications of the forest. Nature was back, and so the islands turned out to meet National Park Service standards after all. Harlan Kelsey had proven to be a poor prophet.

This in itself would be a fascinating story, and Jim Feldman tells it with a winning grace and style, but it is the larger lessons he draws from the narrative that give this book its far-reaching implications. The Apostle Islands today are a Wisconsin jewel in the wilderness system of the United States, but they are also lands that have been inhabited and modified by generations of human beings.

To experience them as many tourists do as "pristine"— as the embodiment of what Kelsey called a "virgin beauty" untouched "by the hand of man"—is to miss the most instructive thing about them. The stark dichotomies we too frequently make between "nature" and "culture," between "wilderness" and "humanized" landscapes, are neither so obvious nor so permanent as we sometimes imagine. Furthermore, if we imagine that the transition from "natural" to "unnatural" is a one-way revolving door—that once an environment has been modified by humanity it loses all of the attributes we regard as natural—then we are likely not even to notice the ongoing interactions between humanity and the rest of nature that we ourselves must carefully navigate if we hope to live and sustain our human communities without ravaging the world around us. That places like the Apostle Islands can undergo what Feldman calls "rewilding," even after extensive human modification, should be taken as a tale of hope. Far from being solely an inherent property of the nonhuman environment, the naturalness we experience in a place equally reflects our own ability to recognize nature and the human choices we make about the parts of nature we use and protect.

One of my favorite places in the Apostles is Sand Island. Excluded from the Gaylord Nelson Wilderness Area for complicated jurisdictional reasons, which Jim Feldman explores in fascinating detail, it is among the best places I know for observing the complex entanglements of humanity with wild nature. Get off your boat at the National Park Service dock on the east side of the island, and if you know where to look you can find an obscure path heading westward through a thick young forest across wet marshy ground to a place deep in the interior, where the ground gradually rises, the soil becomes dryer, and the woods give way to an open field. The vegetation is grassier here, filled with weeds that bloom beautifully in the late summer. On the north side of the field, apple trees still do their unassisted best to bloom and produce fruit. You are, in fact, in an old orchard, its margins now ragged as shrubs and trees encroach on the cleared ground. Scanning the rest of the field, you'll see rusting farm machinery off to the southwest. Walk toward and beyond it, and you'll find the ruins of the house where the owners of this field once lived, along with the moss-covered bricks of the chimney that helped keep members of the Noring family warm so many decades ago.

Is the Noring Farm wilderness? It was omitted from the wilderness area in part so that active management and interpretation might occur at this location in ways that are legally forbidden in a statutory wilderness. That decision reflects the formal rules we use in law and administrative practice to guide the actions of government agencies tasked with enacting our collective values. From one point of view, it makes good sense to draw lines on a map so that this old farm and other human structures and landscapes on Sand Island can be treated differently from the rest of the Apostle Islands National Lakeshore. But as Jim Feldman demonstrates so persuasively, if one really wants to contemplate the meaning of wilderness in human history, there are few better places to observe the process of rewilding than this old field. Human beings have gathered and hunted and cleared and planted to make homes for themselves here for a very long time . . . yet nonhuman nature is abundantly present as well, and is quickly gaining ground in its efforts to reclaim and overwrite the human stories that are so eloquently visible in these old apple trees and fallen bricks and rusting machines and weedy fields. Over time, it will be harder and harder to see such things on the land—that is among the most important lessons they have for us—but thanks to Jim Feldman, their stories will remain legible on these pages in all their poignant ambiguity and beauty for a very long time to come. ❧

Acknowledgments

IN MY EARLY YEARS OF GRADUATE SCHOOL, AS I CAST ABOUT FOR a topic on which I suspected I would spend close to a decade (or, as it turns out, a little more), I knew that I wanted a place-based subject that met two requirements. It needed to be about a place to which I had a personal connection, and it had to connect to a current environmental issue. I found both in the Apostle Islands. I first went camping on Stockton Island in the early 1980s, and I've returned to northern Wisconsin almost every year since. After I spent the summer of 1999 working for Apostle Islands National Lakeshore, learning more about the islands' past and also about the upcoming wilderness suitability study, I knew that I had found my topic. And the more time that I spend in the Apostles, the more I love the place. I hope that my attachment to the islands and their environments comes through in the pages of this book.

I started keeping a list of people to thank for their help with this project a long time ago, as my debts mounted. Nevertheless, I am as sure that I will forget to thank someone as I am that this book would not have been completed without the assistance of the people mentioned here.

My co-advisors at the University of Wisconsin–Madison, Bill Cronon and Nancy Langston, were encouraging, challenging, and helpful with every step of this project. Nancy commented on drafts and proposals, wrote letters, and offered advice, and she served a fresh fish lunch at her cabin in Cornucopia. She provided the crucial perspective of an environmental historian working in the field of environmental studies—a perspective that has now become second nature to me. Bill has been as kind, generous, and helpful a mentor as anyone could ask for, and he continued to push me in his role as editor of the Weyerhaeuser Environmental Books Series at the University of Washington Press. Bill and Nan Fey let me stay in their Bayfield home whenever I needed it, making my many fruitful research trips possible. This goes far beyond the boundaries of what an advisor or an editor does for a student and well into the realm of what one friend does for another.

As this project gradually became a book, a new group of people provided new types of help. University of Washington Press acquiring editor Marianne Keddington-Lang offered constant support, advice, and reassurance. Every writer should have the chance to work with such a talented editor. Marianne also found two of the most helpful and generous readers one could ask for: Jay Turner read the complete manuscript twice, each time making comments that improved the final result significantly; and David Louter drew on his wealth of experience with the National Park Service to help me draw the most that I could out of this story. Julie Van Pelt also read the manuscript with an incredible eye for detail and style.

A number of others read drafts and offered sound advice. Will Barnett, Mike Rawson, Troy Reeves, Tom Robertson, Kendra Smith-Howard, and Chris Wells read drafts at different stages. Two people did the yeoman's work of reading the whole thing. David Bernstein read every page of the manuscript—sometimes multiple drafts—always with a fine eye for detail and for argument. His fresh eyes and insightful comments made this a far better book than it otherwise would have been. Bob Mackreth worked for many years as the park historian and cultural resources manager at Apostle Islands National Lakeshore, and he has a deeper knowledge of the history of the islands and their many stories than almost anyone else. He opened his archives, his knowledge of the islands' past, and even his house to me. He responded to countless emailed questions, not just with prompt answers but with enthusiasm and encouragement.

Other members of the AINL staff helped, too. Christy Baker took over from Bob Mackreth as cultural resource manager and continued to support my research. Superintendent Bob Krumenaker and Jim Nepstad, chief of planning and resource management, have been welcoming from the start, letting me sit in on numerous wilderness study meetings. Julie Van Stappen has provided answers to my questions about the park's ecosystems and resource management programs and access to numerous surveys and documents. Tam Hoffman, Neil Howk, and several others also helped along the way.

Other people gave tangible help by sharing their knowledge, expertise, and memories. Arne Alanen provided access to stacks of newspaper clippings about the Apostles, saving me hours of squinting at a microfilm reader. Bud Jordahl—a central figure in the designation of Apostle Islands National Lakeshore and in Wisconsin environmental politics—provided access to his files. Julian Nelson and Cliff and Harvey Hadland agreed to be interviewed so that I could hear firsthand their stories of working in the commercial fisheries and their memories of lifetimes spent in the islands. Mary Rice hosted me for a night on Sand Island and shared with me her love of a place that has been in her family for three generations. Senator Gaylord Nelson recounted his role in shepherding the national lakeshore proposal through Congress. Todd Anderson and his family invited me to see the islands from their catamaran—sailing might be the best of all ways to explore the Apostles. The History Department and the Office of Graduate Studies at University of Wisconsin Madison and the Faculty Development Office at University of Wisconsin Oshkosh provided funding. Joel Heiman made the maps for a discounted price and a couple of beers and Tony Pietsch painstakingly compiled the index.

There are many, many others who provided uncountable instances of support, advice, and encouragement. Over the years, I have collected a terrific group of colleagues, friends, and mentors from Utah State University, UW Madison, and UW Oshkosh, all of whom have left their mark on me and on this project.

The last spot in the acknowledgments is usually reserved for family, and for good reason. My parents, Susan and Scott Feldman, and my brother, Mark, have been unwavering in their support. And my wife, Chris, has been involved with the book since the beginning; we met during my first semester of graduate school, and I dedicated my dissertation to her. I would never have finished this book—or much else—without her help, support, and love. The writing of *A Storied Wilderness* spans two lifetimes: I began in the summer that my son Sam was born, and I finished just as Ben was born. I dedicate this book to them. ❧

A Storied Wilderness

Introduction

STORIES IN THE WILDERNESS

IN 2005, A PANEL OF EXPERTS GATHERED BY *NATIONAL GEOGRAPHIC* made a surprising pick as their choice for the most appealing national park in the United States: Apostle Islands National Lakeshore. Many people have never heard of the Apostle Islands, let alone traveled to far-northern Wisconsin to see them firsthand. "In good shape ecologically. Not over-visited," commented one expert. "No man-made lights visible," stated another. "Visitation to the Apostle Islands is limited to boats or other small watercrafts, keeping them in natural, pristine condition," added a third. "The aesthetic appeal of the land and water interaction is both dramatic and comforting." Apostle Islands National Lakeshore ranked far ahead of more well-known parks like Shenandoah, Yellowstone, and the Grand Canyon. These more famous parks confront dire threats from overuse, invasive species, and mismanagement. Fewer than two hundred thousand people visit the Apostle Islands each year, so the park does not face the crowds found elsewhere. This has helped maintain the park's appeal.[1]

The twenty-two islands off Wisconsin's Bayfield Peninsula are surrounded by the cold, blue waters of Lake Superior. Distinctive red sandstone cliffs jut from the lake at several points around the archipelago. Pounding waves have carved caverns and arches where the sandstone faces the open lake. Quiet

I.1 Aerial view of the Apostle Islands, looking southwest from the Rocky Island sandspit. In 2004, Congress designated 80 percent of Apostle Islands National Lakeshore as the Gaylord Nelson Wilderness. Photograph by William Cronon.

beaches line the shore in more protected areas. A rich forest mosaic covers the islands, including several patches of old growth — among the only remnant stands in the Great Lakes basin. Bob Krumenaker, the park's superintendent, explains that "some of the islands in this park are literally snapshots — very rare ones — of the original forests that once covered vast parts of this state and the larger Great Lakes region." The islands mark the border of two of North America's most important forest ecosystems: the boreal forest, which stretches down from Canada and is dominated by white spruce and balsam fir; and the hemlock/hardwood/pine forests that cover much of the central and eastern United States. With few deer to browse the understory, most of the island forests are dark, overgrown, and nearly impenetrable, distinguishing them from most other forested areas in the region. Lake Superior envelops cliff and forest alike, with its characteristically ferocious storms and magical sunsets.[2]

The island environments are whole and healthy, an ecological integrity that amplifies the islands' allure. The islands have relatively few invasive species and provide a home for several endangered and threatened ones. Nature writer Jeff Rennicke describes what he calls the "natural rhythm" of the islands. "It is a wildness found in . . . the rasp of storm waves on a beach, a skein of shorebirds moving low along the water, the slow groan of ice or the sparkle of northern lights. It is embroidered in bear tracks, in the rumor of wolves, and the ancient music of a bog." Few places in the Midwest evoke such language.[3]

The opportunity for solitude lies at the heart of the wilderness experience in the Apostles. Only the most intrepid sailors and kayakers venture to the outermost islands; only the most persistent bushwhackers penetrate the island interiors. As one writer explains, "the islands' inaccessibility and rugged nature, the fickle weather, the dense forests and bugs—in short, all the exigencies of a wilderness condition—render most of the Apostle Islands a sanctuary for solitude." Another visitor comments that the "Apostles are one of my favorite places on Earth. . . . You can still have an island almost to yourself for short periods of time."[4]

As is often the case in such places, the promise of solitude attracts visitors. They come by kayak, sailboat, or powerboat, exploring the caves and coves and picnicking on the shoreline. Sailors gather at Stockton Island for its sheltered harbor and beaches. Fishermen trolling for salmon and lake trout head to Rocky Island. Kayakers, wary of the quick-rising storms on the open lake, typically stay in the innermost, smaller islands like Sand, York, and Basswood. The bluff on Oak Island's north shore—one of the highest points in the park— attracts hikers. Lighthouses guard six of the islands, legacies of the shipping trade that flourished on Lake Superior in the nineteenth century but that today serve as a destination for kayakers and boaters. The National Park Service (NPS) maintains campgrounds, which concentrates most visitor use in a few places and makes it easy to find isolated parts of the park, especially among the outer islands.

The village of Bayfield, tucked into the bluffs inside Chequamegon Bay, serves as the gateway to Apostle Islands National Lakeshore. Bayfield has retained its small-town feel, largely by excluding chain restaurants and motels and by preventing the runaway development that mars so many other national park entry points. Restaurants, restored homes, and shops selling local artwork and souvenirs line the town's main street. The ship *Island Princess* departs from the docks at the foot of town, taking visitors on a cruise or to Raspberry Island for a tour of a beautifully restored lighthouse.

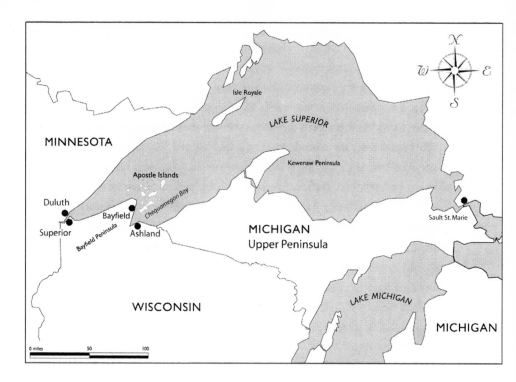

Map 1 Apostle Islands Region

Visitors come to the region to enjoy Bayfield's rustic charm and to explore the island wilderness. What they do not see — and do not expect to see — is evidence of the islands' rich and deep human history, a history that often seems at odds with the apparently pristine environments of today. Native Americans used the islands for centuries, and the Ojibwe Indians regard Long Island as a sacred site for its role in their migration to northern Wisconsin. French traders and missionaries arrived in the 1600s and Fort La Pointe on Madeline Island served as a center of the fur trade through the 1830s. Euro-American residents of the Chequamegon Bay fished, farmed, and logged in the islands after the 1850s. All of these people made homes and workplaces in the islands. Their actions — their stories — remain embedded in the wilderness.

It once seemed like this history would disqualify the islands as a national park. In 1930, landscape architect Harlan Kelsey evaluated the Apostle Islands as a potential addition to the national park system. Civic and business leaders from the surrounding towns hoped that a favorable report from Kelsey would lead to the creation of a park and the solution to a worrisome early Depression question: As timber resources ran out and sawmills shut down, what would replace logging at the heart of the region's economy? A park would anchor a new economy based on tourism. Local leaders prepared a lavish welcome for their guest—an aerial tour of the islands, a sailing excursion aboard the luxurious yacht of one of the area's wealthiest summer residents, and a visit to an old-growth forest on distant Outer Island.

Kelsey was not impressed. "What must have been once a far more striking and characteristic landscape of dark coniferous original forest growth has been obliterated by the axe followed by fire," he reported. "The ecological conditions have been so violently disturbed that probably never could they be more than remotely reproduced." Kelsey concluded that a half century of destructive logging had robbed the area of its value to the NPS. During his visit, fires raged on some of the islands, and he predicted the whole area would soon become "a smoldering, desolate waste." He continued, "The hand of man has mercilessly and in a measure irrevocably destroyed [the islands'] virgin beauty . . . the project does not meet National Park Service standards." Kelsey's comments effectively ended any chance that the proposal would succeed.[5]

But Kelsey was wrong, at least in his assessment of the area's future. In 1970, Congress established twenty of the twenty-two islands as the Apostle Islands National Lakeshore. Kelsey would no doubt have been surprised to learn that the "primitive conditions" and "wilderness character" of the islands provided the primary motivation for the creation of the park. When NPS administrators published the lakeshore's first management plan in 1977, they determined that the vast majority of the park should be managed as a wilderness. In November 2004, Congress gave this management plan the force of law when it designated 80 percent of the national lakeshore as the Gaylord Nelson Wilderness.[6]

Pristine though the islands may seem, evidence of the logging and other extractive activities that so disturbed Harlan Kelsey remains in the island wilderness. The composition of the mature second- and third-growth forests bear the unmistakable imprint of logging, particularly in the absence of white pine and hemlock on most of the islands. Logging camps lay buried in the woods of Outer, Bear, Oak, and Stockton islands. In some places, little remains but the ruined foundations of a building or two; in others, rusting machinery and bulldozer blades provide additional clues to the resource production of the past.

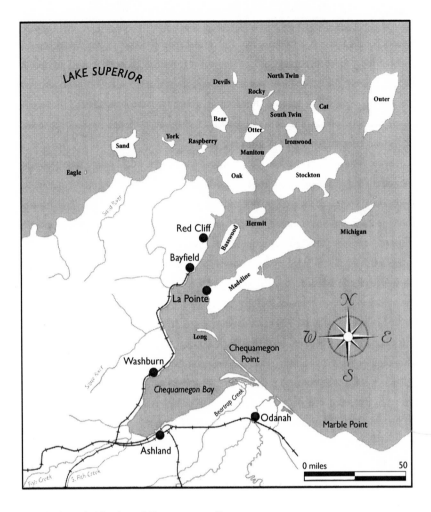

Map 2 Apostle Islands and Chequamegon Bay

The bedrock sandstone of three islands reveals the geometric lines of quarries last active over a century ago. Forest clearings filled with wildflowers mark the site of farmsteads on Sand and Basswood islands. Fishing camps, some in use as recently as the 1980s, still line the shores of Rocky and South Twin islands. Even the lake trout chased by today's fishermen testify to the history of resource extraction—they descend from fish introduced in an effort to rebuild stocks devastated by overfishing and exotic species. The ruined landscape viewed by Harlan Kelsey endures—obscured by today's wild, vibrant, and healthy island environments, but present nonetheless.

Wilderness in the Apostle Islands is deeply layered with stories. Changing social and cultural conditions led to the creation of the national lakeshore and defined its boundaries; histories of logging and farming shaped the modern forest of each island; escaped garden plants mark the homesites of long-departed fishing families. Each story contributed to the rewilding of the islands, to the return of wilderness characteristics in ways continually informed by both natural and cultural processes. To understand—and to protect—this wilderness, we need to recognize the role of both elements.

How do we describe what has happened at places like the Apostle Islands, places where wild nature has returned after long periods of intensive human use? Neither environmental historians nor wilderness managers have an accurate word to explain the process. Terms such as *exploitation, degradation,* and *destruction* are usually used to describe the impact of industrial activity on the landscape; *healing* and *recovery* portray the return of wilderness characteristics to a once-degraded place. These terms apply in places where industrial resource extraction has left behind massive clear-cuts or open mining pits. But surely not *every* human action is one of degradation. What about the fishermen and farmers who made a home in the Apostle Islands for over a century? If the choices they made did not lead to degradation, then recovery does not explain what has happened since those activities ceased. The term *rewilding* is a better fit.[7] The Apostle Islands have become wild again not simply because nature has muted the signs of human abuse. Rewilding landscapes should be interpreted as evidence neither of past human abuse nor of triumphant wild nature, but as examples of the ongoing impact of human choices on natural processes and of natural conditions on human history. These landscapes represent both history *and* nature, working simultaneously and together.

How did the logging- and fire-scarred wasteland viewed by Harlan Kelsey in 1930 become a wilderness in just a few decades? Forest regeneration alone cannot explain the origins of this wilderness. The rewilding of the islands was not accidental, not simply the result of ecological processes left to play out on their own. The forests regenerated in ways profoundly influenced by their history of human use. Ongoing choices about how to value and use the islands shaped the rewilding of the Apostles too. As the state consolidated its authority in the region, it managed the islands to create a landscape valued for its recreational and scientific qualities, a landscape we today call wilderness. During the twentieth century, government land managers promoted some activities at the expense of others, isolating nature tourism from other economic activities. This segregation of the recreational use of nature and the land-use choices associated with it created the conditions necessary for rewilding.

Tourists started visiting the islands and Chequamegon Bay before the Civil War, when Lake Superior captured the nation's romantic fascination with the frontier, Native Americans, and violent, powerful nature. The arrival of the railroads in the 1870s made the islands and their environs more accessible to midwestern urbanites. Railroad companies promoted the Apostles as a summer destination, a place for tourists to find clean air, romantic scenery, and distance from dirty and congested cities such as Chicago, Milwaukee, or Minneapolis. Tourists enjoyed sport fishing, picnicking on the lighthouse lawns, and yachting amid the sea caves, beaches, and sandstone cliffs. By the turn of the century, the Apostles ranked among the Midwest's most popular tourist destinations.

Today, we tend to see landscapes of tourism and landscapes of production as mutually exclusive. This was not always the case. In the Apostles, the fishing, farming, logging, and tourism industries supported and reinforced each other. Farmers depended on summer residents and resorts as a market for their produce. Fishermen worked in logging camps during the winter and ferried tourists during the summer. The railroads that brought the tourists also carried lumber, salted fish, and cut stone harvested from the islands. Only in the twentieth century did tourism come to stand apart from these other uses of nature, the result of a growing separation between the acts of production and consumption. Production-oriented uses of nature left their marks on island environments—logging scars, plowed fields, damaged and unstable fish populations—while tourism emerged as a way of using nature, of consuming nature, without such obvious impacts. The islands transformed from a place valued for production of natural resources to one valued for recreation.

Viewing tourism as a distinctive economic activity has had consequences for the ways modern Americans use and understand the environment. Nature has become a place for leisure and recreation—not a place in which to live or work. We have persuaded ourselves that as tourists we have little or no impact upon the places we visit. We can and should "take nothing but pictures, leave nothing but footprints." The corollary to this way of thinking is that working and living in nature necessarily cause harm or degradation. We see humans as being outside of nature, not as part of it. But kayaking and nature photography *do* have an impact on nature, even though complicated producer-consumer relationships of modern society obscure these impacts and make them difficult to trace. As the history of the Apostle Islands reveals, even wilderness tourism shapes the environment by dictating how people use and manage it.[8]

The idea that wilderness recreation has little or no impact on the natural world is the product of ideas that crystallized in the second half of the twentieth century. The meaning of wilderness has changed over time, especially in its relationship to consumerism and the commercialization of nature. In the 1930s, Aldo Leopold, Bob Marshall, and other founders of the Wilderness Society lobbied for the protection of wilderness because of their discomfort with an increasingly consumer-oriented society. To these wilderness advocates, the auto campers and the roads built to carry them stood out as the greatest threat to the nation's diminishing reserves of wild country. Wilderness should be a refuge from modernity, a place where people experienced nature firsthand, without reliance on—or interference from—the gadgets and comforts of modern society.[9]

After the 1950s, wilderness advocates used the growing public enthusiasm for outdoor recreation to win political support for the permanent protection of wilderness. They traded the critique of modernity—so central to the wilderness concept expressed by Leopold and Marshall—for public support and received in return a highly successful national wilderness preservation system. In so doing, however, they tied the wilderness movement more closely to consumer society. To accommodate the large number of wilderness visitors and to maintain the qualities that made wilderness special, campers used nylon tents, lightweight backpacks, and other high-tech gear. They also adopted an ethic that stipulated that they "Leave No Trace" as they trekked through what they considered to be a pristine landscape.[10]

This transition had significant implications for places such as the Apostle Islands. The islands became valuable not just as a site for primitive outdoor recreation but also for the way that recreational opportunities could revitalize the regional economy. The movement for state acquisition of the islands—culminating in the designation of Apostle Islands National Lakeshore in 1970—coalesced around these attributes. In contrast to the Leopold generation's discomfort with the commercialization of wild areas, the commercial potential of nature protection drove the creation of wilderness in the Apostles.

Valuing the Apostles as a wilderness brought changes in the way people used and altered the islands. Although tourism had long functioned as part of an integrated economy—a balance of fishing, logging, farming, and other forms of resource extraction—the new valuation of the islands as a wilderness demanded the cessation of those activities. As state authority in the region grew, government resource managers ensured that the islands conformed to the needs of wilderness recreation by strictly regulating some of the activities—such as logging and commercial fishing—that had taken place there for decades.

The emerging wilderness character of the Apostle Islands thus ties into another important story of the twentieth century: the growing power of the bureaucratic state. In this, the management of the islands as a wilderness was a relatively late step in a process that had been accelerating for nearly a century. Starting with regulation of the commercial and sport fisheries in the late 1800s, the state gradually extended its management authority, eventually obtaining the power to segregate tourism from other economic activities.

This authority demanded a condition that anthropologist and political scientist James C. Scott calls "legibility," or simplification for easier state management. Scott uses the concept of legibility to explain practices as diverse as the creation of permanent last names, the standardization of weights and measures, and the codification of property division. He explains each of these as a part "of the state's attempt to make a society legible, to arrange the population in ways that simplified . . . classic state functions." In all of these cases, efficient management required the simplification of complex social systems. This requirement intensified as the state became more powerful and more modern, and as the systems it sought to control grew more complicated.[11]

In the Apostles, state officials used the concept of legibility to simplify and organize island environments. In the commercial fisheries, for example, the Wisconsin Fisheries Commission required in 1909 that all fishermen obtain a license. This enhanced the ability of the state to control and manage both the fishermen and the fisheries. Fisheries experts could tabulate the number of fishermen, the equipment they used, and the types and amount of fish they caught. Licenses made the fishery more legible. Officials from many levels of government allocated increasingly scarce resources in the Apostles, determining how those resources could be used to maximize goals such as nature protection, economic stability, and opportunities for outdoor recreation. One of the land manager's most effective tools for this purpose was the division of the landscape by use; specifying which activities could occur in any given area made the landscape more legible. Outdoor recreation as a consumption-oriented use of nature separate from the resource-production economy thus derived not just from changing ideas about wilderness but also from the needs of an increasingly powerful and modern state.

The American system of federalism—which divides power among levels of government—complicated the growing power of the state to regulate the use of resources and to organize the landscape.[12] In the Apostles, many public agencies played a role in both the development of the islands for resource extraction and their transition to wilderness. The federal government funded the construction of locks, railroads, and other internal improvements that connected the Chequamegon Bay to national markets. The Wisconsin Conservation Department regulated the Lake Superior fishery, first to promote commercial production but eventually to boost the region's value as a tourist destination. At the same time, local governments such as the Ashland County Board resisted the shift from production to consumption so central to the rewilding of the islands. Tribal governments struggling to protect their sovereignty at different times supported and opposed the creation of a park in the Apostles. There were many manifestations of state authority in the Chequamegon Bay, and they often came into direct conflict with each other. Nevertheless, the clear trend in the Apostles was toward the expansion of state power, represented by the creation of legible landscapes to more easily control both humans and nature.[13]

The expansion of state authority had consequences for the people who lived, worked, and played among the islands. Creating a wilderness in the Apostles meant restricting some activities and uses of nature in favor of others. Wisconsin fisheries managers, for example, slowly tightened the regulation of commercial fishing in the islands while encouraging the development of a sport-fishing industry. Local residents, who had relied on island resources to support their economy since the mid-nineteenth century, did not always support the shift to wilderness. This was especially so when wilderness advocates—often people from outside the region—sought to shut down the parts of the local economy that depended on resource extraction. The Ojibwe Indians, too, saw their customary uses of nature prescribed, as the state fostered an economy based on consumption rather than production.

As state authority and the value of wilderness waxed during the twentieth century, Wisconsin and NPS land managers worked to make the islands conform to the emerging wilderness ideal. They shut down the last vestiges of the production economy and even prescribed the types of recreational activity that could take place. Resorts, restaurants, and summer cottages had once been the bulwark of the islands' tourist economy. As postwar wilderness users came to value the islands as a place without a human imprint, the state restricted this type of development too.

The process of rewilding accelerated in 1970 with the creation of Apostle Islands National Lakeshore. The NPS managed 97 percent of the park as a wilderness area, which meant the adoption of the agency's standardized wilderness management policies. The NPS removed visible signs of human activity, including fishermen's cabins, logging camps, and other remnants of the extractive economy. These actions followed an emerging NPS goal of restoring wilderness characteristics to places marked by human use, and the agency's intent was to make the islands seem more wild by erasing evidence of past resource extraction. These management choices combined with the regenerating forest to hide the scars that had tarnished the islands for Harlan Kelsey in 1930. A wilderness without evidence of human use is easier to manage. A clean, pristine wilderness is more legible than a messy, storied one.

But removing the evidence does not change the islands' history or diminish the role of past island residents in influencing the wilderness encountered by today's visitors. The old farm fields remain, masked by wildflowers and encroaching woody vegetation. Logging camps and rusting machinery still lurk in the regenerated forest. Today, NPS managers struggle to manage a forest mosaic that has been profoundly shaped by human use, with patches of old growth that survived the threat of logging and exotic species introduced by farmers and lighthouse keepers. The fisheries bear the stamp of 150 years of commercial fishing and management. The stories in this wilderness run too deep to remove.

Places like the Apostles complicate the way we understand wilderness, and the way we manage it. Since the 1990s, academics and wilderness advocates have engaged in a critical rethinking of the meaning of "wilderness" and its usefulness as a conservation strategy. These debates have focused largely on the relationship between wilderness and history. What has been the human role in the wilderness, and what should it continue to be?[14]

One of the central themes of this critique is the concern that the wilderness idea is essentially ahistorical. The idea of pristine wilderness is historically inaccurate, argue scholars of Native American history, who have demonstrated that

Native Americans everywhere directly and consciously shaped their environments with their agricultural practices, their use of fire, and their residential patterns.[15] Other scholars have critiqued wilderness as a cultural construct. Wilderness, they argue, is an idea created in opposition to modern, urban, industrial society, not a real, physical place that somehow avoided the influence of human activity.[16] Scientists have joined the debate, arguing that the goal of wilderness preservation emerged from a discredited ecological model that held that ecosystems moved in ordered progression toward a stable climax and there rested in equilibrium. In the 1970s, ecologists replaced climax theory with a model that stressed dynamism and constant change. Variations ranging from the fall of a single tree in the forest to epochal shifts in temperature ensure that nature will never reach a state of stable equilibrium but, rather, remains in constant flux. These insights complicate wilderness management, which critics charge aims to preserve a supposedly stable environment that existed prior to human, particularly Euro-American, disturbance.[17]

The critiques of wilderness and its assumptions have prompted an equally cogent and passionate response. Wilderness advocates caution that the academy's criticism will have devastating real-world consequences; wilderness is a place to be cherished, not an idea to be attacked. Wilderness activist Dave Foreman worries that these intellectual critiques undermine wilderness areas "by attacking the idea behind them, and others will reap the whirlwind [the critics are] sowing to try to open existing Wilderness Areas to clear-cutting, roads, motorized vehicles, and 'ecosystem management,' and, more dangerously, to argue against the designation of new Wilderness Areas." Others worry that the academics' tendency to relativize, to deconstruct, and to describe a world of constant change strips us of the ability to make morally sound decisions about environmental management. In the mid-1990s, the wilderness debates spilled outside the academy into popular periodicals, conference halls, and classrooms. This only magnified worries about the effects of criticizing the wilderness idea.[18]

The tension between wilderness and history is complicated by the abstract nature of the discussion. Terms like *wilderness* and *wildness* are slippery, subjective, and difficult to define. Part of the problem is that wilderness can refer to a place and an experience or state of mind. And the meaning of wilderness has changed over time. Puritan theologians viewed the wilderness in biblical terms; nineteenth-century Romantics imbued it with the sublime power of the godhead; the founders of the Wilderness Society valued it as a critique of consumer society. The Wilderness Act provides still another definition, one backed by the power of law: "an area where the earth and its community of life are untrammeled by man, where man himself is a visitor who does not remain."[19] *Wildness*, too, is a difficult term to define. Even the *Oxford English Dictionary* struggles with the word, defining *wild* by what it is not: not tame, not domesticated, not civilized. The tendency to use these two terms interchangeably confuses matters still further. Much of the analytical energy of the wilderness debates has been devoted to discerning the meaning and the significance of these words.[20]

Making the wilderness debates less abstract by focusing on a specific place like the Apostle Islands—a place rich in both wilderness and history—points a way out of this dilemma. The history of wilderness in the Apostles reveals the central role of both natural and human processes in creating wild places. It demonstrates the folly of trying to separate nature and culture—or wilderness and history—whether for analysis or for management.

The sandstone quarries of the Apostle Islands provide an example of the intellectual riddles and management questions raised by rewilding landscapes. The red sandstone found on the islands and at several points around Chequamegon Bay anchored one of Bayfield's most important early industries. Nineteenth-century boosters pointed to the stone as a key resource certain to garner national attention and lure economic development. "This beautiful sandstone, now coming into such popular use throughout the northwest and extending well to the south and east," exclaimed the Bayfield newspaper in 1872, "can nowhere be quarried and shipped at so little cost as from the islands and main shore in this vicinity."[21]

At first, it looked like the quarry industry might live up to the boosters' predictions. In 1870, a firm called Strong, French & Company began quarrying on Basswood Island. The Chicago fire of 1871 opened a huge new market, and cut stone from the island and other Lake Superior quarries became a favored building material as a new city rose from the ashes. The cut-stone industry, however, soon fell victim to the boom and bust cycles that so frequently marked peripheral resource economies. The nationwide financial crash of 1873 ruined Strong & French, forcing the closure of the Basswood Island quarry. Quarrying boomed again in the 1880s, prompting another bout of economic optimism. The Basswood Island quarry reopened, as did quarries on Hermit Island, Stockton Island, and at several points on the mainland. The Stockton Island

I.2 Workers at an unidentified Chequamegon Bay quarry prepare sandstone blocks for shipment. Quarrying served as one of the region's most important industries in the late nineteenth century, and it left indelible marks on the landscape. Courtesy of the National Park Service.

quarry produced over two hundred thousand cubic feet of stone per year in the 1890s, but the crash of 1893 shut down most of the quarries once more. Shifting architectural styles — especially a preference for white stone inaugurated by the grand buildings of the 1893 Columbian Exposition in Chicago — guaranteed that the red-stone quarries of Chequamegon Bay would not reopen.[22]

Although active for just over twenty-five years, Chequamegon Bay's quarries had a lasting environmental impact. Stone blocks still sit, perched on the edge of the water, ready for shipment to some distant construction site. Remains of the industrial equipment that once moved the giant blocks rust in the resurgent forest. And the rewilding quarries now serve as an attraction for visitors to Apostle Islands National Lakeshore.

The brief era of quarrying left a riddle for modern resource managers. In the 1980s, the task of crafting a management plan for the quarries fell to park historian Kathleen Lidfors, who wrestled with the question of whether the quarries should be managed as historic resources or as natural sites. The problem was that the two management goals seemed to come into conflict. The forest had begun to reclaim the quarries, and Lidfors recognized that if "reforestation is allowed to continue, quarry faces will eventually be obscured, building remains and artifacts will succumb to natural processes, and clearings and roads created for quarry-related activities . . . will return to the forest." But the quarries represented an important chapter in the history of the region and a chance to interpret for visitors what life on the islands had been like in the past. The Basswood Island quarry, listed on the National Register of Historic Places, exemplified the problem. A cultural site significant enough to receive national recognition deserved interpretation, and the island's accessibility to boaters made it the ideal location for NPS development plans. But such plans required cutting trees that were close to a century old, clearing vegetation, installing trails, and possibly reconstructing buildings and equipment—exactly the kind of development that threatened the wilderness values that visitors and park managers cherished in the Apostles.[23]

Lidfors also recognized the problematic legacy for the island wilderness left by the quarries. "Because of the quarries' shoreline locations and the huge quantity of bedrock removed from these sites," she realized, "these areas will never fully regain their pristine appearance." Buildings might decay, clearings might close, the regenerating forest might obscure the quarry walls and stone blocks, but evidence of human activity would not be erased from these landscapes.[24]

From an ecological perspective, one could argue that the quarries enhance the wildness of the islands. Old quarry sites often contain a particularly diverse flora, and they can provide unusual ecological conditions that create microclimates favored by rare species. Although few scientific studies have evaluated the island quarries, NPS resource management staff report that the Basswood Island quarry has become an exceptional habitat for amphibians. At least fourteen species of lichens are found at the quarry that exist nowhere else in the park. Some of the species are rare and serve as important indicators of air quality. The quarries certainly qualify as self-willed and free—a frequently used definition of wildness—in the sense that there has been no attempt to manage them for over a century. But the impact of human use could not be clearer: the bedrock has been cut into perfectly square blocks. Nevertheless, the quarries on Stockton and Hermit islands lie within the designated wilderness, while those on Basswood remain outside of it. Places such as the abandoned quarries break down the seemingly dichotomous categories of wilderness and history—a reminder that understanding these landscapes demands attention to both the human and natural processes that created them.[25]

Places like the Apostle Islands provide the opportunity to reframe our discussions about the relationship between wilderness and history. For most of the twentieth century, conversations about American wilderness have been conversations about the American West. The large tracts of wilderness with alluring names lie west of the Mississippi—Desolation Wilderness in California, Wrangell–St. Elias Wilderness in Alaska, Frank Church River of No Return Wilderness in Idaho. Great political battles have been fought over western landscapes, too, such as those over the old-growth forests of the Pacific Northwest and the red-rock canyon lands of Utah. With these spectacular and relatively undisturbed locations as a backdrop, wilderness conversations have focused

I.3 By 1982, the Basswood Island Quarry had been unused for nearly a century, creating a management dilemma for the National Park Service. Wildness thrives in this historical landscape. How can the agency best manage and interpret a place valuable for both its cultural and natural history? Courtesy of the National Park Service.

on the protection of pristine nature against the encroaching and destructive forces of civilization. This has been the general narrative of wilderness politics from the fight to protect Hetch Hetchy in the opening decades of the twentieth century to the battle over oil drilling in the Arctic National Wildlife Refuge in the beginning of the twenty-first.

Eastern wild places provoke different conversations. When wilderness characteristics return after decades or centuries of human use, the story of an advancing and degrading civilization does not make as much sense. Forests reclaiming once-cultivated fields, trees growing through abandoned founda- tions, and the return of long-extirpated species seem to indicate that nature, not civilization, is on the offensive. These places require us to rethink the relation- ship between nature and culture, with provocative results. John Elder, who has written extensively about these issues from his Vermont home, explains that the "stories of this long-settled landscape may help us to imagine a more inclusive paradigm for American conservation." As we recognize the importance of his- tory in understanding wild places, long-humanized landscapes such as Elder's Vermont mountains or the Apostle Islands take on a new meaning. They point to a more open way of thinking about human-natural interactions over the long term. The narrative of rewilding—as it has taken place in the Apostles and in many other places—facilitates these new conversations.[26]

Rewilding is occurring in every corner of the country, and the management dilemmas it poses are equally widespread. New York's Adirondack Mountains have a history with much more deliberate attention to the maintenance of wild- ness than the Apostles. Since 1894, when the state legislature declared that the forest preserve "shall forever be kept as wild forest lands," conservation offi- cials, timber industry executives, sportsmen, and residents have negotiated the meaning of "forever wild."[27] The creation of Virginia's Shenandoah National Park in 1926 meant the displacement of people who had lived in the area for generations. For the park's first fifty years, NPS managers sought to erase all evidence of these people from the landscape. They removed fences, burned cabins, and replanted old fields, until in 1976 Congress designated 40 percent of Shenandoah as wilderness. Since 1990, however, NPS officials have recog- nized that the policy of re-creating a "natural" environment at Shenandoah threatens the park's cultural and archaeological resources.[28] Even at Olympic National Park—a large western park with 96 percent of its area designated as wilderness—human history complicates wilderness management. NPS officials struggle over how to manage historical forest clearings and dilapidated Adirondack-style shelters that have long served as elements of the park's recreational landscape. These places, each rewilding in its own way, tell stories about the ongoing interactions of nature and culture. So do the Apostle Islands.[29]

The management of these places depends on recognizing the stories that explain them. The scars from logging and resource extraction in the Apostle Islands that so disturbed Harlan Kelsey in 1930 might be hard to see today, but they are there. These scars provide an apt metaphor for the management dilemmas faced by park officials. It would be easier to manage the islands by pretending that the scars do not exist. Narratives of pristine wild nature or even nature recovering from abuse are easier to tell than those of rewilding. But such stories miss the chance to draw deeper, richer meanings from the islands, quieting the conversations about the relationship between nature and history so central to understanding rewilding landscapes. They also fail to provide answers to the most challenging management questions posed by these places—maintaining and nurturing wild, healthy environments, balancing competing demands on resources, mitigating visitor impact on places valued for both natural and cultural reasons. These challenges can only be met by keeping past uses and ways of valuing the islands always in front of us. ❧

1

Lines in the Forest

AS ITS NAME SUGGESTS, OUTER ISLAND IS HARD TO REACH. TWENTY-four miles from Bayfield at its closest point, Outer is the most vulnerable of the Apostle Islands to Lake Superior's violent weather. It stands, in the words of one writer, "like a clenched fist directly in the path of Superior's worst fury." Only the most skilled and experienced kayakers venture this far from the mainland, and the distance and unpredictable weather deter most sailors and powerboaters. Those who do reach Outer Island find two primary attractions: a lighthouse at the northern tip and a long, graceful sandspit on the southern end.[1]

The lighthouse draws the most attention, as lighthouses always do. With their manicured lawns, beautiful views, and stories of isolation and adventure, the lighthouses of the Apostles have served as tourist attractions since the mid-nineteenth century. The U.S. Lighthouse Board constructed the Outer Island lighthouse in 1874, with an 80-foot brick tower that commands a view of the open lake. True to its romantic image, the station has a daring rescue story. In the ferocious storm of September 2, 1905, keeper John Irvine watched as wind and waves tore apart a disabled 338-foot ore barge, the *Pretoria*. The crew abandoned ship, but their lifeboat capsized before they could reach the island. "Captain Irvine, who, though sixty years old, is still hale and strong, started to their rescue," reported a newspaper account. "By almost superhuman effort, while his life was endangered every minute, he brought the five who still clung to the lifeboat safely to shore." The romance and history make the Outer Island Lighthouse a rewarding destination for those who make the long trip to see it.[2]

The island forest also has a history, one that powerfully represents the rewilding of the Apostles. The seven-mile trail that runs from the lighthouse to the sandspit sees little in the way of foot traffic. Sections of the trail are virtually impassable, inundated by water backed up behind beaver dams. The trail passes through three distinct forest types. A nearly straight line divides the northern and southern portions of the forest. North of this line, hemlock—once one of this forest's dominant trees—joins yellow birch and sugar maple in the forest canopy, while it is almost completely absent to the south. The northernmost tip of the island is different still: a 185-acre patch of old-growth hardwood/hemlock forest with trees over 350 years old, among the largest and most important original stands of this forest type in the Great Lakes basin.

The lines running across the Outer Island forest are far more important than they may at first seem. They bring into subtle relief questions about the future of this forest that have everything to do with its past. As is the case in most of the forests in North America, this past involved axes and chainsaws. Logging started late on Outer Island, due to its isolation and distance from Bayfield. The forest remained largely uncut until the 1920s, when the John Schroeder Lumber Company built a railroad on the island and established a large logging camp. The trail that today carries hikers between the sandspit and the lighthouse follows the old railroad grade.[3]

The Outer Island forest owes its peculiar composition in part to the logging that the railroad allowed. Schroeder lumberjacks clear-cut the southern half of the island and transported the sawlogs to the company's Ashland mill. It was a tour of the Outer Island logging camp—and the uncut forest that remained on the island—that so disturbed Harlan Kelsey when he evaluated the islands as a potential national park in 1930. But the Great Depression swallowed the Schroeder Lumber Company, and logging on Outer Island ceased by 1931. Following a well-established pattern for cutover landscapes throughout the region, the piles of slash and logging refuse dried in the sun and wind and caught fire in 1936. Aerial photographs of the island taken in 1938 show the destruction caused by the fire. They reveal a stark line across the middle of the island: the cutover, southern portion of the island burned, the unlogged hardwood-hemlock forest did not. The resulting line would have been hard to miss in the ensuing years.[4]

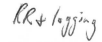

1.1 This 1938 aerial photograph of the western portion of Outer Island demonstrates the extent of the forest fires of the early 1930s. Modern vegetation maps of the island reveal the lasting impact of the fire, as well as other forms of past human use. The burned-over area has almost no hemlock, a tree that is still present in the unburned, northern portion of the island and was once the dominant species in the island forest. Courtesy of the National Park Service.

Although no longer visible from the air—or to most modern hikers—the line drawn by the 1936 fire still divides the Outer Island forest. Hemlock regeneration is particularly vulnerable to fire, and the blaze burned away the seed sources for the tree on the southern portion of the island. As the forest returned, hemlock was strikingly absent. Instead, the forest was dominated by white birch, quaking aspen, balsam fir, red oak, and red maple. The hemlock/hardwood forest on the northern portion of the island fell to the axe in the 1950s, although far more selectively than in the south. Today's forest dominants include hemlock, yellow birch, and sugar maple. The beaver that make hiking wet and difficult on the Outer Island trail owe their existence to the 1936 fire, too. Beaver first colonized the island in the 1940s as an early successional forest dominated by aspen—a highly preferred food source—grew out of the fire scar.[5]

The patch of old growth at the northern tip of the island owes its existence to a different set of historical circumstances. For 150 years, patterns of landowner-ship in the Apostles have been as complicated and varied as the islands' forest mosaic. Federal, state, county, and tribal governments, land speculators and logging companies, homesteaders and reclusive millionaires owned different parts of the archipelago. Each of these owners placed a different kind of value on island resources. For some, the islands and their forests were never more than a speculative investment. Others purchased land to build a home, the value of the timber a secondary concern. State and tribal ownership brought still different valuations—and led to different uses. Ownership patterns created boundaries on the island landscapes, boundaries evident today in the composition of the modern forest.

These jurisdictional boundaries explain Outer Island's remnant old growth. Although ownership of Outer Island changed hands frequently (at least three logging companies and two land speculators owned the majority of the island at different times), the northern tip of the island never left the public domain. In 1874, when the Lighthouse Board established the lighthouse, it reserved 240 acres for the lighthouse keepers and their families to use as a fuelwood reserve. Although it takes no small amount of wood to stay warm throughout the long Great Lakes shipping season, limited logging occurred only near the lighthouse complex. The rest of the reserve remained uncut.[6]

These long-ago historical events—the creation of a lighthouse reserve, the relatively late arrival of lumberjacks on Outer Island, the Schroeder Lumber Company's Depression-era shutdown, the 1936 fire—continue to shape the Outer Island forest. They also inform management of the islands as a whole, creating both opportunities and dilemmas for NPS resource managers. Since 1970, one of the national lakeshore's primary goals has been restoration of vegetation and natural processes to their prelogging conditions. One of the park's early management plans stated this objective succinctly: "rehabilitate . . .

resources and processes recently altered by human activities." This is a management goal shared by many other NPS units, especially those that administer lands with long and varied histories of human use—the result of the agency's dedication to protecting and restoring the lands under its control.[7]

In the early 1980s, the responsibility for realizing this management goal at Apostle Islands National Lakeshore fell to Robert Brander, the park's chief ecologist. In accordance with NPS policies, Brander compiled an environmental assessment of possible management strategies in 1981. He identified three potential alternatives: to allow forest vegetation to evolve on its own; to manage vegetation using a large restoration and rehabilitation program; or to implement a more limited restoration program, aimed at creating "vignettes" of the prelogging forest. Brander took into account a variety of factors in crafting these alternatives, including potential visitor response to NPS restoration activities and the availability of funding. But he also considered history and the manner in which that history still lingered in the modern forest.[8]

Outer Island provided for Brander—as it still does for NPS managers—a laboratory in which to evaluate the extent of human intervention needed to restore natural "resources and processes." Will the unburned, northern section of the forest approach its prelogging condition without intervention? Will forest managers need to plan for the restoration of hemlock on the southern portion of the island? The uncut portions of the forest on Outer and six other islands create different management considerations. They provide a benchmark against which to measure the health and composition of maturing island forests with different histories of logging and fire. They also deserve protection in their own right. Apostle Islands National Lakeshore is one of the few national parks in the Midwest with a strategy to manage old growth.[9]

History has shaped the rewilding of Outer Island and still determines NPS management there. The same is true of the rest of the national lakeshore. Hemlock grows on some of the islands, but not others. Logging began on some islands in the 1850s, but in other places not until after 1900. And some islands were not logged at all and retain their original old-growth cover. Local conditions like accessibility, species composition, and landownership patterns combined with national factors such as technological advances and market demand to determine where and when logging took place. These intersections created a landscape of patches and boundaries that, in turn, influenced forest regeneration and still inform management of the national lakeshore.

The Once and Future Forest

Lumberjacks did not simply start cutting at one end of the forest and methodically work their way through it. The composition of the forest shaped their decisions. Some tree species were more desirable than others, and lumberjacks sought the most valuable trees. Access to the forest—determined by island shorelines, rivers, and topography—also played a role. Even the tallest, straightest, thickest trees remained uncut if access proved too difficult. But extralocal factors determined where lumberjacks worked too. The value of each species depended on fluctuating markets and the degree of access to the forest changed with technological innovation. Local geographies and national economies combined to determine the patterns of logging.

The Bayfield Peninsula marks the northernmost boundary of a region once called the Wisconsin pinery. In the late nineteenth century, white pine was considered Wisconsin's single most important natural resource. Tall, straight, free of knots, lightweight, and easily worked, white pine was the nation's premier building material. Demand for white pine intensified as Euro-American settlers rolled onto the treeless prairies of the midcontinent. The Wisconsin pinery offered one of the country's most abundant supplies of this essential resource. The term *pinery*, however, can be misleading. The quality and the amount of white pine varied greatly from one part of the state to another. Only a few areas could claim white pine as a dominant forest species. Any tract of several hundred acres with an average of only one or two large pine trees per acre received the designation of "pineland." The forests of the Apostles were classified as pinelands: the occasional white pine surrounded by a forest dominated by other species.[10]

The Apostles lay in a transitional zone between the boreal forests to the north and deciduous forests to the south. Northern conifer forests were dominated by balsam fir, spruce, and white birch. Deciduous forests were more complex, with a greater number of tree species, including oaks, beech, sugar maple, and hickory. In between these two forest types lay a distinct forest dominated by hemlock, yellow and white birch, and white pine. Reconstructions of early nineteenth-century island forests have concluded that a mixed coniferous/hardwood forest dominated by hemlock, white pine, sugar maple, and yellow and white birch covered 90 percent of the islands. Scattered stands of red oak grew in well-drained areas. Balsam fir and white cedar were more prominent in poorly drained areas and on the portions of the islands most exposed to windthrow. Forest conditions such as these were consistent throughout the mesic (relatively wet) forests of northern Wisconsin, although the specific composition of the forests varied from place to place with factors such as elevation, soil composition, and frequency of windthrow. In many parts of the islands, the soils contain thick red clay, the depositions left by a retreating Lake Superior in the postglacial period. The lake also shapes the region's climate. The immediate area has more moderate temperatures in both summer and winter and a high incidence of windthrow from the lake's often violent storms.[11]

Determining the early nineteenth-century forest composition of the Apostles helps explain how and why logging in the islands developed as it did. Environmental historians typically use the notes of the U.S. General Land Office surveyors and later scientific surveys to establish a baseline against which to judge the changes wrought by logging and Euro-American settlement. But the presettlement forest composition can serve as more than a baseline. It can also explain the history of logging in the islands. The specific composition of any forest stand—the prevalence of pine, oak, hemlock, or cedar—combined with geographical factors like proximity to water and topography determined the course of logging.

Most of the loggers who cut the island forests staged their operations out of Bayfield. The Bayfield Land Company founded the town in 1856, its investors hoping to capitalize on the Chequamegon Bay's potential as a transportation hub and plentiful natural resources—especially white pine. But as in any frontier lumber town, the products of the earliest logging supplied the local rather than the national market. A steam-powered sawmill was one of the first buildings erected in Bayfield, which the *Bayfield Mercury* dubbed the "most useful" building in town. Several other small mills opened around the Chequamegon Bay in the 1860s, and lumbermen quickly turned their attention to the national market. With this shift, the logging industry took on a distinct character. By 1880, the Chequamegon Bay had a more diverse trade than did other parts of the western Great Lakes. This diversity resulted from the intersection of local geography and national market demand particular to this specific place.[12]

The logging industry of the Chequamegon Bay started late relative to other parts of Wisconsin. The eastern shore of Lake Michigan provided a home for the first large-scale logging in the state, propelled by the demand for building materials and wood products in Chicago; by midcentury, lumbermen had erected mills all along the shore as well as along the Fox and Wolf rivers. The logging industry along the Mississippi and the large rivers at the center of the state was already well established when the Civil War stimulated a massive increase in production. By the time commercial operations commenced along Lake Superior in the early 1870s, the mills along the Wisconsin River already produced two hundred million board feet of lumber each year, and the mills at La Crosse churned out three hundred million.[13]

The vast majority of this tremendous amount of wood came from a single species—white pine. Because white pine provided such malleable, easily worked wood, it brought the best price; few other species proved worth the trouble of logging on a large scale. But buoyancy proved to be the pine's most important characteristic. Until the advent of railroad logging in the 1870s, rivers provided the only feasible method of transporting logs, and only softwoods like white and red pine floated well enough to travel in this manner. In the woods, then, lumberjacks cut pine—and little else. They cut the trees closest to the river first and then moved back into the forest, moving the logs to the riverbank and then floating them en masse to the downstream mills. In most of the Great Lakes forests, lumberjacks ignored hardwoods like maple, birch, and oak, and even conifers like hemlock and cedar, because they did not float well.[14]

Different conditions applied in the Apostles. Rafts of island pine still floated to the mills and, as in the rest of the region, pine became the most important commercial species. But unlike the mainland interior, the cedar, hemlock, and hardwoods that grew along the shore could be easily brought to the mills and sold at a profit. Lumberjacks simply loaded logs onto barges or scows and towed them to mills in the Chequamegon Bay cities. Andrew Tate, one of Bayfield's earliest settlers, explained the situation to one potential investor in Chequamegon Bay lumber: "The most of the wood cut the last winter has been cut on the islands Oak and Basswood. . . . It is cheaper because it is a short distance to the water."[15]

Ease of access provided a host of different opportunities in the Chequamegon Bay. For example, cedar shingles rather than pine lumber served as the first commercial product. Taff & Dunn established a shingle mill on Pike's Creek in 1860, the first truly commercial operation on the bay. Two other shingle mills operated in Bayfield by 1870. Cedar was the wood of choice for shingle manufacturing. The tough, durable wood was highly water resistant and made ideal shingle material, and cedar abounded in the lowland forests of the islands and shoreline.[16]

The same characteristics made cedar desirable for more industrial uses. Cedar grows in swampy environments, and its wood resists damp conditions. It also lasts well underground, making it perfect for railroad ties, telegraph poles, and mining supports. West from Ashland, along the Lake Superior shore, prospectors found bountiful supplies of copper and iron, and mining emerged as a key industry in the region. Chequamegon Bay cedar also helped grade the railroad bed south from Ashland when construction began on that route in 1872. An average mile of railroad track required 2,700 cross ties, 125,000 board feet of lumber per mile. Because island forests could be easily reached and logs could be cheaply sent down the lakes, ties from the Chequamegon Bay appeared in Chicago in the 1870s. From Chicago, they traveled west via rail to help extend the railroad networks onto the prairies. National market forces combined with local environments and geographic conditions to make cedar ties a marketable product.[17]

The steamship trade provided another opportunity. As steamers began to ply the south shore of Lake Superior, James Chapman and William Knight recognized the need for fuelwood stations along the most traveled routes.

1.2 The John Schroeder Lumber Company transferred its logging crews, equipment, and railroad to Outer Island in 1924, and over the next five years removed forty million board feet of hemlocks and hardwoods from the island. The logs here await shipment to the Schroeder Company's mill in Ashland. Courtesy of the National Park Service.

In 1857, they established a station at Oak Island. By 1870, they had built a four-hundred-foot dock to accommodate all sizes of boats and ran a semiper-manent lumber camp on the island. Knight and Chapman did not sell white pine as fuelwood—they could sell that at much higher prices for conversion to finished lumber. Instead, they supplied the steamers with hardwood and hem-lock. Oak Island provided the logical place for such activity. It has the highest elevation of the islands, and its steeper topography meant a well-drained for-est and, therefore, more long-burning hardwoods—the preferred type of fuel. Nearby York Island, also on the steamship route, never hosted a fuelwood sta-tion, since its low and swampy conditions and different forest composition made it a far less suitable location.[18]

The combination of island geography and nationwide economic trends created a market for Chequamegon Bay hemlock too. In the mid-nineteenth century, hemlock bark became the preferred source of tannin, an essential chemical in the process of turning animal hides into leather. Because hemlock bark spoiled easily and broke into pieces from extensive handling, it was usually shipped via water. Like the rest of the logging industry, tanneries shifted west during the course of the nineteenth century. They moved across New England and into New York, then into western Pennsylvania, Michigan, and Wisconsin. Between 1860 and 1880, Wisconsin emerged as a center of the tanning industry because its extensive hemlock forests could be easily accessed along the shore-lines of the Great Lakes. By the 1880s, Wisconsin ranked fourth in the nation in the production of leather products, and the industry continued to expand.[19]

The islands provided an ideal place to harvest tanbark. Hemlock dominated the forests, and the miles of shoreline ensured access to trees whose bark could be secured with a minimum of handling. Because the preparation of hemlock bark did not require milling, these operations were often small scale. In 1871, John Buffalo—a member of one of the most prominent Ojibwe families in the area—secured a contract with a St. Paul tannery. Buffalo received $3.75 per cord for one hundred cords of tanbark, which he shipped to Duluth via steamer and then to St. Paul on the railroad. Throughout the 1880s, Basswood Island farmer Charles Rudd had a team of men harvesting several hundred cords of tanbark per year for shipment to a tannery in Duluth.[20]

The advantage of accessibility that shoreline forests of hardwoods and hem-lock provided did not last long. Technology helped lumberjacks overcome the obstacles of geography. No single technology had as large an impact on the economy and organization of the lumber industry as the railroad, which came into widespread use in the late 1870s. Railroads changed everything from the location of the mills to the site and season of logging to the type of tree cut. Railroads hauled small portable mills deep into the forest; logs could be roughly cut and then transported by rail for finishing elsewhere. Rail transportation opened forests previously inaccessible for their distance from navigable watercourses. Even the season of logging changed. Bogs, hills, and windthrow made summer movement of logs virtually impossible, so until the late nineteenth century almost all logging took place in the depths of winter, when ice and snow eased the skidding of logs. But railroads obviated the need for winter logging. Railroads solved the transportation dilemma presented by hardwoods, profitably bringing oak, maple, and birch to market. Entire forests already stripped of pine regained their value with the development of new markets for previously useless trees. Logging in other parts of the western Great Lakes began to more closely resemble the diverse trade of the Chequamegon Bay.[21]

And yet, the railroad meant much less in the Apostle Islands than it did elsewhere. Lumberjacks already cut hardwoods and hemlock without the aid of railroads. Besides, it made little financial sense to haul locomotives, rails, and other equipment to smaller islands that could only support a few seasons of logging. But even on Oak Island—large enough to employ five large camps over several decades—lumberjacks relied on horsepower well past the turn of the century. Loggers used railroads only on Michigan and Outer islands, and even there not until the 1920s, when timber exhaustion around the state increased the value of remnant stands and made the transport of equipment to the islands financially viable. Ease of access, forest composition, and economic opportunity combined to determine when logging began, how it occurred, how long it lasted, and when it ceased.

The combination of local and national factors that determined the course of logging has had a cascade of consequences for modern forests. Ecologists are increasingly recognizing the role of human history in shaping ongoing ecological processes. David Foster and his colleagues at the Harvard Forest in western Massachusetts have conducted long-term studies on the impact of past land use on modern environments. They are learning that even a season of selective logging or the single turn of a plow by a long-ago landowner has profound implications on forest composition almost two centuries later. The conclusions drawn there apply equally well to the Apostles: "The maples, oaks,

1.3 The Schroeder Company's Outer Island logging operations were among the most industrial in the Apostles. At its peak in 1930, Schroeder had more than forty miles of track and two railroads working on the Island. Courtesy of the National Park Service.

and hemlocks that constitute our woods establish, grow, and are shaped over time by a wide range of conditions; the effects of past windstorms, climates, or human effects become embodied in the shape and structure of the trees and the appearance of the forest, which are then carried forward through time as the forest grows." It is difficult to speculate what accessibility, stand composition, and local economic opportunities meant for individual forest stands of the Apostles, much less for the region as a whole. Studies of the long-term impact of logging in the western Great Lakes and New England have demonstrated how the selective logging of pine reduced forest diversity by altering the seed sources available for forest regeneration. Small variations in forest composition, accessibility, the date of the first and last logging activities have set each island, each forest stand, on its own course.[22]

These conclusions mean that land managers and conservationists *must* consider history in their attempts to understand and steward modern landscapes. "We must always invoke a detailed knowledge of the history of the land and its people," Foster explains. "Similarly, our attempts to project or guide future changes in these ecosystems are always improved by considering the ecological processes that have operated in the past." These conclusions ring particularly true in the Apostle Islands and other places where wild conditions are returning after decades or centuries of intense human use.[23]

Nowhere are these historical influences more evident than in the hemlock/hardwood forests of Outer Island and the lines that still divide the forest there. Accessibility proved to be the most important factor in the logging of the island—and in the composition of the modern forest. Although loggers culled the white pine that grew along the shore in the 1890s, the southern portion of the island remained uncut until the 1920s and the northern portion into the 1950s. The logging history of Outer Island is relatively uncomplicated. This helps to make the relationship between past land use and modern forest composition easier to discern.

NPS management of the Outer Island forest has been particularly concerned with hemlock, once one of the dominant tree species across the entire island. The former lighthouse reserve has retained its original vegetation; it is considered one of the best examples of northern hardwood/hemlock old growth in the western Great Lakes. Hemlocks in this stand are a variety of different ages, and hemlock is expected to remain as a dominant canopy species. On the rest of the northern portion of the island, hemlock is still a forest dominant, but it is poorly represented in the reproductive layers of the forest, which means the relative importance of the species will decline in the future. The southern portion of the island has no hemlock whatsoever, with no prospects for future growth.[24]

The patterns of hemlock growth on Outer Island—and the future position of the species in the forest—have been crafted by the island's history of logging and fire. Logging in the northern half of the island in the 1950s did not remove all of the hemlock, explaining the continued dominance of the tree in that portion of the forest. But hemlock needs shade and moisture to reproduce. The selective logging of the 1950s opened the canopy, exposing the forest to the sun and wind and damaging prospects for future hemlock regeneration. The fires that swept the southern half of the island in the wake of logging by the Schroeder Lumber Company burned away seed sources for hemlock, ensuring that the tree would be absent from the forest that grew out of the fire scars.[25]

Poor prospects for hemlock regeneration complicate NPS management goals of restoring the island forests to their prelogging conditions. "Reforestation, if left to natural succession would take a very long time and some species, such has hemlock, may never regenerate," stated one management document in 1981. These problems are not isolated to the Apostles; by some estimates, hemlock has been eradicated from 95 to 98 percent of its former range. With such a forecast, NPS managers have had to consider extensive intervention to foster the regeneration of hemlock and other species damaged by logging and fire.[26]

But to have a chance at success, even the most aggressive management techniques need to consider history. Hemlock regeneration occurs best in damp conditions, under a closed hemlock canopy, and in places with a large amount of dead, rotting wood. One 1984 study recommended that the NPS take active steps to create this kind of microenvironment on Outer Island. The report suggested stocking the forest with rotting wood and hemlock saplings, removing leaf litter and maple seedlings, and suppressing fire. But such a policy would not make sense everywhere; even aggressive management is bound by the past. The report recommended intervention only on the northern half of the island. On the southern portion of Outer Island, the history of fire has produced conditions unfavorable to hemlock regeneration—warmer, drier soils and a more open canopy—despite the original importance of hemlock in the prelogging forest. The NPS did not act on these suggestions due to the cost and their highly invasive nature. But resource managers continue to regard Outer Island and its tripartite forest as a bellwether for their long-term goal of returning the forest to its original condition.[27]

Land managers everywhere face this kind of dilemma. The future of the forest is dependent on a history of fire, logging, and land use, a past that is often difficult to recover. In each place, in each time, local ecological and geographic conditions integrated differently with changing technologies and the expanding lumber market. Only by paying attention to these local intersections can we determine why logging occurred as it did, where it did, when it did—not just in the Apostles, but anywhere. These intersections continue to shape the modern forest, and discerning them is vital to our ability to understand and manage the places we want to protect.

The Stockton Island Dilemma

Elsewhere in the Apostles, factors other than accessibility determined the course of logging. The forest history of Stockton Island depended on the economic calculus of two men: John H. Knight and William Freeman Vilas. The pair had purchased the majority of the island as a speculative investment in the 1880s. They did not necessarily intend to harvest the island's resources themselves; instead, they hoped to capitalize on the rising value of its timber and stone as western Lake Superior became more connected to the national economy. This speculation determined Knight and Vilas's plans for Stockton Island. Should they sell only the stumpage rights and retain ownership of the land for possible future development? Should they sell the island's pine timber alone, or find a way to package the pine with the more extensive but less marketable hemlock and hardwoods? While Knight and Vilas sought to answer these questions, both tax bills and the threat of forest fire mounted.

Stockton Island provides the opportunity to consider how the decisions of individual landowners shaped both the history and the future of the forest. Working intermittently from the early 1880s until 1920, it took lumberjacks forty years to clear the forests of Stockton Island. Their actions reveal how institutional factors such as tax policy, the economic conditions of the national lumber market, and seemingly natural influences like fire determined when and where logging occurred. Tax policies and lumber prices no longer matter much on Stockton Island, but fire—and the changes to the fire regime that resulted from Knight and Vilas's choices—shape current and future management of the island forest.

The prelogging forests of Stockton Island—also called Presque Isle or Presquisle Island in the nineteenth century—followed the patterns of forest composition across the archipelago. At slightly over ten thousand acres, Stockton is the largest of the islands included in the national lakeshore. It consists of a patchwork of different ecosystems and natural features, three of which played key roles in determining human use of the island. A forest particularly rich in hemlock covered 80 percent of the island. Sandstone outcroppings surface on the southwestern shore, at Presque Isle Point on the southernmost tip, and as steep and rugged bluffs along the northeast shore. The island's most distinctive feature is a tombolo—a low sand deposit that connects Presque Isle Point to the rest of the island. White and red pine grew in the areas with the driest, sandiest soils, such as those along the east side of the tombolo lagoon and the north side of Quarry Bay. One of the best blueberry patches in the islands carpeted the ground beneath the pines, making Stockton for many years (and still) a destination for berry pickers.[28]

It is difficult to trace landownership patterns on Stockton Island because many of Ashland County's early tax rolls are incomplete or have been destroyed. The local newspaper reported that a contractor named William King logged the island for pine in the mid-1880s. King might have been logging land that he owned outright. More likely, he had purchased the stumpage rights to the pine, or he worked on a contract for the landowner. At about the same time, John Knight and William Vilas began to acquire land on the island. Knight and Vilas—or their heirs—owned most of Stockton Island for the next seventy years.[29]

Knight and Vilas invested in land all over Wisconsin and Minnesota. In 1873, Vilas—a rising star in the Wisconsin and national Democratic Party—took a vacation tour of Lake Superior. His trip included a visit with Knight in Bayfield and a sail around the Apostles. Shortly thereafter, Knight and Vilas began to purchase northern Wisconsin timberlands. Knight had arrived in Bayfield in 1869 to serve as the federal Indian agent, but he engaged in a variety of business activities, including real estate speculation, hotel management, and quarrying. He also was the registrar for the Bayfield Land Office from 1871 until 1885.[30]

1.4 and 1.5 William F. Vilas (*left*, in 1900) and John H. Knight (undated) attended law school together in New York in 1858 and later formed a lucrative partnership in land speculation and other investments in northern Wisconsin. Their decision to purchase Stockton Island as a speculative investment in the 1880s determined the course of logging on the island—and its rewilding. Courtesy of the Wisconsin Historical Society, WHi-10712 and WHi-54990.

The two men made a potent team. Vilas, with his political and business connections, had access to far more capital than Knight. Knight's multiple business interests and his position in the land office provided information that the partners used in making investment decisions. Knight culled information on the location of choice timber tracts from the registrants who came through his office, and he used the knowledge to acquire good land for Vilas. The pair became among the largest landowners in northern Wisconsin, and they made some very lucrative investments. For example, between 1881 and 1885, Knight made nearly fifty purchases in Vilas's name at the Bayfield Land Office, paying $17,634 in cash for 8,854 acres of timberland—an average price of $1.99 per acre. In 1881 and 1883, Knight and Vilas sold 480 acres of this land to timber baron Frederick Weyerhaeuser for $15.62 per acre. In 1887, the partners sold another 1,062 acres for a similarly high price. Knight and Vilas extended their investments beyond mere speculation, incorporating the Superior Lumber Company in 1881. They built a mill in Ashland in 1882 and logged over ten million board feet of lumber per year before selling the mill in 1889 and disbanding the company. The partners purchased land on Stockton Island as a part of this speculative portfolio. By 1900, the two men owned 7,739 acres on the island.[31]

More than timber lured Knight and Vilas to Stockton Island. The island contained a prime quarry site at the fittingly named Quarry Bay. A quarry opened there in the early 1870s, but it closed after only a few years of operation. In 1886, with Chequamegon Bay quarries booming once more, Knight established the Ashland Brown Stone Company and used his connections with the Wisconsin Central Railroad—he was its local attorney—to secure the contract to supply stone for the company's depot in Ashland. He did not intend, however, to remain in the business for long. "This stone business is growing into a most important and valuable industry," Knight explained to Vilas in 1891. "I am inclined to the belief that we will very soon be able to sell the stone lands at very nearly as much as we can get for all the balance of the lands." Knight soon sold the company to a firm based in Chicago. Production at the Quarry Bay site continued until 1897 before shutting down for good.[32]

As quarrying operations picked up, Knight and Vilas tried to determine how best to dispose of the rest of their Stockton Island holdings. They had the choice of selling the land outright or simply selling the stumpage rights. In 1891, a timber scaler hired by Knight estimated that the island contained less than three million feet of pine. What the island lacked in pine, it made up with hemlock, but hemlock was worth considerably less. Knight figured that they could receive at least $4.50 per thousand feet of pine but doubted that hemlock would yield more than $1.50 per thousand feet. Still, he had high hopes for a sale that would bring a significant profit. "I think if we can [get] 50 or 60 thousand dollars for the Presque Isle Lands . . . we ought not hesitate to sell," he advised Vilas.[33]

The question of when to sell lay at the heart of the speculator's strategy. Knight and Vilas knew that holding timberlands presented a serious financial risk. The longer they held onto the lands without cutting them, the more taxes they paid. Wisconsin's tax system did not make it easy to hold on to timberland. The combination of institutionalized tax policy and prevailing opinions about land use created a set of incentives for quick, rash, and wasteful logging. Throughout the nineteenth century, Wisconsin taxed landowners on the value of the standing timber. The longer they held the land, the more times they paid taxes on the timber before realizing a profit. This policy rested on two widely shared beliefs at the center of American ideas about forests. For most of the century, people believed that the country owned a virtually inexhaustible supply of wood, and most people thought that the best use of forested land was clearing it to make way for farms. These beliefs, as well as the financial imperative caused by high taxes, led timberland owners to pay more attention to short-term advantages of timber production than the long-term consequences of wasteful and inefficient logging.[34]

Knight found the tax obligations on Stockton Island particularly onerous. "In regard to the Ashland Co. taxes which are so outrageous . . . payment of such taxes for a few years takes all there is of the lands." Only limited logging took place on Stockton Island from 1890 to 1900, so Knight and Vilas recognized little return on their investment. Their tax obligations, however, mounted each year; they paid an estimated $4,057 in taxes on land with an assessed value of $7,187. The tax burden pressured Knight and Vilas to find a buyer for their land or to hire someone to log the island for them.[35]

Forest fires also threatened the investments of timberland owners and further encouraged rapid logging. Fires decimated the Great Lakes forests throughout the lumbering era. Loggers left behind piles of slash—branches, small trees, and other refuse—that turned to bone-dry kindling. Even the slightest spark could ignite a potentially catastrophic blaze. There was no shortage of sparks—lightning, passing locomotives, steam-powered sawmills, campfires, and land-clearing operations of farmers generated a constant risk of fire. George Hotchkiss, one of the first chroniclers of the Wisconsin logging industry, estimated in 1898 that as much timber had been destroyed by fire as had reached the market. He suggested a staggering total of 110 billion board feet of lumber lost to the flames. Despite their watery surroundings, the islands were no exception to this pattern, and fires routinely burned the islands after logging.[36]

Cognizant of the increased threat, Knight and Vilas hesitated to sell the pine separately from the other timber on the island. Selective cutting increased the risk of fire to the remaining timber. This forced the landowners to weigh the tax burden against the likelihood of fire. Knight laid out the dilemma: "Cutting the timber will reduce taxes but of course makes it hazardous for the other timber. These chances have to be always taken by the owners of timber & we are no exception. The question is should we sell, and reduce taxation & interest account on investment." The increasing activity at the quarry exacerbated the problem by providing a new source of sparks. The best solution: finding someone to buy their Stockton Island land.[37]

Lands rich in hemlock—like those on Stockton Island—presented a particular dilemma for speculators. "I am at a loss when it comes to dealing in hemlock," Knight complained. In 1891, Knight and Vilas had decided to hold off on selling their Stockton Island land, waiting for a better price. When the nationwide financial panic of 1893 gutted the midwestern lumber industry, they had little choice but to wait for prices to improve. Even as the lumber industry revived in the mid-1890s, hemlock had little value. Hemlock prices in Chicago did not return enough to provision a camp, pay wages, transport logs to the mill, and then deliver them to Chicago. Still, Knight and Vilas hoped that their Stockton Island investment would pay off. The key lay in attracting a tannery to Bayfield, and with it a steady demand for hemlock bark.[38]

Rumors of the imminent establishment of a tannery in Bayfield—rumors that had been circulating almost since the founding of the town—convinced Knight and Vilas to hold onto the land. The best thing, Knight explained in 1895, "is to wait the development of the tannery business up here which is sure to accrue sooner or later." Knight's hopes lifted again in 1896, when he learned that the U.S. Leather Trust had decided to build a large tannery in Bayfield. "I do not believe I exaggerate or come up to the figure when I predict that in a very short time we will get over $100,000 for our Presque Isle" and Bayfield Peninsula lands. The rumors proved untrue; Bayfield never did secure a tannery.[39]

By the winter of 1896–97, Knight and Vilas decided that they could no longer wait on the price of hemlock. They needed to earn revenue; otherwise, taxes drained all value from the investment. Although hemlock prices remained low, pine prices rose consistently as supply dwindled. Despite the increased risk of fire, Knight and Vilas sold a portion of the island's white pine for $3,500. This was not a big transaction, but it allowed the partners to continue to pay taxes while they waited for a more lucrative deal.[40]

Finally, in 1905, Vilas found a buyer for the rest of the Stockton Island timber (John Knight had died in 1903). Vilas sold stumpage rights for all timber on the island to the Milwaukee-based John Schroeder Lumber Company. Schroeder Company executives valued the island differently than Knight and Vilas. Rather than speculating on the future value of the stumpage rights, they intended to harvest the timber for commercial production. The company had purchased a large Ashland mill in 1901 and needed to secure a steady supply of sawlogs. The company bought land along the shore of Lake Superior, as well as land and stumpage rights to timberland around Chequamegon Bay, including on some of the largest islands: Michigan, Oak, Stockton, and Outer.[41]

The Schroeder Company established large camps on Stockton Island in 1911. Each of these camps employed as many as one hundred men, and the company often had more than three hundred men on the island. This represented a far larger operation than anything else in the islands up to that point. In 1915 alone, Schroeder transported ten million board feet of hemlock and hardwood from Stockton Island to the Ashland mill.[42]

Why had Stockton Island's hardwood and hemlock stands finally become worth the trouble of logging, forty years after the inception of the lumber industry in the Chequamegon Bay? By 1900, lumberjacks had stripped the pine from virtually all of the forests in the region — only hemlock and hardwoods remained. The ever-spreading network of railroads provided a way to get hardwoods to mills in quantities not possible when river drives and log rafts had been the only means of transport. This helped generate a market for previously unmerchantable species. Hardwoods like maple, beech, and oak replaced softwoods as the preferred wood for flooring, and they became an important source of the charcoal that fired the iron smelters along the shores of Lake Superior. The advertising and sales techniques of Northwoods lumbermen also helped create a market for

1.6 The Schroeder Company's railroad, dock, and boom at the southern tip of Outer Island in 1930, where rafts of hemlock and pine were assembled before being towed to the Ashland mill. Courtesy of the National Park Service.

hemlock. Pulp mills in central Wisconsin turned hemlock, paper birch, aspen, and jack pine into paper. With the development of these new markets, Stockton's remaining hemlock and hardwoods increased in value.[43]

After eight years of extensive logging, in 1920 the Schroeder Company shut down its camps on Stockton, the timber resources of the island exhausted. The company moved its men and equipment to nearby Michigan Island, but there faced entirely different conditions. Michigan Island's exposed location on the southeastern edge of the archipelago meant that it could not be logged in the winter—solid ice never formed between the island and mainland, making transport of men, equipment, and supplies dangerous if not impossible. So Schroeder built a railroad to cut the previously inaccessible timber—the first use of the railroad in the Apostles, over a half century later than on the mainland. When the company finished logging on Michigan in 1923, it tore out the tracks and moved them to Outer Island.[44]

The Schroeder Company had purchased only the stumpage rights to Stockton, so it simply abandoned the island once the trees were gone. The question of what to do with the island and its tax burden returned to the landowners. John

Knight and William Vilas did not have to wrestle with the issue; their descendants inherited the Stockton Island dilemma. The two businessmen would not have been happy with subsequent developments. "It is a question as to what will become of this island," commented the local newspaper. "Will it lie unproductive or will some further use of its natural resources be made?" Bayfield boosters hoped the island would be converted to farmland, as had happened in so many other places. This did not occur; no one again used the island for resource production, and fires soon swept Stockton Island.[45]

The fires of the 1930s might have been the predictable result of logging, but they were quite abnormal in Stockton Island's history. The island's two most prominent ecosystems had very different fire regimes. In the white pine/red pine forest of the tombolo, regular, low-intensity fire maintained the ecosystem by keeping the understory open and soil conditions dry and by preventing the growth of competing species. Pollen and tree-core analysis reveal evidence of at least nine fires on the tombolo between 1765 and the 1943. Some of these were anthropogenic, whether sparked accidentally by itinerant fishermen or intentionally by people trying to improve the blueberry crop. This suggests that fire played a significant role in shaping the tombolo landscape well before the inception of logging. In contrast, the hemlock/hardwood forest that covered most of Stockton Island had no evidence of fire for over 250 years. The high humidity, limited amount of fuel, and damp conditions on the forest floor meant that fires ignited by lightning had little chance of spreading. The prelogging forests over most of the archipelago fit into this latter category.[46]

Logging changed these fire regimes. Logging increased the amount of potential fuel and opened the canopy, drying the forest floor and creating conditions more conducive to hot, severe fires. Records of fires on the islands are anecdotal, drawn from newspaper accounts, lighthouse logbooks, and the records of the Wisconsin Conservation Department. Between 1934 and 1975, fires were reported on Stockton, Outer, Rocky, Sand, Hermit, Oak, Michigan, Cat, Raspberry, Devils, North Twin, and Otter islands. The pattern of logging followed by fire repeated itself across the Great Lakes well into the twentieth century.[47]

These fires were suppressed whenever possible. Lighthouse keepers fought fires as a part of their regular responsibilities. The Wisconsin Conservation Department and the Civilian Conservation Corps sent crews to fight large fires on several of the islands, including on Stockton Island in 1934. And when the National Park Service began administering the islands in 1970, the agency instituted a policy of aggressive fire suppression. Although ecologists were beginning to suspect the role of fire in maintaining ecosystem health, NPS policy required fire suppression unless research clearly demonstrated the prehistoric presence of fire. No such research existed for the Apostles. As a result, only three island fires since 1970 have burned more than one acre, and most fires were extinguished immediately.[48]

Altered fire regimes created a dilemma for NPS managers, since the "natural" role of fire in the islands had been significantly disrupted. The fires necessary to maintain some environments — such as the pine forest of the Stockton Island tombolo — had been suppressed. At the same time, the risk of severe fires had become far higher than in the past, due to the changed conditions brought about by logging. Both situations complicated the NPS management goal of restoring natural conditions and processes to the islands. In 1981, park ecologist Robert Brander identified fire management as one of the most important issues facing the park: "Some native vegetation species owe their existence to fire. . . . A policy of total fire suppression may make it biologically and economically impossible to maintain those species at Apostle Islands National Lakeshore. Research has shown that some vegetative fuels are accumulating in abnormal amounts. . . . Those fuels will continue to accumulate if periodic fires do not consume them and the threat of uncontrollable conflagration will increase as years pass."[49]

Lakeshore officials made fire and disturbance history one of the primary goals of the park's research program. They needed to determine how often fires had burned in the past, which environments had burned, and how human activity had changed these fire regimes. Until this information could be acquired, NPS staff suppressed all fires, aggravating the problem of heavy fuel load and the risk of catastrophic fires. Like the question of reseeding hemlock, choices about the future of the island forest had been shaped by the past.

In 2005, the NPS created a fire management plan with the goal of restoring fire to park ecosystems. NPS officials realized that this was necessary "to restore, protect, and propagate the Park's presettlement vegetation, maintain ecological integrity and biodiversity, and mitigate hazardous fuel conditions, reducing the potential for resource damage due to fire." Most of the islands have been placed in the "Natural Fire Management Unit." This does not mean abandoning fire suppression and letting all fires run their course, regardless of origin — history precludes this option, because of the heavy fuel loads that have built up over decades and the risk of particularly severe fires. Rather, it means compiling the research and information necessary to make decisions on an island-by-island, fire-by-fire basis. Some fires will be allowed to burn, especially those in ecosystems historically shaped by the presence of fire. But others, those that threaten human safety, private property, or valuable resources such as the lighthouses, will be suppressed. The plan also suggests that the use of prescribed burns and mechanical treatments might be necessary to reduce the heavy fuel loads, an intervention designed, ironically, to increase the "naturalness" of the modern park's fire regime.[50]

The dilemma faced by NPS managers parallels the one that confronted John Knight and William Vilas more than a century ago: the altered fire regimes created by human action endangered what each hoped the forest would become. Knight and Vilas sought to capitalize on the future value of the forest, a value threatened by the increased risk of fire. NPS managers also encountered the altered fire regimes as a threat, although they of course had a very different notion of how the forest should be valued. Instead of profit, they hoped to make the forest a model of prelogging ecological conditions. The fire-suppression policies of the previous decades (intended in part to protect the investments of landowners like Knight and Vilas) had removed fire from the park's ecosystems. To maximize their conception of the value of the islands' forests, NPS managers sought to restore fire to its natural role. For both the businessman and the manager, fire was just one element that factored into a complicated calculus of how to value the island forest in the present and to plan for its future.

Valuing the Forest

If species composition, water access, and the decisions of individual landowners determined which parts of the forest lumberjacks entered first, the federal government determined which areas they avoided. The transfer of public land into private hands served as one of the chief goals of nineteenth-century land policy, to the advantage of men like Knight and Vilas. By 1900, white pine had been removed from most of the islands, and the logging of the hemlock and hardwood stands was well underway. But in several parts of the archipelago, the forests remained virtually untouched. A series of jurisdictional boundaries drawn by the federal government kept valuable timberlands off the market, out of the hands of land speculators and away from the lumberjack's axe.

Lighthouses established to guide the Great Lakes shipping trade inadvertently protected some of the most accessible islands. The reservation of the Red Cliff Band of the Lake Superior Chippewa, located along the shore of the Bayfield Peninsula, retained its heavy forest cover into the twentieth century. This had nothing to do with the economics of the logging industry, but with attempts to assimilate Native Americans into mainstream society. The lands marked off by these jurisdictional boundaries have had different histories and subsequently different modern forest patterns and management concerns.

In the mid-nineteenth century, the Ojibwe signed three treaties with the United States that established the modern political landscape of northern Wisconsin. In the "Pine Tree Treaty" of 1837, the Ojibwe ceded a vast territory of north-central Wisconsin and eastern Minnesota—an area desired because of the access it provided to valuable pinelands. In the 1842 Treaty of La Pointe, the Ojibwe ceded the land north of the 1837 cession, including the Apostle Islands and the Chequamegon Bay, as well as the Upper Peninsula of Michigan—one of the richest copper deposits in the world. A final treaty, signed in 1854, secured for the United States access to the Mesabi Iron Range on the north shore of Lake Superior and also established four reservations in Wisconsin: Bad River and Red Cliff on the Chequamegon Bay and Lac Courte Oreilles and Lac du Flambeau in north-central Wisconsin. In negotiating these treaties, the Ojibwe retained usufructuary rights in the ceded territories—that is, the right to hunt, fish, and gather wild rice. The political boundaries established by these treaties, as well as future contests over the meaning and extent of reserved rights, played crucial roles in the establishment of Apostle Islands National Lakeshore and the management of the island wilderness.[51]

The heavily timbered Bad River reservation stretches for over 124,000 acres to the south and west of Ashland, including the rich wild rice areas of the Kakagon Sloughs and a two-hundred-acre parcel of land on Madeline Island with access to important fishing grounds. The Red Cliff reservation runs north from Bayfield along the shore of the Bayfield Peninsula. The 1854 treaty set aside 2,500 acres at Red Cliff, but President Abraham Lincoln enlarged the reservation by executive order in 1863 to roughly 14,000 acres. The reservation includes most of the shoreline that faces the Apostle Islands. Both reservations contained extensive and valuable timberlands.[52]

The Bureau of Indian Affairs (BIA) strictly managed the timber resources under its control.[53] As on the lighthouse reserves, government officials withheld Indian timberlands from the market because they had a higher value when put to a different purpose. The BIA tied its timber policy to the larger goal of assimilation. The paternalism characteristic of nineteenth-century Indian policy informed every element of BIA forest management. Indians were not allowed to sell reservation timber and could only clear land for agricultural purposes. In the 1870s, the BIA began to allot the Ojibwe reservations; that is, to divide tribal lands into individual ownership with the goal of assimilation through training in agriculture. Despite private ownership, the BIA retained tight control over the ability of Indians to sell their timber.[54]

The Ojibwe bands had no uniform opinion about allotment and logging. Ethnic, religious, and racial lines divided the Ojibwe bands. Some Ojibwe had closer ties to the white community—by marriage or ancestry—than did others. This put some people in a position to more fully embrace the market opportunities and private property represented by allotment, while others remained committed to tribal ownership and subsistence. And many mixed the two paths. In any case, the opinions of individual Ojibwe often mattered little to BIA officials.[55]

As the logging industry in the Chequamegon Bay expanded, officials at the La Pointe Agency—which administered most of the Wisconsin Ojibwe reservations—strayed from BIA policy and initiated small-scale logging on the Red Cliff reservation. In 1871, the BIA opened a mill at Red Cliff, as well as a cooperage, a carpenter's shop, and a boardinghouse for the mill workers. The mill produced 250,000 board feet of lumber a year—roughly the same amount as the other small commercial mills in the area. The Indian agents who permitted this logging pushed the limits of the federal policy that restricted the sale of timber to that which fostered agriculture, but rationalized that these activities cleared land, supplied timber for fencing and agricultural use, and provided a way for Red Cliff members to earn money.[56]

Although the Chequamegon Bay timber trade continued to grow, an important shift in federal Indian policy halted logging on the reservations in 1876. The treaty of 1854 had provided the president with the authority to assign reservation lands to family heads, and in 1876 the Red Cliff band became the first of the Wisconsin Ojibwe to have their lands allotted. As they prepared to shift tribal lands into individual ownership, BIA officials stopped all logging on unallotted land. Logging operations on the Red Cliff Reservation through 1875 had taken place on land held communally by the tribe; these activities ceased with allotment. Although thirty-one 80-acre parcels were allotted in 1876, a delay in processing the patents held up the transfer of these lands, forcing the suspension of all logging activity at Red Cliff.[57]

As the BIA processed allotments, the logging of Indian timber resumed. By 1884, over five hundred Ojibwe from the Bad River, Red Cliff, and the Lac du Flambeau reservations had received individual patents. Many Ojibwe demanded the right to sell the timber on land that they now owned as individuals. Agent William R. Durfee devised a plan for logging allotted lands. Durfee did not want the Ojibwe to simply sell the stumpage rights. Doing so would provide money, but Durfee believed that Indian timber had an additional social value as a tool for assimilation. He established a system that allowed Indians to log three-quarters of the timber from their allotted lands, reserving the rest as a woodlot for home use. White laborers would not be allowed on the reservations; the Ojibwe were required to complete the work themselves. Durfee did not base this system on the economics of the lumber market, or even the financial interests of the Ojibwe. Rather, he believed that woods work could be a source of education:

> It was not to the advantage of the Indian to have all his pine cut off, to sell his stumpage, and get a large amount of money without labor, because he would not know the value of money coming to him in that way and it would soon be squandered; that all he would have left would be the land covered with stumps and would be in a poorer condition than when he began . . . [Under this plan the] work would last for a great many years . . . the younger ones growing up in the community might improve and become self-supporting men.

Durfee's system received approval from the BIA in 1883.[58]

The system was quickly turned to the advantage of land speculators. James T. Gregory, who succeeded Durfee as the head of the La Pointe Agency in 1885, disregarded many of the policies established to regulate reservation logging. He allowed the Ojibwe to sell their stumpage rights to white contractors and freed contractors from the requirement of hiring Indian labor. He permitted the loggers working on the reservations to selectively cut the best timber from individual allotments, leaving the remainder devalued and at significant fire risk. He also finalized these contracts without the approval of the Washington, D.C., office of the BIA. Gregory's interpretation of BIA timber policies led to a dramatic increase in logging on Wisconsin reservations. From 1882 to 1885, under Durfee, Wisconsin Ojibwe signed 206 contracts for close to 77 million board feet of lumber. With Agent Gregory in charge from 1885 to 1888, these numbers increased to 1,203 contracts for close to 383 million board feet.[59]

That Gregory had administered so dramatic an increase in logging was hardly surprising; he had received his appointment at the behest of lumbermen John Knight and William Vilas. Gregory started work for the Vilas-owned and Knight-managed Superior Lumber Company in 1881. In 1885, Vilas secured an appointment for Gregory as the Indian agent at the La Pointe Agency. In 1887, Knight wrote to Vilas concerned that the delays in allotting lands on Wisconsin reservations were threatening the investments of their industry colleagues. Knight wanted Vilas to use his influence to grease the wheels of the BIA bureaucracy. "[Local lumbermen] have undoubtedly invested a large amount of money in the project and they are very anxious — indeed much alarmed. . . . These men are our friends and have been honest and upfront in their dealings with these Indians and if you feel you can help them out by asking the Secy. of the Interior to take the subject up. . . . I am sure that the approval will not be a mistake." The Superior Lumber Company did not hold any contracts for reservation timber. But D. A. Kennedy, an employee of the company, had extensive contracts for Bad River timber, many of them printed on Superior Lumber Company letterhead.[60]

The logging activities on the Ojibwe reservations became the subject of a congressional inquiry. Lumbermen from central Wisconsin accused Gregory of favoritism in doling out timber contracts to friends and former colleagues like D. A. Kennedy, and in March 1888 the Republican-dominated Congress appointed a committee to investigate allotment and timber sales on Wisconsin Ojibwe reservations. After collecting over 1,300 pages of testimony and documentary evidence, the committee issued a damning report. It declared findings of "inexcusable neglect of duty" by the commissioner of Indian Affairs and "willful and deliberate disobedience of laws and orders, and gross abuse of official power" by Gregory. The committee further concluded that "a plan originally designed to benefit the Indians . . . has been perverted into a system under which greedy contractors have rushed upon the reservations." The onslaught had "already absolutely denuded the finest timber tracts." The committee ordered an immediate cessation of all reservation logging until a new regulatory system could be devised.[61]

The inquiry had more to do with partisan politicking than Indian welfare. The committee did not find any specific wrongdoing on the part of John Knight, and held William Vilas responsible in his role as secretary of the interior (a post to which he was appointed in January 1888), but not for his connections to the Superior Lumber Company. The scandal demonstrates that some methods of valuing land had more power than others. It also illustrates how some people were more effective than others at using the power of the state for their own ends.[62]

But a strange thing had happened at Red Cliff during the years that Gregory had encouraged widespread logging on the Ojibwe reservations: almost no logging took place. Red Cliff had been spared the rush of white lumbermen. The government lacked the authority to allot most of the lands in the Red Cliff reservation, and the Ojibwe were only allowed to sell the stumpage rights on lands that they owned individually. The treaty of 1854 had provided authority to allot the lands in the original four sections of the reservation as well as on the other reservations created by the treaty. These original sections were parceled out in 1876. But the BIA did not have authority to allot the eleven thousand acres added to the Red Cliff reservation by executive order in 1863. No new timber sales were permitted throughout the 1880s. The majority of reservation lands remained untouched.[63]

The delay in allotment of the Red Cliff reservation altered the economics of the logging industry in the Chequamegon Bay. The unallotted portion of the reservation stretched north from Bayfield around the edge of the Bayfield Peninsula. Lake Superior provided the same advantages of accessibility and transportation as on the islands—felled trees had to be hauled only a short distance for easy shipment to the mills. One 1874 estimate noted that the "pine on the reservation averages a good quality . . . it [is] one of the most favorable points for manufacturing and shipping lumber on Lake Superior." The value of the reservation timber increased with time, as the pine trees throughout the region disappeared. By 1898, when Wisconsin State forester Filibert Roth visited the area, the Red Cliff reservation contained the last large block of uncut pine timber on the Bayfield Peninsula and one of the best stands left in the state.[64]

As the value of the Red Cliff timberlands increased, pressure mounted from all sides to authorize logging. Lumbermen wanted access to the rich pinelands. Many Red Cliff residents, cognizant of the money being made by Ojibwe on other reservations, demanded their allotments and the right to sell their timber. In 1888, they petitioned for allotment under the authority granted to the government by the Dawes Severalty Act of 1887. But due to the ongoing Senate investigation of timber sales at other La Pointe Agency reservations, the BIA took no action. The agents who succeeded James Gregory at the La Pointe Agency repeatedly asked the BIA to hasten the allotment process, to no effect.[65]

All parties recognized the cost of delay: fire could destroy the valuable pine forests before anyone had earned a penny. "The pine timber should be disposed of without delay, as it is rapidly going to destruction by wind and fire," explained Agent M. A. Leahy in 1889. Leahy and his successors issued similar warnings on an annual basis. These predictions came true in 1896. In mid-October, a fire raged through the heart of the Red Cliff reservation, severely burning over seven million board feet of prime pine. The burned timber retained a portion of its value, but only if it was logged immediately. If left to stand for the entire winter and following summer, insects and rot would destroy what good logs remained.[66]

The fire prompted the BIA to allot the remaining Red Cliff tribal lands. The BIA directed La Pointe agent W. A. Mercer to devise a plan for the immediate salvage logging of the burned region as well as for the standing unburned timber. The entire Red Cliff Reservation — over fourteen thousand acres — now lay in the hands of individual Indians, parceled out to 204 household heads. Agent Mercer set up a system for Red Cliff that mirrored those at other Wisconsin Ojibwe reservations. In the 1890s, in the aftermath of the congressional hearings, the BIA had developed a system for reservation logging called the La Pointe Plan. A single contractor purchased stumpage rights to all timber on the reservation. The contractor faced stiff rules and regulations designed to protect Indian interests. Each individual allottee signed a contract, but with a uniform price for each type of timber. The standardized contracts were easier to police than the multitude of different contracts used in the 1880s. The plan also required the contractor to erect a mill on the reservation, to cut all timber logged on the reservation at that mill, and to give Indians preference in hiring in the mills and camps. The BIA began soliciting bids for the 7.5 million board feet of salvaged pine and 100 million board feet of standing timber on the Red Cliff Reservation in August 1897.[67]

Duluth lumberman Frederick L. Gilbert won the contract, and his newly formed Red Cliff Lumber Company (RCLC) began logging in the winter of 1897–98. The company cut over eight million board feet of white pine in its first year. By June 1898, the company had constructed a mill on the reservation as well as a store, a boardinghouse, additional employee housing, an electrical plant, docks, and wharves. The RCLC cut and milled an average of more than seven million board feet of pine over the next five years. The company's lumberjacks were aided, not only by the accessibility offered by Lake Superior, but also by railroads that reached every corner of the reservation, allowing the lumberjacks to cut both pine and hardwoods. Unlike many of the islands, which were logged first for pine and then later for hemlock and hardwoods, the Red Cliff Reservation was clear-cut. After reaching a peak of 12.3 million board feet in 1902–3, the total cut on the reservation fell steadily.[68]

Despite containing the last large stand of virgin timber on the Bayfield Peninsula, the timber reserves of the Red Cliff reservation did not last long. After just one decade of intensive logging, very little merchantable timber remained. A 1910 estimate placed the total standing timber at eleven million board feet. What good timber remained stood in widely scattered, isolated areas, making it hard to log and decreasing its value. When a fire destroyed the Red Cliff Lumber Company mill in 1906, Gilbert decided not to rebuild and defaulted on his contract. Thereafter, individual Red Cliff residents arranged for logging on their own allotments. These small-scale operations continued into the 1920s.[69]

Following the allotment and rapid removal of the timber, Red Cliff band members were quickly alienated from their land. Without timber, the land had little financial value. As people all over northern Wisconsin learned in the early twentieth century, poor soils and a short growing season ensured that farms rarely followed forests, despite the high hopes of town boosters and Indian agents. Indian landowners often struggled to pay their taxes and were forced to sell their land or watch it be condemned by the county. Others sold a portion of their lands to raise money for other purposes, such as fixing up houses or purchasing boats. The BIA encouraged these land sales, hoping to attract white homesteaders to the region. They saw Red Cliff lands that fronted Lake Superior as particularly marketable because of their potential use for summer cottages. By 1933, nearly 11,000 acres of Red Cliff lands (out of 14,000) had fallen out of Indian ownership. Of a population of six hundred, 505 Red Cliff residents owned no land at all. This mirrored patterns around the state and the nation. Allotment, and the land alienation that almost inevitably followed, dealt a devastating cultural and economic blow to most Native American groups.[70]

As timberland, the Red Cliff reservation had little remaining value. Logging had left behind a ravaged landscape, one with less forest cover, drier soil conditions, and an elevated fire risk. One evaluation stated that the "entire reservation is a slashing from which practically all the timber was supposed to have been removed, fires have run through much of this and killed it making it dry and inflammable fuel in which fires will easily start and spread destroying any timber of value standing in its path."[71]

But reservation lands had never been valued purely for financial reasons—certainly not by the Ojibwe themselves, but also not by the BIA officials who managed the reservations. These lands took on a new meaning in the 1930s, when federal Indian policy underwent a dramatic shift. For decades, Indian policy had sought assimilation, urging Native Americans to join mainstream society. Early logging operations at Red Cliff were guided by this principle, an attempt to encourage Indians to take up farming or to teach them "American" habits and skills. This policy culminated in allotment, which aimed to sever tribal relationships to land in favor of individual ownership. In the 1930s, federal policy instead tried to reinvigorate and support Indian cultures. Ending allotment and reinstating tribal landownership emerged as a central tenet of this agenda. The 1934 Indian Reorganization Act (IRA) enabled Indians to formalize tribal governments and appropriated two million dollars per year to reestablish the Indian land base. Land would no longer be used as a tool for assimilation, but rather for tribal independence.[72]

Red Cliff band members overwhelmingly voted to accept the IRA (138 to 1), primarily because of the potential the act held for the return of alienated lands. In 1937, BIA officials used IRA funds to purchase 5,086 acres of tax-delinquent reservation land from Bayfield County for the Red Cliff band. The timber on this land had little financial value. But officials hoped that it could serve as a source of fuelwood and that, with proper management, it could become a source of commercial pulpwood. BIA officials also hoped to use the newly acquired land to teach the principles of conservation and land management, to "[instill] in the youth the need for protection and maintenance of our forest resources." This meant limiting sales of the remaining timber and inaugurating tree-planting programs and other forest management techniques. By returning the land to Indian control, BIA officials believed that "we have gone a long ways down that road which points to a self supporting Indian community." In other words, the land still had greater social than financial value. BIA officials a half century earlier had used similarly paternalistic logic to promote the logging and sale of Indian lands in the first place. The policies of the 1880s thus constricted the management options for BIA foresters and Ojibwe leaders in the 1930s.[73]

The cultural goals of timber management on the Red Cliff reservation have left an ecological footprint. Although little research has been done on this subject at Red Cliff, research at the Bad River Reservation, thirty miles to the south along the shore of Chequamegon Bay, has revealed significant differences between off- and on-reservation lands. Early attempts to force Ojibwe into farming lifestyles (and Ojibwe resistance to these efforts) and later management for pulpwood production have ensured that, as forests in the area have regenerated after the logging era, aspen/paper birch and balsam fir/aspen forests dominate the Bad River Reservation, while agricultural lands and hardwood forests predominate off of it. Location inside or outside the reservation boundary is the single most important factor in determining modern forest type.[74]

The legacy of BIA timber management has had a social and cultural component as well. The resulting patterns of Indian and non-Indian landownership on the reservation played an important role in the creation of Apostle Islands National Lakeshore. Almost two-thirds of the lakeshore's mainland unit, 1,573 acres, lies within the boundaries of the Red Cliff Reservation, alienated land once allotted to the Ojibwe. In the 1960s, Indian distrust of the federal government scrapped initial plans for a much larger park that would have included Indian-owned land on the Bad River and Red Cliff reservations. Subsequently, the NPS and the Red Cliff Band have been cautious in their interactions with each other. This relationship is further complicated by the enduring Ojibwe goal of regaining control over all land within the reservation boundary, a goal obviously threatened by the presence of the NPS.[75]

The overlap between the boundaries of the Red Cliff Reservation and the national lakeshore has created a series of special management considerations. The first full management document for the park states that one of the administrative goals of the park is "to cooperate with the Red Cliff band, Lake Superior Chippewa Indians, in formulating plans, law enforcement, and managing resources on the mainland unit." This cooperation has resulted in an agreement on the exercise of Ojibwe treaty rights within the park and has altered NPS plans for the interpretation and development of the national lakeshore. The reservation boundary complicates fire management in the park as well. The 2005 Fire Management Plan divided the park into two categories: the islands are in the Natural Fire Management Unit, and the mainland is in the Special Use Fire Management Unit. While the goal of fire management on the islands is to restore fire to its natural role in the ecosystem, on the mainland the goal is "intensive protection for human life and property within and outside Park boundaries." This means that all fires, regardless of their cause, will be suppressed. Although the resource management goal remains the restoration of prelogging conditions in the park, including a natural fire regime, the political realities created by the overlap between national lakeshore and reservation boundaries serves as a higher priority.[76]

This history shaped the boundaries of the designated wilderness as well. When NPS officials initiated the wilderness management process in 2001, they immediately ruled out wilderness designation for all portions of the mainland. In part, this was because the NPS only controls a narrow strip of land along the shore, an area close to (and occasionally crossed by) roads. But it was also because of the history of the relationship between federal land managers and Native Americans—both at Red Cliff and elsewhere in the nation. When BIA officials tied the cultural goal of assimilation to forestry policy in the 1870s, they set the forests of Red Cliff on a different course, in both ecological and political terms. Well over a century later, NPS wilderness planners wrestled with the legacies of this decision.

The Last Whistle

By the 1920s, many of the mills around Chequamegon Bay, and around the state, had shut down. They simply ran out of wood. The lumber companies either went out of business or moved their operations to more productive lumbering regions. They left behind a landscape plagued by forest fires, poor soil, and erosion—a wasteland. Or so it seemed at the time. As forests regenerated in the ensuing decades, they grew as well a new kind of value—as a place for recreation and ecological study, as a wilderness. When NPS personnel tried to manage this new wilderness, they found their choices about the future of the island forests shaped by the past.

Bayfield's largest mill, the Wachsmuth Lumber Company, reflected industry trends. The mill had originally been owned by R. D. Pike, one of Bayfield's earliest residents, who had established his lumber company in Bayfield in 1869. The mill had grown with the town and served as one of its most important institutions. Wachsmuth lumberjacks logged the Bayfield Peninsula and some of the smaller islands until the mid-1920s. When the end approached in 1924, the *Bayfield County Press* offered what amounted to an obituary:

> Practically all the large timber on the Peninsula, owned or purchased recently by the company, has been cut and but a few remaining logs in the slip are yet to be sawed up, and the big whistle at the mill will announce the completion of its work. . . . Millions of feet of the best North Wisconsin pine, hemlock and hardwood timber have passed over the great chain to the log deck of the mill during the years of operation here, and Bayfield Peninsula lumber had gone into construction throughout the entire western hemisphere. . . . We will miss the familiar sound of the big whistle at morning, noon, and night, and the familiar hum of the whirring saws as they cut their way through the logs.

On September 9, 1924, at exactly 7:30 PM, fifty people gathered to watch the last hemlock log go through the Wachsmuth Company's Bayfield mill. The plant engineer blew the mill's whistle for nine minutes. That final log provided 410 board feet of lumber.[77]

The Schroeder Lumber Company followed a similar path. When it had stripped Stockton Island of its hemlock and hardwoods, the company moved its employees and equipment first to Michigan Island and then to Outer Island. It had 225 men stationed at its Outer Island railroad camp heading into the winter of 1930, with plenty of standing timber still waiting to be cut. But as the Great Depression deepened, Schroeder could not maintain its operations. It closed the Outer Island camp, and the Ashland mill shut its doors soon thereafter. Other logging and milling companies around Chequamegon Bay shut down at the same time, doomed by the combination of dwindling resources and a stagnant economy.[78]

By the 1920s, the landscapes of the Apostle Islands looked much the same as those in almost every other part of the northern Great Lakes. The region had come to be known as the cutover. Stumplands and fire scars had replaced the dense forests that had covered the area just eighty years earlier. These ruined landscapes prompted conversations across the region and the nation about the future of the cutover. Some people hoped that a network of small farms would replace the forests, fulfilling a long-held agrarian ideal. Others believed that the trees should be regrown and that the area could become once again the site of productive forestry and tourism. As economists and planners debated, a new forest emerged from the cutover landscapes.[79]

Seen from the air or water, the modern forests of the Apostle Islands and the rest of the northern Great Lakes seem homogenous, all having followed a similar path of logging, fire, and regeneration. The seeming uniformity of this forest masks important local variations in forest history. In each place, geography, economics, and politics came together in different ways to shape local patterns of logging. At Outer Island, limited access and a history of fire created ecological conditions unique to that place. Stockton Island's history as a speculative investment for timber barons determined the time and place of logging. And on the Red Cliff Reservation, the cultural goals of federal Indian policy took precedence over other factors in shaping forest history. Each of these variations left its mark. The forests of the Apostles — like those everywhere — are not uniform. They are a collection of patches and boundaries, a network of different landscapes, each one created differently. These differences have revealed themselves in the dilemmas faced by land managers who found their choices prescribed by history.

Nowhere is this clearer than in the lighthouse reserves. The U.S. Lighthouse Board erected the first lighthouse in Chequamegon Bay on Michigan Island in 1856. As the shipping trade increased, the agency established lighthouses on several of the other islands: Long Island, 1858; Raspberry Island, 1863; Outer Island, 1874; Sand Island, 1881; Devils Island, 1891; and Long Island/Chequamegon Point, 1893.[80] The agency reserved a plot of land at each station as a fuel source for the use of lighthouse keepers and their families. Some of these reserves were quite small: 111 acres on Sand Island and just 77 on Michigan Island. But elsewhere, the government reserved entire islands, such as on Raspberry (295 acres) and Devils (320 acres). The reserves had a higher value in the service of maintaining shipping lanes than as timberlands, and this dictated a different kind of land use. Some logging occurred in the immediate vicinity of the light stations, but commercial logging was prohibited. The reserves today provide some of the best examples of old-growth forest in the Great Lakes region. The lighthouses and their reserves stand as the preeminent cultural and natural resources of today's Apostle Islands National Lakeshore.

The lighthouse reserves demonstrate once again the ways that history confines modern management. The mainland is not the only area that receives protection from fire. The islands, although designated as the Natural Fire Management Unit, contain over forty Fire Exclusion Zones. These are areas where NPS personnel will suppress all fires, regardless of origin, because they contain resources too valuable to risk. This primarily means cultural resources, like lighthouses and other historical structures. But areas of old growth, such as the hemlock forest protected by the Outer Island lighthouse reserve, also receive this classification. This makes sense, considering the ecological and scientific value of the old-growth stands. But it creates a richly ironic management situation: the goal of reinstating a fire regime unhindered by human intervention does not apply to the areas of the park most prized for their naturalness. Lines in the forest drawn a century ago still inform management options today.[81]

National Park Service officials were not the first government representatives to face management dilemmas created by human choices. These issues surfaced with the earliest attempts at resource management in the islands. This is most clearly evident in the attempts by the state of Wisconsin to manage the fisheries of the Apostle Islands. Beginning in the late nineteenth century, state fisheries experts sought to protect—and also to control—both the state's fisheries resources and the people who depended upon them.

2

Creating a Legible Fishery

IN APRIL 1997, THE WISCONSIN DEPARTMENT OF NATURAL RESOURCES (DNR) brokered a controversial deal with the fishermen of Lake Superior. State managers cut the number of commercial fishing licenses for lake trout by more than half—from twenty-one to ten. The trout quota for the commercial fishery dropped from 15,000 to 7,140 per year. Opposition to the plan arose primarily because the DNR agreed to pay the eleven displaced fishermen more than $1.5 million over the course of ten years in return for their licenses. Opponents of the buyout worried that the plan set a poor precedent by treating a public resource like trout as private property, requiring the state to purchase the right to regulate. The state legislature addressed these concerns by passing a law guaranteeing that the buyout could only happen once.[1]

Wisconsin DNR officials saw the plan as a political solution to a complicated natural resource management problem—the need to reduce commercial fishing pressure on lake trout. The fish had only recently rebounded from a collapse caused by overfishing and the impact of the sea lamprey, an invasive predator that had devastated the fishery in the 1950s. Fisheries experts wanted to further protect the still-fragile species. Other groups wanted to catch the fish: sportsmen, whose disposable income provided a key part of the local economy, and Ojibwe fishermen, who had won a series of court cases in the 1980s affirming their treaty-guaranteed right to harvest lake trout. Commercial fishing had long served as the most important and reliable industry in the Apostle Islands region and formed a central component of the town of Bayfield's identity. State fisheries managers believed that the buyout plan recognized the historical significance of the commercial fishery while at the same time alleviating pressure on the lake trout so that other demands could be met.

The ability of state managers to retire more than half of the commercial fleet and to reallocate the fishery to other uses represented the maturation of a process that had begun well over a century earlier: the growing authority of the state to determine how natural resources would be used and valued. In 1874, the Wisconsin legislature created the Wisconsin Fisheries Commission (WFC).[2] Initially, the commission measured the state's fisheries and started an artificial propagation program. It had little responsibility or power. But as the managerial authority of the state increased, the state acquired the ability to regulate and restrict who fished, what type of equipment they used, and for what reason.

State managers sought to bring what scholar James C. Scott calls "legibility" to the fishery; that is, they tried to organize the fisheries in a way that made them easier to control. A chaotic fishery, with uncounted, unregulated fishermen using the resource for a variety of competing reasons, was difficult to manage. Fisheries managers sought to counter this chaos by using state authority to create license requirements, closed seasons, and spawning sanctuaries. These actions ordered the fishery and made it easier to control—they made the fishery more legible. In the late nineteenth century, as the Progressive conservation movement gained momentum, the state took an ever more active role in regulating the use of natural resources such as timber, water, and wildlife.[3]

The task of making the fisheries legible fell to James Nevin, the state superintendent of fisheries from 1882 to 1921. When Nevin assumed his post, the state's fisheries faced a crisis. The lucrative whitefish fishery seemed on the verge of collapse. Whitefish harvests on Lake Michigan had dropped by over 25 percent since 1870, and experts predicted that Lake Superior's production would soon follow. Nevin recognized that unlimited, unregulated fishing had pushed the fish stocks to their breaking point. Too many fishermen, using too many different kinds of equipment, fishing for too many different reasons and for too many different species had created a chaotic, disordered fishery, a system that could only lead to disaster. "The number and variety of nets used for fishing are appalling, and their destructive character, supplemented by the spear, are rapidly exterminating the white fish and salmon trout," stated the WFC in one of its early reports. To fight this problem, Nevin and his colleagues sought to bring order to the fishery—to regulate and restrict how and when fishermen could harvest whitefish and other commercial species. "It is only through timely legislation and a vigorous enforcement of the law that such a calamity—for a calamity it would be—can be averted."[4]

The use of state authority to make the fisheries legible was but a first step. In the decades that followed, state managers extended their authority to include regulation of sport fishing, timber harvests, and outdoor recreation. This expansion of state authority had significant consequences for the Apostle Islands, as the state reshaped the very environments it sought to manage. On both land and water, the state segregated production- and consumption-oriented uses of nature. By the mid-twentieth century, the state managed the Apostle Islands as recreational wilderness, actively suppressing activities based on the extraction of resources. The 1997 retirement of commercial fishing licenses and the ensuing reallocation of lake trout quotas to the sport fishery represent a late step in this process—and an ironic one, considering that the state first exercised its power to protect commercial fishing.

Although James Nevin and his colleagues argued that conservation measures would maximize public utility, not everyone benefited from the increase in state power. In the Apostle Islands, the well-capitalized, full-time fishermen and large fish dealers benefited from the state's attempt to bring order to the fishery, while the Ojibwe Indians found their uses of the same resources restricted. Ojibwe had participated in commercial fishing in the Apostles since the 1830s, but they moved in and out of the industry, sometimes fishing for wages and other times for subsistence. They used a variety of methods to fish—spears, nets, and lines through the ice. These changing methods and motivations were exactly the kinds of activity that state resource managers such as Nevin found difficult to control. Beginning in the 1880s, the state conservation bureaucracy forced Ojibwe fishermen to obey a growing list of regulations. Activities that the Ojibwe had pursued without interference for generations became criminalized. The Ojibwe were the first group to have their access to island resources limited by the growing power of the state, but not the last. The regulation of the fishery created an important framework for restricting economic activity that foreshadowed the arrival of the National Park Service and the management of the islands as a wilderness free from the scars of industrial activity.

A Chaotic Fishery, 1850–1890

Before the 1880s, when state authorities began regulating the island fisheries, environmental and market conditions governed the fisheries of the Chequamegon Bay. Market prices determined which fish the fishermen sought, but fishing techniques and seasons depended on the habits of the fish. Underwater environments and available technology also shaped patterns of fishing. None of these factors remained constant; underwater environments and fishing technologies fluctuated. It was the very multitude of these governing factors that led fisheries managers such as James Nevin to conclude that the commercial fishery needed regulation.

Commercial fishing emerged as one of Bayfield's most important industries in the years following the establishment of the town in 1856. The *Bayfield Mercury* reported in 1857 that shipments of fish had been sent to several cities on the southern Great Lakes. The lumber camps and copper and iron mines that developed around western Lake Superior provided additional markets. The Bayfield fleet grew dramatically in 1870, when the fishing company N. & F. Boutin moved from Two Harbors, Wisconsin, fleeing the depleting harvests on Lake Michigan. The firm brought 550 gill nets, 12 pound nets, a variety of small fishing boats, and a large schooner named the *Alice Craig*. Like several other companies in Bayfield, N. & F. Boutin processed, packed, and sold salted fish.[5]

The Boutins chose Bayfield for a reason. With its bountiful fish stocks, easily accessed fishing grounds, and the protective ring of the Apostle Islands, the Chequamegon Bay had already earned a reputation as one of Lake Superior's most productive fisheries. The islands provided a particularly good location for catching whitefish (*Coregonus clupeaformis*), the most prized and marketable of all Great Lakes fish. Whitefish frequent shallow-water habitats, moving in schools as they comb the lake bottom for small fish and crustaceans. The Apostles project into the largest area of shallow water on Lake Superior, making the islands the premier whitefish grounds on the lake. The Boutins were not alone in taking advantage of the island fishing grounds. In 1880—the first year for which this type of statistic is available—414 fishermen plied Lake Superior; at least 160 of them lived in Bayfield and Ashland.[6]

Fishermen sought lake trout as well as whitefish, and the islands provided good trout grounds too. Trout (*Salvelinus namaycush*) could be caught off the deepwater ledge that surrounds the Apostle Islands archipelago, a preferred feeding area. Bayfield fish dealers like the Boutins sent their boats as far away as Isle Royale (over 120 miles) in search of lake trout. In October, the trout headed for shallower waters to spawn, and the Apostles were prime spawning grounds. Fishermen depended on these midautumn runs to catch trout in large quantities.[7]

Fishing equipment and techniques depended on the habits of the fish and the environments they inhabited. Pound nets provided the most reliable catch but required a significant investment in equipment and labor. Fishermen set pound nets (also called pond nets) at fixed locations in shallow water. A straight, long leader guided fish through a tunnel and into an enclosed area called a pot, from which fish found it hard to escape. Every few days, fishermen scooped out the entrapped fish. The key event in the poundnet season was the setting of the nets. In the Apostles, this usually occurred in late May. Once set, the nets could not be easily moved—they stayed in place through the summer and sometimes into the autumn spawning season. Pound nets required more capital than other netting technologies, especially in labor costs. A team of three men could set and tend three to five nets. Only well-capitalized operations could fish in this manner. A federal investigator assessed Great Lakes poundnet fisheries in the mid-1880s: "The nature of the apparatus used in pound-fishing and the outlay which it involves make it impossible for men of limited means to engage in it. The industry is therefore largely carried on by men who possess considerable capital and capacity." Not until the Boutin brothers moved to Bayfield did poundnet fishing become popular among the islands.[8]

But pound nets could not be used everywhere. They could only be employed in relatively shallow water with a sand or clay bottom, because fishermen had to drive the posts into the lake bed. The shallow channels of the Apostle Islands archipelago and the Chequamegon Bay made pound nets a more popular technology in the Bayfield fishery than elsewhere on Lake Superior. In 1885, Bayfield fishermen used 124 sets of pound nets, while Ashland fishermen used 20. Only 86 other pound nets could be found on the entire lake.[9]

Gill nets required less capital and could be used almost anywhere. Fishermen dropped gill nets into the lake, weighing down one end with stone or lead and boosting the other end with floats made of cork or wood. They returned to the nets after several days, hauled them in, and picked out the fish. New nets were then set—in the same location, or they could be easily moved if the fisherman thought he would have better luck elsewhere. Fishermen brought the wet

2.1 Sand Island fishermen Peter Hansen, Frederick Hansen, Lenus Jacobsen, and Herman Johnson Sr. in 1914. In the late nineteenth century, Sand Island became a center of the island fishing industry and the home to a settlement of fishermen and farmers who emigrated from Norway. Courtesy of the National Park Service.

nets to shore, dried them on reels, and readied them for the next round. A typical fisherman had four gangs of fifteen to twenty nets, keeping three gangs in the water at any one time. These lighter, more mobile rigs cost less to purchase and maintain than pound nets.[10]

Itinerant and part-time fishermen used far simpler technologies. Seine nets— long, sling-shaped nets fixed to the shore at one end and swept in a half circle by a row boat to entrap nearshore schools of fish—could be operated by a single person. These were among the most popular nets in the early stages of the Great Lakes commercial fishery, but as the industry grew, and technology improved, seine nets declined in use. Still, they remained an easy, inexpensive option for people who did not have the money to invest in pound nets or gill nets.[11]

Fishermen who used these simpler technologies often fished part-time, but they made up a significant percentage of fishermen. An 1885 survey found that 62 percent of Lake Superior fishermen prosecuted their trade on a full-time basis, while 38 percent combined fishing with jobs in lumber camps, mines, or on the farm. Even those who listed their full-time employment as fishermen often spent time in other trades. Others fished full time, but only for a couple of years, hoping to earn enough money to purchase land or go into some other business.[12]

The relationships between the fishermen and fish dealers often dictated the fishing technology and extent of operations. These relationships were loose and fluctuating but fell into three categories. Some fishermen worked on a fixed wage, using the dealer's boats, nets, and other equipment. Others owned their own equipment and sold their catch to whichever dealer offered the best price. Still others fished on shares—they bought nets, supplies, and equipment from the dealer and promised to pay with two-fifths to one-half of their catch, sold to the dealer who had advanced them the equipment.

Fishermen and fish dealers in Bayfield used all of these arrangements. A big firm like N. & F. Boutin employed people directly or on shares, stationing them on the islands and sending their schooner, the *Alice Craig*, around the islands to pick up the catch. As the *Alice Craig* picked up fish, it also dropped off barrels and salt so that fishermen could preserve their catch until the next run. With such a large territory to cover and a heavy dependence on the weather for transportation, collection of fish from some island fish camps sometimes occurred only once a month. The Boutins also ran a dry goods store in Bayfield, from which they sold provisions to fishermen on credit. In 1879, for example, N. & F. Boutin put in over 1,200 gill nets (close to ninety linear miles of net), 28 pound nets, and 7 seine nets and that year marketed at least 11,000 half barrels of fish. The firm employed about seventy men, making it one of the largest fishing outfits on the lake, and also bought fish from independent fishermen.[13]

Wageworkers, independent fishermen, and large dealers populated the islands with small, seasonal fish camps. These camps consisted of little more than small shanties and perhaps a few net reels. Little evidence remains of these camps, scarcely more than scattered references in the local newspapers and the occasional comments of federal investigators who periodically assessed the fishery. Preferred locations for pound nets included the east bay of Sand Island, the channel between Rocky and South Twin islands, the shallow regions of Chequamegon Bay, and along Madeline Island. Gillnetters often camped on Stockton Island, the Rocky/South Twin channel, and Madeline Island. Oak, Bear, and Outer islands were also used as temporary fish camps.[14]

Only the most general picture of the lives of early fishermen can be drawn. French Canadians dominated the Chequamegon Bay commercial fishery. The Boutin family, for example, had emigrated from Canada earlier in the century.

Twenty-five of the forty-five people who listed their occupation as full-time fishermen in the 1880 census traced their ancestry to Canada. Many of these families had lived in the Chequamegon Bay area for several generations, arriving to work in the fur trade but staying after this trade declined. These statistics likely did not cover the part-time fishermen or the women who picked, cleaned, and dried nets on shore.[15]

The Ojibwe, too, played a key role in the Apostle Islands commercial fishery. Indian men and women had worked as wage laborers in the 1830s for the American Fur Company, the first commercial fishing venture in the islands. They continued in this role as the fishery expanded in the 1870s. One 1887 estimate counted a quarter of the Chequamegon Bay fishermen as either "Indians or part Indian," and officials at the La Pointe Agency reported through the end of the century that Ojibwe found regular work in the commercial fishery.[16]

As they integrated into the expanding American economy, Ojibwe blended subsistence pursuits with the new opportunities presented by the market. Fishing stands as an example of this balancing act. The ice that formed over the

2.2 Fishermen of lesser means used gill nets and seine nets, and populated the islands with small itinerant fishcamps from the 1870s through the 1950s. The National Park Service has restored this Manitou Island fishcamp to its appearance in the 1930s. Photograph by William Cronon.

shallow channels between the nearshore islands provided ideal conditions for spear fishing. The Ojibwe of the Red Cliff and Bad River bands were so successful in this enterprise that they made the Chequamegon Bay the only site of commercial spear fishing on Lake Superior. The Ojibwe used other techniques, including hook-and-line, seine nets, and gill nets. "The Indians lie down on the ice and cover their head over and watch, and when they see a trout coming, they coax him to take the hook," described one observer. In the 1890s, one white fisherman estimated that winter fishing was "done by Indians and other fishermen. Considerable many half-breeds—Indian blood. There would be probably upwards of 150 people engaged in this fishing in the winter. There will be ⅓ of that number who do not sell any fish—just fish for their own use." The mixture of subsistence and market activity constituted an essential component of Ojibwe economic life.[17]

Market price, available technology, and the feeding and spawning habits of whitefish and lake trout determined the organization and operation of the commercial fishing industry. As the nineteenth century drew to a close, however, the rules began to change. The arrival of the railroad at Bayfield and the development of new fishing technologies fueled a significant expansion of the industry. Until the 1880s, fishermen depended on the wind for transportation and their own strength for hauling heavy nets, and Bayfield's fish dealers had limited market options. Packing fish in barrels of salt for shipment by boat was the only way to transport fish. When the Wisconsin Central Railroad completed the line to Ashland in 1877, Bayfield dealers began to sell small amounts of fresh fish but still worked primarily with salted fish. The arrival of the railroad in Bayfield in 1883 ushered in a new era of commercial fishing in the Apostles. "Boutin & Mahan are shipping large quantities of fresh fish by almost every train" reported the *Bayfield County Press* in November 1883, only a month after the opening of the town's depot.[18]

Transportation technology improved on the water as well as on land. The first steamboat began toiling in the Lake Superior fishery in 1871. In 1879, the Boutins bought a steam tug, the *N. Boutin*, and used it along with their schooner to pick up fish and drop off salt and barrels to the island-based fishermen. Steamers allowed fishermen to reach fishing grounds farther away from Bayfield and also freed them from dependence on the wind to keep a regular schedule. Firms could more easily station their fishermen on outlying islands, and a fresh catch could be immediately put on ice, picked up by a steamer, and

2.3 Sand Island fishermen Jacob, Paul, and Fred Hansen set nets through the ice in the winter of 1933–34. Because of the shallow water in the channels around the islands, the Apostles were one of the most productive winter fisheries on Lake Superior. Courtesy of the National Park Service.

shipped to the railroad depot in Ashland or Bayfield. By 1885, four steamers docked in Bayfield.[19]

The railroad helped Bayfield catch the biggest fish of all: A. Booth Packing Company, the largest fish-packing firm in the Great Lakes, opened a dealership in Bayfield less than a year after the arrival of the railroad. The Chicago-based company ran a vertically integrated operation, catching, collecting, processing, and selling fish. As Chicago's railroad network stretched across the continent, Booth supplied more distant markets. At first, Booth could supply these markets from the waters of southern Lake Michigan, but as the company expanded and whitefish became scarcer, Booth looked farther north. When Lake Michigan's whitefish stocks declined, the company moved its fleet to Lake Superior. With its new railroad connection and well-known fishery, Bayfield emerged as the best spot for a highly capitalized fishing operation. "Bayfield is *the* point on this lake for successfully conducting this business," proclaimed Alfred Booth. The Bayfield Businessmen's Association donated a prime site in the center of town for a dock, and the company installed packinghouses, icehouses, and a freezing plant.[20]

The railroad and freezing technology changed the basic operations of the fishing industry. Fresh fish became the most important product. Where collection boats once dropped off salt and barrels for the preservation of fish, now they dropped off flaked ice to keep the fish fresh. The Booth Company could freeze up to ten thousand pounds a day and its four freezers at the Bayfield plant could hold close to one million pounds of fish. This gave the company a significant market advantage, because it could hold a large quantity of fish while it waited for a good price.[21]

The scale of island fishing operations expanded to supply the new packinghouse. In 1888, Booth stationed a steam tug on Rocky Island, with a crew of eight. The steamer allowed Booth's employees a far greater range than had been possible in the past. They could fish up to and beyond a distance of twenty miles from the island on a daily basis, almost all the way to the lake's north shore. Booth had a second steamer, the *Barker*, which it used as a collection boat. The *Barker* made regular runs to Rocky Island, stopping at the other island fish camps along the way.[22]

Other technologies transformed the fishing process between 1870 and 1900 and ensured that fishermen caught more fish with less effort. For example, fishermen switched from cotton to linen nets, which packed tighter and weighed less. The same number of fishermen could now handle a greater quantity of nets in a single lift. The size of the mesh on both pound and gill nets decreased, meaning that the fishermen snared smaller fish. The addition of steam-powered gillnet lifters in the 1890s enhanced fishing intensity still more. The switch from sail- to steam-powered boats significantly increased the capacity and range of each boat. While a sailboat used for gill nets handled an average of six linear miles of netting, a steam tug averaged twenty-nine miles. The number of fishermen employed in the islands and on the rest of Lake Superior increased, too, jumping from just over four hundred in 1880 to over nine hundred in 1903. One federal investigator estimated a 500 percent increase in the efficiency of fishing apparatus between 1870 and 1880. Fishermen had their own estimates, quantified in terms of pounds of fish caught, miles of net used, or number of boats. In any case, more fishermen used better equipment to catch more fish over a greater area of the lake.[23]

The amplified intensity of fishing translated into much higher production figures. In 1889, Great Lakes fishermen caught a whopping 146,284,000 pounds of fish—a record exceeded only twice since. The greatest expansion came between 1880 and 1885. The total catch for Lake Superior between those years expanded from 3.8 million pounds to nearly 9 million. Production levels did not remain at this high level, but in 1893 the Lake Superior catch again topped 8 million pounds, and in 1903 it surpassed 13 million pounds.[24]

With the arrival of the railroad and the expansion of the town's fleet, Bayfield secured its position as the most important fishing locale on Lake Superior. In 1885, 167 of the lake's 622 fishermen sailed from Bayfield, over 40 more than any of the other fourteen American ports. Bayfield had 209 of the lake's 510 fishing vessels, and the town's fishermen caught 2,832,500 pounds of fish in 1885, close to one-third of the total for the whole lake. Duluth, with just over 2 million pounds, came in a distant second. Bayfield's gillnetters had 2,000 gangs of nets, putting them in second place on the lake, but the town's 124 pound nets totaled more than all other ports combined. Bayfield's whitefish grounds remained particularly productive. In 1885, Chequamegon Bay fishermen accounted for 49 percent of the lake's whitefish harvest.[25]

The bloated production figures that followed the arrival of the railroad and the conversion to steam power masked disturbing changes under the water. The increased intensity of fishing in the Chequamegon Bay had an almost immediate impact: whitefish populations crashed in the 1890s. Most of the fishermen agreed that they had no one to blame but themselves.

Although there is no method to quantify the statistical relationship between fishing effort, commercial catch, and the health of the fish populations in the nineteenth century, contemporary observers agreed that that harvest levels were not keeping up with the increased fishing intensity. Despite increasing effort, production figures remained relatively stable. The fish, in other words, were becoming harder and harder to find. Whitefish— the most desirable commercial species—showed the first signs of stress. In 1880, whitefish made up 59.1 percent of Lake Superior's commercial catch, measured in pounds (2.257 million pounds). In 1885—despite record highs in total pounds of fish caught—this proportion fell to 51.8 percent (4.572 million pounds) and then dropped precipitously. In 1893, whitefish represented only one-third of the total catch (2.732 million pounds), and by 1903, a mere 6 percent (794,000 pounds). Similar changes occurred on the other Great Lakes.

As fishing intensity increased, the fish population lost its ability to replenish itself. Whitefish, which swim in discrete schools, are particularly vulnerable to this pattern of overfishing and collapse.[26]

The rapid decline of the whitefish catch was not unexpected. James Milner, who conducted the first federal survey of the Great Lakes fisheries in 1871, reported on the declining whitefish populations of the lower lakes at a time when the Lake Superior fisheries had barely been touched. A decade later, Chas W. Smiley compared Milner's 1871 findings with a second investigation conducted in 1880. He concluded that the tremendous increase in intensity of commercial fishing, declines in the average size of fish arriving at market, and continued fishing pressure portended the imminent collapse of the Great Lakes fishery: "[In] the natural order of events, remarkable diminution if not complete collapse is to be anticipated in the coming decade." In 1887, another investigator reported that "year by year men engaged in fishing have seen their feeding grounds almost deserted and the numbers still deminishing [sic], until at last to find a large whitefish in their nets is indeed a curiosity." By the 1880s, experts regularly expressed their concerns about the Lake Superior whitefish fishery.[27]

Although it is hard to accurately trace the health of the fish populations of so localized a region as the Chequamegon Bay, little doubt exists about the fate of the Bayfield whitefish industry.[28] The fishery showed signs of stress as early as 1880. State fish warden James Chapman reported unusually poor harvest years in 1886 and 1887, when the whitefish catch dropped from over two million pounds to under five hundred thousand pounds. The year 1888 started off poorly as well, when a series of spring storms kept the fishing fleet in Bayfield. By the end of the year, however, the fishermen reported an excellent harvest. Of course, Chapman and other observers commented not on the health of the fish population but on the economic status of the commercial fishery, related but distinct concerns.[29]

The observations of the 1880s foreshadowed the exhaustion of the Chequamegon Bay whitefish fishery. In 1885—the largest catch on record—whitefish made up over 73 percent (by weight, at 2.252 million pounds) of the Bayfield commercial harvest and nearly 70 percent again in 1890 (1.082 million pounds). But then the bottom dropped out. By 1899, whitefish made up a scant 4 percent of Bayfield's catch (61,000 pounds). James Smith, an independent fisherman with twenty years of experience fishing in the Apostles, observed that "the fishes are not as abundant as they were ten years ago . . . there is not one whitefish now to where there was 100 then . . . there has been a corresponding decrease in size, as well as numbers, and that not only are large fish much fewer, but that the general average is at least one pound lighter." The whitefish fishery of the Chequamegon Bay collapsed faster and more thoroughly than at any other point on Lake Superior. The region dropped from first to fourth in total production statistics and counted a lower percentage of whitefish than anywhere else on the lake.[30]

Many fishermen believed that the decline in whitefish could simply be attributed to overfishing. "The fishermen have cleaned them all out," one explained. "There has been too much fishing here, which has killed off the fish. The decrease began when the tugs came here." Another pointed out, "[Years] ago when fish were plentiful there were a great many small ones uselessly caught and thrown away. We have done that ourselves." The fishermen recognized that although the size of the commercial harvest had increased over the years, this came only in combination with more extensive and more efficient equipment. Other fishermen blamed the collapse of the whitefish on a decrease in the mesh size of gill nets and pound nets, which caught fish too small to sell on the market while wiping out whole schools of young fish before they matured. Still others believed that the fishing of the spawning grounds prevented the fish from reproducing. The fishermen "were killing the goose that laid the golden egg," lamented Duluth fish dealer M. F. Kalmbach, a forty-year veteran of the Great Lakes fisheries.[31]

Why had the Bayfield fishery suffered a more severe collapse than others on the lake? The intensity of fishing contributed to the decline. So, too, did the type of nets preferred by the fishermen. The sandy, flat lake bottom of the Chequamegon Bay and among the islands had long provided perfect conditions for setting pound nets. This had provided island fishermen with a competitive advantage in the whitefish fishery and had given the more well-capitalized fishing operations an advantage over smaller ones. But pound nets, the fishermen agreed, did far more damage to the fishery than gill nets. "[Pound nets are] much more detrimental to the fishes than gill nets, since they take a great many more young fish," commented one fishermen. "Especially is this true for whitefish." The repeated harvest of the young fish in the Chequamegon Bay and among the islands inhibited whitefish reproduction and contributed to the collapse of the Bayfield whitefish fishery.[32]

Other factors, in addition to overfishing, contributed to the collapse. The sawmills that rimmed Lake Superior dumped sawdust into the lake, fouling whitefish spawning grounds. Duluth and Ashland developed heavy industry based on the milling and transporting of coal, iron, and other metals. Pollution from these industries, as well as sewage and refuse from the growing cities of western Lake Superior, threatened water quality and whitefish health. Watershed changes from deforestation and agricultural land use degraded the underwater environments of Lake Superior. Some fishermen blamed these other potential causes for the whitefish crash, but most recognized their own role in the collapse.[33]

By the mid-1890s, little doubt existed about the state of the Chequamegon Bay whitefish fishery. What had been the most valuable component of the area's most important industry had disappeared almost entirely. Whitefish stocks in other parts of Lake Superior were showing similar signs of trouble. Fishermen could not seem to stop themselves from overharvesting, and no regulations prevented them from doing so. Something needed to be done protect whitefish and other commercial species from further decline.

Regulating and Restricting the Fishery, 1890–1920

This, then, was the situation when James Nevin assumed his post as the state superintendent of fisheries in 1882. Fishermen of many types plied the waters of the Great Lakes, fishing with a wide variety of equipment for a range of reasons. Such a disordered and unregulated fishery, Nevin believed, could not be sustained. Nor did this unregulated system allow for Wisconsin's natural resources to be put to their best use. As whitefish harvests plummeted on Lake Michigan, and as experts predicted a similar collapse for Lake Superior, Nevin set out to bring the chaotic commercial fisheries under control. He needed to make the fishery more legible—to make it easier to track and control by restricting and limiting the activities of the fishermen. The state used the opportunity provided by the declining whitefish harvests to increase its role in the regulation of the fisheries. By 1910, the Wisconsin Fisheries Commission held the power to determine who could fish for commercial species and when and where this activity would take place.

In the late nineteenth century, resource managers across the nation championed the ideology of progressive conservation, which called for the maximization of public utility from public resources. The expansion of state regulatory authority—in the economy, governance, and other areas as well as conservation—was a defining feature of the Progressive Era, and Wisconsin was among the most progressive of states. Historians have explained these reforms as an attempt to establish order and efficiency through reliance on scientific expertise and government regulation. Experts such as James Nevin sought to use state power to make the production of natural resources more efficient and profitable. In so doing, they manipulated the environments that produced these resources and the people who harvested them. The actions of state managers working to achieve their interpretation of the greater good emerged in the twentieth century as a driving force in the rewilding of the islands.[34]

Nevin sought to apply the principles of conservation to Wisconsin's commercial fisheries. As he faced this situation, he was certain of one thing: the fishermen themselves could not be trusted to act appropriately. "The fishermen as a class will not and can not," he wrote, "in the nature of things, successfully overcome through organization the evil I have pointed out [harvesting immature fish] without the aid of good laws. Many fishermen would gladly protect and foster the immature fish, but a large number of them seem to prefer the present destructive policy."[35] Only a regulatory state, acting on the advice of technical experts and for the benefit of the general public, could solve the fishermen's problems. This, to Nevin, was the essence of conservation: "Conservation does not mean hoarding fish or game as a miser does his gold; it means to permit the taking, catching, and killing of fish and game in such a manner, at such times, and in such quantities, as will conserve the supply for future years."[36]

State regulation of the commercial fishery grew slowly during the last third of the nineteenth century. Wisconsin took the first step toward regulating its fisheries in 1866, when the legislature created the position of Great Lakes fish inspector. Lake Superior fisheries had barely been tapped, but Lake Michigan fisheries had been exploited for decades and were already threatened by overfishing. These inspectors did little more than estimate each year's commercial harvest. The legislature created the Wisconsin Fisheries Commission in 1874, with the charge "to prevent or delay the exhaustion of fish." The commission had two tools to achieve this goal: supplementing fish stocks with artificial propagation and changing how fishermen caught fish.[37]

Of these two options, both fisheries experts and fishermen far preferred propagation. Just after their 1874 appointment, the commissioners announced plans to plant 5 million fry (recently hatched fish) in Lake Michigan. Although the commissioners focused on the more intensively harvested Lake Michigan, they cautioned that Lake Superior must not be ignored. In 1887, the state established a fish hatchery in Madison—the first state-run fish hatchery in the country. Artificial propagation began on Lake Superior in 1885, when 2.25 million whitefish fry were released into Chequamegon Bay. The commission subsequently planted fry at various points along the Superior shore. Artificial propagation represented the first steps by state managers to actively shape the environments of the Apostle Islands, steps that grew more powerful and wide-ranging in the twentieth century.[38]

Bayfield became the center of the propagation effort for Lake Superior. In 1895, the state built a fish hatchery just south of town. "Hereafter we shall be able to increase the output and prevent the practical extermination of this choicest product of our waters," pronounced Nevin. With the help of the new Bayfield Fish Hatchery, the WFC released staggering amounts of fry in the Apostle Islands: 11.5 million lake trout in 1899; 22 million in 1900; 13.8 million lake trout and 8 million whitefish in 1901; 13.5 million lake trout and 18.8 million whitefish in 1902.[39]

Fishermen also participated in propagation. During spawning season, they routinely stripped their catch of milt and eggs for the hatchery or volunteered their time to distribute fry and fingerlings (young fish reared in the hatchery). Many fishermen also practiced a form of propagation of their own. As they caught fish during spawning season, they mixed eggs and milt directly on their boats and dumped the fertilized mixture back into the water on the spot. The fishermen recognized that their industry stood to gain from the state-sponsored propagation program. Plus, they preferred propagation to regulation.[40]

Many pisciculturists believed that they could produce fish more efficiently than nature itself. "Nature's provisions for the survival and increase of the several species of fish are not adequate," Nevin explained, since only small percentage of eggs ever produced mature fish. "To rectify this apparent error in nature's laws, we have resorted to artificial propagation." Nevin earned his position as Wisconsin's superintendent of fisheries on the strength of his reputation as a pisciculturist, and he made fish propagation the WFC's main focus. If human ingenuity could transform the technology and economic structures

2.4 The opening of the Wisconsin State Fish Hatchery in Bayfield in 1895 signaled the increasing role of the state in the protection and regulation of both sport and commercial fisheries. Courtesy of the Wisconsin Historical Society, WHi-29123.

of the commercial fishery, it could also improve the underwater environments of Lake Superior.[41]

But even the most devoted pisciculturist recognized that artificial propagation alone would not restore badly damaged fisheries. The habits of fishermen needed to be changed too. "What we need is protection for the small fish," Nevin recommended, "and artificial propagation will keep the lakes and streams well supplied." It was a difficult task. Fishermen supported artificial propagation far more enthusiastically than regulation, and laws outlawing certain kinds of equipment and the sale of small fish were notoriously hard to enforce. Nevertheless, the state legislature passed the first laws regulating the fishery in 1879, when it set the minimum weight for the sale of fish at three-quarters of a pound and banned nets with a mesh size smaller than three inches. By enforcing these laws, experts like Nevin believed, the fishery could be restored to Lake Michigan and protected on Lake Superior. "If all, or practically all, unlawful fishing should be stopped," Nevin claimed in 1886, "our hatchery could, within five years or less, make the waters of Wisconsin swarm as they did when the country was first settled."[42]

Regulations did not necessarily change fishing practices. The WFC had little real power. Even with wardens supposedly policing the commercial fleet, enforcement remained lax. Lake Superior is an awfully large lake to patrol, and wardens faced pressure from the fishermen—often their neighbors or relatives—to ignore what violations they might have seen. Rolla Baker, the first warden for Lake Superior, explained that "the enforcement of laws for the preservation and protection of fish and game meets with much opposition, and the laws are continually violated, while the offenders are seldom brought to justice." Wardens encountered district attorneys who refused to prosecute fish and game violations, justices of the peace who ruled such laws unconstitutional, and judges who returned guilty verdicts without punishment. In 1889 and 1890, the Lake Superior wardens reported only twelve violations, and none of these resulted in a conviction. "We have neither the means nor the power to proceed against a single offender not possessed by every other citizen of the state," complained the commissioners in 1887. The fisheries were regulated in the law books more strictly than on the water.[43]

The problem of multiple jurisdictions in the Great Lakes fisheries impeded regulation as well. Each state had its own set of rules and regulations. Lake Superior had regulations imposed by the states of Michigan, Wisconsin, and Minnesota as well as by the Canadian province of Ontario. The U.S. government lacked the constitutional authority to regulate the American fisheries, inhibiting prospects for uniform regulation across state and international boundaries. Fishermen from one place often fished in the waters of a different jurisdiction to take advantage of less restrictive laws or to circumvent regulation entirely.[44]

Concerns about uniform regulations did call attention to the continuing problems facing the Great Lakes fishery and provoked a renewed dedication to state-based regulation. In 1887, the Wisconsin legislature prohibited the setting of all types of nets in the Chequamegon Bay, an area considered essential spawning grounds for whitefish, before reopening the area in 1891. Lake Michigan's commercial harvest had plummeted in the 1880s, and the state acted to protect its remaining resources. Despite the closure, harvest levels remained distressingly low. In 1895, the Wisconsin legislature again closed the Chequamegon Bay to all nets, a direct response to the collapse of Bayfield's whitefish fishery. The repeal of the 1887 closure law had prompted fishermen to flood into the Chequamegon Bay in search of whitefish. "Small white fish have been taken by the tons in Chequamegon Bay," reported James Nevin. Netters "drew load after load of white fish to the shore, of a size so small that it would take three or four of them to make a pound." The Wisconsin commissioners hoped that the ban on setting nets in the spawning grounds would allow whitefish stocks to rebound.[45]

The state legislature gradually tightened regulations governing commercial fishing. This included establishing minimum net sizes, minimum weights for marketable fish, and closed seasons for whitefish and lake trout. In 1887, the legislature passed a law prohibiting possession or sale of whitefish weighing less than 1.5 pounds, punishable by a fine. By 1891, fishermen could not fish for lake trout from October 1 to January 15 or for whitefish from November 10 to December 15. Regulations six years later further increased the minimum size limits to 2 pounds and extended the closed season for both species. Enforcement of these regulations, however, remained problematic well into the twentieth century.[46]

Quantification became an important tool in the control of the fisheries. After 1887, fishermen were required to make annual reports to their local wardens of the amount of fish they had caught each year, the value of the catch, the number of nets and boats used, and the number of men employed. At first, the WFC used this information simply to tabulate the harvest, but keeping track of who was using the resource was also an important part of regulation. Over the next two decades, this information became an instrument of control, an essential component in the state's drive to make the management of natural resources legible. It allowed the commissioners to assess the mesh size of nets in use, a frequent target of restrictions. After 1905, commercial fishermen were required to mark their nets with a white flag and a tag bearing their name or company, to allow for easier enforcement of regulations. The ability to quantify the use of the fisheries or other natural resources served as a key component of the conservation movement. By 1909, all commercial fishermen needed to purchase a license, and fisheries experts—men like James Nevin—knew who was fishing, they type of equipment they used, and what they had caught. They had made the fishery legible.[47]

Regulation Winners and Losers

The growth of state conservation authority privileged some fishermen over others. Full-time fishermen and the large packing and dealing firms like the A.

Booth Packing Company benefited the most from state control. Among those who lost access to the declining resources of Lake Superior were the Ojibwe fishermen who had participated in both commercial and subsistence fishing for generations. Conservation in the Apostle Islands followed a pattern replicated elsewhere. In places as diverse as Yellowstone National Park in Wyoming, Minnesota's Superior National Forest, western Pennsylvania, and the rural South, the last decades of the nineteenth century brought the restriction of access to resources that had once been used as a commons. Those who sought to use resources for reasons other than sport or market production, or who produced at small scales, often found their uses of nature prescribed or even criminalized. Game laws prevented the hunting of birds and wildlife; grazing permits and fencing restricted the common use of pastures; and trespass laws prevented the gathering of firewood on public land. In other words, conservation had winners and losers. Those with social, economic, and political power successfully used the ideology of conservation to secure for themselves control of resources or advantages in the marketplace. Those able to use the state's managerial authority for their own ends won access to limited resources at the expense of those who could not.[48]

As the nineteenth century drew to a close and after the collapse of the white-fish stocks on both Lake Michigan and Lake Superior, fishermen increasingly supported the regulation of their industry. In 1886, 156 Lake Superior fishermen signed a petition asking the federal government to expand its regulation and propagation work. In the early 1900s, the Commercial Fishermen's Association recommended that the Wisconsin legislature pass tighter restrictions on mesh size in commercial nets. Fishermen supported the regulation of the fishery—despite the potential damage to their own economic fortunes—because they recognized their own role in the destruction of the whitefish.[49]

Some fishermen had less altruistic reasons to support regulation: they saw it as a way to guarantee their own access to a declining resource. Regulations that forced some fishermen off the water worked in the interest of those who remained. C. W. Turner, the western manager for the A. Booth Packing Company, wrote the Wisconsin Fisheries Commission in 1893, demanding that "some means be determined to prevent the wholesale catching of smaller fish." Turner was particularly concerned with the fisheries of the Apostle Islands, one of his company's key points of supply. Booth had invested heavily in Bayfield, and Turner wanted the state to protect that investment:

I would kindly ask what has been done, or what is going to be done, in reference to the breeding grounds of the whitefish at Chequamegon Bay. Certainly something must be done, as the present and past modes of fishing is very fast depopulating the waters, owing to the unprincipled people employed in fishing . . . Now this is getting to be a serious question with us. We have invested over $200,000 in the state of Wisconsin at Bayfield and Ashland and would therefore ask protection from the fish commissioners, as something certainly must be done to protect our industry, as we are not there for today, but we are there for the future. . . . Now, certainly some stringent measure must (or should) be taken immediately to offer us some protection, also to protect the fishing grounds, otherwise there will not be any white fish on the south shore of Lake Superior.

In Turner's eyes, Booth's investment in Wisconsin industry gave the company the right to expect preferential treatment from the state.[50]

State regulation did privilege some fishermen over others. A limit on the mesh size that applied to seine, gill, and pound nets thus affected fishermen of different means disproportionately. Independent, part-time fishermen who had recently invested in new nets—only to have those nets declared illegal—could not easily refit their rigs. Closed seasons allowed large fish dealers like Booth to sell frozen fish while no fresh fish reached the market. James Nevin recognized the unequal benefits of state regulation: "I consider the close season for fishing on the Great Lakes as being in the interest of the syndicate of fish dealers . . . to the disadvantage of the small fishermen on the lakes." Most independent fishermen accepted minimum mesh sizes for nets but resisted the gradual tightening of other regulations.[51]

By the turn of the century, the state of Wisconsin had made significant headway in enforcing these regulations. In 1897, the legislature appointed five wardens to focus solely on the enforcement of fish and game laws, and these appointments made an immediate impact. In 1898, the state fish and game warden reported 614 arrests, 511 convictions, $6,415 in fines, and the confiscation of over $15,000 worth of nets, boats, and other fishing gear. In 1899, the legislature approved the appointment of an additional thirty deputy wardens around the state.[52]

The unequal impacts of the extension of state authority are most clearly seen in the way that state agents sought to control the fishing of Ojibwe Indians. Ojibwe had participated in the Chequamegon Bay commercial fishery since its inception, often blending commercial and subsistence opportunities. They took wage-paying jobs in the area's fishing, logging, and mining industries but sometimes left these jobs when other opportunities presented themselves—much to the chagrin of the federal Indian agents who had set as their goal the training of Ojibwe men for "civilized" occupations. This pattern held particularly true in fishing, where Ojibwe continued to mix independent fishing, wage work, and subsistence, with little regard to reservation boundaries. These activities often ran counter to state-imposed closed seasons, sanctuary laws, and minimum weight requirements. Ojibwe fished nonetheless, confident that the treaties they had made with the federal government protected their rights to do so. Wisconsin's conservation authorities believed differently.[53]

As fishing regulations tightened, conflicts with Ojibwe fishermen increased. For their part, the Ojibwe consistently maintained that the land cession treaties guaranteed their right to hunt and fish both on and off the reservations. Two Ojibwe arrested in 1889 claimed "that it has been customary from time immemorial for many of the Chippewas to obtain the major part of their subsistence from that source." The 1854 treaty protected Ojibwe rights to hunt and fish in the ceded territory until otherwise ordered by the president. This clause, the Ojibwe argued, had never been revoked. Agent W. A. Mercer reported the Indian reaction when wardens prevented several Red Cliff band members from using their nets under the laws regulating mesh size in 1894: "The Indians all feel that they are entitled to hunt and fish as they may choose and that the stipulation of the treaty with the Government granting this privilege has never been changed." Until they heard from the president, the Ojibwe would continue to fish.[54]

Both commercial fishermen and state officials saw Indian fishing as a direct threat to the fishing industry. M. B Johnson, the Booth Company's assistant manager in Bayfield, explained in 1894, "They claim that the Indians by treaty with the government, can fish anywhere they want to. . . . They claim [it] is their treaty that they can fish everything and anything they want to at any time and that the state laws have no effect upon them whatever." This meant, Johnson explained, that regulations could be easily circumvented: "If the Indians can fish anything they want to what can we do? It is like this: suppose I own 2 or 3 three pound nets. I can give them to an Indian for a couple of months, and say, you fish them and turn the fish in your name, and the Indian says, all right, he will fish them for me in that way, and if a fish warden comes along he tells him 'these are my nets,' and so they get around the law." Johnson believed that if the Ojibwe had a treaty right to fish, the state could not adequately protect the fishery.[55]

Others saw Ojibwe activities as a threat to sport fishing, a rapidly growing sector of Wisconsin's economy. Here, the concern lay with fishing methods, especially spearfishing. "Under the head of usages which are destructive to the finny tribe, I would call your attention . . . to that nefarious practice 'spearing,' " explained one Wisconsin fish commissioner. State experts objected to spearing because it killed fish when they were most vulnerable and it took place during the spawning season, thus threatening the reproduction of important species. James Nevin joined the chorus of criticism of Indian fishing when he claimed that spearing was not a "sporting" method of taking fish: "[If] those who wish to spear fish wish to get fish, let them pursue a more honorable course. Give the fish a fair show." Protecting fish and game for sportsmen provided an additional motivation for curtailing Ojibwe usufructuary rights.[56]

In 1896, wardens arrested and confiscated the equipment of two prominent Red Cliff residents, Antoine Buffalo and Michael DePerry, for fishing off the shore of the reservation and for selling fish below the legal size limit. The arrests became a test case for the status of Ojibwe treaty rights. Both the state warden and the Bureau of Indian Affairs wanted a definite legal opinion and asked Wisconsin attorney general W. H. Mylrea for direction. Mylrea offered an unequivocal opinion: "The power of the state to regulate and control the taking of fish and game is unquestioned." Mylrea argued that the federal government had not reserved the right to manage wildlife when Wisconsin became a state in 1849, so this right remained with the state. "The state is entitled," Mylrea continued, "to punish Indians as well as others for the violations of the fish and game laws." Mylrea provided the first legal opinion on treaty-guaranteed fishing rights in Wisconsin and his comments prompted a concerted campaign to curtail these rights.[57]

The state's authority to restrict Indian hunting and fishing received an important test in federal court in 1901. A warden arrested Bad River band member John Blackbird for illegally setting a net in Bear Trap Creek, deep in the heart of the reservation. Blackbird was convicted in municipal court and fined $36.75. When he refused to pay, he was thrown in the county jail and put to hard labor for thirty days. Blackbird maintained that the treaty of 1854 protected his right to fish on the reservation, regardless of state law; he appealed to the U.S. district court for a writ of habeas corpus. The Wisconsin attorney general advanced the argument proposed by Mylrea in 1896: the state had the unquestioned right to manage the game and fish within its borders. Federal judge Romanzo Bunn disagreed, ruling that the federal government maintained jurisdiction on Indian reservations and that on-reservation fishing remained outside of state law. He also chided Wisconsin State authorities for their actions: "After taking from them the great body of their lands in Minnesota and Wisconsin . . . and stipulating that they should always have the right to fish and hunt upon all the lands so ceded, it would be adding insult as well as injustice now to deprive them of the poor privilege of fishing with a seine for suckers in a little red marsh-water stream upon their own reservation." The decision represented only a temporary setback in the consolidation of the state's regulatory authority.[58]

Wisconsin authorities continued to press for absolute control over the fish and game resources of their state. In June 1907, wardens arrested Red Cliff member Michael Morrin for fishing with gill and pound nets in Red Cliff Bay, adjacent to the reservation but in violation of state laws preventing the use of nets within one mile of shore. Morrin appealed his conviction, and the case traveled to the state supreme court. The case differed from the circumstances of the *Blackbird* case. In *Blackbird*, the courts wrestled with the question of subsistence fishing within reservation boundaries. But Morrin had set his nets in Lake Superior, technically off the reservation, and had sold his catch to a Bayfield fish dealer. In addition to claiming the state's right to manage wildlife, the Wisconsin attorney general argued that because Morrin had received his citizenship under the Dawes Severalty Act of 1887 he was subject to the same laws as other citizens. Morrin claimed that the treaty of 1854 protected his right to fish and that the federal government alone held jurisdiction over crimes committed on reservations. The Wisconsin Supreme Court ruled in the state's favor, stating that Morrin's "status is like that of every other citizen, and subjects him to penalties of the violation of any state law." The ruling extended the state's regulatory authority over Indian fishing and hunting, both on and off the reservations, and restricted Ojibwe rights to hunt and fish for the following seventy-five years.[59]

As with the regulatory laws, court decisions did not necessarily translate into changed behavior. Much as they had before the state attack on their treaty rights, Ojibwe continued to rely on the fish of Lake Superior for both wage work and subsistence. They sold their catch commercially or worked for other fishermen, but they either complied with state fishing laws or risked further run-ins with state wardens. The intermittent cases concerning Indian violations of fish and game laws that appeared in Wisconsin courts throughout the twentieth century testify to Ojibwe resistance to state authority. Flaunting fish and game laws—often called "violating"—became an important part of reservation life for many Ojibwe.[60]

The state's growing control over both commercial fishing and Ojibwe usufructuary rights was part of the larger process of bringing legibility to the management of natural resources. Quantification and regulation systematized fishing, making it easier for the state to control. The state had a similar motive in curtailing Indian fishing. Ojibwe had argued that the treaties had reserved for them access to the state's fish and game resources, but legibility required that the state force the Ojibwe to comply with the same simplified rules as everyone else. Exceptions for subsistence fishermen made the extension of the state's regulatory authority more difficult.[61]

Reasons other than the resource manager's need for legibility contributed to the curtailment of Ojibwe fishing. Racism and a desire for social control played a part too. Many wardens believed that Indians spent so much time hunting and fishing simply because they were lazy. Indian agency officials still maintained a goal of training Indians for stable jobs within the market economy; access to subsistence resources hindered this goal. Wardens and conservation experts perceived fish and game resources as finite. Fish and game caught by the Ojibwe were no longer available to white hunters and fishermen, who used these resources for what the conservation authorities saw as more creditable pursuits. Legibility was not only the result of the needs of a managerial state but also of decisions of individuals seeking to turn state authority to their own ends. The result of these decisions was a shift in the way that both whites and Indians interacted with the natural world. The state now had a far greater ability to control these interactions.

Over the rest of the twentieth century, the role of the regulatory state continued to grow. Regulation expanded from the fisheries to land use and economic development. With each new regulation, the state—first in the form of the state of Wisconsin and then the federal government—further prescribed the actions of the residents of the region. The regulatory authority of the state emerged in the twentieth century as one of the most potent forces shaping the relationship between people and the environments of the Apostle Islands.

The Stabilization of the Twentieth-Century Fishery

The steady growth of state authority served as one of the few constants in the commercial fishery from 1880–1920; other components of the industry changed constantly. As the technology of fishing improved, fishermen of the Apostles and the Chequamegon Bay altered the way they fished and the species they sought. When whitefish harvests declined, fishermen switched to lake trout and herring. These changes, in turn, sparked a reorganization of the economic structure of the fishing industry and a period of growth and stability. The industry looked much the same in 1950 as it did in 1920—an apparent success for James Nevin's goal of using state authority to make the fishery more legible.

Between 1880 and 1900, lake trout replaced whitefish in the fishermen's nets. On Lake Superior, the percentage of lake trout in the overall catch grew from 38 percent in 1880 to 43 percent in 1890 to 61 percent in 1899. In Bayfield, trout made up 20 percent of the catch in 1885, when whitefish still accounted for 73 percent of the total. By 1899, lake trout constituted 45 percent of the catch. Booth Company employee M. B. Johnson stated in 1894 that he did "not expect the tug 'Camp' . . . has caught 10 lbs. of whitefish all the season so far. It is all trout."[62]

The new importance of trout brought shifts in the organization and apparatus of the industry. Pound nets had once provided the best chance for catching whitefish and made the Apostle Islands the center of Lake Superior's whitefish fishery. When whitefish stocks collapsed, pound nets lost their competitive edge.[63] "There are not as many pounds now as there used to be simply because they cannot get enough fish to pay," explained one fisherman. Meanwhile, with the advent of steam tugs, mechanical net lifters, and linen nets, the effectiveness of gill nets had increased. Where pound nets had once been the gear of choice for the larger, more financially secure fishermen, this was no longer the case by the mid-1890s. The Booth Company invested in gillnet steamers rather than pound nets. The more versatile gill nets offered a better chance at catching lake trout, which swam in deeper waters and with a greater range than whitefish. In 1890, the fishermen of Ashland and Bayfield owned 1,723 gill nets, valued at $16,745. By 1903, these numbers had climbed to 2,598 nets valued at $29,588.[64]

Herring, too, became increasingly important. Much as with the whitefish fishery, geography and environmental conditions made the Apostle Islands the premier herring grounds on Lake Superior. Lake herring (*Coregonus artedii* Lesueur) feed primarily on plankton, which they find in deep water during the summer. But as winter approaches, herring move toward shallower waters, congregating in tremendous numbers. Spawning season occurs at the end of autumn—in the Apostles, typically in November. "At that time they appear in millions . . . over the great muddy bottoms in the shallower Wisconsin waters at the extreme western end of the south shore of the lake," recorded one observer. The massive numbers and shallow water made herring an easy target for commercial nets during the two- to three-week spawning season. Almost 90 percent of the annual catch of herring occurred during this time.[65]

Lake Superior fishermen did not start catching herring until the 1890s. Herring spoil easily, especially from overhandling; until the perfection of curing and freezing techniques, the fish could not be sold commercially. One 1892 report noted that the "lake herring is abundant throughout [Lake Superior], but, being regarded as a cheap fish, it has little market value at the present time." As whitefish disappeared and technology improved, fishermen turned to herring. And as the Lake Superior region became more populated, a new use for herring emerged: farmers purchased large amounts of the cheap fish for fertilizer.[66]

Herring became a key component of the commercial harvest, especially in Bayfield. In 1890, herring made up 6.1 percent of the catch by weight. By 1899 this number had climbed to 44 percent and then to 63.7 percent by 1903. Just as they had dominated Lake Superior's whitefish trade, Bayfield fishermen emerged as the lake's largest suppliers of herring. Although tremendous amounts of herring passed through Bayfield's packinghouses, the fish did not command that high a price. The first several hauls in November paid well, but the markets were soon glutted. In 1903, for example, 3,046,025 pounds of fresh and salted herring brought in only $18,870 (just $0.60 for 100 pounds of herring). In contrast, fresh and salted whitefish combined to value $4.12 per 100 pounds, and trout sold for $3.78 per 100 pounds.[67]

The whitefish collapse in the 1890s also reshaped the organization of the fishing industry. Throughout the 1890s, the Booth Company extended its market dominance on the Great Lakes, purchasing the fish dealerships that failed during the decade. The economic distress caused by the whitefish collapse and the financial panic that swept the country in 1893 aided in this endeavor. In many places, fishermen had little choice but to sell their fish to Booth—at Booth's prices—because no other dealers remained. Bayfield, with its proximity to the rich island fishing grounds, continued to provide a home for two or three small dealers. As the Booth Company grew, it regularly sparred with federal, state, and Canadian regulatory agencies wary of its monopolistic behavior. It suffered, too, from poor commercial catches in 1905 and 1906. The Wisconsin Fisheries Commission described 1906 as one of the worst years on record; the Lake Superior fishing tugs stopped running early in the season because the nets continually came up empty. In 1908, the company declared bankruptcy before reopening in 1909 as the Booth Fisheries Company.[68]

Booth's 1908 bankruptcy marked a major transition in the Bayfield fishery. The company ceased employing fishermen directly and focused solely on collecting, processing, marketing the catch. The fishermen stationed at Rocky and South Twin islands became independents, selling their catch to Booth or other dealers. Booth's collection boats visited the island camps on a regular schedule, dropping off ice and picking up the daily catch. Bayfield's other dealers worked the same way or simply waited for fishermen to bring the catch to them at the end of each day. The industry followed this model for the next half century.[69]

Technological developments made the new economic organization possible. In 1899, a Michigan fishing firm attached gasoline engines to sailboats as a form of auxiliary power. The idea quickly caught on, and gasoline boats dominated the industry by 1910. Even the most primitive gasoline engines made the work of fishermen far easier. A crew of one or two could now more easily take advantage of other technological innovations like mechanical lifters. Gasoline engines increased the fishermen's range, the number of nets they could handle, and their ability to combat inclement weather. Steam tugs had required a much larger crew—and significant capital to pay for labor and maintenance. Gasoline engines provided the advantages of steam tugs to fishermen of more limited means. In most other American industries, technological innovation paved the way for increasing scale and corporate organization; the reverse was true in the Great Lakes fishery. The environmental changes that favored gill nets over pound nets and the evolution of gas-powered boats meant that smaller, independent fishermen took the place of corporations like Booth on the waters of the Lake Superior.[70]

Meanwhile, Wisconsin's conservation bureaucracy continued to grow in size and power. The governor of Wisconsin appointed a Conservation Commission in 1908 to gather information and to produce recommendations on the management of the state's natural resources. In 1915, the legislature created a permanent commission staffed by three conservation experts—with James Nevin as commissioner of fisheries. The new commission centralized conservation efforts, assuming the responsibility to manage fish, game, parks, and forestry resources. In 1927, the legislature created the Wisconsin Conservation Department (WCD) to carry out the policies crafted by the Conservation Commission. Legislation in 1933 further empowered the commission by granting it full decision-making authority in natural resource management—the power to set closed seasons, bag limits, create sanctuaries, and so on. The new structure, read the 1927 Wisconsin Conservation Act, would provide "a system for the protection, development, and use of forests, fish and game, and other outdoor resources." This fit the pattern established in the commercial fisheries over the previous half century: state managerial authority grew ever more centralized and powerful.[71]

The WCD immediately stepped up the enforcement of fish and game laws and did so far more effectively than had its predecessor agencies. "A larger force of better trained wardens is in the field today than there has ever been before in the history of the state," observed the conservation commissioners in 1928. By the late 1920s, the WCD averaged nearly 1,700 arrests for conservation violations each year; this number had been in the single digits in the 1890s and not much higher in the early twentieth century.[72]

When James Nevin retired in 1921, the commercial fishing industry looked far different than it had when he had assumed his post in 1882. Fishermen used different equipment to catch different species of fish, preserved their catch in new ways, and prosecuted their industry under the guard of a powerful regulatory state. What had seemed in the 1880s to be a chaotic, disordered fishery had seemingly been brought under control. Harvest figures for Wisconsin's Great Lakes fisheries in the 1920s dwarfed those of the 1880s. In 1885, the state's fishermen had caught 5,151,054 pounds of fish, valued at $158 million. By 1918, these numbers had jumped to 21,659,302 pounds of fish, with a value of $1.3 billion. The combination of propagation and regulation, Nevin believed, had secured this bounty from nature: "It is something remarkable, the great numbers of fish that have been taken from year to year from our great lakes system, and then to remember that the numbers caught annually have not diminished." So long as his successors maintained an active role in management, Wisconsin's fishermen could expect continued results. "The planting of millions of fish," he wrote, "with regulations governing the size, limiting the number to be taken each day, and the season that they may be taken from our waters will make it possible to maintain the fish supply for all time to come."[73]

Nevin's comments seemed prophetic, as after 1920 the industry entered a period of stability and financial security that lasted for three decades. Both on Lake Superior as a whole and in the waters around Bayfield, lake trout harvests remained remarkably constant for the next thirty years, averaging just over three million pounds and rarely deviating from this norm. Fishermen benefited from this stability, a condition that had not been possible when harvest figures fluctuated wildly from year to year.[74]

Even the whitefish made a comeback. By the 1930s, the conditions that had caused the whitefish collapse had changed. Lumbering and milling had ceased, fishermen used fewer pound nets, and the state protected spawning sanctuaries and enforced closed seasons; whitefish returned to the islands. In 1936, the Chequamegon Bay whitefish catch topped 100,000 pounds for just the second time since 1908. Harvests climbed steadily, surpassing 700,000 pounds in 1948.[75]

Lake Superior fishermen enjoyed extremely favorable market conditions in this period as well. In 1925, the Lake Erie herring fishery crashed, ruining what had been the largest herring fishery on the Great Lakes. Demand for Lake Superior herring increased, as did the price and size of the harvest. Collapses of the lake trout fisheries on Lake Huron in the 1930s and Lake Michigan in the 1940s produced a similar result: a near monopoly on trout for Lake Superior fishermen. With strong demand and steady harvests, the fisheries of Lake Superior thrived through midcentury. Proponents of state regulation claimed credit for bringing stability out of the chaos that had marked the industry in the nineteenth century.[76]

Not all fishermen, however, shared in the bounty. Ojibwe fishermen bore the brunt of the Wisconsin Conservation Department's increasing authority. As the WCD grew more powerful, its wardens increasingly interfered in Indian life to enforce fish and game laws that had been designed to police commercial fishermen and urban sportsmen. In the late 1920s and 1930s, clashes between Ojibwe and WCD wardens grew more frequent and more heated. Fines, jail terms, car impoundments, and the confiscation of hunting and fishing equipment became commonplace. A 1931 legal victory restored the right to hunt and fish on the reservation. Off the reservation, however, WCD officials took a hard line on what they regarded as violations of state conservation laws. In the 1930s, the WCD stationed four special wardens at the boundaries of each of Wisconsin's three largest Ojibwe reservations. The continued clashes with state officials demonstrated that the Ojibwe claimed their hunting and fishing rights, despite the risks.[77]

The WCD effort to curtail Indian hunting and fishing rights occurred at the same time as the state government's first concerted effort to promote northern Wisconsin as a resort destination. Beginning in the late nineteenth century, sportsmen began frequenting Wisconsin's lakes, rivers, and forests, putting a new set of demands on the state's fish and game. Sportsmen brought a different set of assumptions and priorities to their use of the fisheries and other island resources, and this required a different kind of management from the state.

The growing demands of sportsmen prompted the Wisconsin Department of Natural Resources—the successor agency to the WCD—to retire the licenses of half of the state's Lake Superior fishermen in the 1990s, despite a century-long tradition of protecting the commercial fishing industry. Sportsmen and anglers frequently argued that they deserved prioritized access to the limited number of lake trout because their means of using the resource caused far less environmental damage than did commercial fishing. The recreational economy might not have had the dramatic environmental impacts of clear-cutting or overfishing. But in managing to meet the demands of tourists and sportsmen, state authorities reshaped the environments of the Apostle Islands. They created a wilderness. ❧

3

Consuming the Islands

FOR OVER TWENTY-FIVE YEARS IN THE MID-TWENTIETH CENTURY, Grace and Laurie Nourse ran one of the most unusual and authentic tourist operations in the Apostle Islands, a restaurant and resort called the Rocky Island Air Haven. Laurie Nourse or his son captained an excursion boat that departed from Bayfield. Passengers boarded the boat and placed a lunch order, which was radioed to Grace, who had the meal ready when the ship arrived at Rocky Island. The menu included fried or boiled fish, scalloped potatoes, salad, bread, and pie, which visitors enjoyed in an old net house that Laurie had converted into a dining room. The Nourses decorated the dining room with fishnet curtains and hung old ring buoys and floats on the walls. They converted other buildings at their old fishing camp into cabins, which they rented to sportsmen who wanted to spend several days in the islands trolling for lake trout or hunting deer.[1]

The Air Haven flourished because the Nourses capitalized on the connections between tourism and other industries. The restaurant got its start because the Booth Company's collection boat arrived at Rocky Island three times a week, often carrying tourists on a scenic tour of the islands. In the early 1940s, the Nourses started serving coffee and pie to the tourists, and they soon realized that this might be more lucrative than fishing. "We could hear those passengers say

'If I could just get a cup of coffee, I wonder how long we are going to have to lay here.' So an idea was born. . . . [So] many people were lined up clear down to the boat up to the building so we decided that this was going to be a pretty nice thing." The Nourses bought fresh fish from the commercial fishermen who still used Rocky Island as a base. The deer hunt also depended on island history and a connection to resource extraction. Few deer lived on Rocky until the mid-1940s. But the edge environments that grew up in the logging sites and burned-over areas provided excellent deer habitat and led to a spike in deer numbers. Every autumn Rocky Island became the center of a distinctive island hunt.[2]

Despite its charm and local flavor, the National Park Service shut down the Rocky Island Air Haven in 1974. The Air Haven represented a brand of tourism grounded in the islands' past, not their future. The NPS intended to manage the Apostles as a wilderness, a place for primitive recreation and scientific study valued because evidence of human history seemed so hard to find. Such a wilderness required severing the ties between tourism and resource-production activities like commercial fishing and logging. As in the fisheries, the management of the island tourist industry required legibility, in this case a strict separation between activities of production and consumption. A restaurant and cabin-rental service like the Air Haven, with its historical connections to resource production, did not fit into this management scheme.[3]

In the late nineteenth and early twentieth century, the state took an ever more active role in fostering the tourist trade. At first, this meant little more than introducing game fish and promoting Wisconsin as a tourist destination. But as the managerial authority of the state grew, and the demands of resource management became more complicated, state planners encouraged the segregation of tourism from other economic activities. Setting tourism apart has had tangible consequences for island environments. It has led to the perception that the islands represent pristine wilderness and to a federal management regime designed to maintain this perception. In the long run, the impact of tourism on island environments has proven at least as enduring as the extractive industries once so common on the Chequamegon Bay.[4]

An Escape into Nature

As soon as the locks at Sault Ste. Marie opened in 1855, the Apostle Islands and the rest of Lake Superior became accessible to tourists, and tourism joined fishing, logging, and quarrying as pillars of Bayfield's economy. Early visitors arrived by steamer, but as in fishing and logging, the railroad transformed every aspect of the tourist trade. The number of visitors who traveled to the islands jumped as the railroads engaged in a promotional campaign to lure passengers out of the crowded, noisy cities and to the clean air and scenery of the Chequamegon Bay. In doing so, the railroads built the impression that a trip to the Apostle Islands meant a step away from the cares of modern life, an escape into nature. The people who worked in the island tourist trade experienced tourism differently, not as an escape from reality but as an economic activity inextricably tied to other elements of their economy.

Soon after the completion of the tracks into Ashland and Bayfield, the railroad companies erected grand, luxurious hotels to lure tourists to the region. Early railroad hotels often imitated European architecture and resort style. At the Wisconsin Central Railroad's Hotel Chequamegon, built in Ashland in 1877, "broad piazzas on three sides give an unequaled promenade over 1,000 feet in length," noted a promotional pamphlet. "The *cuisine* is perfect, not excelled by any hotel in the world." The hotel had room for five hundred guests and had "all the modern conveniences," including running water, electricity, fountains, bowling alleys, a billiard parlor, croquet, and an archery range. When the Chicago, St. Paul, Minneapolis & Omaha Railway reached Bayfield in 1883, it constructed the Island View Hotel in similar style.[5]

Tourists could now travel easily from Milwaukee, Minneapolis, Chicago, and other midwestern cities. The railroad companies promoted tourism in the northern Great Lakes, with the Apostle Islands at the center of these efforts. Railroad promotional campaigns became an early and loud voice promising that an escape into nature meant an escape from the concerns of modern life. While others had certainly voiced this perspective, the railroads popularized the trend and made such an escape more accessible (if still only to the wealthy). Tourists did not expect to find an untouched wilderness at the end of their journey. Over the next century, however, these expectations changed dramatically.

The anti-urban, anti-industrial, anti-corporate tenor of promotional campaigns conducted by the corporate, industrial railroad companies stands as one of the great ironies of nineteenth-century tourism. As living conditions in American cities deteriorated, a search for healthful places motivated American travelers. They wanted vacation destinations to have clean air,

3.1 and 3.2 Railroad companies like the Wisconsin Central promoted the Apostle Islands and other parts of northern Wisconsin as an escape from the pressures of modern life, a place where middle-class urbanites could find clean air, sporting opportunities, and a touch of wilderness, all while staying in luxuriously appointed hotels. The belief that a trip to the Apostles meant an escape into nature helped build the islands' reputation as a wilderness. From the Wisconsin Historical Society pamphlet collection.

spas, refreshing climates, mineral springs, and other restorative attributes. In the 1870s, Dr. George Miller Beard diagnosed a condition he called neurasthenia, or nervous exhaustion. Beard believed that neurasthenia derived from the pressures of modern urban living. Doctors around the country recommended long stays at healthy spots and resorts as the standard cure for neurasthenia as well as for other diseases such as consumption and tuberculosis. While railroad companies were indisputably complicit in sullying city environments, they eagerly promoted their resort hotels as the cure for the nervous, the sick, and the stressed.[6]

The railroad companies trumpeted Bayfield for just this kind of escape. Promotional brochures described it as "the most healthful spot in the state. It is supplied with pure spring water . . . [possessing] many of the properties of our most noted mineral waters without their unpleasant taste. . . . Bayfield As a Health Resort has superior claims. It is a Mecca for all who are troubled with catarrh, asthma, bronchitis and throat diseases of all kinds. Consumption before it has progressed too far easily yields to the influences of our pure dry air and pine forests." Those suffering from hay fever found that a trip to Lake Superior took them away from the pollen and ragweed of more developed regions. Bayfield's boosters called their town the Fountain City to emphasize the clean water and the many fountains that enlivened city streets.[7]

Those not suffering from neurasthenia, hay fever, or some other health problem also wanted to escape the cities to explore the nation's natural landscapes and wild areas. Throughout the nineteenth century, American attitudes toward the natural world had changed dramatically. Following intellectuals and artists like Henry David Thoreau, Ralph Waldo Emerson, Thomas Cole, and Albert Bierstadt, Americans came to appreciate the wild, natural qualities of North America. Tourists sought out sublime, picturesque, and pastoral landscapes — landscapes similar to those depicted with paint and pen. The expanding railroad network made western landscapes ever more reachable, and traveling to destinations remarkable for their scenery and wilderness became a central feature of upper-middle-class tourism.[8]

Tourism in the Apostles hinged on connecting island scenery to the fascination with the American landscape. Railroad brochures described the scenes their passengers could expect to find in terms borrowed directly from the romantic thinkers and landscape painters:

Lake Superior has at times not only the varied interest, but the sublimity of a true ocean. Its blue, cool, transparent water . . . undisturbed by tides, lies during a calm, motionless and glassy as those of some secluded lake, reflecting, with perfect truth of form and color, the inverted landscape that slopes to its sandy beach. But when the inland sea is stirred by the rising tempest, the long sweep of its waves and the curling white-caps that crest its surface give warning not only to the fragile boat, but also to sloop and schooner and lake steamer.

RR land L. Superior

Gem Island, Apostle Islands, Lake Superior.

3.3 Promotional materials for the Apostles, like this undated postcard, portrayed the islands with words and images that relied heavily on the Romantic fascination with water, nature, and wilderness. Courtesy of the National Park Service.

With their caves, cliffs, bays, and beaches, the islands were especially rich in the water-meets-the-land picturesque scenery sought by travelers. Exploring offered days of entertainment, "and one can never exhaust the delightful and changing panoramic features, which in infinite variety continually pass before the eye in ever new and wiching [sic] forms of beauty."⁹

Promoters tied the lighthouses of the Apostles to this romantic sensibility. Excursions to the lighthouses had been a centerpiece of island tourism since the 1860s. The *Ashland Daily Press* called Sand Island "one of the Beauty spots on our coasts." The *Press* used the language of color and light typical of the picturesque to describe the scene: "From the tower the view is indeed grand, the great sea stretching away to the north and west where the blue outline of the north shore can be seen from thirty to seventy miles distant. East and southeast lay the islands spread out in a beautiful panorama, their green shores casting shadows upon the clear channels which surround them, forming a most interesting and charming picture." Albert Bierstadt himself reportedly once visited the island—a sure indicator of Sand Island's romantic bona fides.[10]

Many tourists wanted to do more than sightsee. They also wanted to escape into nature, to live the sporting life, to go camping and fishing. As the nineteenth century drew to a close, Theodore Roosevelt forcefully advocated the virtues of the outdoor life. His rhetoric added a layer of racialized and gendered meaning to the pleasures of camping and sport fishing. Roosevelt and many of his contemporaries believed that the white race—particularly white men— risked becoming soft and weak if they remained too long within the structured confines of civilized society. The outdoor life provided the necessary remedy to these ills, just as clean air cured those afflicted with neurasthenia.[11]

The railroads portrayed the lakes and rivers of northern Wisconsin as a sportsman's paradise. Fishermen would find the creeks and rivers flowing into the Chequamegon Bay "literally swarming with the finest brook trout. . . . Five hundred of the epicurean dainties in one day is by no means an extraordinary catch." Hunters would find deer, bear, wolves, and "every imaginable species of wild fowl and small game. . . . There is no occasion for a sportsman to crawl back into camp empty-handed from these hunting grounds; his only dilemma will be to procure a game-bag sufficiently capacious to contain his booty." The channels between the Apostle Islands also offered a form of fishing found nowhere else between the ocean coasts: trolling, or fishing for lake trout with a hook and line. "Parties who have tried it say there is no finer sport to be had than that of trolling for lake trout among the islands during the months of June and July," commented the *Bayfield County Press*. Trolling became an increasingly popular activity after the turn of the century. The railroad companies often included the fish and game regulations of Wisconsin or other Great Lakes states in their published timetables to make planning a vacation that much easier for their passengers.[12]

History lured tourists to the Apostles, too, as an escape to an earlier, simpler time. La Pointe, a small village on Madeline Island that had been the site of French, British, and American missionary and trading efforts since the late 1600s, became the centerpiece of this promotion. Railroads promised that visitors could explore "the ruins of the historic city of La Pointe, one of the places settled by Father Marquette and the base of the operations of the American Fur Company in early days. The ruins of the old church built by Father Marquette may yet be seen." It mattered little that Father Marquette had not built the church. Visitors to the island could share in the romance and adventure of the voyageur, the trader, and the missionary: "The old life of the missions and the legends of the fur trade have thrown a mellow flavor of adventure about the shores of the northern lakes to be found nowhere else. . . . To the curious traveler familiar with their *patois*, the few antiquated voyageurs now living in [La Pointe] relate many a stirring tale." On Madeline Island, tourists could not only see historical sites but also could speak with living relics of the romantic past.[13]

Tourists were fascinated with the primitive—not only the primitive wilderness, but also the so-called primitive Indians who lived in that wilderness. They traveled to Indian villages, filling their diaries with commentary on what they regarded as the barbarous and uncivilized conditions of the reservations. Railroads and resort companies arranged for vacationers to attend dances, ceremonies, and cultural performances. Observing Indians gave tourists the chance to reaffirm their own class status and racial identity. Tourists in other regions did the same thing by observing Native Americans, Chinese immigrants, or Chicanos. For the Lake Superior country, Henry Wadsworth Longfellow's poem *The Song of Hiawatha* defined the experience. Tourists traveled to Lake Superior hoping to find among the Ojibwe the real-life analog to the poem.[14]

With Ojibwe reservations flanking the Chequamegon Bay at Red Cliff and Bad River, tourists found ample opportunity to explore their fascination with the native and the primitive. "For those who have never seen a similar town," promised one brochure, the town of Odanah on the Bad River reservation "can hardly fail to be of interest. . . . The natives number about five hundred and are a quiet, industrious people. Belonging to the once large and powerful Chippewa tribe, they continue to indulge in many of their primitive customs. . . . They build their own canoes, which are made of bark, are partial to bright colors and in general possess in personal appearance the characteristics of their race." For those who did not make the trip to Odanah or Madeline Island, the Hotel Chequamegon arranged to have Bad River band members perform dances at the hotel. Camping, too, served as an escape into the primitive conditions of the past. Tourists magnified the frontier experience by hiring Indian guides for camping and fishing excursions or by paddling birch-bark canoes along the shores of Lake Superior. All of these activities replicated tourist behavior at other spots around the country, particularly in the West.[15]

The desires of nineteenth-century tourists to experience the primitive wilderness cannot be taken too literally. The primitive became more powerful

adoration of Indians

when placed in contrast to the luxury that tourists expected in their hotels. Even when camping on the islands, tourists did not risk real threats and privations like disease or hunger. The tourist wanted, according to one brochure, an

> easily-get-at-able, strictly-first-class wilderness, with all modern improvements . . . the anti-malarial, non-venomous, highly-medicated, thoroughly-oxygenized, ozone-impregnated, piney-perfumed, damp-devoid, health-reviving, rest-inviting, appetite-constructing, intellect-elevating, devotion-developing, vice-destroying, virtue-strengthening, brain-expanding, sense-sharpening, idea-evolving, fashion-forgetting, lake-embellished, stream-meandered, fish-abiding, game-inhabited, sun-kissed, delightfully-diversified, fragrant, cool and inviting wilderness, where his ear will not be pained, and his soul will ne'er be sick.

Tourists sought to escape the stress of modern life, not its conveniences and comforts. They wanted what the railroads called "tame" wilderness.[16]

While tourists might have viewed the islands as an escape from their daily cares, the residents of the Chequamegon Bay region had a different perspective. Tourism was not an escape; it was an integral part of their economy. Everyone benefited from the increased business brought by the surge in summer visitors. "The advent of the summer tourist season is generally a welcome occurrence to Bayfield merchants, and in fact to all Bayfield people," reported the *Bayfield County Press*. "The number which spend the season in or near this city has reached up into the hundreds and the marketing they do does much to enliven the merchants' business during the summer." Farmers found a ready market for their produce. Even fishermen took advantage of the summer season, a traditionally less productive part of their year, by ferrying tourists on fishing expeditions or tours of the islands. By one estimate, each visitor who traveled to Bayfield would spend an average of one thousand dollars a day on room, board, and other services. Although this was certainly an exaggerated figure, it reflects the economic importance of tourism.[17]

From the start, the Chequamegon Bay tourist trade functioned within a regional economic framework, overlapping and complementing the extractive industries that flourished at the same time. In addition to his interests in lumber and quarrying, for example, John Knight ran one of Ashland's large hotels. Many of the people who catered to tourists also worked in the lumber camps and on the fishing tugs, and the wives and daughters of fishermen and lumberjacks worked in the hotels. Bayfield lumberman Henry Wachsmuth's dry-goods store sold not just supplies for loggers but also "boots, shoes, and gent's furnishings" and "fine goods for the resort trade." Excursions to the islands—whether for sightseeing, berry picking, lighthouse picnics, or fishing—often took place on the boats in Bayfield's fishing fleet. As in the commercial fisheries, many of the region's Ojibwe residents folded work in the tourist trade—as guides or as dancers at the hotels—into the fabric of their economic life, blending subsistence and wage work.[18]

Visitors to the Chequamegon Bay imagined that they were escaping the material concerns of the modern world. But on the ground, in the places they visited, tourism functioned as one part of an integrated economy that also relied on resource extraction. Nevertheless, railroad companies and tourism promoters encouraged the perception that a trip to northern Wisconsin provided a way to evade the perils of modern life. Over the course of the twentieth century, the idea of an escape into nature became an ever more central part of the tourist experience, in the Apostles and elsewhere. The concept that one may leave a tourist landscape behind—to travel into it and then to return home—contributed to the perception that tourism has a lesser environmental impact than resource extraction. But this was never the case.

The Making of Madeline Island

The steadily growing influence of the tourist trade transformed island environments every bit as much as if the tourists had wielded axes. As sport fishing grew more popular in the nineteenth century, fisheries experts and tourism promoters shaped nature to meet the demands of anglers. These actions had a lasting impact. Beginning in the 1870s, growing popularity as a summer destination transformed the social, economic, and physical landscapes of the Apostles and other wilderness retreats.

When the state legislature established the Wisconsin Fisheries Commission in 1874, its primary concern lay with the declining commercial fisheries. The commissioners focused their initial propagation and stocking efforts on commercial species. Within just a few years, however, the commissioners turned their attention to the inland sport fisheries. In 1879, they announced plans to supplement natural reproduction of game fish such as brook trout, walleyed pike, and black bass, and to begin introducing sport fish popular elsewhere. The motivation for this transition was explicitly economic. "Hundreds of sportsmen from beyond our borders annually visit [northern Wisconsin], and leave thousands of dollars within our confines," the commissioners explained. The commissioners believed their work vital to the continued expansion of the state's tourist trade. "These summer dwellers and throngs of transient sporting tourists who bring so large a revenue to our state, seek not only fine scenery, boating and fresh air. Our lakes and rivers are also attractive to them because of their fish supply. This supply needs continual protection as well as reinforcement."[19]

The WFC complemented its stocking programs with a continual call for the regulation of sport fishing. Beginning in the 1870s, the legislature set closed seasons on sport fish, prohibited the use of nets on inland waters, and outlawed the sale of game species. Like the regulation of commercial fishing, the restrictions on the catch of game species had the result of privileging some activities — and some people — over others. The commissioners were quite explicit in this goal: "While these inland waters have a local importance as yielding food, their value as a means of sport and recreation is much greater, both to the state and to the community in which the lake is situated. For this reason, the aim of legislation for many years has been to preserve the fishing rather than to cause the lakes to yield a maximum amount of food." The commissioners believed that sporting provided a better use of game fish than did subsistence or market sale. Rural residents of northern Wisconsin — who often depended on fish and game to supplement their meager incomes — saw their access to commonly held resources restricted. The protection of game fish provided an essential and complementary motive for the campaign to restrict Ojibwe hunting and fishing rights.[20]

The actions of the state in enhancing and controlling sport fisheries did not simply change the way that residents and tourists interacted with the environments of northern Wisconsin; they changed the environment itself. The WFC supplemented native species with other game fish, particularly rainbow trout and brown trout, especially after the construction of state fish hatcheries in the 1880s. Anglers particularly favored rainbow trout because the fish prefer fast-moving water and put up a good fight when hooked. The WFC introduced German and Scotch brown trout imported from Europe in the 1890s. Brown trout were considered particularly intelligent and difficult to catch — and so grew to larger sizes than rainbow trout.[21]

The Bayfield Fish Hatchery became the central point for dispersal of sport fish in northern Wisconsin. Periodically in the 1890s and yearly after 1900, state workers planted rainbow, brook, and brown trout fingerlings and fry into Fish Creek, the Onion, Sand, and Little Sioux rivers, and other waterways that emptied into the Chequamegon Bay. Rainbow and brown trout established self-perpetuating populations in these rivers. The fish commission also introduced several varieties of salmon, grayling, and perch, but none adapted to Wisconsin rivers like the rainbow and brown trout. The constant introduction of new species combined with changing land-use patterns to reshape the fish populations of the state's waterways.[22]

The Brule River, which empties into Lake Superior just east of the Bayfield Peninsula, serves as an example of the complicated interconnections of social class, sport fishing, and environmental transformation. The Brule is perhaps the most famous trout stream in the Midwest, known equally for the abundance of its trout and for the high social standing of its fishermen. With the Apostle Islands, the Brule was the most renowned tourist attraction in northern Wisconsin. Early descriptions of the river heralded a sportsman's heaven: "I have seen [brook trout], upon a clear day, in these lakes, as thick as minnows in a common pond. . . . It has been aptly said that this is the angler's paradise. One may capture in a short time all that he can carry." By the turn of the century, locals and tourists alike regarded the Brule as "the king of the Lake Superior trout streams."[23]

The Brule attracted fishermen from all over the country, earning a reputation as a gathering spot for the nation's most powerful politicians and businessmen. The river even served as the seat of the U.S. government in 1928, when President Calvin Coolidge spent his summer fishing the river. Presidents Grover Cleveland and Ulysses S. Grant tested their angling skills on the Brule too. Many fishermen established permanent camps and lodges on its banks, mimicking similar camps in New York's Adirondack Mountains. Lumbermen John Knight and William Vilas constructed the first of these exclusive lodges in the 1870s, and sportsmen from St. Paul, Chicago, and other cities soon joined them. These men purchased land along the river, established private fish and game reserves, and built lavish clubhouses and stately summer homes. In so doing, they transformed the environment of the river and the way it was used.[24]

Cedar Island, the private estate of St. Louis oil and railroad tycoon Henry Clay Pierce, exemplifies these transformations. Pierce began acquiring land

3.4 President Calvin Coolidge spent the summer of 1928 at Henry Clay Pierce's lodge on the Brule River. On August 22, 1928, he visited the Apostles. At Devils Island, fisherman Charlie Benson presented the president with fish; later in the day, Coolidge picnicked on Madeline Island with the Gary and Woods families, two of the most prominent families of the Madeline Island summer colony. Local boosters hoped that the president's visit would bolster the regional tourist trade. Courtesy of the National Park Service.

along the Brule in the 1880s, and by the 1890s he owned close to four thousand acres of riverside property. He erected a luxurious lodge on Cedar Island and reportedly employed a retinue of forty servants and assistants during the summer. President Coolidge spent the summer of 1928 as Pierce's guest. Pierce also established one of the largest private fish hatcheries in Wisconsin, which raised and released native brook trout as well as rainbow trout, Scotch and German brown trout, and other species. The Wisconsin Fisheries Commission supplemented this work by planting game fish. By 1910, rainbow and brown trout established self-perpetuating populations on the Brule.[25]

Pierce was a notorious recluse. He aggressively guarded his property, posting signs warning off trespassers, both anglers of his own social class and residents of the region who strayed onto his property in search of fish or game for their tables. For decades, the forests and waters of the Brule watershed had served as a commons, providing food, firewood, and a source of supplemental income in the form of woods work for people who lived on the fringes of the market economy. Pierce and other clubhouse owners sought to privatize these resources. When Wisconsin pisciculture experts stocked the rivers of the state with game fish, they had the interests of men like Pierce in mind; when legislators passed laws limiting the use of these species for subsistence or market purposes, they hoped to restrict the activities of the men and women who trespassed on Pierce's land. The growing importance of private property, and the use of state regulatory authority to protect the interests of property owners, brought a gradual closing of what had been common resources.[26]

Brule River landowners tried to keep trespassers off their land to preserve their ability to escape into nature. The chance to throw off the stresses of modern life, of course, had attracted sportsmen to the Brule in the first place. Once they had achieved this escape, these men were determined to protect it. Nowhere is this more evident than in a court battle between Henry Clay Pierce and lumbermen John Knight and William Vilas. In 1897, Knight and Vilas logged timberlands they owned along the banks of the upper Brule. To get the timber to market, the logs were floated down the river, past Pierce's Cedar Island retreat. Pierce resented the intrusion and filed suit in Wisconsin state court. The log drive, argued Pierce, represented an act of trespass that prevented the "actual, peaceable and undisputed possession and enjoyment" of his land. Pierce lost his suit, for state law allowed log drives along all navigable watercourses. But the case demonstrates how men like Pierce viewed their wilderness property and the extent to which they would go to protect their ability to retreat into nature. It also demonstrates that some tourists—especially those from outside the region—were beginning to see recreation and resource extraction as incompatible.[27]

Pierce and his contemporaries transformed the nature into which they sought escape. Artificial propagation combined with shifting land use in the Brule River basin to reshape the river ecosystem. Both rainbow and brown trout became well established. By the early twentieth century, these species had largely displaced native brook trout. A 1944 survey revealed that these exotic species made up 75.2 percent of all trout caught on the river. The closer to the river's Lake Superior mouth one fished, the less likely one landed native fish.[28]

Changing land-use patterns contributed to this transformation. Knight and Vilas were not the only ones to cut the forests that flanked the Brule River. Lumber baron Frederick Weyerhaeuser logged large tracts of land within the watershed. Logging removed forest cover and increased erosion, thereby

raising the temperature and silt load of the river. These changes benefited introduced species like the brown trout at the expense of the native brook trout,
which preferred cooler, clearer water. Sportsmen contributed to the problem
by removing downed logs and snags to create the manicured clubhouse lawns
from which they enjoyed their wilderness retreats, further exposing the river
to the warming sun. In the first decade of the twentieth century, the Brule's
sportsmen-landowners complained about the decline of angling opportunities and demanded that the state step up its propagation program, crack down
on illegal fishing, and limit logging and other development on the river. State
authorities complied with these requests.[29]

The Brule River retained its reputation for both trout and wealthy anglers
well into the twentieth century. The environments of the river and riverbank,
however, had been transformed. Dignified mansions and rustic clubhouses
lined the shore of a river that housed species of fish imported from California, Scotland, and Germany. Similar ecological changes occurred in the rivers
that emptied into the Chequamegon Bay. Although wealthy sportsmen did not
build clubhouses on these rivers, they did cast their lines in search of exotic
game fish, and some of them traveled to these rivers from the summer homes
they erected on Madeline Island.

Madeline Island is at once similar to the rest of the Apostles and also markedly different. It has similar soils, forests, and topography and, at close to twelve
thousand acres, is the largest island of the archipelago. As on the other islands,
people came in search of resources, but on Madeline the farmers, fishermen,
lumberjacks, and tourists stayed. Only Madeline and Sand islands developed
permanent, year-round communities, and Madeline's proved the more enduring of the two. After the turn of the twentieth century, Madeline Island emerged
as an exclusive summer destination. The permanent community and summer
residences ensured that when Congress created Apostle Islands National Lakeshore in 1970, it excluded Madeline Island from the park.

After its utility as a trading and missionary outpost ended in the mid-
nineteenth century, a small community persisted on Madeline Island. Census
takers counted 319 people there in 1860. Commercial fishing was the primary
occupation, along with ancillary activities such as boatbuilding and cooper-
ing. Islanders engaged in logging and farming too. Even while lumberjacks
stripped the island of its white pine, the accessibility of the island provided an
opportunity for summer woods work to harvest cedar railroad ties, hemlock

bark, and hardwoods. Farmers, often clearing fields in the cutover areas left behind by logging, mixed subsistence farming with limited market production, selling their surplus in the lumber camps or in the emerging markets of Bayfield and Ashland. The intermittent opportunities provided by the tourist trade also played an important role in the island economy. Tourists made the short trip from Bayfield to investigate the village, the old trading post, several Indian cemeteries, and the buildings left behind by the missionaries. Often, islanders mixed and matched among the activities, finding seasonal work in many different industries.[30]

Madeline Island's development as a resort community had an unlikely impetus: the vacation needs of Congregational ministers. In 1897, the Reverend Edward P. Salmon purchased the property of the Methodist mission that had been established in the 1830s but had long since fallen into disrepair. He renovated the buildings and in 1898 opened the Old Mission, a resort intended to cater to the needs of Protestant ministers and their families. Although the resort retained a set of strict rules about appropriate behavior and decorum, the clientele expanded beyond families of the cloth. The Old Mission became the focal point of the Madeline Island summer community for the next forty years. Families returned year after year, eventually persuading Salmon to construct cabins that they could rent for the length of the summer, taking their meals at the Old Mission dining hall.[31]

Once summer residents had secured a beachhead on the island, they began a process perhaps best described as colonization. After spending one season at the Old Mission, Omaha businessman and hay-fever sufferer Frederick M. Woods purchased land of his own and built a summer home. He then convinced many of his relatives and business associates from Nebraska to join him. The group of summer residences that developed just north of the town of La Pointe came to be known as Nebraska Row. A second set of summer homes coalesced around the residence of John D. O'Brien, populated primarily by urbanites from St. Paul and known as O'Brien Row. O'Brien had spent his childhood on the island, while his father served as a teacher in the 1850s. He had returned to the area in the 1880s as a sporting enthusiast and became a founding member of the Winneboujou Club—one of the Brule River's most exclusive hunting and fishing clubs. Throughout the teens and 1920s, the summer community of Madeline Island expanded. The prosperous years of the late 1920s brought a flurry of construction.[32]

Madeline Island summers offered the same antimodern appeal that had drawn tourists to the islands for decades. Summer residents arrived in the end of June or in early July and often stayed through the first week of October. Longtime summer visitor Hamilton Nelson Ross remembered berry picking, sailing, and fishing: "Some of these cruises consumed several days in the waters of the adjacent archipelago, convincing the visiting city dwellers that they were truly experiencing pioneer life. . . . Some of the more venturesome experimented with Indian birch bark canoes, a few of which were still in existence."[33]

Madeline's emergence as a tourist destination prompted Chequamegon Bay entrepreneurs to establish resorts on other islands. The Lake Superior Land and Development Company put together the most comprehensive resort scheme. In 1910, the Minneapolis-based company announced plans to develop Hermit Island for tourism and agriculture. The company planned to carve the island into ten-acre shoreline parcels for the construction of private homes, with the interior of the island designated for fruit orchards and a "natural reserve forest." Central to these plans was the odd three-story mansion on the island, the Cedar Bark Lodge, once the summer residence of a prominent Ashland businessman. The lodge ran as a resort for several years, but the plans for private homes and orchards never came to fruition.[34]

Madeline Island remained the hub of summer activity in the Chequamegon Bay, with increasing consequences for island economic and social life. Islanders gave up occupations like fishing and logging for work in the tourist trade. In 1930, nineteen permanent residents listed their full-time occupations as service-oriented positions like gardener, caretaker, or housekeeper. These occupations made up the second-largest category of employment on the island, behind only common labor. Not a single person had listed this type of occupation in 1900. Island farmers benefited by selling produce, butchered meats, and dairy products. In some cases, the relationship between farmer and summer visitor was more formal. In 1929, Nebraska Row resident Hunter S. Gary purchased an island farm and hired the Anderson family as year-round tenants. The Andersons ran a produce-delivery service, providing summer residents with standard orders of eggs, milk, cream, meat, and other fresh food. By 1930, summer residents owned three interior farms and employed year-round residents in similar arrangements.[35]

The ongoing productive work of fishing and farming was not a disincentive for summer residents, but rather an advantage. Madeline Island thus provides an example of how the spaces of production and consumption overlapped. This overlap began to change the nature of island life, as islanders depended more and more on the seasonal opportunities of the tourist trade. The perils of seasonal labor and dependence on wealthy tourists, of course, occurred everywhere that tourism made up a significant part of the economy.

Madeline Island's landscape reflected the growing economic importance of tourism. Nebraska Row stands as an example. When Frederick Woods constructed the first summer home there in 1899, he built in an open pasture. The area had once been the site of cabins and merchant's shops, built in the wings of the American Fur Company post, and had been completely cleared of its forest cover. A severe fire in 1869 burned down the homes, shops, and the warehouses, many of which had remained vacant since the demise of the fur trade. As Woods and his colleagues erected summer homes on the site, they also began to plant trees. Early photos of the area show the handsome mansions with virtually no surrounding vegetation; by the 1940s, Norway pine and other ornamental trees shaded these same houses. The grounds of Coole Park Manor, a summer residence built by former Old Mission guests Albert and Cora Hull in 1913, underwent the most complete transformation. Beginning in 1920, the Hulls created a tiered English garden, with 450 rose bushes, a teahouse, pergolas, stone paths, and a small pool and fountain. The formal gardens of Coole Park Manor and the manicured lawns of Nebraska Row that replaced the pasture represent the ways that development for the summer tourist trade transformed the physical environment of Madeline Island.[36]

The alteration of the Madeline Island's landscapes to satisfy the needs of tourists radiated outward from La Pointe. In town, summer residences replaced the more modest homes of year-round residents. The managers of the Old Mission tore out the apple and cherry orchard to the east of La Pointe for a golf course and a tennis court in the 1920s—a powerful symbol of the transition from production to consumption as the driving force of the island economy. Another entrepreneur dredged the lagoon on the southwest tip of the island in the 1930s to build a marina large enough to dock the powerboats and yachts of the summer visitors.[37]

These changes accelerated in the twentieth century. Between 1900 and 1940, the average number of farms on Madeline fluctuated but hovered around thirty. In 1935, 32 farms dotted the island. After World War II, the number dropped quickly: 18 farms in 1945; 12 in 1950; 8 in 1954. By 1960, only one working farm

3.5 This early twentieth-century postcard shows the summer homes built to the west of La Pointe on Madeline Island, known as Nebraska Row. When Omaha businessmen Frederick W. Woods built the first summer home on the shore in the 1890s, the area was an empty pasture. By the mid-twentieth century, formal landscaping and forest growth had transformed it, and it is now covered in thick woods. Courtesy of the National Park Service.

remained. The capital demands of mechanized agriculture and the rising taxes that followed summer development forced farmers to sell their property. The fields lay fallow, but the farmhouses became summer homes. One observer counted 125 summer homes on the island in 1960. As plans for a national lakeshore in the islands progressed in the 1960s, the pace of tourist development on Madeline Island quickened.[38]

The environmental transformations wrought by the summer tourist trade are obscured by a century-long tradition of viewing tourism—especially the brand of nature tourism available in the Apostles—as a way to escape from the pressures of modern life. Tourists wanted to see nature unsullied by the society they sought to escape. Wealthy summer visitors could sit on the porches of their hotels and summer homes and enjoy the view of what they saw as a wilderness, blind to the transformations that their presence had necessitated. They viewed nature as a place to be visited, not a tool with which to work or a place in which to live. The tourists had help in coming to this seemingly contradictory perspective. For most of the twentieth century, the state both fostered the tourist trade and segregated it from other forms of economic activity.

The Promotion and Segregation of Tourism

Government assistance—in the form of the construction of internal improvements, tax codes, or regulation—encouraged logging, commercial fishing, and other extractive industries in resource-producing areas like the Chequamegon Bay. The same held true in the tourist trade. The state indirectly fostered tourism in many ways, most notably through federal subsidies for internal improvements that allowed first steamships and then railroads to carry tourists to the islands, and also in the restriction of Ojibwe fishing rights to clear the way for sport and commercial fishing. During the twentieth century, state involvement in the tourist economy became more explicit. In the teens and 1920s, Wisconsin initiated a coordinated program of road building, with the attraction of tourist dollars a primary motivation. In the 1930s, with other extractive industries struggling, the state used its regulatory authority to rearrange the landscape and maximize the region's potential as a tourist destination.

In 1923, business leaders throughout northern Wisconsin began planning for the Apostle Islands Indian Pageant, performed for the first time in August 1924. Staged in an outdoor amphitheater just a few miles north of Bayfield, the pageant depicted the history of the Chequamegon Bay from prehistory through the arrival of American treaty commissioners in 1854. Over four hundred actors dramatized this story through the presentation of thirty-five scenes viewed over three consecutive days. These scenes depicted events in the region's history, such as "The Arrival of Jean Nicolet, at the Chequamegon, 1634," and "The Arrival of the American Fur Traders." Although purportedly about Native Americans, the Chequamegon Bay's journey from barbarism to civilization emerged as the central theme of the pageant. Pageant organizers catered to the tourists' interest in escape. The dramatic scenes did not mention boosters, farmers, lumberjacks, or quarrymen—the people who had wrought so much change on Chequamegon Bay environments in the previous fifty years. The pageant offered a trip to the romantic past of the voyageur and the explorer, not a reminder of the region's ongoing economic stagnation. Organizers planned to run the pageant for two or three weeks every August.[39]

In the early twentieth century, towns all over the country staged historical pageants as statements of civic identity and patriotism and also for the
economic benefits the shows provided. Editors of the *Bayfield County Press* predicted that the pageant would establish Bayfield as "a gateway through which in
the single summer more tourist visitors may pour than during all of the history
of tourist travel in Northern Wisconsin." They estimated a tenfold increase in
visitors, all of them traveling with the incentive of "going back to the wilderness
of James Fennimore Cooper." Organizers publicized the opportunity to explore
America's romantic past, to see primitive Indians firsthand, to experience the
beautiful outdoors. They hoped that close to one hundred thousand people
would take in the spectacle each year.[40]

The Apostle Islands Indian Pageant differed from earlier attempts at tourist
promotion in its focus on automobile tourism. "Come by automobile," encouraged one pamphlet, "over long graveled and concrete highways. Drive through
virgin lands of forests, lakes, and rivers. Enjoy wild life in its primitive haunts,
for you will startle deer, and grouse, and partridge, all along the way." Once
they arrived, visitors would find an array of services catering to the needs of
auto campers: "Visitors to the Indian Pageant will find plenty of accommodations to suit their particular likes and needs. Near the Pageant Grounds is a
large tourist camp with cooking grates, running water, fire wood and comfort
stations." Ashland, Washburn, Bayfield, Duluth, and Superior offered similar
facilities as well as garages, gas stations, and restaurants. Those who attended
the pageant would touch the primitive and the wild while also enjoying the
comfort and convenience of modern automobile travel.[41]

In targeting auto campers, pageant organizers hoped to tie into a wildly popular national trend. As cars became more affordable and middle-class incomes
rose during the 1920s, urbanites from around the nation took to the roads,
in the process inventing an entirely new type of tourism. Only the wealthiest
Americans could afford the time and expense of railroad journeys to remote
destinations, but auto touring made vacations more broadly available. A new
pattern of vacationing emerged, called "gypsying"—touring the countryside
with no particular itinerary, freed from the confines of a railroad timetable. New
destinations and wayside attractions sprang up as auto campers explored the
countryside. Traveling by car became the quintessentially American vacation.
By the early 1920s, rural towns and larger cities around the nation established
municipal auto camps, which attracted potential customers to town centers and

kept them from pitching their tents in the fields and yards of farmers. One 1923 survey determined that on a single August day, 29,409 out-of-state cars toured Wisconsin roads, from as far away as New York and California, and that tourists spent an estimated one hundred million dollars each year. The organizers of the Apostle Islands Indian Pageant hoped to profit from this trend.[42]

The state played a direct and essential role in luring auto campers to Wisconsin. In 1911, the legislature passed the State Aid Road Law. The law provided for road development, cooperatively funded by county and state governments, and also created the State Highway Commission to supervise highway construction. The Wisconsin highway network grew rapidly. In 1918, the legislature established a state highway system, which included 5,000 miles of improved roads. This number jumped to 7,500 miles in 1919 and 10,000 miles by 1926. The federal government contributed to the improvement of Wisconsin roads with matching funds provided by the Federal Highway Act of 1921. During the 1920s, highway engineers discovered methods of finishing and improving roads to help them withstand Wisconsin's long winters. By 1926, Wisconsin claimed one of the best road systems in the nation.[43]

Recreation provided a key motivation for the burst in highway construction. In the 1890s, urban bicyclists lobbied for road improvement so that they could better enjoy their sport. Rural residents of the state, however, often opposed state-sponsored road improvements, fearing an increased tax burden and a loss of control over local decision making. Road-building advocates directed much of their promotional efforts at the state's rural areas. They argued that road improvement would help farmers and loggers get their products to market, but recreation provided an underlying motivation for this rhetoric. When the bicycling fad died in the 1890s, motorists picked up the mantle of the good roads movement. By the 1920s, road advocates had succeeded in convincing most Wisconsinites of the need for state aid for road construction.[44]

The organizers of the Apostle Islands Indian Pageant depended on the support of state road building to make their venture profitable. Just one week after the creation of the pageant corporation in 1923, Bayfield businessmen attended a hearing before the State Highway Legislative Committee to urge that forty-four miles of Highway 13 between Bayfield and Superior be improved and designated a part of the state highway system. The Chequamegon Bay's major roads had been included in the original state highway system in 1917: Highway 10, between Ashland and Superior, and Highway 13, between Ashland and

Bayfield. An improved state highway along the shore of the lake between Bayfield and Superior, promised pageant manager L. E. McKenzie, would create an appealing scenic drive. He argued that successful development of the region as a tourist destination depended on the state's willingness to improve this road: "Immediate completion of a state highway between Superior and Bayfield is the prime essential for development of the Lake Superior region." McKenzie recognized that the success of the pageant depended on good roads. Without them, even a threat of rain might prevent thousands of visitors from making the trip to Bayfield. Highway 13 was included in the state system and improvement was underway by 1925.[45]

During the 1920s, tourist ventures throughout Wisconsin and the western Great Lakes hoped to take advantage of new, improved roads. With timber resources gone or disappearing and the prospects for cutover farming increasingly grim, businessmen hoped that tourism would take the place of logging in the region's economy. Northern Wisconsin residents established several organizations to help promote the tourist trade. In 1922, the Northern Wisconsin Resort Association formed with the goal of improving services and luring tourist dollars to the state. The organization claimed two thousand members in its first year and in 1923 changed its name to the Wisconsin Land O' Lakes Association. Organizers of the Indian pageant built on this publicity, encouraging tourists to "travel though the scenic wooded sections of Minnesota and Wisconsin, through the beautiful Land O' Lakes region, and on up to the Pageant grounds . . . where you may tour concrete highways through a virgin wilderness, or camp at modern summer resorts and tourist playgrounds." Attracting motorists remained a central part of this promotional strategy, and the Land O' Lakes Association, like other similar groups, lobbied repeatedly for state assistance in improving Wisconsin's highways.[46]

Despite the high hopes of its organizers and promoters, the Apostle Islands Indian Pageant did not provide the expected financial windfall. In its first run, from August 1 to 20, 1924, poor weather kept the potential audience off the road. The second season had a higher turnout, but still only twelve thousand people attended the show. By the end of the 1925 season, the pageant had failed to cover expenses for two years running and announced a debt of sixty thousand dollars. The production survived only one more year.[47]

The significance of the pageant lies not in its brevity but in the way that its organizers looked to the state to create the essential link that would bring tourists to the islands. After the 1920s, Wisconsinites and other Americans increasingly turned to the state to organize and supplement the tourist economy. Tourist promoters found willing listeners in the offices of the State Highway Commission and the Wisconsin Conservation Department. State fisheries experts such as James Nevin had recognized the value of tourism since the 1880s, and they stocked the state's rivers with game fish to bolster the tourist economy. In 1915, administration of state parks had been brought under the control of the Conservation Commission. In the 1920s, the commission made the protection of the state's recreational resources an ever more central part of its mission. The WCD adopted the motto "Relax in Wisconsin, where friends and nature meet," to better promote the state's resources. In 1936, the WCD created its own recreational publicity department. But the state did not stop with promotion. In the 1930s, it took an increasingly direct role in shaping the tourist economy as well as the environment on which that economy depended.[48]

Government and academic planners saw tourism as a savior in a time of economic distress, the one industry that would allow the residents of northern Wisconsin to earn a living. They called for the state to take a more active role in planning for tourism. This meant applying the bureaucrat's logic of legibility to the tourist trade and rearranging the landscape to maximize the region's potential for tourism. Legibility required segregating tourism from the resource production that had anchored the economies of places such as the Chequamegon Bay for decades.

A crisis of tax delinquency motivated an increased state role in planning for tourism. Since the late nineteenth century, settlers had tried to carve farms out of the forests of northern Wisconsin, following the developmental path of New England, the Ohio River valley, and the southern parts of the state. But poor soils, a short growing season, and limited access to markets made the Wisconsin cutover unsuitable for agriculture. When the bottom dropped out of the farm economy in the mid-1920s, many settlers of the cutover could no longer pay their taxes. Nearly one-quarter of all land in seventeen northern Wisconsin counties entered into tax delinquency in 1927 alone. Removing that amount of land from the tax base severely strained county governments and made the provision of public services to remaining settlers untenable.[49]

In response to these deteriorating conditions, state planners turned to the new discipline of land economics for solutions. University of Wisconsin economist Richard T. Ely, who founded the discipline in the 1920s, believed

3.6 In the 1920s, the state of Wisconsin took an ever more active role in the promotion of tourism. The Wisconsin Conservation Department adopted the motto "Relax in Wisconsin, where friends and nature meet." Rural zoning initiatives helped to ensure that tourists would find the "nature" they sought in northern Wisconsin. Courtesy of the Wisconsin Historical Society, WHi-37927.

that statistics and modern scientific methods could ascertain the best possible use for land and natural resources. Wisconsin's cutover was one of his first laboratories. Ely determined that the region was unfit for agriculture and best suited to reforestation and use for forestry and recreation. He urged the resettlement of farmers away from northern Wisconsin, a concentrated effort at forest regeneration, and a dedication to tourism as the center of a new, more robust economy.[50]

George S. Wehrwein, another land economist, came to similar conclusions. In a study of Vilas and Oneida counties, just to the southwest of the Apostle Islands, Wehrwein found that recreation provided by far the most profitable use of land. Oneida County, for example, had only 8.5 percent of its land classi-fied as recreational in 1929, but this land contributed 37.2 percent of real estate value. In Vilas County, recreational land made up 15.7 percent of the area but generated 63.1 percent of real estate value. "Wisconsin has the scenery, the cli-mate, and the location to be one of the outstanding playgrounds of the Middle West," asserted Wehrwein. But Wisconsin had not fully tapped its recreational potential. Doing so would rejuvenate the economies of depressed regions and solve the crisis of tax delinquency.[51]

Part of the problem, Ely and Wehrwein believed, lay in the fact that rec-reational lands were not being used to their fullest. Wehrwein suggested that the "farmer resorts" of northern Wisconsin demonstrated the need for more efficient planning in the tourist industry. His survey of Vilas County found that forty-six farmers reported owning 102 rental cottages in 1930. These farmers no doubt hoped to tie in to the regional tourist trade and supplement their farm income. Tourism in northern Wisconsin had often functioned in this man-ner, integrated with other economic activities. "Theoretically, a combination of farming with a resort or cottages seems feasible," Wehrwein explained. Farmers could build and maintain their resorts during the less-busy periods of the agri-cultural calendar. But in reality, he argued, "the operating of a resort and a farm do not mix. The resort season falls in the very months when the farmer is busy with his crops and harvest. Summer guests demand many services and a great deal of attention which only a trained 'hotel man' knows how to render satisfac-torily." Farmers would do much better to focus full-time on growing produce and dairy products to serve the resort trade, rather than trying to engage in both industries at once. Farmland and recreational land in proximity to—but segregated from—each other would create the ideal situation.[52]

At the urging of planners like Wehrwein and Ely, Wisconsin adopted rural zoning ordinances that employed the power of the state to realize this goal. In 1929, the state legislature conveyed to county governments the right to zone land for exclusive forest, agricultural, or recreational use. Counties could pre-vent agricultural settlement on lands deemed too poor for farming, relieving the burden of providing costly roads, schools, and services to scattered and isolated farm families. Wisconsin's rural zoning law was the first in the nation, and it became a model for New Deal management of submarginal agricultural lands. Oneida County adopted the first ordinances in 1933, and the rest of the cutover counties followed by 1940. In all, county governments closed nearly five million acres to farming and settlement. Although at first resistant to these initiatives, town boosters and businessmen in rural Wisconsin by the 1930s saw a greater state role in collective planning as the path out of the crisis of tax delinquency and depression. Farmers—the men and women being told that their lands were unfit for agriculture and asked to leave their farms—were less enthusiastic.[53]

Zoning for recreation and tourism became a central tenet of economic recovery for the cutover. County planning boards, with the assistance of state extension agents, classified lands for agriculture, forestry, or recreation. A typical recreational area might prohibit such industrial activity as quarries, sawmills, or mines but would allow development for summer homes. An early state publication explained the benefits of recreational zoning: "Recreational land means taxable wealth. A zoned area dedicated to recreation insuring a quiet, beautiful, undisturbed area in which to build a summer home will help to attract the recreation seeker to the zoned counties of Wisconsin." Some areas were zoned to allow for forest products industries as well as for recreational use. But more significantly, the county used this authority to segregate recreational land use from other types of economic activity.[54]

Rural zoning resulted from the same drive for legibility that took place in the commercial fisheries. Faced with the disorder and inefficiency of settlement on submarginal lands and widespread tax delinquency, state officials responded by using the zoning ordinances to create a more ordered and easily managed landscape. State planners argued that segregating tourism from other economic activities made for the most efficient use of natural resources. Rural zoning provided a mechanism to utilize state authority to achieve this segregation. State and county governments assumed a far more powerful role in determining economic activity.

Ashland County adopted rural zoning ordinances in 1934. La Pointe Township—which includes all of the Apostle Islands but three—faced a different situation than the rest of the county. In 1930, only 1.25 percent of La Pointe Township was in delinquency; the rest of the county averaged 26.3 percent. The state held title to only one 80-acre parcel on Basswood Island, while the rest of the Apostles remained in private ownership. Island landowners continued to see value in their property, and continued to pay their taxes, despite the fact that most of the islands had been stripped of their timber. Recreational potential provided this value.[55]

When it created land-use areas in 1934, the Ashland County Land Use Planning Committee divided the Apostle Islands into two categories. It designated Madeline Island as "agricultural and recreational" and the other sixteen islands under its jurisdiction as "forestry and recreational." The county closed these islands to potential agricultural settlement, to all uses other than forestry and tourism. Even Madeline Island's agricultural land use depended on recreation—on the local markets created by the extensive summer home development. By 1934, then, the county had begun the process of segregating the Apostle Islands for their recreational value and had set Madeline Island into its own land-use category.[56]

This separation of tourism from other economic activity marked a turning point in the environmental history of the Apostle Islands. State and county planners conceived of the Apostles as a place valued only for recreation. Over the rest of the century, the state further prescribed the activities permissible in the islands. This process culminated in the view of the islands as a wilderness, as a place valued for only a specific type of recreation. When the National Park Service shut down the Rocky Island Air Haven in 1974, it did so because of the ways that the Air Haven blurred the lines between consumption and production, between recreation and extraction. Blurry lines and bureaucratic authority do not mix.

The segregation of tourism did more than make for easier management. It also changed the way that people viewed recreational landscapes. It made the idea of an escape into nature an easier illusion to maintain. When nineteenth-century tourists traveled to the Chequamegon Bay, they responded to the promotional imagery that urged them to escape the pressures of modern society. When they arrived in the Apostle Islands, they found a tourist economy firmly embedded in an integrated economic system that treated tourism as an activity indistinguishable from resource extraction. But with tourism segregated from other industries, these connections became harder to see. The image of an escape into nature became more convincing. ❧

4

Sand Island Stories

MOST VISITORS TO SAND ISLAND DISEMBARK AT A GRASSY CLEARING at the base of a long dock in the middle of the island's east bay. From the clearing, visitors have a choice of three trails. The northernmost trail winds through a small field of wildflowers and a remnant pine forest on its way to the tip of the island and a stunning view of the open lake. A second trail heads into the interior of the island, to one of the few open clearings in the island forest. The third trail — the most clearly defined of the three — skirts the shoreline to the south, although it rarely leaves the forest. Each trail has a different destination, and each tells a different story.

The northern trail ends at the red sandstone lighthouse built in 1881 to guide ships into Chequamegon Bay. Like all of the lighthouses of the Apostles, the Sand Island Light evokes stories of lonely lighthouse keepers, ferocious storms, and disastrous shipwrecks. The trail to the center of the island runs to the site of the Noring farm, the last year-round residence on an island once home to a community of Norwegian fishermen and farmers. Not much remains but some abandoned farm equipment and a pile of moldering boards. The southernmost trail once served as the county road connecting the islands' farms and houses. The rusted bodies of two cars sit off the side of the trail, their upholstery long since rotted away and their wheels three-quarters buried in the mud. One of the cars belonged to Gert Wellisch, a school teacher from St. Paul who spent nearly fifty summers on the island. A quarter mile south of the cars, in the woods to the west of the trail, lie the ruins of a one-room schoolhouse—once the center of the island community. The school closed in 1928, and fifty-year-old trees now grow through its crumbling foundation. With each passing year, the ruins become harder to see.

Stories are embedded in the Sand Island landscape, although the returning wilderness makes their details difficult to discern. These stories are some of the most precious resources of the rewilding islands. Between 1880 and 1945, fishermen, farmers, and tourists created a community on Sand Island, building homes, lives, and landscapes. They also created the stories still evident in the island's ruins, trails, and fields. These stories provide a place to recast the relationship between wilderness and history.

Today, the National Park Service holds the responsibility for determining which of Sand Island's stories will be told. This task has proven remarkably difficult. Sand Island could be a place to learn about the creation of a community; the history of the fishing, farming, and tourism; the environmental consequences of resource extraction; the transition from production to consumption; or the return of wilderness characteristics to a humanized landscape. Each of these stories represents an important strand of the island's history. But NPS management policies pit some of these story lines against each other, dictating a choice between the activities of the island's past and its management as a wilderness. It is hard to tell stories about farming, logging, and one-room schoolhouses when NPS policy demands that the physical evidence of these activities be removed from areas valued for their wilderness characteristics. How the stories should be told—whether through trails, signs, brochures, guided walks, or some other option—creates an additional management dilemma. These questions surfaced in 2001 when NPS planners initiated a suitability study to determine which parts of Apostle Islands National Lakeshore should be designated as wilderness. Sand Island—and also Basswood Island, with its equally rich human history— lay at the center of the debate. Wilderness status for these islands depended on how the story of rewilding might be told.

As the suitability study progressed, most wilderness advocates pushed for as large a wilderness designation as possible. In the initial public comment period, the NPS received 4,512 written comments, 80 percent of which supported wilderness designation. When NPS planners published the draft environmental

4.1 By the twenty-first century, signs of Sand Island's human history were visible only for those who knew where to look. The car once driven around the island by summer resident Gertrude Wellisch rusts in the woods off the side of the East Bay trail. Photograph by William Cronon.

impact statement (EIS) in 2003, their "preferred alternative" was to designate 33,500 acres, or 80 percent of the park's land base, as wilderness. Sand and Basswood islands were excluded from this proposal. In subsequent public comments, 78 percent of those who responded to the draft urged the NPS to expand the area designated as wilderness.[1]

But an extensive wilderness designation would handcuff the NPS, making it difficult to include rewilding as one of the stories told about the islands. Wilderness designation would bring the application of park service–wide management policies and the removal of what the NPS calls "nonconforming conditions"—the physical signs of past human activities, such as fishermen's cabins and summer homes. It would also prohibit, or at least significantly limit, the development of an interpretive program focused on the stories of the people whose lives informed the modern Sand Island landscape. Interpretive signs, in particular, are prohibited in wilderness areas. Such policies are intended to enhance the park's wilderness character by making the human imprint less noticeable—by making park environments seem pristine and untouched. Wilderness designation, the EIS explained, "would likely . . . foreclose potential interpretive opportunities." Stories about the human use of places like Sand Island would become harder for visitors to discern and harder for NPS interpreters to point out.[2]

This struck some observers as a critical missed opportunity. Environmental historian William Cronon—himself a Bayfield summer resident—urged the NPS to adopt a more flexible wilderness management policy. "What makes this landscape come alive are the tales we tell about it," he explained. "Management policy in the National Lakeshore should seek to protect *stories*—the stories about human history as well as stories about wild nature—as much as it protects wilderness values and historic structures." By removing the evidence of human history to create the appearance of pristine wilderness, the NPS would forfeit the chance to tell stories about how islanders shaped the environments of both the past and the present. If the NPS could not tell these stories, Cronon recommended the exclusion of Sand Island from the wilderness.[3]

The disagreements about how to best preserve and interpret the stories and the environments of the Apostle Islands led to ongoing discussions between wilderness advocates, community members, and other interested parties. The resulting proposed compromise, known as the "Shared Vision," recognized three key goals: the protection of wilderness, the interpretation of history, and limits on future development. To achieve these goals, the compromise proposed the addition of most of Basswood Island to the wilderness area but the exclusion of Sand Island. "Sand Island represents an especially rich opportunity for historical and cultural interpretation, given the concentration there of sites representing most phases of Apostle Islands history. The management and interpretation of these sites should emphasize the mingled stories of human and natural history as expressed in the physical landscape, while always respecting the surrounding wilderness context."[4]

Endorsement for the compromise came from the Wilderness Society, the local chapter of the Sierra Club, and many other groups and individuals, with the largest single block of comments on the draft EIS supporting the "Shared Vision." Ultimately, NPS administrators settled on their original preferred alternative, citing the management flexibility that resulted from excluding both

Sand and Basswood islands from the wilderness. In the formal record of decision, they nevertheless made clear the intention to continue to manage Sand
and Basswood as wilderness.

Land managers all over the country struggle to determine which stories to
tell about the landscapes they protect. At the Phillip Burton Wilderness in California's Point Reyes National Seashore, NPS officials manage wilderness in an
area with a long and diverse human history. Observance of national guidelines has led to the removal of historical structures, the promotion of natural
over cultural resources, and a refusal to interpret human history within designated wilderness. At Congaree National Park, in the South Carolina floodplain,
the NPS has only limited interpretation of rare and significant archeological
resources called cattle mounts—large earthen masses built by slaves in the
nineteenth century to create dry havens for cattle—that lie within a wilderness
area. The managers at Great Camp Sagamore, an Adirondack camp once owned
by the Vanderbilt family but now run by a nonprofit organization for educational purposes, have taken a different approach. They worked with New York
conservation authorities to include the ruins of a historical hydroelectric dam,
"subject to the forces of nature," in the management plan for the Blue Ridge
Wilderness and Wakely Mountain Primitive Area. Old mines in Death Valley
National Park, the removal of the Cascades Diversion Dam from the Merced
River inside Yosemite National Park, and a host of other examples testify to the
challenges of managing wild places with complicated human histories.[5]

How are we to understand the presence of the past in places that today seem
wild? Does calling attention to human stories detract from the value of wild
places? Questions like these lie at the heart of the wilderness debates, and the
answers point a way out of them. With its wild characteristics returning in ways
continually shaped by human choices, Sand Island provides the perfect stage to
tell such stories: of making a home in nature, of the consequences of human
actions, of the connections between human and natural processes. These
stories of connections and consequences are what the narrative of rewilding
helps illuminate. Sand Island's stories teach us that while all human choices
have long-term effects on nature, these choices are not always destructive, and
they do not necessarily cause irreparable harm. Wild nature does not disappear
from places touched by human history. Today's Sand Island landscapes testify
that wild places, too, have human pasts.

Early Connections

Sand Island's earliest stories left the lightest marks on the landscape and prove the hardest to recover. Through the mid-1880s, the island provided a base for seasonal fishing, logging, and tourism, activities that were only loosely connected to each other. But as Sand Island integrated into the nation's expanding economy, the activities of the island's residents developed a more permanent character—and a more lasting impact.

Sand Island received few visitors until the 1870s. Archeological surveys have revealed only the slightest traces of early Indian use of the island—a few quartz flakes and fire-cracked rocks, nothing more. Archeologists have surmised that these few signs might mark the island's use as an itinerant fishing or hunting camp. When General Land Office surveyors arrived 1857, they found no evidence of human activity.[6]

In 1870, fisherman Frank Shaw acquired land on Sand Island's southeast corner with his Civil War veteran's bonus. Shaw and his wife, Josephine, had moved to the Chequamegon Bay region from Ohio in 1867. The Shaws lived in La Pointe during the 1870s and in Bayfield in the 1880s. Frank Shaw fished among the Apostles while Josephine ran a Bayfield boardinghouse and their children attended school. By the early 1880s, Frank Shaw used Sand Island as a base for his summer fishing. He hired several men during the summer to help drive poundnet posts and tend nets. Shaw and his men salted their catch and either transported it to town themselves or waited for one of the collection steamers sent by Bayfield's fish dealers. Shaw fished in this manner throughout the 1880s, with Sand Island as his summer residence.[7]

Frank Shaw, however, did more than catch fish. He and his hired men also grew crops on Sand Island, mostly for home use but also to sell in Bayfield. In the mid-1890s, with the children no longer in school, the Shaws made Sand Island their year-round home. They expanded their fishing and farming activities over the rest of the decade. The farm earned a particular reputation for its strawberries. "The finest strawberries that have been brought into market this season are arriving daily from Frank Shaw's farm at Sand Island," reported the local newspaper. The farm looked like other farmsteads in rural Wisconsin, complete with cows and sheep, hayfields and apple orchards. Frank Shaw's fishing operation grew, too, and by 1899 his fleet included four vessels and he kept three to four hired men on hand at all times.[8]

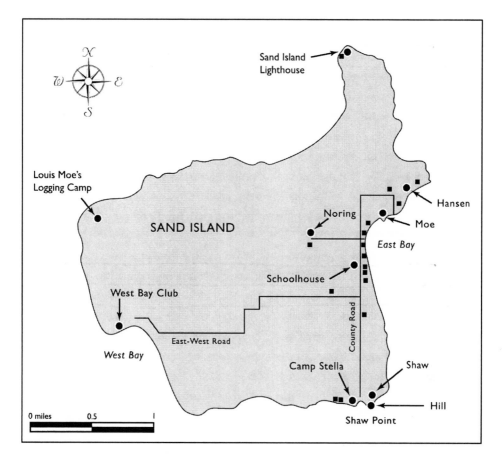

Map 3 Sand Island

Other fishermen used Sand Island as a summer fishing camp too, some of them perhaps even predating Shaw. The underwater ledge around the outside of the archipelago was one of the area's most important fishing grounds, easily accessed off the northern and western points of the island, while the sandy east bay provided shelter and an easy approach. Few of these itinerant fishermen owned land on the island and most built nothing more than shacks for shelter. Little remains to record the character of these fishermen's lives. Their names occasionally appear in the local newspapers, enough to prove their existence but little else. Justice Bay, on the island's northeast side, bears the name of fisherman Jean Baptiste Justice, who lived there with his family for several years. The name remains as the only trace of their tenure.[9]

Through the 1880s, Sand Island remained a seasonal fishing station and, as autumn turned to winter, lumberjacks replaced the fishermen. In December 1884, the local firm of Boutin & Holston established a logging camp on the island. The company estimated that it would remove over 2.5 million board feet of lumber, mostly high-grade white pine. The following June, another Boutin tug arrived at Sand Island to pick up equipment and to tow a raft of the winter's work to the Ashland mills. Boutin & Holston reestablished the camp in November 1885. That the Boutins—Chequamegon Bay's biggest fish dealers—doubled as logging contractors represents an early indication of the ways that seemingly distinct industries intersected at a peripheral point of production like Sand Island.[10]

In 1881, the federal government provided another form of seasonal employment on Sand Island when it established a lighthouse to guide the region's growing commercial traffic through the shoals off York and Sand islands. Contractors built the new lighthouse and its fifty-foot tower out of locally quarried red sandstone. The *Bayfield County Press* pointed out that the new lighthouse added yet another feature to the region's growing tourist trade: "Among the many attractions in and around Bayfield and the Apostle Islands should be numbered the new Light House, in course of construction on Sand Island. Superintendent Louis Lederle, and family, have located to the island and will be pleased to point out the various points of interest."[11]

Several of the region's most wealthy and prominent citizens sought out the island as a spot for summer fishing and camping. Samuel Fifield—one-time editor of the Bayfield and Ashland papers, former state senator and lieutenant governor, and the Chequamegon Bay's most prominent booster—spent part of the summer of 1881 camping on the island. Fifield liked it so much that he returned on a permanent basis. In 1886, he established the Apostle Islands' first summer resort, Camp Stella, on the south shore of the island, just to the west of the Shaw farm.[12]

Fifield had very different plans for the island than did his neighbors. Next to the Shaws' hayfields and market garden, he constructed a landscape of leisure—a "street" lined with white canvas camping tents, several permanent cottages, a large dining space, and even gas-powered streetlamps. For Fifield, Sand Island became an escape into nature and a hay-fever retreat for his suffering wife Stella. "Beneath the evergreen boughs the white tents glisten through the open spaces of a beautiful grove," he described. "The sun finds its way among the tree tops that cast a welcome shade where the hammocks are hung, while a gentle breeze, cooled by the waves of the sparkling bay, plays summer airs that lull and soothe the happy campers to delightful dreams." At first, Camp Stella's visitors consisted mainly of the Fifield's local friends and relatives. But as the camp developed and Fifield's promotional efforts took hold, it attracted more out-of-state visitors. Fifield's political connections lured a series of high-profile visitors, including at least two Wisconsin governors. Many of Fifield's guests returned year after year.[13]

By 1890, Sand Island served as the seasonal base for a loose collection of people: summer fishermen, late-summer campers and tourists, the lighthouse keeper and his family, and the occasional winter lumberjacks. One would be hard pressed to call this a community—these people were only loosely con-nected to each other, bound by little more than geographic proximity. But even at this early stage, the seasonal residents had begun to modify the Sand Island landscape. The Shaws had established a farm, lumberjacks had stripped pine from the island forest, and Samuel Fifield had transformed Camp Stella into a landscape of leisure. As the island community developed in the 1890s, the pace of these changes accelerated.

Island Connections

The Sand Island community grew with the town of Bayfield. When the railroad connected the Chequamegon Bay to the national economy, the types of activities possible on Sand Island broadened. The scale of logging, fishing, farming, and tourism expanded, and the connections between these industries solidified. In the 1890s, Norwegian immigrants joined the Shaws and transformed Sand Island from a seasonal outpost into a year-round community. They created an economic and social network that tied the island's different parts—tourist and resident, fishing and logging, human and natural—closely together.

In 1890, Louis Moe left his native Norway for the United States and three years later filed a homestead claim on Sand Island. Soon after, in a common pattern of chain migration, others from the same region of Norway followed. Although noticeably short on fjords, the Apostles offered the chance to rep-licate the mixed fishing and farming economy that many of the immigrants had practiced in Norway. When the Wisconsin state census taker arrived on the island in June 1895 he counted 46 residents. Nineteen of these were single men, indicating the island's continuing importance as a seasonal fish camp, but seven families also called the island home. The local papers took notice: "There is a settlement of Swede and Norwegian fishermen-farmers, on East bay, which bids fair to increase in numbers and prosperity, for Sand Island contains much rich soil for farming which only needs clearing and improvement." After the turn of the century, the Sand Island population hovered between 35 and 55. In his diary, Frederick Hansen names over 75 year-round residents, although not all of them lived on the island at the same time. In January 1911, Louis Moe traveled to Bayfield with news of a growing Sand Island community. "He reports everybody on the island feeling fine and enjoying life," noted the *Bayfield County Press*. "He says an especially pleasant Christmas was enjoyed by the residents on the island, and that a large Christmas tree in the school house was a pleasant event." The 1920 census listed 45 people on the island, but only two single men—everyone else lived in a family group.[14]

In 1910, the growing island population built a one-room schoolhouse for grades one through eight, which meant families would no longer need to move to Bayfield during the winter to send their children to school. Several of the older daughters of the island families served as teachers, while other teachers came from the mainland and boarded with island families during the school year. Sixteen students attended the school in 1911, and that number grew to twenty-five by 1914. Older islanders used the school too, for social gatherings and community meetings. Islanders also established a post office, a cooperative store, and a short-lived telephone company with connection to the mainland. These institutions signified a growing community.[15]

A less organized community life existed too. The diaries, memoirs, and oral histories that document life on Sand Island describe a vibrant social life— dances, card games, picnics, and socials marked weekends and special occasions. Islanders went on camping and hunting trips on the mainland or on the other islands. They took advantage of the lighthouse gardens and grounds for picnics and parties. In their recreational activities, islanders replicated patterns of rural life experienced elsewhere. The confines of the island and the short distance between homes in some ways allowed for a more active social life than experienced by residents elsewhere in rural America in the early twentieth century.[16]

As it did in so many places, the railroad enabled the development of the Sand Island community. It brought the ability to get frozen fish to market, prompting an expansion of the fishing industry that made settlement on the island viable.

4.2 By 1914, twenty-five students attended Sand Island's one-room schoolhouse. The schoolhouse was once the center of the island community; today nothing remains but the foundation, which can be found just off the East Bay trail. Courtesy of the National Park Service.

Booth and Boutin company boats arrived on a regular schedule to pick up fish and drop off ice. Commercial fishing anchored the Sand Island economy.

Some of the island's permanent residents were primarily farmers, and their impact on island environments is easier to trace. The Noring and Loftfield families established farms in the years following 1910, growing a variety of crops, but especially berries. "The strawberries that [the Loftfields'] raised were large berries and delicious. They were about the size of eggs—you could put them in an egg carton and sell them by the dozen, they were that large," remembered islander Harold Palm. The cooling effect of Lake Superior ensured a longer berry season on Sand Island than on the mainland, providing a market advantage. The Loftfields and Norings grew a variety of vegetables too—potatoes, rutabagas, carrots, and cabbages. The Norings kept dairy and beef cattle and sold cream and butter to the Bayfield Creamery as well as beef and sausage.[17]

After 1910, Burt and Anna Mae Hill ran the most extensive farm on the island. Hill worked as an editor for the *Bayfield County Press* and was one of the

Bayfield community's most visible citizens. In 1894, he married Frank Shaw's daughter, Anna Mae. In 1910, Hill resigned from the *Press* and purchased his father-in-law's farm. He used Frank Shaw's pound nets for several years, but in 1919 he sold the fishing gear and focused on farming. For the next two decades, the Hills expanded their farming and dairying operations. Like the other Sand Island farmers, Burt and Anna Mae grew a variety of crops and kept livestock to cobble together a yearly income. They had three small apple orchards scattered around the property and sold apples and cider. The Hills also raised and sold chickens and eggs. They owned eight dairy cows and a cream separator, and over half of their farm income derived from the sale of milk, butter, and cream. They sold dairy products to the Bayfield Creamery and agricultural produce to a Bayfield grocer. The Hills also sold farm products to their island neighbors.[18]

Farming rendered an obvious physical change to the island landscape. The Noring farm serves as an example of the on-the-ground transformations wrought by the settlement process. The Norings worked a forty-acre farm, all of which had to be cleared for agricultural production. Like other settlers of rural Wisconsin, the Norings utilized the trees they felled in the process to construct their first house and other farm buildings. They then used fire to clear the understory and stumps. The Norings replaced the original forest vegetation with a suite of crop plants—potatoes, rutabagas, cabbages, strawberries—and forage plants such as timothy and clover. The Noring farm is the farthest of the Sand Island homes from the shoreline, about a quarter mile inland from the island's east bay. Building the farmhouse and clearing land meant removing some trees and planting others. The Norings transplanted several spruce trees, dug up from one of their fields, to the northeast side of the house to form a windbreak. They planted lilac bushes along the west side of the house and rose bushes elsewhere nearby. The physical changes to the land persist more than a half century after the Norings left their farm.[19]

To consider the farmers and fishermen as distinct from each other, however, misses an essential aspect of Sand Island life. No one on Sand Island was only a fisherman or only a farmer. All worked together, with daily tasks, seasonal changes, and personal lives overlapping in intricate ways. These intersections are difficult to trace, but it was in the intersections of seemingly distinct industries that the people of Sand Island made their living.[20]

Burt Hill serves as an example. Despite selling his fishing gear in 1919, he remained tied to the fishing industry. He often accompanied Fred Hansen or one of the other fishermen out on their boats, as did other island farmers. Hill rented space at his dock to fishermen during the herring season, and Anna Mae Hill provided room and board to entire herring crews. In 1915, the Hills boarded a crew of herring fishermen for the S. L. Boutin Fish Company, as they did intermittently through the 1930s. In 1933 and 1936, they boarded the crew hired by fellow Island resident Carl Dahl. In 1936, this meant housing up to thirty men for most of the month of November, earning a total of $502.20. Hill also took part in the fishing industry in his capacity as the island's handyman—fixing boats, motors, and other gear.[21]

Almost all of the Sand Island fishing families engaged in limited agricultural activities too. Fred Hansen's diary details the completion of constant agricultural tasks. The Hansens planted an extensive garden as well as fields of hay, oats, and millet. The Hansen women and children most likely tended the vegetable garden and helped with the couple of dairy cows always on the farm. Entries that indicate trips to town or the shipment of produce occur regularly in the diary but with no consistency; fishing clearly required the most time and produced the most reliable income.[22]

Most of the island families also kept livestock. The Hansens always had at least one cow (and sometimes two or three) and at other times had hogs, chickens, and sheep. Most of the island families owned a few cows, for both milk and meat. The women and children generally tended the livestock. Cattle were often turned loose to fend for themselves. The area around Justice Bay, near the lighthouse, served as a common pasture, much to the chagrin of the lighthouse keeper who recorded in his logbook in 1917 that "cattle came over and ruined my haystack." This practice no doubt had other environmental consequences as well. Cattle grazing hastened the spread of weed species and encouraged the growth of woody, thorn-bearing vegetation that the cows would not eat.[23]

The Hansens and other island families merged farm labor into a daily and seasonal schedule dictated by their primary work of fishing. Most of the year, the seasonal nature of the two activities complemented each other: the fall harvest of root vegetables like potatoes and rutabagas occurred in October, before the start of the November herring season. Winter provided time to fix nets or work in the barn. The biggest labor crunch developed in the spring, when the fishermen struggled to work the early trout season as well as plow and plant their gardens and fields. Fred Hansen's daily diary entries from May 6 to

May 22, 1913, reveal the competing demands of fishing and farming as well as the multiplicity of tasks completed by Sand Island fishermen/farmers:

MAY 1913

6   About 300 lbs. [fish] today. Planted in hot bed.

7   About 500 lbs. today. Nice weather but cold.

8   Nothing doing—no fish.

9   Stretched some fence.

10 Lifted [nets] as usual.

11 About 350 lbs. fish today.

12 Foggy, so we could not lift—finished our fence.

13 Lifted.

14 Nothing doing—stormy. Moved boat to Shaw's.

15 Brought boat back. Raised the barn roof.

16 Lifted—no fish.

17 Went to town and came back today.

18 (Sun.) Played cribbage and whist all day.

19 Lifted.

20 Plowed some—had to stop for rain.

21 Finished plowing—foggy.

22 Best lift of the season so far—about 1100 lbs.

The weather helped determine where Hansen spent his time. Foggy, windy days that made for difficult fishing offered the chance to work around the farm.[24]

The most important intersection between fishing and farming came on the boats that transported fish and produce to Bayfield. When the fish boats stopped at the island to pick up the daily catch, they also took on board bushels of potatoes, jugs of cream, and crates of berries, all bound for the Bayfield market. The time and expense of transporting produce to Bayfield certainly hindered market agriculture; without the scheduled stops by the collection boats, this kind of activity would not have been viable. But by dovetailing fishing and farming, island residents protected themselves against the vagaries of the market. At times, prices for fish dropped so low that it made no sense to start up the boats; islanders could then work on their farms. The collection boats traveled the intersection between fishing and farming that allowed the mix-and-match economy of the island to function.[25]

4.3 Frederick Hansen, pictured here around 1900, kept a log of his daily activities for nearly twenty-five years, recording the varied tasks necessary to participate in Sand Island's multifaceted economy. Courtesy of the National Park Service.

4.4 The Booth Fisheries Company boat *Apostle Islands* approaches a dock at Sand Island's East Bay in the early 1940s, with tourists aboard for an island cruise. The fish collection boats run by Booth tied the varied parts of Sand Island's diverse economy together, carrying not just fish but also agricultural produce and tourists. Courtesy of the National Park Service.

The Moes are another family that demonstrates the varied nature of Sand Island economic life. Louis Moe worked primarily as a fisherman, but the Moes had twenty-five acres of cleared land, with about twenty acres in hay. They had an orchard and grew potatoes and berries to sell in Bayfield, and they kept cows, hogs, and chickens. Moe also ran a logging camp on the west side of the island for over two decades. He started on his own land in 1897 but then secured stumpage rights on the west end of the island by working out arrangements with absentee owners. Moe paid half the taxes due to Bayfield County in return for the right to log. Logging in the 1880s had cleared most of the white pine from the island; Moe cut the remaining softwoods and then turned to hardwoods like birch and maple, hiring a scow each spring to bring the logs to the mills.[26]

A winter logging camp required considerable logistical support, and so Moe's operations affected other island families too. Moe hired between eight and ten loggers each winter, usually men from Bayfield but also the sons of island fishermen. Carl Dahl and Bill Noring both worked as sawyers, and Bill Palm worked as a swamper—identifying trees to be cut and finding routes for the skidways that led cut lumber to the shoreline for shipment. Bergitt Noring worked as the camp cook one year. Moe relied on his small herd of cattle to provide meat. He also had a blacksmith shop on his farmstead, where he could repair logging equipment, shoe horses, and take care of other small-scale metalwork.[27]

Fishermen and farmers all over the Great Lakes replicated the seasonal labor patterns evident at Sand Island, hanging up their nets or plows and looking for work in the logging camps during the winter. This proved particularly true for hired hands, as opposed to fishermen who owned their own gear and boats. Farmers, too, found employment in the lumber camps. Often, they rented out their oxen and horses to haul logs, and they received wages themselves for tending the animals. Farmers frequently sold the timber that they cut in the process of clearing land. Although Frank Shaw did not run an extensive outfit like Louis Moe, he occasionally sold sawlogs to Bayfield lumbermen on a contract basis.[28]

When describing the nature of island life, former residents stress this varied, self-sufficient lifestyle. "My dad was a fisherman but he also had a great big garden, fruit trees and we had berries," remembered Fred Hansen's daughter. Melvin Dahl said of his father, "Then, of course, he commercial fished and we had two to three milk cows and a barn and everything. And then we grew our own vegetables and potatoes and practically grew our own meat, too." Another islander had a similar report: "All of the people in East Bay . . . raised everything under the sun that you could possibly raise." Living on an island made self-sufficiency imperative.[29]

Viewed from Sand Island, a peripheral point of production, the intersections between various industries take on added importance. Fishing, farming, and logging reinforced each other. Overlapping transportation methods made each individual activity economically feasible. The seasonal nature of the different industries complemented each other too. Winter logging, spring and fall fishing, and summer fieldwork allowed the residents of Sand Island to patch together their livelihoods. There were conflicts among the elements of this economy—sawdust fouled the spawning grounds, log drives intruded on the tranquility of the Brule River retreats, anglers complained about the overfishing of lake trout, and the constant demands of commercial fishing meant that some agricultural tasks went unattended. Nevertheless, these interconnections made each industry possible.

Sand Island's isolation—and the very fact that it is an island—exaggerates these connections and makes them easier to recognize and trace. But these local conditions and economic intersections defined life throughout rural America in the late nineteenth and early twentieth centuries. In northern Wisconsin, for example, over half of all farmers in 1930 took on additional off-farm work in mining, logging, tourism, or wage work. The sale of produce sometimes provided as little as 18 percent of a farm family's income. Historian Mary Neth calls this local, family-based economic system "making do," a key strategy employed by rural people as they dealt with the changes wrought by the expanding market economy. Throughout the hinterland regions of the West and Midwest, local interconnections and overlap between seemingly distinct industries determined how and when people engaged in economic activity.[30]

It might be tempting to view Sand Island as exceptional or irrelevant because of its isolation and the small scale of the market production that occurred there. But all aspects of Sand Island's diverse economy functioned as parts of a larger regional whole. The commercial fishery of the Apostle Islands and Bayfield vicinity emerged in the 1870s as one of the most productive on Lake Superior, and it maintained this position for close to a century. In 1927, Frederick Hansen caught 23,478 pounds of lake trout and whitefish; the Bayfield area's 142 other fishermen totaled 608,276 pounds (meaning Hansen caught far more than most). Sawmills all over the region bought logs from independent farmer-loggers and from contract loggers like Louis Moe. Some mills secured half of their supply of sawlogs in this manner. John Knight and William Vilas owned land on Sand Island and sold stumpage rights to Louis Moe. When islanders sold crates of berries or bushels of apples in town, they participated in an effort to establish the Bayfield Peninsula as a nationally important fruit-growing district. In all of these cases, activities on Sand Island contributed to the regional economy.[31]

A Sand Island Summer

Vacationers and tourists joined the year-round residents on Sand Island in the summer. In the teens and 1920s, wealthy residents from the Midwest's urban centers built summer homes on Sand Island, much as they did on Madeline Island. The tourists and summer residents integrated into the island's social and economic network. Tourism, like fishing, farming, and logging, functioned on a seasonal, contingent basis, flourishing at the intersection of seemingly distinct industries. But as the extractive economies on the island ceased, tourism persisted. In this way, too, Sand Island reflected its region.

Camp Stella prospered and expanded after its founding in the 1880s. Samuel Fifield added several permanent structures to the original tent pads, building a capacity for over sixty guests. Fifield used his skills as a writer and connections as editor of the Ashland newspaper to promote the resort, and the comings and goings of prominent guests received constant coverage in local papers. Promotion of Camp Stella mirrored the rhetoric of the railroad companies, emphasizing the opportunities to hunt, fish, and explore the islands, "at rest from the treadmill and trials of life." Indeed, Fifield had a direct tie to railroad tourism—he had served as the first manager of the Hotel Chequamegon, the Wisconsin Central Railroad's luxurious Ashland establishment.[32]

Camp Stella's guests pursued a different type of fishing than Sand Island's permanent residents. Whereas the commercial fishermen set their nets for lake trout, whitefish, and herring, summer tourists traveled to the nearby mainland streams in search of game fish. Fifield did what he could to ensure his guests' success with the rod and reel. In 1904, he secured 22,500 rainbow trout fry from the state fish hatchery in Bayfield and released them into the mouth of the Sand River, just across the channel from Camp Stella. Fifield's actions mirrored those of other wealthy sportsmen in their quest to modify fish populations in the name of sport fishing.[33]

As a summer resort, Camp Stella did not survive the death of Sam Fifield in 1915. Independent entrepreneurs tried to run the resort, but none lasted more than a few seasons. Camp Stella remained vacant until 1934, when the Jensch family—who had first come to Sand Island as Fifield's guests—bought it for use as a summer home. The Jensches sold part of the property to two other families, also for summer use. The change from resort to summer home tied tourism more concretely into the lives of the permanent Sand Island residents. The same people came to the island each year, integrating more directly into the island's social life and economy.[34]

Sand Island emerged as a popular site for summer home construction. The West Bay Club, built on the southwestern corner of the island, followed the model of the private clubhouses established on the Brule River, in the Adirondacks, and in other wilderness retreats. O. H. Neegard visited Camp Stella in 1910 and liked the island so much that he determined to build a home of his own. He and several friends bought land there in 1912 and erected a large Adirondack-style lodge called the West Bay Club. In 1922, club member Frank

4.5 This undated photograph shows life at Sand Island's Camp Stella—the first resort in the Apostle Islands—in the late nineteenth century. Samuel Fifield founded the resort in 1886 and tied Sand Island into the region's flourishing tourist trade, creating a landscape of leisure next to the fields and homes of Sand Island fishermen and farmers. Courtesy of the National Park Service.

Eha bought out his partners and used the club as a family summer home for the next forty years.[35]

Others built less-substantial summer homes. Year-round resident Edwin Bonde promoted the area for just this purpose. He divided his land into farming plots on the interior and small 1.5-acre plots along the East Bay road for sale as summer homes. In 1914, nine people owned the fifteen lots of section 24—the land along East Bay. The following year, after Bonde's subdivision, the same acreage had been divided into thirty-eight plots, with thirty-two separate owners. Some of these new owners chose not to build on their new land, and permanent residents of the island bought some of these lots too. Most of the new owners intended to build summer homes.[36]

Like fishing, farming, and logging, the summer tourist trade at Sand Island might have looked slightly different because of its island setting, but it also functioned as a part of a larger regional economy. Sam Fifield patterned his promotion of Camp Stella after the large railroad hotels, luring guests to his resort by advertising its natural and healthful qualities. The burst of summer home development on the island from 1910 through the 1920s had analogs not just on Madeline Island but on lakes and rivers around the region. As homesteaders realized the challenges of market agriculture in the cutover region, many of them sought to supplement their incomes by building tourist cabins or taking on additional wage work. This became more common in the 1920s, when the automobile helped bring vacations within the financial means of the middle class. This tourism, too, was the result of conscious promotion, often with the aid of state and county road building and zoning ordinances. Resort owners, state planning officials, and vacationers were in the process of reinventing the western Great Lakes, transforming the region from the cutover into the Northwoods. In the early stages of this transformation, production and consumption inhabited the same landscapes.[37]

Summer residents merged into the social and economic networks of the island. They depended on year-round residents for food, transportation, and the upkeep of their homes. First Camp Stella, and then the individual summer residents, provided an important home market for Sand Island fishermen-farmers. Summer families like the Andersons, Disens, and Jensches show up regularly in Burt Hill's account books. They bought dairy products, meat, chickens, eggs, fruit, and produce. Summer visitors either arranged for travel to the island on one of the Booth or Boutin company boats or with one of the island fishermen.

Harold Palm remembered, "We were dependent on them for transportation. When we came out to the island, the only way we could get across would be to have someone from the island come to get us." Summer residents paid islanders to serve as caretakers for their property and to cut wood, repair roofs, and open their homes for a new season. Such payments added significantly to the Sand Island economy.[38]

Anna Mae Hill performed the most lucrative work by cooking for some of the summer residents that lived close the Hill farm. Especially in the late 1930s,

4.6 and 4.7 Burt and Anna Mae Shaw Hill in the early 1900s. The Shaw-Hill farm was the first permanent residence on Sand Island, and the landscape of the farm has endured the most profound and lasting changes of any location on the island. Sand Island's multifaceted economy required the work of both Burt and Anna Mae. The farm site is still used as a summer home under a use-and-occupancy agreement with the National Park Service. Courtesy of the National Park Service.

when the Hills had curtailed their farm work due to advancing age, meals and boarding receipts made up the largest portion of their income. In 1938, boarding work accounted for more than the combined income derived from the sale of chicken and dairy products, apples, and money earned by Burt Hill through labor and renting his horse team and plow. The Loftfields also provided board to summer visitors, although on a smaller scale than the Hills.[39]

Islanders played a dual role in the tourist economy: they functioned as both purveyors of the tourist trade and objects of it. The city dwellers who frequented Camp Stella relished the opportunity to watch the fishermen return in the middle of the day with a load of fresh fish. And when tourists took passage on the Booth and Boutin fish boats for an island cruise, they had no choice but to wait on the island while their boat took on the daily catch. One observer described her trip on the Booth Company boat named the *Apostle Islands*: "While waiting for the fishing boats, the passengers explore the little fishing community, peering into unpainted sheds, where dry nets are hanging in big rolls from the rafters, and where trays of floats and sinkers are kept; examining the great wooden reels outside, on which the wet nets are spread to dry; and picking the raspberries that are so thick in the islands in the latter part of summer."[40]

Segregating tourism from the more obviously productive activities on the island obscures an essential component of the tourist trade. Extractive activities like fishing and farming did not preclude tourism on Sand Island. On the contrary, it was these other activities that made tourist endeavors possible in the first place and allowed them to continue. Although tourism relies on different resources and relationships than do productive industries like fishing and farming, on Sand Island all of these activities remained tightly connected.

The Rewilding of Sand Island

Despite these connections, tourism persisted long after other activities at East Bay ceased. One by one, families began to leave Sand Island. Year-round houses were converted into summer homes or fell into disrepair. Fishing sheds filled with cobwebs. Fields lay fallow, and the forest encroached on their margins. Wilderness slowly returned to Sand Island. Although the fishing, farming, logging, and tourism that had dictated economic life on the island stopped, the impact of these activities on island landscapes persisted. Today, the fields appear to be peaceful, even pristine, forest meadows filled with wildflowers; only a trained ecologist or someone already familiar with Sand Island's history would know differently. But to view this transition, this returning of the wilderness to Sand Island, as only a result of ecological succession, as purely a natural and not a human phenomena, misses an essential part of the process.

Rural communities around the country declined in the early twentieth century, and Sand Island was no exception. The increasing mechanization and corporatization of agriculture made family farming more difficult. Fewer farms and a decreased demand for labor combined with the allure and opportunity of the cities to plague rural areas with chronic out-migration. Across the country, 6.25 million people—predominantly the young and unattached—left rural areas for the cities in the 1920s alone. The farm crisis of the 1920s depressed the prices for basic agricultural commodities and made life in rural America still more difficult.[41]

The East Bay community faced the same dilemma, as few children chose to stay on the island as adults. The isolation of island life exaggerated these problems. The closing of the school in 1928 for lack of students foretold the imminent decline of the community. With their children grown, farming and fishing proved more and more taxing for the settler generation. As they aged, islanders needed to be closer to the facilities and services found in town. The Palm family left in the 1920s when Anna Palm developed tuberculosis. Olaf Loftfield died in July 1930, and his widow Jonette joined her children in the Twin Cities shortly thereafter. Frederick Hansen died of cancer in 1939. Burt Hill suffered from diabetes, and as he and Anna Mae grew older life on the island simply became too difficult. Hill's memoir records his increasing health problems and struggles with the isolation of island life. In 1942, the Hills sold their farm to one of the summer families and moved to Bayfield. Even the lighthouse shut down—the station was automated in 1921 and rented to Gert Wellisch, the daughter of a founding member of the West Bay Club, who used it as a summer home. The Norings were the last family to leave the island. One islander remembered, "When the Norings family was raised—all the kids were on their own—the Norings abandoned the farm and built another house down by the lake near the shore. They lived there for a few years until they started getting older and weren't able to live on the island anymore. They wanted to live in town—be closer to medical help if they needed. Which is what all of them do eventually."[42]

Sand Island was empty in the winter of 1944. An *Ashland Daily Press* headline proclaimed: "Sand Island Utterly Deserted." The story lamented the end of an important part of the region's history: "For the first time in more than half a century, Sand Island . . . will be utterly deserted this winter. The seagulls will keep a lonely vigil at Swallow point. The new-fangled gas light in the steel tower in front of the lighthouse which was home to the veteran Emmanuel Luick for so many years will blink on in solitude till the close of navigation. The waves will lash against the fishermen's docks, but there will be no one to care." Sand Island would never again serve as a year-round home. Sand Island's reconfiguration as a wilderness had begun.[43]

Although the Hills, Norings, Hansens, and other families had left the island, the decisions that they made in the process of making Sand Island their home continued to shape the landscape. The Shaw-Hill farm serves as an example of the ties among human choices, ecological processes, and the modern landscape. First the Shaws, then the Hills, lived on the southeast tip of Sand Island from the 1870s through the 1940s, the longest inhabitance of any spot on the island. The landscape still reveals the physical evidence of this long tenure.

Apple orchards and field boundaries demonstrate the ongoing impact of earlier choices. Hill planted three apple orchards, each still identifiable by their row planting and the drainage ditches that flank each row. Today, occasional apple trees have sprung up elsewhere on the farm. The oldest of the orchards, dating to 1920, stands close to the farmstead on the southwest end of the property. The age of the trees—some of the oldest on the site—suggests that Burt Hill planted them just after he dedicated himself to farming. The other two orchards date to 1940, the very end of Hill's time on the island. Both are located on spots originally too wet for apple trees—they required drainage ditches to remove the excess water. One orchard lines the county road, perhaps planted for its beautiful blossoms as much as for its apples. The trees have been joined by other plants that moved in after productive work ceased. An alder thicket has grown up around the apple trees along the road, and the eastern orchard trees have been joined by American plum, mountain ash, and serviceberry, along with dense thickets of red osier dogwood. The apple trees remain, but wild nature has flourished in the time since the Hills departed.[44]

Changing field boundaries further illustrate the legacy of past land-use decisions. Aerial photos taken since 1938 and vegetation surveys conducted since the national lakeshore was created in 1970 reveal three distinct human-induced boundaries on the farm. The oldest part of the clearing lies at the southernmost tip of the property, the area around the original home. The dry soils around the

4.8 Harvesting apples at Burt and Anna Mae Shaw Hill's farm in the 1910s. The apple trees remain, but woody vegetation has grown up around them. Courtesy of the National Park Service.

house required the least maintenance and labor for the limited crops grown by Frank and Josephine Shaw in the 1880s and 1890s. A second zone, cleared between 1900 and 1920, surrounds the original area. The most recently cleared land, dating to Hill's expansion in the 1930s, extends north and west to the historical edge of the fields. By 1982, native woody vegetation—alder, dogwood, and young aspen trees—had encroached into the clearings. These shrubs had moved in from the north, invading the wettest parts of the old fields first, with alder in the wettest areas. Aspen and birch trees have encroached more slowly, moving in from the existing boundaries. In some areas of the clearing, willow, hawthorn, mountain ash, and serviceberry have moved into the meadow in straight, regular lines, following the drainage ditches dug by Burt Hill. The for-

4.9 This aerial view of Sand Island, looking north, shows the docks of the Shaw-Hill farm site and Camp Stella on the southern end of the island and two of the remaining docks in East Bay. The straight line that cuts through the trees marks the path of the old East Bay road. The remaining clearings of the Shaw-Hill fields can be seen on the southeast corner of the island. Photograph by William Cronon.

est is reclaiming the fields, but these straight lines underscore the continuing human role in the process.[45]

Some of the boundaries on the Shaw-Hill farm remain quite stark. A barbed-wire fence marked the northern edge of the farm; vegetation surveys conducted in 1982 discovered a sharp differentiation in forest composition and age on each side. South of the fence, in the area once completely cleared, investigators found a stand of twenty-year-old aspen trees. Aspen are among the first trees to grow into an open, disturbed area, and they began their invasion when active clearing of the fields ceased in the 1950s. To the north of the fence, Park Service investigators found a mixed birch and balsam fir forest, with trees approximately sixty years old. Although never fully cleared for agriculture, this area had been subject to selective logging and fire.[46]

The impact of human choices made sixty or one hundred years ago can be found all around the East Bay. The Norings were the last family to live on Sand

4.10 The trail from East Bay dock on Sand Island leads to the site of the Noring farm, once the most extensive agricultural landscape on the island. Rusting equipment now lies in the fields. The well and a pile of moldering boards are all that remain of the Noring home, although many of the plants that mark the home site can still be identified. Photograph by William Cronon.

Island year-round. All that remains of their homestead is a pile of decaying boards and some rusting farm equipment. But the spruce trees they transplanted to the northeastern side of their home to form a windbreak still mark the site, as do lilac bushes that Bergitt Noring planted by the side of her house. The drainage ditches dug by the county to keep the road dry today flank the most developed trail on the island. In the southern, wetter part of the road, those ditches now provide a home for dense alder thickets and wetland plants like fringed loosestrife and late goldenrod. Farther north, in drier areas, a colony of a rare sedge plant, *Carex pallescens*, grows along the roadside. Wildness thrives here, and humans have not actively managed or altered these places for decades. But ecological processes alone cannot explain these Sand Island environments. History—the choices of individual men and women—helped create this landscape too.[47]

Not all island environments have been so completely transformed. Reconstructions of the precontact forest have delineated three major vegetation types on Sand Island: A mixed-deciduous forest dominated by yellow birch, white pine, and hemlock in the dry areas and white cedar in the wetter areas covered 92 percent of the island. White pine grew on the northernmost tip of the island. Black spruce and tamarack bogs made up the third vegetation type. Despite the extensive human use of the island, the latter two cover types have been only slightly modified. The establishment of the lighthouse reserve protected the white pine forest on the northern tip of the island from commercial logging; this area is today designated a state natural area for its ecological significance as a remnant of precontact forest conditions. The black-spruce bogs also retain their original character, these areas protected by their lack of utility.[48]

The western and central portions of Sand Island look very different than East Bay. With its more intensive human use, and more varied land use history, the eastern portion of the island today contains a patchwork of different vegetation types. The rest of the island, however, has larger areas covered by similar forest types. A 1982 NPS survey produced a crude vegetation map of the island. The largest cover type, 860 acres, was dominated by large yellow birch and white cedar. The third largest forest type, 331 acres, held a higher number of mature trees per acre but had a similar composition, although with slightly more balsam fir. The second largest cover type, 699 acres, consisted of a similar composition but a lighter density.[49]

Landownership changes help explain this pattern. Louis Moe owned the land on the western coast of the island, which he logged in the 1920s. When Moe died in 1929, his family stopped paying taxes on the land. By 1935, Bayfield County acquired the property and logging ended. No logging occurred on the southern shore of the island either, owned after the 1920s by the families of summer residents Samuel W. Campbell and Daisy Jensch. These areas show up in the 1982 vegetation survey as the more densely forested portions of the island. The center of the island once belonged to summer resident Frank Eha. In the 1950s, two small logging companies purchased the property and selectively logged for white cedar and yellow birch. In some parts of the island, logging persisted into the 1970s—even after the creation of the national park. A more recent vegetation map, compiled in the 1990s, echoes these landownership patterns, with vegetation types roughly conforming to old property lines. Certainly, the processes of forest regeneration and succession shaped these patterns. But so too did the needs and decisions of Louis Moe, Daisy Jensch, and Frank Eha, choices that still shape the composition of the forest.[50]

Sand Island and places like it require a rethinking of the traditional understanding of wilderness. We typically conceive of wilderness as a pristine state that can only be degraded and exploited. Over time, such places might recover or even be actively restored. This way of thinking might describe places where large lumber companies logged virgin forest, leaving behind ugly piles of slash, refuse, and fuel for forest fires. But what about at Sand Island? Is it right to characterize the choices of Frank Shaw, Burt Hill, or Bergitt Noring in this way? Were their decisions to plant apple orchards or lilac bushes acts of destruction and degradation? If not, then perhaps *recovery* is not the correct word to explain what has happened to the landscapes that their lives helped to shape. The narrative of rewilding provides a more nuanced telling of the Sand Island story, one that blurs the boundaries between wilderness and history. History and nature, working simultaneously and together, created these rewilding landscapes.

Rewilding points toward a narrative that explains the history of places like Sand Island without characterizing all human activity as a wound in need of recovery. Human action certainly can be destructive and degrading, but it is not necessarily so. The Apostles are becoming wild again because of human choices—the choices made by the Hills, Norings, and other families to leave Sand Island, but also the choice to designate the islands as a national park, to manage them as wilderness, to allow some kinds of activity but not others. These choices have provided a space for wilderness characteristics to return. The narrative of rewilding helps explain human action that is not always destructive and exploitative but it also underscores the ongoing environmental consequences of past choices. It points toward a concept of conservation and land management that recognizes the human role in nature.

The stories that we tell about places like Sand Island—and the way we treat the landscapes that stage these stories—provide a commentary on our ideas about the proper relationship between humans and nature. As William Cronon explains, it is through stories that we make judgments about past human choices: "Human interests and conflicts create *values* in nature that in turn provide the moral center for our stories. We want to know whether environmental change is good or bad, and that question can only be answered by referring to our own sense of right and wrong." In so many places, we judge past environmental change as bad—clear-cutting, open-pit mining, and other industrial uses of nature have done irreparable harm. It is not so easy to characterize the actions of Sand Islanders in this manner. Their fishing, farming, and recreating changed island environments, but we can also celebrate the way that wildness has returned to the landscapes shaped by their lives. Cronon believes that the task of environmental historians is to find stories that "increase our attention to nature and to the place of people within it." The stories of Sand Island help us do this.[51]

This is why the rewilding of Sand Island is so important, because of the conversations about the relationship between history and wilderness that its landscapes provoke. The trails that depart from the East Bay dock travel to places that provide evidence of rewilding at every turn. The grassy clearing at the foot of the dock once served as the site of Herman Johnson's home. The trail to the lighthouse passes through a field filled with swaying purple stalks of fireweed. Few hikers realize that they pass through the Moes' old farm fields. The other trails lead to places where the story of rewilding is more clearly evident. Those who walk inland from the dock on the faint track to the Noring farm find rusted farm equipment, ruined buildings, and Bergitt Noring's lilac bushes. And those who know where to look can see Gert Wellisch's car and the foundation of the school in the woods off the old county road. Wilderness is returning to all of these places in ways powerfully informed by the choices made by islanders fifty, eighty, or one hundred years ago. As it returns, the wilderness obscures the evidence of these choices, making the narrative of rewilding—and the lessons of rewilding landscapes—more difficult for today's visitors to see. 🌿

5

A Tale of Two Parks

REWILDING THE ISLANDS, 1929-1970

IN AUGUST 1970, KRISTINE JENSCH WROTE A LETTER TO THE EDITOR OF the *New York Times*, complaining bitterly about the prospect of losing her family's Sand Island property to the national lakeshore proposed for the Apostle Islands. She regarded the whole project as unfair and unnecessary, a refrain that Jensch and her neighbors had sounded frequently during the ten years of discussion and planning for the park. Two weeks later, Wisconsin senators Gaylord Nelson and Robert Kastenmeier responded in their own letter to the *Times*. Jensch's comments, they explained, were "typically characteristic of the attitude expressed by landowners to national park proposals when such projects propose to incorporate some private land within new park boundaries." For the senators, the losses suffered by a few property owners were a small price to pay. "For a very modest investment," they wrote, "the Apostle Islands bill promises to preserve in perpetuity a unique collection of 20 islands in Lake Superior unrivaled by any other island chain" in the country. Everyone would benefit. "This beautiful and unspoiled Lake Superior country will bring much needed recreational pleasures not only to the citizens of the Midwest but, indeed, to the entire nation."[1]

As the senators suggested, opposition to Apostle Islands National Lakeshore followed a familiar pattern. When methods of using and valuing nature come into conflict, some people have their access to resources prescribed in favor of others. The different needs and perspectives of locals and outsiders often lie at the root of these disputes. Gaylord Nelson and other park supporters valued the islands as a wilderness—as a site for primitive recreation and ecological study—but they faced stiff resistance. Some opponents of the lakeshore, like Kristine Jensch, feared the loss of their property. Others worried that a wilderness park would inhibit the multifaceted economy that had supported Chequamegon Bay communities for more than a century. Members of the Red Cliff and Bad River bands opposed the park because they saw it as yet another attack on tribal sovereignty.

The question of control lay at the center of the debate. Who had the authority to determine how the islands would be used? What kinds of activities and economies should the island resources support? Would activities of the past—the very activities that had created the landscapes now valued as wilderness—be allowed to continue? Gaylord Nelson's challenge as the chief architect of the park lay in uniting a coalition in support of his vision of wilderness. The proponents of nature protection projects everywhere have faced similar challenges.[2]

Locals and outsiders had disagreed over the value of the Apostles as a park once before, and these two national park movements were bookends in a dispute over the proper relationship among nature, tourism, and the state. In the 1920s, local boosters and businessmen called for the creation of a national park in the islands as a means of stimulating a stagnant economy. The proposal brought National Park Service investigator Harlan Kelsey to the islands in 1930, but he refused to endorse the project because the scars left behind by decades of logging were simply too severe.

When the NPS rejected their proposal, residents of the Chequamegon Bay had little choice but to resume the logging, fishing, and tourism that had supported their economy in the past. These activities continued, however, amid constantly changing environments. Forests regenerated without human interference, but in ways constantly informed by their long history of human use. Fish populations continued to change, pressured by overfishing and the arrival of exotic species. Wildlife populations shifted in response to the new environments created by logging, land clearing, and fire. The natural and cultural systems of the Chequamegon Bay shaped and responded to each other. These changes provided a new set of economic opportunities for residents of the

Chequamegon Bay, opportunities that depended on the century-old tradition of valuing the islands for the resources they contained.

Even as traditional uses of island resources continued, a new way of valuing the islands emerged: as a wilderness. What had happened in the Apostle Islands in the forty years between the two park proposals? Forest regeneration gave the islands a new appeal. But far more had happened in the Apostles than just forest growth. As a wilderness, the islands were valued as a recreational and ecological landscape more than an extractive one. Surging demand for recreation, especially in a primitive setting, and a newfound concern for the environment made the wild landscapes of the Apostles particularly appealing. The "natural condition" of the islands—the seeming absence of human interference in forest regeneration and other ecological processes—provided the basis for this value. When Wisconsin Conservation Department and then NPS officials looked at the islands again in the 1950s and 1960s, they found a landscape worth protecting for these new reasons.

To be sure, the islands still had economic importance as a site for primitive recreation, but the new wilderness value severely restricted other types of economic activity. Many residents of the region resisted plans for wilderness management in the islands because they wanted to use the islands as they always had—as an economic base, suitable for both resource extraction and tourism. They did not see these activities in conflict. Wilderness advocates disagreed. They believed that the islands could only be valued as wilderness if resource extraction ceased, and only as a wilderness could they generate the tourism revenue needed to support the region's faltering economy. Wilderness management would replace the multifaceted, production-based economy with a consumer-oriented one. Both supporters and opponents of wilderness saw economic value in the islands. The question was how to maximize this value.

The transition to wilderness, therefore, required the growth of a regulatory state with the power to encourage some economies and to shut down others. Throughout the twentieth century, state authority had grown steadily. The process that had begun with the regulation of the commercial fishery in the nineteenth century and the zoning of land for tourism in the 1930s continued; the state took an ever more active role in segregating tourism from other economic activities. Important checks existed on the growth of this authority. The American federalist system, with power shared between different levels of government, hindered the ability of the state to dictate economic activity. Even as those who valued the Apostle Islands as wilderness used the WCD and the NPS to advance their goals, opponents of wilderness turned to other levels of government to protect their interests. Tribal governments resisted the growth of state authority in the Chequamegon Bay for different reasons. When Gaylord Nelson and other park proponents approached the Ojibwe for their support in creating a park in the Apostles, Indian leaders bargained for the federal government's assistance in their ongoing battle with the WCD over treaty-guaranteed rights to hunt and fish. The result was a turning point in the ability of Native Americans to control reservation resources, and also a park with far different dimensions than Gaylord Nelson had envisioned.

A Park in the Cutover

As the 1920s drew to a close, businessmen and civic leaders in the Chequamegon Bay recognized that they faced an economic crisis. The logging industry had collapsed, and the farm economy was struggling. Only commercial fishing offered stable economic prospects. Many people believed that tourism could solve the region's economic ills, but for tourism to flourish they needed something to attract visitors. They needed a national park.

Just as residents of the region began to explore the possibility of a park, the Pike-Wachsmuth mill—long a key part the Bayfield economy—burned to the ground, a powerful symbol of the need for economic revitalization. "At that time, we were in an economically very poor shape," remembered Charles Sheridan, president of the Apostle Islands National Park Committee. "[The park] was looked on as an economic boon. It would bring in thousands of people and it would increase property values and it would give us business." Park boosters hoped to capitalize on the nationwide attention generated by the Apostle Islands Indian Pageant and by President Calvin Coolidge's stay in the region in the summer of 1928. Coolidge had toured the islands and reported that "the fishing around here, I can testify, is fine. The climate is wonderful. . . . We are returning to Washington refreshed and invigorated." The president stated his belief that the islands were "a coming region for those who are seeking recreation."[3]

Noneconomic motivations fueled the park movement too. As summer home construction expanded on Madeline and Sand islands, and development schemes on other islands became more common, some area residents worried that the Apostles might become the reserve of wealthy summer dwellers from outside the region. John B. Chapple, editor of the *Ashland Daily Press*, sounded the alarm in 1930: "Do we want the Apostle Islands grabbed from under our nose and plastered with 'Private—Keep Out' signs? These islands which we have loved so long belong primarily to us of the Chequamegon Bay region." A national park would preserve local access to the islands. Chapple's comments highlight the local origins of the proposal; these local origins distinguish the park movement of the 1920s from that of the 1960s.[4]

Representatives from Ashland, Bayfield, and Washburn formed the Apostle Islands National Park Committee to shepherd the idea to fruition. Wisconsin congressman Hubert H. Peavey corresponded with the National Park Service and in January 1930 submitted a bill to Congress to fund an investigation of the proposal. Peavey's bill sailed through Congress, and the NPS agreed to send a representative to the islands. "National Park Looks Certain on Islands" proclaimed a *Bayfield County Press* headline.[5]

Peavey, Sheridan, and other park promoters placed Madeline Island at the center of their proposal. Madeline represented all of the advantages offered by the islands: it had history, scenery, and recreational opportunities. It was easily accessible from the mainland and already possessed the framework for a good road system and the area for future development. Congressman Peavey believed that 40 to 50 percent of Madeline Island might be combined with several other islands to create a strong proposal. The island's wealthy summer residents evidently agreed, for they actively supported the project.[6]

That Madeline Island served as the centerpiece of the plan reveals the type of park that the promoters hoped to establish. They did not want a wilderness park—far from it. Rather, they wanted a park that followed the well-established patterns of the tourist trade, a park that showcased the area's history and scenery, and most importantly one that would help revive the slowing economy. They expected that gas stations, hotels, restaurants, and other services would quickly follow the creation of the park. It was exactly this vision of the national parks that prompted Aldo Leopold and others to form the Wilderness Society in 1935, an organization dedicated to saving wild areas from this type of development.

The National Park Service hired landscape architect Harlan Kelsey to investigate the Apostle Islands park proposal. While on his visit to the western Great Lakes, Kelsey also evaluated the Quetico-Superior country in northern Minnesota, the Menominee forest in Wisconsin, and Michigan's Isle Royale, all

initial idea of park → Madeline Island

under consideration as national parks. In August 1930, Kelsey enjoyed a six-day whirlwind tour of the Apostles. His hosts on the Apostle Islands National Park Committee ushered him to the region's most scenic spots, and Madeline Island summer resident Hunter Gary took Kelsey aboard his yacht for a trip around the islands. The John Schroeder Lumber Company supplied transportation to Outer Island, where Kelsey toured both the lumber camp as well as the remaining uncut forest. Kelsey also enjoyed an aerial tour of the islands and a banquet in his honor in Bayfield.[7]

The hospitality made little difference: Kelsey was profoundly disappointed by what he found. He conceded that although spectacular forests might have once sheathed the islands, logging and fire had left behind a ruined landscape. "The second growth on the Islands which I visited," Kelsey explained in the report that he filed on the conclusion of his trip, "is now in the jungle stage, making it difficult to walk over them even following the abandoned logging roads which criss-cross them in every direction." Stockton Island, Kelsey reported, had "a good safe harbor with deep water, but for several miles the adjacent shore has been recently fire-swept and fairly ruined." Kelsey came to a damning conclusion: "This project does not meet National Park standards." He pointed out that no one on the local committee had ever visited a national park or understood what these park standards might be—subtly explaining the promotional efforts for a proposal that had little chance of success.[8]

Fire scars were not the only reasons that the Apostle Islands failed to qualify as a national park. NPS policies also played a role. In the years since its creation in 1916, directors Stephen Mather and Horace Albright had used two primary arguments to promote the expansion of the National Park System. First, they argued that the agency should administer America's most spectacular and unique places, like the Grand Canyon and the Grand Tetons. Second, Mather and Albright desperately wanted geographic diversity. They recognized that most potential park visitors—as well as important political support—lived east of the Mississippi River. This logic propelled creation of parks like Acadia in Maine and Shenandoah in Virginia. At the same time, Mather, Albright, and their allies worked to guard the park service's reputation as protector of the nation's most important and spectacular places. They worried that allowing "inferior" parks into the system would tarnish the agency's reputation and limit its power. When Harlan Kelsey commented in his report that the Apostle Islands "did not meet National Park Service standards," he touched

5.1 Harlan Kelsey included several photographs in his report to the National Park Service with the proposal to make the Apostle Islands a national park. The caption for this photo reads: "At Railroad in Primeval Forest, Ready for next years' operations on Outer Island. Unless stopped, 6 yrs. will see the entire destruction of this marvelous woodland." Courtesy of the National Park Service.

on this ongoing debate. Furthermore, Kelsey determined that Isle Royale fit NPS standards far better than did the Apostles, primarily because its forests had not been logged. Sometimes, NPS leaders bent the "standards" rules, especially when they saw political advantage in doing so. The Shenandoah Valley, for example, might not have been spectacular or unique, but including such a large eastern area within the system represented a clear gain for the agency. The Apostles provided no such political advantage.[9]

Both Kelsey and Arno Cammerer (a future director of the NPS who investigated the Apostles in 1931) believed that the islands should be preserved, but as a state park rather than a national one. The reason, they argued, lay in the islands' recreational potential. Cammerer explained, "The whole bay region is a wonderfully scenic region and has untold possibilities for recreation." In 1930, however, the NPS was not interested in recreational parks. The agency certainly catered to tourists, but its leaders believed that maintaining NPS standards mattered more than expanding the system to include inferior areas better suited to state park management. As much as the regeneration of the forests, it was a change in this attitude that created the conditions needed for a national park in the Apostles.[10]

Changing Environments, Changing Economies

When the NPS rejected the proposal to establish a park in the Apostle Islands, residents of the region had little choice but to accept this decision. They continued to pursue the varied economic strategy that had sustained them in the past. Fishing remained the most important economic activity in the islands, but it was still supplemented by logging, tourism, and farming. But both under the water and on the land, island environments continued to change. Forest composition and fish and deer populations shifted dramatically during the mid-twentieth century, each change providing new opportunities and challenges for residents of the region. Intersecting natural and human systems continued to shape each other.

Commercial fishing remained at the core of the Bayfield economy and community. The organization of the Bayfield fishery looked much as it had since the early twentieth century. The Booth Fisheries Company and two or three smaller packing firms sent collection boats to the island fishing camps, picking up fresh fish and dropping off ice. Other fishermen sailed from Bayfield, dropping off their catch at the packinghouses each night. Fishermen spent the summer catching trout and whitefish, switching to herring for the brief autumn season. The years from 1920 from 1950 proved remarkably stable and profitable, as trout harvests stabilized, whitefish stocks rebounded, and market conditions remained strong.

The good years came with a cost. Although production of lake trout, white-fish, and herring from Lake Superior either remained stable or increased after 1930, the intensity of the fishing effort rose steadily. The high prices and consistent demand drew more and more fishermen onto the lake. Technological innovations like nylon nets and depth finders made these fishermen more effective. Contemporary observers recognized the implications of steady harvests from intensifying effort: the relative abundance of lake trout had declined. Comforting though recent good years might be, experts warned, "the general situation must be recognized as dangerous. . . . Fishing intensity and production must be expected to drop abruptly. Only a reversal of the present trend in the abundance of lake trout can save the fishery from disaster." These experts suggested that the decline in abundance might be due to overfishing, but it might also be due to a natural cycle in lake trout populations. The former meant the imminent decline of the fishery; the latter theory at least provided hope.[11]

Other industries persisted as well. The fish collection boats continued to carry tourists on excursions through the islands. The fishermen-farmers of Sand and Madeline islands carried on their mixed economies. Fishermen supplemented their income with wage work in lumber camps, the Ashland iron mills, or the Great Lakes shipping trade. Small-scale logging continued on several of the islands, in some cases based on second-growth timber and in others on the remaining old growth stands. In the late 1930s, for example, the Lullabye Lumber Company purchased the unlogged portions of Outer Island and selectively logged for large birch and maple. Logging continued on Madeline and Sand islands as well.[12]

The Rocky Island Air Haven exemplifies the persisting connections between industries and the diverse island economy. Rocky Island had been a summer fishing camp since the late nineteenth century. Grace and Laurie Nourse had started serving lunch to tourists who rode on the fish collection boats running out of Bayfield, and by the 1950s they had a dining room capable of seating one hundred guests. The Nourses also provided cabins and meals to fishermen who wanted to spend several days in the islands. In the late 1940s, deer

5.2 The Lullabye Lumber Company logged on Outer Island from the 1930s through the 1950s, evidence of the persistence of the Chequamegon Bay's extractive economy. Here, chainsaw operator Lyle Yancy prepares to cut a large yellow birch in 1956. Courtesy of the National Park Service.

hunters joined the fishermen. Every autumn Rocky Island became the center of a distinctive deer hunt, and the Nourses provided hunters with room and board. Some years they housed forty hunters at once. Other island landowners established deer camps or fishing resorts on South Twin, Basswood, and Bear islands. Madeline Island also emerged as a favored hunting ground; several people built hunting camps on their property and at least ten mainland hunting clubs erected cabins. One mid-1940s count estimated nearly three hundred hunters on Madeline in a single day.[13]

If deer camps provided a new source of income to island landowners, it was because deer had only recently arrived on the islands. Prior to logging, deer populations in the dense hardwood/hemlock forests of northern Wisconsin remained below ten deer per square mile. The edge environments and early successional stands of aspen in areas regenerating after logging and fire provided more favorable habitat. The elimination of wolves and other predators enhanced conditions for the rapid growth of deer populations. The conservation

5.3 In the 1950s, Rocky Island became the site of a distinctive deer hunt. Hunters could camp on the island or rent a cabin from the Rocky Island Air Haven. The deer were a recent arrival to the islands, surging as the regenerating forests created ideal habitat. Wisconsin Conservation Department officials promoted sport hunting as a way to control the deer population, which they worried would quickly exceed the islands' carrying capacity. Courtesy of the National Park Service.

movement led to bag limits, license requirements, and closed seasons—deliberate attempts to protect and increase the deer herd. By the mid-1930s, some scientists recognized that they had a problem: deer herds had grown beyond the carrying capacity of their range. Overpopulation meant damage to crops and die-offs during harsh winters or necessitated winter feeding programs.[14]

The Apostle Islands followed this trajectory. A biologist who visited the islands in 1919 reported very light deer populations, including on Madeline Island. By the 1930s, however, Madeline had a reputation as a spot for good deer hunting, and by the late 1940s, island deer herds had reached problem proportions. Rocky Island had a remarkably fast transition. Deer were only occasionally sighted on the island in the 1930s, and as late as 1946 the deer population remained quite small. The island had a dense cover of Canada yew, a preferred food, as well as ample winter shelter and forage. Then, the deer population exploded. One state deer ecologist called the Rocky Island irruption "the fastest buildup of a deer population and the fastest degeneration of a habitat I've seen." Hunters killed 124 deer on Rocky in 1954, a startling figure for an island that measured just less than two square miles in size.[15]

Both deliberate and accidental human action contributed to the quality of the deer habitat. Deer fared particularly well in recently burned-over areas. Fires burned on Stockton Island at least five different years between the cessation of logging in 1920 and 1954. Oak, Outer, Rocky, and several other islands burned during the same period. Lightning set some of these fires; escaped campfires from fishing and hunting camps caused others. But humans deliberately set some of these fires too. Berry pickers started the Stockton Island fires in 1934 and 1936. The island had been a favored site for blueberry picking for decades, frequented by both local whites and Indians, as well as by tourists seeking a pleasant spot for a picnic. Madeline Island also had large berry patches. Regular burning kept these patches productive; without fire, young trees shade out the berry bushes. Fires might have had the unintended consequence of improving deer forage, but the fires themselves were often intentional. Whether deliberate or not, human actions had altered the fire regimes and elevated both deer populations and berry-picking opportunities.[16]

The deer irruption on the Apostle Islands presented a familiar problem to state game managers. As biologists recognized the impact of deer irruptions in the 1930s, they lobbied for the reduction of the deer herd through the use of extended hunting seasons and antlerless hunts (hunts for does instead of bucks, which control population by limiting reproduction). The Wisconsin Conservation Commission authorized a special "any deer" season for the Apostle Islands in 1954 and carried out a publicity campaign designed to lure hunters to the islands. "For the adventurous and skilled deer hunter, young in body or spirit, the Apostle Islands offer thrills, rugged conditions, and good hunting success!" proclaimed one publication. Hunters responded by taking 411 deer from the islands in 1954 (excluding Madeline, which did not have the special season), 254 in 1955, and 209 in 1956. The Conservation Commission kept the special hunting regulations for the Apostles in effect for the next two decades. Hunters from around the state and the region traveled to the Apostles to participate in the distinctive hunt, solidifying the islands' reputation as a destination for outdoor recreation in a rugged and primitive setting. The *Milwaukee Journal* reported that a hunting trip to the Apostles offered "a taste of the primeval" and "could be something like a trip to Africa or Alaska at a small percentage of the cost." This reputation became an essential factor in the transition of the Apostles into a wilderness.[17]

The economic opportunities provided by the deer irruption on Rocky and the other islands proved fleeting, forcing the Nourses and the other island landowners to adapt yet again. State game managers had hoped that hunters would help keep the deer population from exceeding the carrying capacity of the islands and thereby would prevent the die-offs that had plagued portions of the mainland. Even the special hunting seasons failed to keep the deer herd in check. Browse conditions deteriorated rapidly on the islands with large herds, and by the early 1960s observers noted signs of starvation. Harsh winters exacerbated the problem. Hunting slowed as deer became less numerous and more sickly; the total number of deer killed on the islands (excluding Madeline, where numbers remained higher) topped one hundred only twice after 1958, falling to nine in 1972, the last year records were kept for the islands.[18]

Fish populations fluctuated as much the deer herds. Exotic species and overfishing threatened the most important commercial fish species. Rainbow smelt (*Osmerus mordax* Mitchill) was the first of several problematic exotic species. Pisciculturists had introduced smelt in Michigan in the early 1900s as food for stocked salmon. By 1930, smelt appeared in eastern Lake Superior, and they reached the Apostles by the 1950s. The silvery, seven-inch-long fish had an immediate impact on the commercial herring catch. Herring and smelt competed directly with each other for food. As smelt populations grew, they often concentrated on herring spawning grounds in late autumn and impaired herring reproduction. Herring numbers and harvest levels dropped. Fisheries biologists have speculated that competition with smelt rather than overfishing prompted this decline, although fishing took its toll as well.[19]

The collapse of the lake trout fishery was more rapid, more complete, and more disastrous for the fishermen. The parasitic sea lamprey (*Petromyzon marinus* Linnaeus) took much of the blame for the destruction of the lake trout fishery on the Great Lakes.[20] Over the course of the twentieth century, the sea lamprey moved into the Great Lakes basin from the St. Lawrence River, enabled by the locks and canals built for the shipping trade, decimating commercial fisheries along the way. Lamprey reached Lake Michigan in the 1930s and Lake Superior in 1946. The impact of the lamprey was hard to miss. The parasitic sucker attached itself to the sides of adult and juvenile lake trout, pulling out their insides. Lamprey preyed upon trout before they reached maturity, drastically limiting trout reproduction. Fishermen in the Apostles first noticed lamprey-scarred trout in the early 1950s.[21]

At first discovering only an occasional scarred trout in their nets, fishermen in the Apostles soon found that lamprey had ruined the entire haul. In 1955, 36 percent of trout caught in Wisconsin's Lake Superior waters had lamprey scars; this percentage increased to 56 in 1956 and 79 in 1957. Commercial production plummeted by 27 percent per year after 1953, with harvests falling progressively from the eastern to the western edge of the lake. The lamprey infestation threatened to ruin stocking and research programs, simply because healthy trout could not be found. "Imagine, only two females were caught in the course of netting the important spawning reefs [in the Apostles] which have always been a dependable source of eggs," lamented Wisconsin fisheries biologists.[22]

The lamprey halted commercial fishing in the Apostles. The Booth Fisheries Company stopped sending collection boats to the islands in 1958 and closed its Bayfield packinghouse soon after. Many fishermen had little choice but to retire or look for other work. The State of Wisconsin took the extraordinary step of closing the trout fishery altogether in 1962, with the hope that lamprey control and reduced fishing pressure might save the lake trout from extirpation. "We fished as long as we could, and then in '62, the state closed the lake for trout," remembered one long-time island fisherman. "And of course by that time, everybody realized that they had to do something different to make a living. And so we, a lot of us just walked away from it." A few fishermen persisted by focusing on herring, smelt, and chubs (deepwater herring), but with lake trout and whitefish—the two highest-priced fish—devastated by the lamprey, fishing became even more tenuous an occupation than it had been in the past.[23]

Other economic blows battered northern Wisconsin in the 1950s. Iron mining along the south shore of Lake Superior, and smelting and shipping in Ashland, declined sharply. The area's farm economy remained stagnant, the victim of poor soils and a short growing season. The Chequamegon Bay communities of Bayfield, Washburn, and Ashland (as well as other northern Wisconsin towns) suffered from chronic unemployment, out-migration of labor and capital, and economic depression. In 1965, the U.S. Department of Commerce declared northern Wisconsin one of the most economically distressed regions in the country.[24]

These setbacks seemed to signal the end of the varied economy that had persisted in the islands for over a century. The fishermen who used Sand Island as a base retired, and the last production-oriented economic activity there ceased. A few fishermen continued to work out of Rocky and Madeline islands, but in smaller numbers and with poorer prospects than before. Only a single farm remained on Madeline Island. Although logging continued on several of the islands—by this time often in second-growth forests—the scale of these operations remained relatively small. By 1960, resource extraction in the islands had ground to a virtual standstill.[25]

Creating a Legible Landscape

Even as the multifaceted economy dwindled, a new and more exclusive use of the islands grew in its place. In the prosperous years that followed World War II, the nation as a whole and Wisconsin in particular experienced a boom in outdoor recreation. Wisconsin Conservation Department officials responded to the resulting pressure on park and forest facilities by dramatically increasing the role of the state in planning for recreation. The WCD acquired new lands, improved parks, and built campgrounds. In doing so, state planners organized and simplified Wisconsin's recreational landscape, making it more legible and more easily managed. This state simplification had striking implications for the Apostle Islands. WCD officials saw the islands as a wilderness, an undeveloped and wild area valuable for its recreational and ecological characteristics. Residents of the Chequamegon Bay region maintained a markedly different view, one far more in keeping with economic patterns of the past. As state management authority in the islands grew, these two perspectives came into increasing conflict.

In the 1950s, the United States transitioned from depression and war into a period of unprecedented economic growth. Armed with disposable income, leisure time, and a pent-up consumer demand that had accumulated for two decades, middle-class Americans headed indoors to shopping malls and outdoors to beaches, hiking trails, and campgrounds. By every measure, demand for outdoor recreation surged between 1950 and 1960: visits to national parks jumped 86 percent; outboard motors in use, 94 percent; fishing licenses, 25 percent; and visits to recreation areas, 143 percent. Existing resources could not meet this newfound demand. Congress labeled the situation a "crisis in outdoor recreation."[26]

postwar recreation

The way people enjoyed the outdoors changed too as wilderness recreation became more popular. Visitors to places like the Apostle Islands sought a camping spot in nature rather than a hotel in town. They were enabled in this transition by close ties between the environmental movement and the outdoor recreation industry, which produced lightweight tents and other high-tech gear that made wilderness recreation easier and more comfortable. Bayfield's hotels and excursion services continued to thrive, as did the stores that provided equipment and supplies to wilderness campers. The summer tourist trade had reshaped the environments of Sand and Madeline islands in the first half of the twentieth century; this new form of outdoor recreation had even more dramatic implications in second half of the century.[27]

Wisconsin's recreation crisis was particularly acute. Since the days of railroad tourism, the state's lakes, resorts, and sporting opportunities had earned it a reputation as the playground of the Midwest. Even before the boom of the 1950s, some people believed that Wisconsin did not have enough publicly owned recreational lands and facilities, and they accused the legislature of underfunding the state park system. Pressure on state parks and forests increased significantly in the 1950s. Visits to state campgrounds exploded by 243 percent during the decade, and total visits to state parks jumped from three million in 1951 to over five million in 1956. Funding for the parks, meanwhile, remained constant. The WCD did not have money to build and maintain facilities in the existing parks, let alone to acquire new land. "If we continue at our present rate of acquisition and development we cannot possibly hope to supply the demand," explained one state official. The situation had reached crisis conditions. "[No] matter how clever our planning and development, the point may soon be reached when every camping unit is occupied every day of the camping season. What will we do the following year?"[28]

State officials recognized in this situation an opportunity to ameliorate the chronic economic depression that stifled the northern part of the state. If the recreationally starved urbanites of Chicago, Milwaukee, and other cities could be connected to the resources of northern Wisconsin, two problems could be solved at once. Many state planners believed that *only* by developing a recreation industry could the south shore of Lake Superior be rescued from economic stagnation. To accomplish these twin goals, they recommended the creation, expansion, and improvement of parks, roads, and forests throughout northern Wisconsin.[29]

Gaylord Nelson built his political career in Wisconsin in part on the recognition that recreational tourism could help solve northern Wisconsin's economic ills. As a state senator in the early 1950s, Nelson worked to inject New Deal values of planning and centralized research authority into the state's resource management programs. When he became governor in 1958, Nelson accomplished this with several ambitious initiatives. Nelson built a reputation—for himself as well as for his state—as a leader in the emerging environmental movement. In both its use of modern planning techniques and its focus on outdoor recreation, Wisconsin became a national model. This context frames the decision by the WCD to acquire the Apostle Islands and, more importantly, the decision to manage the islands as a wilderness.[30]

The movement for state acquisition of the Apostles began in 1950. That year, the Milwaukee County Conservation Alliance—an affiliation of sportsmen's clubs—submitted a resolution to the Wisconsin Conservation Commission requesting a study of the feasibility of state acquisition of the Apostle Islands "for recreational purposes." Concluding that the large amount of privately held land in the Apostles made state acquisition unlikely, the commission took no action. But the Milwaukee sportsmen were not easily dissuaded. Both deer herds and the Apostles' reputation as a spot for primitive recreation were peaking in the early 1950s, and the sportsmen again recommended public acquisition in 1952. These suggestions differed from the park proposal of the 1930s in that they originated outside the Chequamegon Bay. They served the needs of Milwaukee hunters, not the people who lived near the islands.[31]

In response to this pressure, WCD officials agreed to consider the proposition. In 1952, WCD administrators, conservation commissioners, and a representative of the Milwaukee County Conservation Alliance toured the islands. They liked what they found: a forest recovering after the destructive logging of previous generations; a landscape seemingly tailor-made for scientific experiments in ecology and game management; and a wonderland for the increasingly popular forms of wilderness recreation. The movement for state acquisition of the islands coalesced around these attributes.[32]

How could state officials find so much to value in the Apostles, just two decades after NPS investigators described the islands as a logging- and fire-devastated wasteland? Certainly, the trained scientists of the WCD recognized the signs of logging. "[Madeline] island was once covered with the finest trees the north woods could support," explained one pair of naturalists. "Perhaps not a single giant among the white pines remains, but an occasional badly rotted stump furnishes the evidence of a former luxuriant growth." Even today, large stumps and fire scars are still evident on some of the islands, as are the ruins of logging camps and industrial machinery. Nevertheless, observers valued the islands for their "natural condition." Wisconsin's chief forester described Stockton Island in 1956 as "an island almost in its natural condition; no fires have destroyed the forests. It has not been logged since 1915." By this, he meant not the absence of human activity, but that people had not directly shaped forest regeneration. The island had no roads, no buildings save a few ruins, and no active forest management. As plans for public acquisition of the islands developed, their naturalness—or wildness—became their most important attribute. The prevailing ecological belief that forests inevitably and predictably matured from disturbance to a climax ecosystem increased the islands' ecological value.[33]

Island forests might have regenerated without direct human interference, but past human activity shaped the rewilding of the islands. Colonizing plants like white birch and aspen thrived in the cutover and fire-scarred islands. Maturing second-growth forests had a different composition than prelogging ones: Hemlock and white pine served as two of the most important species in the lumber trade. But these trees made up a much smaller part of the regenerating forests. Heavy deer browse and increased light levels after clear-cutting and fire retarded hemlock regeneration. White pine seed sources often perished in the fires that followed logging. By the 1950s, white pine grew only on a few isolated sandscapes and the areas protected from logging by lighthouse reserves. Red and sugar maple, in particular, benefited from the low regeneration rates of white pine and hemlock and dominated the rewilding island forests. One of the important impacts of these changes was a lessening of landscape diversity— dense stands of hardwood replaced the former mosaic of hemlock, hardwoods, and pine. In some places, such as on Sand Island, changing forest types can be traced to specific human choices to clear fields or plant orchards. But on all the islands, the natural condition masked the ongoing role of past human action in the process of rewilding.[34]

The natural condition of the islands provided an important additional value: an unparalleled opportunity for scientific research. One researcher called the Apostles a "ready made experiment for the ecologist" because of their location, their isolation from each other and the mainland, and their different histories of fire, logging, deer browsing, and agriculture. The islands were particularly suited to the study of the relationship between deer and forest regeneration in a cutover landscape. Some islands (Rocky and Madeline) had high deer populations. Others (Cat and Michigan) had only small numbers of deer, while still others (Raspberry and Outer) had none. In 1955, several University of Wisconsin faculty surveyed Stockton Island and noted its potential for freshwater, forest, entomological, and wildlife research. WCD officials also underscored the islands' scientific value. In 1953, the WCD had used Stockton Island as its base for the experimental release of the pine marten and black grouse, and the agency planned other wildlife research as well.[35]

WCD officials believed that the islands' greatest value lay in the opportunity they provided for wilderness recreation. Visitors to the islands had long noted their beauty, their cliffs and beaches, and the plentiful fish and game. But as the outdoor recreation boom intensified, the Apostles took on a new value. They could provide a type of recreation not possible in most places. State deer ecologist Burton Dahlberg wrote to the director of the WCD in 1955 that

the value of an undeveloped area where it is possible to get away from the hustle and bustle of modern living cannot be overestimated. There are very few places left in the Middle West that offer an opportunity to establish a natural area, where future generations may know the value of natural things. As human pressures increase the value of places like Stockton Island will increase proportionately. One of Stockton Island's greatest assets is its inaccessibility. The fact that a vacation on the island requires some planning and the possibility that one may be stranded for a few extra days makes it all the more desirable.

Although Dahlberg did not use the term *wilderness*, he was one of the first to directly employ wilderness rhetoric in calling for public acquisition of the islands. Dahlberg and others worried that logging and development might soon rob the islands of their wilderness value.[36]

As WCD officials toured the rewilding islands, the national wilderness movement gathered steam. In the 1950s, wilderness advocates rallied around the defense of Echo Park in Colorado's Dinosaur National Monument, a wild and beautiful canyon at the confluence of the Green and Yampa rivers threatened by a federal dam proposal. Arguments based on the scientific and recreational value of wilderness emerged as key points in this battle. Wilderness advocates strategically appealed to the growing demand for outdoor recreation to build a national coalition against the dam project. The momentum generated by stopping the dam at Echo Park led to the submission of the first wilderness bill to Congress in 1956 and the eventual passage of the Wilderness Act of 1964. The rhetoric of the national wilderness movement informed the developing WCD policy on the acquisition of the islands.[37]

For all these reasons—regenerating forests, scientific value, and most importantly wilderness recreation and the potential economic benefits of tourism—state officials began to plan for acquisition of the islands. In 1955, the Conservation Commission unanimously accepted a "Policy on Acquisition of an 'Apostle Islands Wilderness Area,'" which called for the preservation of the islands' scenic, historical, plant, wildlife, and scientific resources. It encouraged further study of these resources and their potential, "especially for their specialized wilderness-type recreational values." WCD officials singled out Stockton, Oak, and Basswood islands for state acquisition. But a chronic budget shortfall handcuffed the state's environmental programs, particularly land acquisition and state parks. The lack of funds clouded discussions from the start and WCD officials recognized that purchase of the islands likely required legislative action, something they considered unlikely.[38]

Despite the financial crunch, WCD administrators discovered a cost-effective method for the state to secure management authority on Stockton Island. Upon hearing of state interest in the islands, the trustees of the William Vilas estate contacted the WCD about a sale or leasing arrangement. In 1955, the WCD agreed to a five-year lease for one thousand dollars per year—just over the annual tax bill—and also secured a purchase option should funds become available. The WCD had no plans to develop the island, instead retaining it "as a wilderness area . . . open for limited recreational use" as well as for research and game management.[39]

Other islands proved more difficult to acquire, primarily because not everyone on the Chequamegon Bay approved of the WCD's plans for wilderness management. In contrast to the 1930s, when local residents had spearheaded the attempt to create a national park, many locals resisted the growing power of state authority to manage the islands. They turned to the county governments, which could protect their interests because of the way the federal system of government splits administrative power, and because the counties owned some of the land in question. The WCD, and then the National Park Service, were forced to engage in a debate over the proper role of the state in the development and management of natural resources. NPS and WCD planners advocating an increase in state authority had to address the continued demands for local control of resources. The local reaction to state acquisition of land in the Apostles paralleled opposition to nature protection in other parts of the country, especially in the West.

When discussions on state acquisition of the Apostles began in the early 1950s, residents of the region supported the project. The Ashland and Bayfield county boards and local chambers of commerce promised to work with WCD officials, who agreed to develop their plans in conjunction with local governments. But as prospects for acquiring the islands solidified, residents of the Chequamegon Bay expressed their displeasure with the WCD. After adopting the wilderness acquisition policy, WCD officials approached the Ashland County Board for purchase options on Oak and Basswood islands and for parts of Stockton—this would allow the state to acquire the islands when funds became available. The Ashland County Board declined and even retained a real estate agent to help sell its island property to private developers.[40]

At issue was the classification of state lands and the WCD's plans for development of the Apostle Islands—or, more accurately, its plans *not* to develop them. WCD officials considered three classifications: state forest, state park, or state forest designated as wilderness. Although the WCD administered state forests under the principle of multiple use, timber production served as the primary function of these areas. State parks were developed recreational sites with roads, picnic tables, flush toilets, concession stands, and other amenities. Wilderness, in Wisconsin state terms, meant areas with little formal management and a primarily "natural" character. Wilderness designation within the state land system was therefore reserved for state forests, as parks typically had too much development to qualify. Despite their history of logging, the Apostles remained in their "natural condition" and could be considered wilderness. Debates over state acquisition of the Apostles revolved around the question of classification—some people wanted the islands declared a state park and developed accordingly; others wanted the islands declared a forest and administered as a wilderness area.[41]

Residents of the Chequamegon Bay region disapproved of the WCD's plans to manage the Apostles as a wilderness. Instead, they demanded a state park. A park, many believed, would bring in more tourists and generate more dollars. Kenneth Todd, chair of the Ashland County Board, believed "it would not help the state, the county, or the islands if they are established as a pure wilderness area. . . . There is already enough wilderness area in the north and that the need is for well-developed state parks." Todd and other members of the county board also worried about the loss of tax revenue if the state acquired the islands; they wanted Ashland County land returned to tax-paying private ownership if it was not going to be developed as a park.[42]

A state park would generate a brand of tourism more in line with past uses of the islands. John Chapple had long supported the creation of a park in the Apostles—he had played a prominent role in the national park proposal of 1929–30. His ideas about the type of park he wanted had not changed. He advocated a park based on Madeline Island, one that would recognize the historical importance and scenic beauty of the islands. This type of park would lure tourists, as well as the roads, hotels, restaurants, and services they needed; it would connect to other industries in the area and stimulate the economy. "[The] people in the Ashland area want something made of the islands so that they will be an attraction for tourists," explained Kenneth Todd. Wilderness would not provide these benefits.[43]

Despite the stiffening opposition, the state forged ahead with its plan for the Apostles. In 1959, the Conservation Commission created Apostle Islands State Forest—formalizing the wilderness acquisition policy adopted in 1955. The forest included Stockton, Oak, and Basswood islands. The WCD purchased Stockton Island from the Vilas estate. The creation of the state forest did not necessarily mean that the WCD would acquire the rest of the land within the forest boundary. Ashland County Board members were not pleased with the creation of the state forest, and they resolved not to sell county lands on Oak and Basswood islands to the WCD until it demonstrated an acceptable development program for Stockton.[44]

The county board's demands did not dissuade the WCD from managing Stockton Island as a wilderness. But what, exactly, did wilderness management mean? The state had no clear plan or policy, no infrastructure to manage the forest, count visitors, or assess visitors' needs. In the first several years after the creation of the state forest, the WCD's annual reports did not even mention the Apostles. By 1966, the WCD had crafted guidelines for the management of Stockton Island: "General development will be kept to a minimum in order to preserve the Apostle Islands as a primitive, wilderness area. Intensive use sites will be minimal and maintained at specific areas in order that such use will not encroach upon the wild aspects of the area." Any future developments that might detract from the island's "wilderness aspects" would be prohibited. The limited facilities provided by the WCD included a pier, a small office, several pit toilets, and a handful of campsites with picnic tables.[45]

Reactions to the limited development split along local and outsider lines. Frederick Goetz wrote from Minneapolis to complain that the piers and tables spoiled the wilderness experience: "Anything which alters the 'wilderness' character of the Islands is a serious detraction. I was therefore distressed to hear that a series of picnic tables has been brought to Stockton Island." Others complained about the buildup of garbage and tin cans near the campground. But those who lived closer to the islands, and favored more extensive development, had an opposite reaction. Some complained of the newly constructed pier "that it is not large enough to accommodate all who wish to use the facility." The limited development certainly did not satisfy the demands of the Ashland County Board, which continued to reject the WCD's efforts to purchase Oak and Basswood islands.[46]

WCD officials responded to these demands by creating Big Bay State Park on Madeline Island, where they again found themselves in the middle of a conflict between locals and outsiders over the protection of nature. The WCD established Big Bay in 1963, with plans for a 2,700-acre park with full recreational facilities featuring the expansive beach on the northeastern end of the island. WCD planners intended the park to complement wilderness management in Apostle Islands State Forest. But as the national lakeshore moved closer to designation in the 1960s, and the exclusion of Madeline from the proposal became clear, the prospects for private development of the island rose. This led island residents to demand that the WCD scale back on its plans for Big Bay State Park. Summer resident Theodore Gary led this opposition and he capitalized on the rising land values with a series of lucrative real estate deals in the 1960s, including the construction of a marina, a golf course, and a lodge. The WCD did create Big Bay State Park, but it reduced the size of the park and the available facilities.[47]

Residents of Bayfield and Ashland resented the interference from people they regarded as outsiders—even though the Gary family had first started using Madeline Island as a summer retreat in the early twentieth century. Supporters of Big Bay State Park charged that the Garys and their allies wanted to keep Madeline Island as a retreat for the rich and well-heeled. The

Bayfield County Press ran a blistering editorial on the issue: "It seems that the general run-of-the-mill family groups which would frequent such a park, would not be in keeping with the high caliber of people THEY are interested in having on their island." Patricia Gary's comment that the "type of people who frequent a state park would not be good for the island" did not help matters. In fact, many year-round islanders opposed the expansion of Big Bay, as did the summer residents. But most citizens of the other Chequamegon Bay communities supported the state park, much as they wanted a similar development on Stockton Island.[48]

In the eyes of WCD officials, plans for Big Bay State Park and Apostle Islands State Forest were tightly linked. The entire south shore of Lake Superior would become a recreational landscape, with park facilities, campgrounds, scenic roads, beaches, public fishing grounds, and primitive areas complementing each other. WCD director L. P. Voigt explained that Big Bay would "be a part of the recreational complex which includes the Apostle Islands State Forest. Intensive recreational developments for this complex would be concentrated on Big Bay and, in general, the adjacent islands would be kept in a wilderness or primitive state." Other nearby areas also played a role in this organized landscape. The WCD improved facilities at Amnicon Falls and Copper Falls state parks and at Brule River State Forest—all within sixty miles of Ashland. The state acquired land on the northern tip of the Bayfield Peninsula for a boat landing to increase access to the Apostles. WCD planners expected that this well-organized landscape would solve the state's recreational crisis and the northland's chronic economic woes.[49]

The recreational development plan of the 1960s illustrates the further expansion of state authority in resource management. Rising environmental awareness, a greater faith in the power of centralized planning, and the crisis in outdoor recreation convinced state officials that recreation provided the best use of Lake Superior's resources. They determined that they could achieve the goals of environmental protection as well as the economic benefits of tourism by devoting increasing acreage to recreation rather than other activities such as logging or even private development. One official explained "that the long-time gain . . . would be greater if the state of Wisconsin were to develop public recreation facilities than if the county-owned lands were to be sold to private individuals to get them on the tax roll." State planners delineated parts of the landscape for specific types of recreational activity.

As they had with rural zoning in the 1920s, state authorities sought a more legible landscape, one that would make management goals easier to achieve. They had segregated wilderness recreation from other forms of tourism and from other parts of the regional economy. And as was the case in the early twentieth century, nowhere was the campaign for legibility more clearly evident than in fisheries management.[50]

The collapse of the lake trout fishery in the 1950s prompted the state to take a stronger role in managing the Lake Superior commercial fisheries. State managers faced the difficult task of balancing recreational consumption and commercial production. As lake trout became harder to catch, competition between sportsmen and commercial fishermen intensified. Sportsmen blamed commercial fishermen for destroying the fishery and argued that recreation brought more money to the local economy. Commercial fishermen blamed the lamprey invasion and believed that their economic needs should take precedence over the leisure-time activities of sportsmen. The Bayfield Trollers Association asked the Conservation Commission in 1950 to reserve an area in the Apostles for the exclusive use of sportsmen by prohibiting commercial nets. The Wisconsin Federation of Conservation Clubs tied the controversy over Apostle Islands State Forest to the decline of the lake trout. They recommended state purchase of the islands on the condition "that commercial fishing operations be curtailed to perpetuate the Lake Trout fisheries, which would be one of the areas major attractions." In 1960, the Ashland County supervisors urged the WCD to prohibit commercial fishing within one mile of the Apostle Islands because they believed that commercial fishing "has been detrimental to the interests of the amateur fishermen and is therefore harmful to the area." In 1962, the state closed the commercial trout fishery, but it allowed continued sport fishing for the species.[51]

As the lamprey infestation worsened on the eastern Great Lakes in the 1940s and 1950s, lake states teamed with the federal government and Canada on an aggressive research and control program. This program focused on Lake Superior, which held the last viable population of lake trout. Researchers experimented with variety of control techniques, eventually settling on a combination of chemical treatments and electronic barriers to restrict access to spawning streams. Lamprey control was combined with massive stocking of lake trout yearlings. These actions brought dramatic results, and lamprey numbers plummeted while trout numbers rose steadily. Fisheries experts saw

5.4 Frank Eha Sr. *(left)* owned the West Bay Club, one of the summer homes on Sand Island, and commercial fisherman Harold Dahl lived on the island year-round. Here, they show off a trophy fish. The summer residents often depended on the islanders for transportation, and the commercial fishermen often earned extra money by taking tourists and summer residents on island cruises and fishing expeditions. Courtesy of the National Park Service.

signs of recovery by 1965, and by 1970 the trout population had returned to its pre-lamprey level. Restoration of the Lake Superior lake trout stands as one of the great success stories of modern fisheries management.[52]

When the WCD reopened the fishery in 1968, it did so with a new set of priorities. Planners expected a resurgent sport fishery to play an essential role in the recreational economy. State authorities implemented a management technique known as "limited entry," strictly regulating the number of commercial fishermen allowed on Lake Superior and the amount of trout each could catch. As many as seventy fishermen had permits to fish the Wisconsin waters of Lake Superior in the 1950s and 1960s, but by 1971 this number had dropped to twenty-one. The state achieved this reduction by issuing licenses only to those who qualified as full-time fishermen (based on number of days spent fishing and the value of equipment). Although bound by bag limits, permit and reporting requirements, and other regulations, sport fishermen clearly enjoyed first priority. The WCD explained its position as an attempt to find "the greatest good recreationally, aesthetically, and economically." This meant "precedence in management is given to sport fishing, since it provides a greater benefit" by supporting the economy of the entire area. As they had in allocating other types of resources, planners determined that recreational consumption rather than commercial production provided the best chance for both protecting trout and stabilizing the economy. This was a very different perspective on production and consumption than had prevailed in the Apostle Islands for the previous century. The days of tourism as but one part of a complex and interconnected economy had disappeared.[53]

Local Demands, National Needs, and the Creation
of Apostle Islands National Lakeshore

During the 1960s, the movement to create a national lakeshore in the Apostles slowly gained momentum. No one doubted the wild and primitive character of the islands. But as the park moved closer to designation, conflict over the proper balance among nature, tourism, and state authority polarized. The promised economic benefits of a national park won the support of many who had opposed the creation of Apostle Islands State Forest. Only the people most directly affected by the park proposal—property owners and residents of the Red Cliff and Bad River reservations—maintained their opposition. Nationwide interest and support widened as federal officials responded to demands for outdoor recreation and nature protection. Local visions for tourist development in keeping with traditions of resource use did not match these environmental aims. It fell to Gaylord Nelson and Harold Jordahl Jr.—chief architects of the park proposal—to craft a project that satisfied an array of often conflicting demands.

The crisis in outdoor recreation that spurred state acquisition of the Apostle Islands also motivated the federal government's interest in the area. In 1958, Congress created the Outdoor Recreation Resources Review Commission. The commission's subsequent report highlighted the importance of places like the Chequamegon Bay in meeting the nation's surging recreational needs: "Most people seeking outdoor recreation want water—to sit by, to swim and to fish in, to ski across, to dive under, and to run their boats over. . . . Camping, picnicking, and hiking . . . are more attractive near water sites." Access to beaches, lakes, and other sources of water-based recreation remained far below demand, especially for ocean and Great Lakes shorelines. These areas had been neglected as a public resource and left open to private acquisition. Only a small percentage of shoreline remained in public ownership. "Immediate action should be taken by Federal, State, and local governments to acquire additional beach and shoreline areas," the report recommended.[54]

The NPS conducted a series of studies on the national coastlines in the late 1950s and reached similar conclusions. The report on the Great Lakes identified the Bayfield Peninsula, Stockton Island, the Brule River, and the Bad River/ Kakagon Sloughs (marshes on the southern edge of the Chequamegon Bay) as areas that might help satisfy the underserved recreational needs of midwestern cities. The shoreline surveys prompted the designation of twelve new units of the National Park System between 1963 and 1972, including Cape Cod National Seashore in 1961 and Pictured Rocks National Lakeshore (on Lake Superior) and Indiana Dunes National Lakeshore (on Lake Michigan) in 1966. These areas, established to both provide recreation and to protect nature, became important models for Apostle Islands National Lakeshore.[55]

Gaylord Nelson moved from the Wisconsin's governor's office to the U.S. Senate in 1962. He took with him his ideas about organizing the landscape of northern Wisconsin to achieve the twin goals of nature protection and economic stimulation. Establishing the region as a national park, rather than a state park, would increase the scale of the project and further advance both goals. Nelson received a warm response from Secretary of the Interior Stewart Udall in 1962 for the idea of creating a national recreation area in the Chequamegon Bay region. In 1963, President John F. Kennedy traveled to Ashland and the Apostle Islands as a part of a national conservation tour. He applauded Nelson's idea: "If promptly developed, recreational activities and new national park, forest, and recreation areas can bolster your economy and provide pleasure for millions of people in the days to come."[56]

The project received an additional endorsement from an unlikely source: the Bad River Ojibwe. In 1962, the Bad River Tribal Council requested the creation of a national recreational area in the Kakagon Sloughs, a beautiful and undeveloped wetland area on the south shore of the Chequamegon Bay. Tribal leaders hoped that such a designation would both provide economic opportunity for the chronically depressed reservation and help protect "the natural resources, the ancient customs and culture" of the band. Like the supervisors of Ashland County, members of the Bad River band resented the way that the WCD had expanded its conservation authority. They hoped to use the lakeshore proposal to secure their treaty-guaranteed rights to hunt, fish, and gather wild rice—rights the WCD had long fought to extinguish.[57]

With wide backing, U.S. Department of the Interior planners assembled a formal proposal for Apostle Islands National Lakeshore. In 1964, Secretary Udall deputized a task force to work on the project that included representatives from the NPS, the Bureau of Indian Affairs, the Bureau of Recreation, the State of Wisconsin, the tribal councils of the Bad River and Red Cliff reservations, and several other agencies. He appointed Harold Jordahl to head the effort. The resulting proposal stated three primary goals: preserving a "splendid remnant" of the Lake Superior shore; improving conditions on the Bad River and Red Cliff reservations; and bolstering the local economy through tourism.[58]

With this proposal, federal planners once again sought to use state authority to organize the landscape in an efficient and legible manner. They delineated exactly what kinds of activities would be permitted in each of the three major units of the proposed lakeshore. The Apostle Islands Unit would be acquired and be "preserved as wild, natural areas" with only limited facilities. The Red Cliff Unit would stretch around the perimeter of the Bayfield Peninsula; all but the westernmost portion of this unit lay within the Red Cliff reservation. This unit would receive the most development, with a scenic road, park headquarters, and extensive picnicking and docking facilities. The Kakagon Sloughs–Bad River Unit included the marshlands and coastline of the Bad River reservation, which would receive a ranger station and docking facilities, with strict controls on boat access to preserve the wild character of the marsh. In 1965, Gaylord Nelson introduced the proposal to Congress.[59]

NPS planners made an important decision when they proposed a national lakeshore rather than a national park. The NPS made wide use of the national recreation area category in the 1960s and 1970s, a direct response to the crisis in outdoor recreation. One policy document clearly stated the intent of these areas: "Outdoor recreation shall be recognized as the dominant or primary resource management purpose." Other activities would be allowed, but only if they were "compatible with fulfilling the recreational mission." Congress used this recreational designation to create twenty-four new national recreation areas, lakeshores, and seashores between 1965 and 1971, covering nearly 1.5 million acres. For the Apostles, national lakeshore status ensured that the hunting, fishing, and trapping carried on by white and Indian residents of the region could continue. This would not be the case in a national park. Protection of

5.5 Secretary of the Interior Stewart Udall (*right*) presents Wisconsin Senator Gaylord Nelson with the first copy of the proposal for Apostle Islands National Lakeshore in 1965. Courtesy of the Wisconsin Historical Society, WHi-30352.

hunting and fishing rights served as the essential component of the proposal for the Ojibwe.[60]

Decisions about where to draw the lakeshore boundaries proved far more contentious. Planners included within the lakeshore the summer colonies on Sand Island and Little Sand Bay (on the mainland, across from Sand Island) but excluded Madeline Island because of its extensive road system, summer homes, high property values, and permanent population. They also wanted to leave Madeline Island open for continued development to ensure that the kind of economic activity demanded by local residents in the dispute over Apostle Islands State Forest remained possible. Madeline Island had served as the centerpiece of the park proposal in 1929; its exclusion signifies how differently planners envisioned the lakeshore in the 1960s.[61]

Sand Island had less development than Madeline but presented a similar dilemma. Did its history of resource extraction and summer homes disqualify the island for inclusion within the lakeshore? From the earliest stages of planning, in correspondence with lakeshore planners and then at public hearings, Sand Islanders maintained that it did. The descendants of the men and women who settled and summered on Sand Island employed their family histories as an argument against the creation of the park. "For three generations my ancestors lived and made their living on the island as commercial fishermen and farmers," explained Fred Hansen's daughter. The Jensches had been using the island as a summer home for six decades; Daisy Jensch still spent time there at age ninety. Howard Palm believed that although the settlers had left the island, their descendants should be allowed to remain: "At one time there was a thriving community on Sand Island comprised of lumbermen, farmers and fishermen who resided there the year round. . . . Their homes and cleared land for farming still remain, and the people who were forced to leave continue to maintain their homes for summer use for themselves, their children and grandchildren." Sand Islanders wondered, as well, why they did not receive the same treatment as Madeline Island property owners. "Now Madeline Island has a lot of estates, and fine roads . . . but to us, Sand Island is just as important," explained Samuel Jensch.[62]

Harold Jordahl and the other federal planners rejected these arguments. They considered excluding Sand Island and Little Sand Bay entirely or including them but using conservation easements or zoning ordinances to limit development. They ultimately decided to acquire these two areas and offer landowners the option to lease their land back from the government. The NPS had traditionally treated the purchase or condemnation of privately owned lands in this manner. NPS planners acknowledged the hard feelings of individual landowners but believed that the condemnation of some lands was necessary to create a creditable national lakeshore.[63]

Between 1967 and 1970, the House and the Senate each held two sets of hearings on the proposal. In these hearings, concerns about the project fractured along geographic lines. A coalition of summer and permanent residents coalesced to oppose the project. This coalition portrayed the proposed lakeshore as an attempt by outsiders to use the federal government to take something away from the communities of the Chequamegon Bay. But just who was considered "local" in this dispute? Some property owners had been spending their summers on Sand Island since the days of Camp Stella but had never identified the island as a permanent home. Others were the children and grandchildren of island settlers but no longer lived in the area. Some park opponents had lived on the Chequamegon Bay for generations; others had just arrived. The prospect of losing access to treasured resources united these disparate interests into a small but vocal group determined to prevent the creation of the park. Over one hundred landowners formed the South Shore Property Owners' Association. Willard Jurgens, a year-round resident of Little Sand Bay, served as chairman of the association, but many of the members lived out of state for much of the year. Other park opponents joined the Apostle Islands Residents Committee.

park opponents

The Ashland Rod and Gun Club circulated a petition seeking the exclusion of the Kakagon Sloughs from the proposal. The club secured over one thousand signatures, primarily from people worried about losing access to favorite hunting and fishing grounds.[64]

Lakeshore opponents offered a variety of arguments against the park, mostly stemming from the fear of losing control over how the islands would be used. Some resented the interference of outsiders. "It seems to me that the southern half of the State should take care of its own responsibilities and let the northerners do likewise," complained one property owner. "All you people in Washington have to do is leave us alone and our economy will improve plenty fast," stated another. Others suggested that a national park would not protect the islands but instead would bring too much development. "I see but one eventual outcome for all of these grandiose plans for this area," explained one member of the South Shore Property Owners' Association. "Tourist facilities and marinas will mar the untouched islands, and make them more accessible for the great influx of the random vacationing populace, many of whom will have no regard for this country." The option of twenty-five-year or lifetime leases to property owners mollified almost no one. The NPS faced a bitter struggle to acquire land from resistant owners for well over a decade after the designation of the lakeshore in 1970.[65]

No one disputed the wildness of the islands. Some lakeshore opponents even argued that the region was *too* wild for consideration as a national park. "The main thing that concerns me about this national park is the safety involved," stated one lakeshore opponent. "Lake Superior, its waves are over 25 feet high and I have seen many people, a lot of casualties . . . you get novice and laymen people out in the lake in 16- and 20-foot boats and they are nothing but trouble." Fishermen Bob Hokenson shared this view: "I've been caught in plenty of [storms] and even did a little praying at times with bigger boats in the 40 ft. class." Sand Islander Carl Dahl's father had drowned in a Superior storm, a fact that he made clear in a letter to the House subcommittee. If Harold Dahl, an experienced fishermen, had succumbed to the violent and wild lake, how well could untrained and unsuspecting tourists possibly fare? The Apostle Islands Residents Committee circulated a brochure publicizing the cold water, dangerous boating conditions, and inaccessibility of the islands. Such a wild place did not make a good tourist destination.[66]

Lakeshore supporters, on the other hand, saw the wild condition of the islands as an amenity, but they disagreed over the best use of the area. Gaylord Nelson, backed by environmental groups from around the country, believed that the lakeshore provided the best chance to protect wild country from development. The majority of Chequamegon Bay residents—at least those that did not face the prospect of losing property—saw the lakeshore as a chance for the kind of economic stimulus that the WCD had precluded by managing Stockton Island as a wilderness. They remained wary of the plans to keep the islands in a wilderness condition, but they eagerly anticipated the development of the Red Cliff and Bad River units of the park.

Even the previously recalcitrant Ashland County Board passed a resolution in favor of the project. Kenneth Todd, a vigorous opponent of Apostle Islands State Forest, had a very different reaction to the national lakeshore. He reasoned that the county could bear the loss of taxable lands because the gas stations, motels, and marinas promised by the creation of the park would provide new revenue. It would be foolish, Todd believed, to pass on "a proposal as major as this one, with a bonanza of island development, booming tourism, and financial gain." The proposal called for exactly the type of development that Todd and others had demanded in their conflict with the WCD over land classification in the 1950s. John Chapple, who had advocated the creation of a state park rather than a state forest, strongly supported the national lakeshore. Chapple estimated that at least three-quarters of the residents of the Chequamegon Bay agreed with him. Opponents of the lakeshore had been reduced to a small but vocal minority.[67]

The scenic road along the Bayfield Peninsula epitomized the development expected by local lakeshore supporters. The president of the South Shore Scenic Drive Association believed that the proposal was "one of the best things that could ever happen to the south shore and the whole area" because of the traffic it would bring to local businesses. Another road enthusiast put the project in the context of several decades of tourism promotion: The proposal would "bring to reality the fond hopes and dreams of the residents of this South Shore area for the past generation and more. It is the firm belief of most of us that this project will make our area the Mecca of hundreds of thousands of beauty and recreation lovers from all parts of the nation and that it will initiate an upsurge of economic development that will benefit the entire region." The planned lodge for Sand Island fit into this category as well. For residents of the

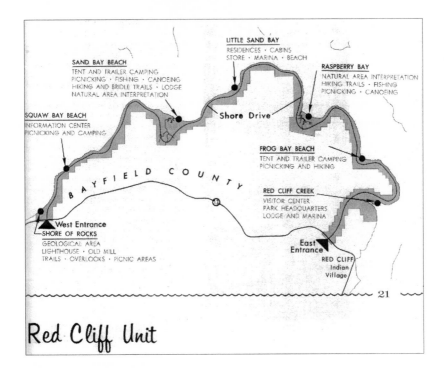

5.6 The 1965 Apostle Islands National Lakeshore proposal contained plans for significant development of the Red Cliff Unit, including a scenic road, campgrounds, cabin rentals, stores, marinas, hiking trails, and visitor centers, as indicated on this map, which was included in the proposal. Most of the unit lay within the boundaries of the Red Cliff Reservation. Courtesy of the National Park Service.

Chequamegon Bay, the islands' greatest value still lay in the economic benefits they could provide.[68]

Those from outside the region valued the islands for entirely different reasons. Nature protection and ecology, not potential development, attracted this support. National conservation groups lined up in favor of the proposal. The National Parks Association, the Sierra Club, the Wilderness Society, the Izaak Walton League, the National Wildlife Foundation, and several other national organizations sent representatives to testify at the congressional hearings. Sigurd Olson, president of the Wilderness Society in the 1960s, grew up in Ashland and knew the islands well. "Here is a great opportunity to preserve this magnificent region for the enjoyment of untold millions of this generation and generations to come," Olson told the House subcommittee. For Olson—not surprisingly—the islands' wild and primitive character provided a more powerful rationale for the park than did economic stimulation. The Wilderness Society and other environmental organizations recommended designating the islands as a part of the National Wilderness Preservation System created by the passage of the Wilderness Act in 1964.[69]

The islands had scientific value as well, but this also depended on the protection of their wilderness characteristics. As the environmental movement gathered strength, ecologists became increasingly interested in determining environmental conditions of the past to establish a baseline against which to measure the degradation caused by human activity. The fusion of ecological study and social commentary represented one of the environmental movement's most significant contributions to the critique of modern society. The islands provided a perfect place for such study. Henry Kolka of the Wisconsin State Board for Preservation of Scientific Areas affirmed the "outstanding scientific contribution that has already resulted from the wilderness quality of the islands and Lake Superior. . . . Because some of the islands have had almost no disturbance . . . they have contributed in a truly incomparable way to our understanding of the probably natural vegetation in other parts of Wisconsin, and the northern Lake States generally, if they had not been so widely disturbed first by cutting and more recently by population pressure."[70]

Outsiders expected the lakeshore to protect the islands from the very development demanded by locals. The alternative to creating the national lakeshore, cautioned Sigurd Olson, "is to see commercialism take over and destroy what is still intact, barring the public from its enjoyment." Wilderness advocates were frustrated with what they regarded as the runaway development of the national parks as a part of Mission 66—the NPS program to expand and modernize roads, visitor centers, and other infrastructure to prepare for the agency's fiftieth year of operation in 1966. They also resented the continued resistance to the designation of wilderness at other parks. Harold Kruse, chair of the Citizens Natural Resources Association, agreed: "We assume that preservation of the wilderness character of the islands and the Lake Superior shoreline is the primary goal of establishing a national park here, and that "improvements" and "developments" will be kept to an absolute minimum. . . . Attracting tourists to the area to bolster its economy is also important, but we hope that tourist accommodations will be provided mainly outside of the park boundaries, and that pressure to develop the park area with too many access roads, campsites, etc., will be resisted." Many environmental groups opposed plans for the scenic road and the lodge on Sand Island for these reasons.[71]

Gaylord Nelson and Harold Jordahl had to ensure that they maintained the support of both those who wanted economic development and those who saw the park as a mechanism for wilderness protection. Nelson recognized the challenge: "Here we must strike a careful balance and we must retain our sense of perspective. If we do not create a park, the wilderness presumably will be lost forever. If the park is created, a certain amount of development is inevitable but under wise management, the over-all effect should be beneficial." Nelson and Jordahl found the correct formula, and an array of local, regional, and national organizations endorsed the lakeshore. Nelson placed in the record of each congressional hearing a list of groups that supported the project: 37 business organizations, 17 civic organizations, 12 national organizations (including environmental groups), 16 farm organizations, 2 labor organizations, 6 regional organizations, 28 newspapers, 12 governmental agencies, and 50 conservation clubs. Nelson had convinced park supporters that the project would provide both nature protection and economic stimulation—a difficult combination to oppose. Balancing these potentially conflicting aims would be a task for the NPS to tackle once Congress approved the lakeshore.[72]

One group of people stood outside the debate about whether to value the islands for economics or wilderness. Members of the Red Cliff and Bad River bands had initially supported the lakeshore, and Gaylord Nelson's decision to approach Stewart Udall with the proposal for a national recreation area stemmed in part from the 1962 resolution passed by the Bad River Tribal Council in support of the idea. Both reservations lagged far behind the rest of the region in a variety of economic and social indicators such as income, education, housing quality, and health standards. Improving these conditions remained an essential goal of the proposal. Park planners hoped that the lakeshore would prompt coordinated resource management, celebrate Ojibwe cultural practices, and revitalize reservation economies. Federal planners had negotiated complicated leasing arrangements to address the needs of both the NPS and the Ojibwe bands. The proposal called for preferential hiring for Indians and included several measures aimed at protecting Ojibwe treaty rights and heritage. But by 1965, both bands opposed the project and lobbied to have their lands removed from the lakeshore. Why had the Indian position changed?[73]

Ojibwe support had always been contingent on securing federal assistance in their battle with the Wisconsin Conservation Department over treaty rights. Members of Bad River and Red Cliff bands sought to pit the state and federal governments against each other, reclaim their treaty rights, and establish tribal authority to manage the resources of their reservations. The debates over the creation of Apostle Islands National Lakeshore provided a venue for the Ojibwe to advance their political claims. Ojibwe attitudes toward the proposed lakeshore complicate the typical understanding of an oppositional relationship between Native Americans and the National Park Service. The Ojibwe sought to work with the NPS at some times and fought against the agency at others, depending on their own changing needs. Their ultimate success in keeping reservation land out of the lakeshore reversed a century-old pattern of Native American land loss and provided an important check on the power of the state to organize the landscape for management.[74]

Since the late nineteenth century, the growth of state conservation authority had come at the expense of Native American access to resources. When the Wisconsin Fisheries Commission sought to bring commercial and sport fishing under its control, it did so by restricting Native American fishing practices. In the late 1950s, the long-simmering conflict between the Ojibwe and the WCD erupted. The boom in outdoor recreation that swept the nation in the 1950s sent record numbers of non-Indian hunters and fishermen into the Northwoods. WCD wardens intensified the regulation of hunting and fishing in the area and once again attempted to restrict Indian activities both on and off the reservations. Conflict between Ojibwe and state officials over treaty rights heightened, with the Bad River reservation at the center of the dispute.[75]

A battle over the right to harvest wild rice sharpened the conflict. When the Wisconsin legislature passed a law in 1959 claiming title to all wild rice growing within the state and requiring a harvest license, the Indian community reacted with angry opposition. The small fee was not the point, argued the Ojibwe. It was the principle of control—who had the authority to manage this resource? "We, the Tribal Council, and the members of the Tribe, are strictly not in favor of State jurisdiction," stated council chair Albert Whitebird. In 1964, twelve members of the Bad River band deliberately flouted state laws by harvesting rice out of season and without a permit, and WCD wardens willingly arrested them. As the case moved through the courts, the Wisconsin attorney general ruled that Public Law 280—federal legislation passed in 1953 to advance the policy of termination in Wisconsin and several other states by making reservation law enforcement a state responsibility—provided grounds for state regulation of all Indian hunting, fishing, and gathering activities. The Ojibwe were losing their fight with the WCD and had scant resources to pursue the matter further.[76]

It was in this context of escalating tension over treaty rights that the Bad River Tribal Council took the unusual step of asking the federal government to assume management of a part of its reservation. Bad River leaders hoped that allegiance with the federal government would aid them in their struggle with the WCD. In the 1962 resolution asking for federal management of the area, the tribal council insisted that the "old and historic treaty rights and customs be allowed the Indians, such as: hunting, fishing, trapping, and gathering wild rice." At the first meeting of the lakeshore planning committee in June 1964, tribal representatives Fred Connors and Albert Whitebird reiterated that the band required guarantees that "their treaty rights and the interests of the tribe in wild rice" be protected. Whitebird described the situation to Gaylord Nelson, reporting that the clash with the WCD "may stalemate the cooperation on the part of the Indians, I sure would like to see this park, but if things continue, I see trouble . . . I sure don't like to see . . . the park stalemated over [the] game dispute. I hope you take necessary action if needed." If the federal government could not aid them in their fight with the WCD, Whitebird cautioned, then Indian support for the lakeshore could not be guaranteed.[77]

Nelson, Jordahl, and the other park planners did what they could. Jordahl urged the Department of the Interior to enter into the wild rice case as a friend of the court and perhaps to assist the Bad River Tribal Council in appealing the Wisconsin attorney general's decision. Nelson, too, exerted his influence. This was exactly the kind of support that the Ojibwe hoped to secure from the federal government. Despite these efforts, Department of the Interior lawyers concluded that the federal government could not extend rights that the state of Wisconsin refused to recognize. Bureau of Indian Affairs attorneys supported this stance. The state held the right to regulate hunting, fishing, and gathering on the reservations, and the Ojibwe would accrue no additional rights even if their reservations were included in the national lakeshore.[78]

When federal planners could not promise to protect treaty rights, Ojibwe withdrew their support. In 1965, the Bad River Tribal Council passed a resolution opposing the project. The resolution accused the federal government of failing to protect the band's treaty rights and labeled the lakeshore proposal "another step by the Government to acquire Indian lands and destroy Indian hunting, fishing, and gathering" rights. Concerns about treaty rights prompted a more general distrust of federal motives, and Indian support for the lakeshore eroded further. Ojibwe doubted that they would ever see the economic benefits offered by the federal planners. Red Cliff band member Idile Duffy wondered, "We have waited over 100 years and not one of the other promises have ever been fulfilled. How can you people ask us to accept your promises again?" Not all of the Ojibwe who testified opposed the bill, but most tribal leaders spoke against it. Red Cliff tribal chairman Philip Gordon called the proposal "more of the paternalistic garbage that the Federal Government has fed to the Indians for far too many years."[79]

Distrust of federal motives and the renewed hunting and fishing controversy took place within the context of rising awareness of civil and Indian rights. Disputes about treaty rights occurred not just in Wisconsin but across the country. In the 1950s and 1960s, the recognition and protection of treaty rights emerged as a core component of Indian identity. Being Indian meant having a set of reserved rights that non-Indians did not share. The insistence of treaty rights and Indian distinctiveness provided the foundation for the American Indian Movement of the late 1960s and early 1970s. While Congress held hearings on the Apostle Islands proposal, activists occupied Alcatraz Island to protest the history of federal mistreatment of Native Americans and the Indians of Taos Pueblo in New Mexico neared the successful completion of their high-profile attempt to reclaim title to sacred lands from the federal government. These identity politics helped sustain the Bad River opposition to the lakeshore, as a younger generation of politically active Ojibwe took a leading role in lobbying against the project. Reservation councils around the country and several national Indian organizations also opposed the lakeshore.[80]

In 1970, the House Subcommittee on National Parks and Recreation spent three days in contentious debate over inclusion of Indian lands in the lakeshore. Mounting Indian opposition imperiled the entire project. NPS director George Hartzog threatened to withdraw his support if Indian lands were removed from the proposal. Nelson and Jordahl tried to salvage the bill, negotiating with the tribal councils and with the National Congress of the American Indian on amendments that might win Indian support. Despite these efforts, both the Bad River and Red Cliff bands maintained their stance against the lakeshore.[81]

In the end, Indian opposition did not prevent the creation of the lakeshore, but it did change its boundaries. Wayne Aspinall, chair of the House Committee on Interior and Insular Affairs, recognized that the lakeshore stood little chance of approval without Ojibwe support. The nation's heightened concern for civil rights gave the Ojibwe cultural authority they had not possessed before. "If you get this bill to the floor with the Indians of the United States against it, you are not going to pass it. Let us just be realistic," Aspinall stated at the hearings. Instead, Aspinall favored deleting Indian lands from the proposal, and the resulting compromise did just that. All Indian lands were excluded from the lakeshore, except for two small plots on the Bayfield Peninsula. The Bad River Unit was deleted entirely and the Red Cliff Unit reduced in size to just 2,568 acres, a narrow strip along twelve miles of shoreline on the western edge of the peninsula. This mainland unit included lands within the reservation that had long been alienated from Indian ownership—the legacy of the quick sale of reservation timber to the Red Cliff Lumber Company at the turn of the century. Long Island was deleted from the proposal, too, because of its religious significance and its proximity to the Bad River reservation and its distance from the other islands. In its new form, the proposal moved ahead quickly. Congress approved the lakeshore on September 11, 1970. Two weeks later, President Richard Nixon signed the bill creating Apostle Islands National Lakeshore.[82]

After nearly a century of having their treaty rights stripped by state agencies seeking to increase their regulatory power, the Ojibwe succeeded in keeping their lands out of the lakeshore. This was a historic victory—the first time that Native Americans had successfully fought the creation of a national park on their land. The debates about the proposal had served as a venue for them to further their political claims, rather than a venue for having those claims refused. Other victories followed. In 1972, the Wisconsin Supreme Court recognized the rights of members of the Bad River and Red Cliff bands to fish off the Lake Superior shores of their reservations, assuring them a share of the lake trout previously divided between sport and commercial fishermen. Eleven years later, in a landmark ruling known as the Voigt decision, the U.S. Court of Appeals affirmed the right of the Ojibwe to hunt, fish, and gather in the forests and lakes in the territory ceded in the treaties of 1837 and 1842—both on and off reservation. The Voigt decision set the stage for the well-publicized spearfishing conflicts of the 1980s, during which Ojibwe won recognition and far broader public acceptance of the reserved rights guaranteed by the nineteenth-century land cession treaties.[83]

The Ojibwe victory also demonstrates an essential component of the federalist system. No level of government has absolute authority; different levels share power, including the authority to manage land. How much power each level of government can assert hinges on cultural norms—such as the civil rights and treaty rights movements—and on interpretations of the courts. The trend over the course of the twentieth century has been an increased role for higher levels of government at the expense of lower ones, but this trend has not been absolute. The local governments of the Chequamegon Bay used their ownership of valuable lands to negotiate for development in keeping with traditions of resource use in the islands. Nor has the trend toward increased state power been unidirectional. In the early twentieth century, tribal governments of the Chequamegon Bay faced attacks from both state and federal administrative agencies, and tribal authority diminished. In the 1960s, this pattern reversed and tribal authority grew, at the expense of the ability of the federal government to organize the landscape for recreation and nature protection.

Gaylord Nelson's challenge as the architect of Apostle Islands National Lakeshore lay in getting the different levels of government—and the competing ideas about how to value nature that each represented—to share power in a way that facilitated the management of natural resources. He did this by crafting a proposal that united two powerful motivations: economic growth and nature protection. That different constituencies might interpret the relationship between economics and wilderness in disparate ways would be a problem for the NPS managers who assumed control of the islands in 1970. The protection of nature and economic stimulation might seem to be in conflict—especially in a place like the Apostles, where economic growth had always stemmed from the extraction of resources rather than the protection of them. But tourism had become separate from other forms of economic activity, split off by the need of the state to organize the environment for easier management. This segregation helped people to envision economic uses of nature that did not compromise wilderness characteristics.

And it was as a wilderness that most people now valued the Apostle Islands. Forests had regenerated, lake trout populations had recovered, and wild nature once again shaped the islands' "natural condition." But the rewilding of the islands was not solely a natural process. Sportsmen had identified the Apostles as a destination for hunting and fishing. Scientists had valued them as an ideal location for ecological study. Politicians had recognized that protecting nature in the Apostles met social and economic goals. Resource managers had isolated the Apostles from other forms of economic activity to ensure that these values had precedence.

When Park Service officials assumed control of the Apostle Islands in 1970, they instituted a management plan designed to enhance the islands' wilderness characteristics. The twentieth-century growth in state authority gave them the power to do so and the imperative to organize a complex and changing landscape to meet managerial needs. But the older way of valuing the islands hindered this management regime. The fire scars, farm fields, and other evidence of past human use remained, threatening the islands' new value as wilderness. ✺

6

Rewilding and the Manager's Dilemma

WITH THE CREATION OF APOSTLE ISLANDS NATIONAL LAKESHORE IN 1970, the National Park Service inherited a rich and evocative landscape. The islands boasted lonely beaches, mysterious sea caves, and bays that could protect boats small and large from the powerful moods of Lake Superior. Island forests contained some of the best remnant stands of old-growth forest in the western Great Lakes. Lighthouses guarded five of the islands. Although automated beacons had replaced the keepers and their families, the romantic buildings and manicured lawns still served as among the biggest tourist attractions in the region.

Establishing the lakeshore, however, proved far easier than managing it. For fifteen years after designation, the NPS engaged in acrimonious disputes with property owners for control of the land within the park. As NPS officials resolved these conflicts and assumed conservation authority for the islands, they made a series of decisions about the development of the lakeshore that consistently elevated the protection of natural resources over other concerns. They established primitive campsites but steered away from commercially oriented developments such as scenic drives, lodges, and restaurants. They drafted a resource management plan that aimed to return the islands—or at least portions of them—to their prelogging condition. Since 1977, the Park Service has managed the Apostles as wilderness, even though formal wilderness designation did not occur until 2004.

Wilderness, in both popular conception and NPS policy, is a place without people, a place where wild nature rather than human influence shapes the land. Evident human use—especially modern Anglo-American use—necessarily degrades wilderness. This is a relatively recent perspective. Wilderness advocates of the early twentieth century had a far more inclusive view of lands influenced by humans. It was only with the growing popularity of wild places for primitive recreation and scientific study in the 1960s and 1970s that the wilderness ideal excluded traces of human activity. This has created a standard that defines and values wilderness as a place without history, an ideal that is often at odds with the wild landscapes the NPS seeks to protect.

NPS management guidelines translate this wilderness ideal into on-the-ground policies that strictly segregate nature and culture. This divide is further reinforced by the demands of the modern bureaucratic state for simplified, easily managed landscapes. Applying wilderness management to the Apostles represented the culmination of a trend that began nearly a century before: the growing authority of the state to specify with ever greater precision the kinds of activities acceptable on the land under its control. By instituting wilderness management in some places but not others, NPS officials determined which landscapes should be valued for their history and which for their wildness. These imperatives have reordered both the natural and the cultural landscapes of the islands. NPS personnel removed fish camps, summer cottages, and other evidence of human activity to create the appearance of pristine nature. They concentrated campgrounds, trails, and other facilities into previously "disturbed" locations, further reinforcing the boundary between the human and the natural. But removing the evidence does not change the past. NPS policy creates a deception—a wilderness without history.

State power and ecological succession make a potent team. They have remade the Apostle Islands into a place that looks ever more like the dehumanized wilderness ideal. Island forests have regenerated, and evidence of the wasteland that so disturbed Harlan Kelsey in 1930 is very difficult to find. But mythologizing the Apostles as a wilderness without history obscures some of the most important lessons places like this can teach. For generations, people lived, worked, and played in the Apostles, and recognizing the human imprint on the returned wilderness allows us to see the consequences of these actions.

Doing so opens new conversations about the relationship between humans and nature, conversations that break down the boundary between these seemingly dichotomous categories.

The Battle for Sand Island

Before NPS officials could take formal steps toward managing Apostle Islands National Lakeshore (AINL), they had to acquire property from landowners who had often fought against the establishment of the park. In 1970, private citizens owned over 25,000 acres of land within the lakeshore, approximately 60 percent of the 42,375 acres in the park, and the State of Wisconsin owned nearly 17,000 acres. The complicated process of land acquisition in the Apostles can be divided into three phases: the purchase from private property owners, the transfer of state lands, and the addition of Long Island to the park. With each new acquisition, the NPS consolidated its control over the islands. But each of these phases prompted NPS managers to elevate the protection of nature over other activities.

In the first planning document created for the new park in 1971, AINL officials announced their intention to purchase land as quickly as possible. This would open the islands to public use and conform to NPS policy on land acquisition. Until 1960, Congress had established most national parks out of lands already in public ownership or donated by private citizens. The creation of Cape Cod National Seashore in 1961 signaled a change in this practice. Many of the parks created after 1960 were chosen because of the recreational opportunities they provided for the densely settled regions of the East and Midwest. Creating parks in such places required the federal government to exercise the power of eminent domain to purchase or condemn privately owned lands. NPS officials strongly preferred the outright acquisition of land to the use of easements or zoning ordinances that would allow private citizens to own property within park boundaries. NPS managers worried that such privately owned parcels, known as inholdings, kept alive threats of logging, commercial development, and other inappropriate use and significantly impaired their ability to manage the parks. Complicated arrangements like inholdings ran counter to the logic of state management, which required legible land-use regimes.[1]

NPS officials began acquiring private land in the Apostles in 1972. The privately owned land within the lakeshore boundary contained 11 year-round residences, over 100 seasonal cottages, 8 rental cottages, and 25 docks. The Park Service offered all owners the chance to lease their lands back from the government for twenty-five years or for the lifetime of the owner. Some landowners sold their lands willingly, or at least without a fight. Others refused, and the NPS initiated condemnation procedures with these landowners in 1973. AINL officials soon found themselves embroiled in fifty condemnation cases involving seventy-two tracts of land.[2]

Sand Island emerged as the center of the struggle. Lying just two miles off the mainland and possessing the protected docking space of East Bay, Sand Island figured heavily in early plans for the lakeshore, making its acquisition a priority. The 1971 park master plan called for a large campsite, hiking trails, a marina, and concession facilities on the island. The same advantages and access, of course, had drawn Norwegian immigrants in the 1890s and summer residents for decades thereafter. Sand Islanders had fought against the creation of the lakeshore, lobbying at the very least for the exclusion of Sand Island from the park and often opposing the entire proposal. Several island families questioned the government's authority to take their lands in the first place and took their cases to the federal courts.[3]

The conflict between the NPS and the Westhagen family was particularly acrimonious. In 1956, the Westhagens had purchased the property that had once belonged to Norwegian farmer-fishermen Fred Hansen, and they lived on the island in the summer. The family strongly opposed the creation of the lakeshore and testified against it at every congressional hearing held on the proposal. The Westhagens refused to abide by the terms stipulated by the use-and-occupancy agreements offered by the Park Service. They wanted the right to maintain a dock, to construct a helicopter pad, to conduct their stockbrokerage business, to cut and collect firewood, to run a market garden, and to keep horses. They also wanted to rent cottages and boats and to sell gasoline from their dock. In short, the Westhagens wanted to conduct the very types of commercial activities that made NPS officials so opposed to inholdings in the first place.[4]

For more than a decade, first through negotiation and then in the courts, the Westhagens and the NPS battled for control of 112 acres on the easternmost tip of Sand Island. Park officials initially offered the Westhagens $106,375 for their property; the Westhagens demanded nearly four times this amount as well as the right to use their land as they saw fit. Negotiations quickly turned sour.

NPS buying land

"I spent the better part of five hours with Mr. Westhagen and his mother trying to find some neutral ground—to no avail," commented one federal negotiator. The case moved to the courts, culminating in a jury trial in November 1980. By this time, the NPS had increased its offer to $250,000, but the Westhagens now asked for $500,000. After the jury set the fair market value of the property at $241,500, the two parties still needed to negotiate the terms of use and occupancy. These disputes were not resolved until 1983. The NPS eventually agreed to many of the Westhagens' demands but refused to allow the construction of a helicopter pad or the renting of boats and cottages. Although NPS managers eventually conceded a number of exceptions to the ordinary conditions of use-and-occupancy agreements, they prohibited the activities most at odds with plans for the management of Sand Island.[5]

Howard "Bud" Peters, a landowner on the other side of Sand Island, posed a different problem. Unlike the Westhagens, Peters had supported the park from the start and had even served on the Citizens Committee for Apostle Islands National Lakeshore, a group that provided logistical support and local connections to federal planners throughout the 1960s. Peters believed that the lakeshore provided "the best long-range use of this land." But he did not consider the recreational use of the Apostles to be in conflict with his own plans to log Sand Island. In fact, Peters suggested that the NPS should consider logging many of the islands in the future, if the value of the timber rose. After all, economic stimulation had been a primary motivation of the park. As if to prove his point, Peters continued logging on Sand Island into the 1970s. NPS officials saw this as a significant threat to the environments they had been asked to protect.[6]

Peters owned Budvic Timbers Inc., a small logging company that had acquired 1,044 acres on Sand Island in 1962. The property had originally been owned by Frank Eha, a charter member of the West Bay Club; Peters purchased the historical Adirondack-style lodge as well as the timberland. He logged on Sand Island for two seasons in the 1960s but then ceased, to wait for better market conditions. When NPS representatives appraised his Sand Island holdings, they concluded that the timber had no commercial value because of the cost of transporting logs and equipment, and they crafted their offer accordingly. Peters disagreed with this conclusion and decided to log his property before relinquishing it. During the summer of 1973, he housed an eleven-person crew in the West Bay Club lodge, using heavy equipment such as cranes and tractors to remove high-quality yellow birch and sawlogs. Peters estimated that he would be able to take as much as three million board feet of timber from the island, despite the NPS valuation.[7]

For NPS managers, the promised economic stimulation would come not from the value of the island timber but from the value of wild nature. Tourists would pay to see wilderness, not the eroded banks, refuse, and roads left behind by logging. When AINL rangers visited the island in the fall of 1973, they found that the "road is extremely deteriorated with ruts in places 5 feet deep. . . . The mud is the consistency of wet cement, and is running into the lake in many places along the road." Other visits revealed that Peters had extended the logging roads, constructed an earth-and-stone landing to prepare logs for shipment, dredged a small stream, and dumped fuel and oil drums directly onto the ground. Peters's logging, in the eyes of NPS managers, presented a direct conflict to the goals of the lakeshore.[8]

The Park Service reacted quickly to the threat. When Peters rejected the initial offer and commenced logging in September 1973, NPS officials filed a declaration of taking in federal district court. This formal procedure expedited the normal condemnation process and provided the NPS with immediate control over the land in question. NPS managers claimed in court that the Budvic tracts were essential for "the proper preservation, development, and administration of that area for the use, benefit, and enjoyment of the people." The NPS assumed legal title of the property in November 1973 but not until after Peters had cut an estimated five hundred thousand board feet of timber. Like many of the other Sand Islanders, Peters appealed the appraised value of his property, and he did not reach a final agreement with the NPS until 1982.[9]

Recalcitrant landowners with plans for logging forced the NPS to secure a declaration of taking three more times in the next six years. In 1974, contractors logged York Island for several weeks before the NPS acquired control of the island. NPS officials acted preemptively to stop planned logging on Outer Island and on the mainland. In each case, the desire to encourage the return of wilderness characteristics motivated federal action. AINL superintendent Pat Miller explained that Outer Island "is returning to a primitive state where human sign is rapidly being obliterated by natural reproduction. . . . A new logging operation on Outer Island would set back natural reproduction and cause scenic damage that would require many years to heal." Logging threatened not only wild nature but also the value of the islands as recreational wilderness: "Since the south end of the island is popular with those Apostle Islands visitors seeking a remote, wild area, the impact of logging would be tragic." Proposed logging on the mainland created a similar threat the park's management goals. Miller explained that logging would leave "little hope for meeting our resource management objective of maintaining, even accelerating the transition from what now exists to what would be, had not modern man interfered."[10]

Landowners across the archipelago fought the NPS acquisition of their lands, although not all of the negotiations were as contentious as those on Sand Island. Of the fifty condemnation cases, a 1976 commission on just compensation resolved six, three were decided by jury trial, and the rest were settled by negotiation. But just when it seemed that the NPS had finally secured control of the islands, politics in Washington, D.C., threatened to strip this authority.[11]

The election of Ronald Reagan as president in 1980 brought revolutionary changes to federal land management. James G. Watt was named secretary of the interior, and among his most controversial ideas was the privatization of federal land. He wanted to reopen the sale of the public domain. In 1982 and 1983, Park Service land acquisitions slowed to a virtual standstill, as Watt directed the agency to reallocate the money Congress had provided for land purchases to construction and maintenance in existing parks. The NPS had completed its land acquisition program in the Apostles, but Watt and his deputies still applied the new logic of privatization: they considered selling previously acquired lands back to the original owners.[12]

The Anderson/Rice family—summer residents of Sand Island since 1935 (when they had purchased a part of Camp Stella) and owners of the Shaw/ Hill farm since 1942—approached officials in the Department of the Interior about reacquiring title to their Sand Island property. The Anderson/Rices had been forced to sell their land to the Park Service in 1981, and they sought to turn the anti-public-land ideology of the Reagan administration to their advantage. They found a willing ear in Ric Davidge, deputy assistant secretary for fish, wildlife, and parks. Davidge had previously served as the managing director of the National Inholders Association, a group that fought against what it regarded as unnecessary state regulation of private property. Davidge agreed to consider the Anderson/Rice proposal and entered into negotiations to resell or exchange portions of Sand Island.[13]

Word of the potential deal sparked a public outcry. Gaylord Nelson called the proposal "an outrageous violation of the whole principle of management of a public lakeshore." The Sierra Club threatened a lawsuit to stop any resale. The proposal, as well as other questions about the sale of public lands, seemed to confirm environmentalists' worst fears about the new administration. "We do not know if the Apostle Islands case will be the first of a wave of disposal actions, but if this sale is completed, every disgruntled person who has sold land to the National Park Service will be trooping into Washington with both hands out," explained Michael McCloskey, executive director of the Sierra Club. Opponents of the resale plan worried about the precedent such an action would set. Faced with such public opposition, Department of the Interior officials backed off from the prospect of reselling the Shaw/Hill farm.[14]

Significantly, AINL staff members were not involved in these negotiations. Watt's policies on NPS land acquisition prompted oversight hearings in 1983 and a stern reprimand by the House Committee on Interior and Insular Affairs. When pressed in aggressive questioning at the hearings to discuss the land exchange, Superintendent Miller explained that members of his staff had not participated in the discussions: "You have to understand that most of the negotiations that occurred [were] at levels above my office." The potential resale or exchange of Sand Island derived from Reagan's and Watt's ideas about the role of the federal government, not the needs of NPS officials. Land acquisition had been the central concern of AINL staff for over a decade, with the goal of unifying park management, not fracturing it further.[15]

The goal of unified management motivated the second stage of land acquisition for AINL. In 1976, the NPS acquired title to the nearly seventeen thousand acres owned by the State of Wisconsin. This included Stockton Island—the archipelago's most popular spot for camping and boating—as well as Oak and Basswood islands.[16] This transfer had its own set of complications. The NPS and the Wisconsin Department of Natural Resources (the DNR replaced the Wisconsin Conservation Department in 1967) initially planned on joint management of the islands. But in the 1971 master plan, NPS officials recommended that all of the land within the lakeshore be brought within a single jurisdiction: "[The] entire archipelago . . . under one jurisdiction and administration is deemed advisable for good management of the lakeshore." With the acquisition of private lands bogged down by contentious condemnation cases, AINL officials issued a renewed call for the transfer of state lands to the federal government in 1973. Wisconsin policy makers, however, demanded financial compensation for state-owned land, free access to the lakeshore for Wisconsin residents, continued state control of hunting and fishing, guarantees about the nature of NPS management, and other considerations.[17]

The compromise that resolved these concerns further elevated nature protection among the park's administrative priorities. Before Wisconsin officials would transfer the islands under their control, they wanted assurances that the NPS would manage the islands to preserve their "wilderness character." The NPS objected to this language, worried that since the 1970 lakeshore legislation had not used the term *wilderness* its use by the state in a formal transfer document might pose legal problems. The Park Service had at first opposed the Wilderness Act because its leaders feared a loss of autonomy in making land management decisions, and it faced this possibility with the transfer of state land to AINL. Wisconsin officials, however, insisted on the right to declare the proposed uses of the land in question; they had spent close to $400,000 to create a wilderness opportunity for their citizens, and they wanted assurances that this wilderness would endure. When the Wisconsin legislature transferred state lands to the NPS in 1976, it declared, "It is the policy of the legislature that the Apostle Islands be managed in a manner that will preserve their unique primitive and wilderness character." Legislators wanted the citizens of their state to "be assured the opportunity for wilderness, inspirational primitive and scenic experiences in the Apostle Islands into perpetuity." This was a far more aggressive stance on wilderness protection than contained in the lakeshore legislation. The State of Wisconsin's strong advocacy for wilderness set it apart from many other state governments. Most western states opposed wilderness for its apparent threat to economies dependent on resource extraction.[18]

The third phase of land acquisition further pushed the NPS toward a policy that elevated nature protection over other uses of the islands. In 1986, Congress added Long Island to the park. Long Island had been a part of the original 1965 proposal but was removed to meet Ojibwe concerns about federal management. In the early 1980s, several arguments emerged for the island's addition to the lakeshore. Long Island's proximity to the mainland meant that it had the potential for heavy recreational use. Adding the island to the lakeshore would increase visitation to the park and make it easier for administrators to acquire funding. Developing the island for tourism would, in turn, benefit the local economy. Resource protection provided a second motivation. Long Island's varied dune, wetland, and forest habitats contained the most diverse collection of plants on the archipelago. It provided a home for the piping plover, a bird on the federal endangered species list, as well as the common bittern, a bird on Wisconsin's threatened species list. The island also had cultural value for its religious significance to the Ojibwe, its lighthouse, and its historical importance in the fur trade. The economic benefits of tourism and the protection of natural and cultural resources had motivated the designation of AINL in the first place; the addition of Long Island would affirm and extend these goals.[19]

Debates over the addition of Long Island to AINL brought the goals of recreational tourism and nature protection into conflict. How could the NPS manage for both increased tourist use and protect the island environment at the same time? "This growing and presently uncontrolled access and use of Long Island by day visitors and overnight campers threatens to destroy sensitive areas of the island," worried the director of the Ashland-based Sigurd Olson Environmental Institute. "Dogs run unleashed chasing birds off their nests, trash is left behind from picnics and all-terrain vehicle tracks and campers leave their impact on the vegetation." Advocates of nature protection wanted the NPS to focus on plover habitat; those arguing for the addition of Long Island for its recreational value wanted to ensure heightened access to its berry patches and swimming spots. Could Long Island be used and protected at the same time?[20]

Mounting opposition from the Bad River reservation complicated the conflict between nature preservation and tourism. Although Long Island was not on the reservation, the island had vital religious significance to the Ojibwe, as it had provided a stopping point on the Ojibwe migration to western Lake Superior. A spokesman for the band informed Congress and the NPS that Long Island held a "sacred and holy place in the history of Ojibwa people." The Bad River Tribal Council passed a resolution opposing NPS acquisition of the island in 1985. The Ojibwe worried that NPS management would increase non-Indian visitation to the island and lead to the commercialization of a place that they considered sacred.[21]

The two families that owned land on Long Island sounded a familiar refrain about the prospect of federal condemnation of land. Both families had owned their land for generations and believed that this history should protect their interests. Archie Wilson explained, "We are not newcomers bent on profit or distruction [sic]. The land is part of our heritage and family tradition. We want nothing more than to be allowed to pass these properties on to our children and grandchildren." The landowners suggested that they could sell conservation easements to assist in plover protection and other NPS management goals.[22]

Negotiation and networking by those advocating NPS acquisition of the island, including AINL superintendent Miller, Harold Jordahl, tribal representatives, and others resolved the conflict by clearly stating the reasons for acquisition of the island. Resource protection, not recreation, would get priority in NPS management of Long Island. U.S. senator Robert W. Kasten Jr. explained the compromise and the clarified the intent of the acquisition: "All interested parties agree that the primary goal must be to protect the natural and cultural resources on Long Island. The secondary goal should be the development of human use and visitation patterns which are compatible with such protection." Clearly stating these priorities earned the support of the environmental groups and met Ojibwe concerns. Only the landowners maintained their opposition. With this agreement in place, Congress passed the boundary adjustment legislation in 1986. The Long Island compromise completed NPS land acquisition at AINL and served as an important statement that the agency had elevated the protection of resources over their use. NPS policy soon established an additional set of priorities, one that further elevated natural over cultural resources. Land acquisition was just one part of a larger process of reordering the environments of the Apostles to meet the goals of wilderness preservation.[23]

Planning for Wilderness

As land acquisition proceeded, NPS officers faced a series of planning decisions about the new lakeshore. Recreation, nature protection, and economic stimulation had motivated the creation of the park. The NPS proposed to meet these goals by developing some areas while preserving others in their "primitive state." In the early years after the creation of the park, however, the NPS consistently veered away from recreational development and toward wilderness management. This meant adapting the park to the wilderness ideal of the 1960s—an ideal that celebrated pristine environments for their ecological and recreational value. Tourism still played an important role in NPS plans, but the primitive recreation encouraged by AINL management decisions differed greatly from the type of tourist development locals had expected when they supported the creation of the park.

The 1965 lakeshore proposal called for several commercial developments, including a lodge on Sand Island, a restaurant on Rocky Island, and a thirty-mile scenic drive on the mainland flanked by hiking trails, picnic sites, and marinas. These proposals secured the support of the residents of the region—including many of those who had opposed the creation of Apostle Islands State Forest in the 1950s because of the WCD's plans for wilderness management rather than tourist development.[24]

Practical concerns prevented some of these plans. Engineers worried that the red clay soils of the Bayfield Peninsula would not support a high-volume road. The erodible, unstable soils meant the road would require costly long-term maintenance. The gullies and ravines along the route posed an additional problem: "Substantial amounts of fill would be required [to bridge the ravines]. Such filling would in itself destroy much of the scenic beauty that the proposed highway is to make available to the visitor." Last-minute changes to the park boundaries—the exclusion of Indian lands from the proposal had shortened the length of the shoreline in the mainland unit from thirty miles to twelve—also decreased the appeal of a road.[25]

There was philosophical opposition to the road as well. From the first congressional hearings on the lakeshore proposal in 1967, national environmental groups pressured the NPS to abandon developments such as the road and the Sand Island lodge. Wilderness Society representative M. Rupert Cutler testified that the Sand Island lodge conflicted with the goal of protecting the islands' natural beauty. A Sierra Club representative argued that the road would "do very serious damage to the very qualities the lakeshore is intended to preserve." The president of the National Parks Association cautioned that the road "could become the familiar monstrosity." Others worried that the road would compromise the ecological value of the lakeshore. A representative of Wisconsin's State Board for the Preservation of Scientific Areas urged NPS planners to keep the road away from the shoreline to protect "biologically unique areas." The environmental organizations recognized the potential conflict between wilderness and recreational development and pressured the NPS to prioritize the former.[26]

The lakeshore's most important proponents shared these concerns. Harold Jordahl had served as the chair of the Department of the Interior committee that had created the initial lakeshore proposal, and he subsequently played a central role in the transfer of Wisconsin land and the addition of Long Island to the park. "I have, as do you, mixed emotions about the road," Jordahl admitted to an ecologist worried about the project's environmental impact. "If I had my druthers, the peninsula would have been kept wild and natural."

Gaylord Nelson expressed similar concerns. He viewed the environmental groups as key allies and wanted to ensure their support. Nelson regarded overdevelopment as a serious threat to the lakeshore, and he "had no interest in teeming masses eating hot dogs and littering the landscape," remembered one of the senator's aides. NPS director George Hartzog also disapproved of the road, suggesting that he viewed scenic drives as "something you would swallow if that was the only way to get the legislation, but would always put it at the bottom of the list for development funding." These opinions ensured that the NPS would err on the side of underdevelopment. With engineering concerns, mounting political pressure, and new park boundaries, NPS planners decided not to build the scenic road and abandoned plans for the other commercial facilities within the park.[27]

The Rocky Island Air Haven stands as an example of the implications of the trend toward wilderness management. By the time Congress created AINL in 1970, the Nourses had run their restaurant for over twenty-five years. The 1971 master plan incorporated the Air Haven into its scheme for visitor access to the islands, calling for the restaurant to "continue to serve its famous Lake Superior fish dinners." The plan also suggested the development of a nature trail to provide a hiking experience on Rocky Island. Early communications between the Nourses and NPS staff indicated that the Air Haven had a continuing place in the lakeshore's future.[28]

As the park moved toward wilderness management, however, NPS officials determined that the commercial activities of the Air Haven no longer had a role in the park. Practical concerns were central in this decision. The restaurant did not meet public health standards, and the NPS was now responsible for bringing it up to code. AINL personnel did not want to spend their limited budget on the restaurant, so they converted it into a public shelter. In 1982, the NPS tore down the remains of the Air Haven, leaving a single building for use as ranger quarters. The commercial nature of the resort did not fit the wilderness experience that the NPS wanted to provide. Its removal reinforced the value of the park as a place for primitive recreation.[29]

The most significant decisions made by NPS officials grew out of the administrative needs of a modern, bureaucratic state. State management requires simplified, legible landscapes. The Wisconsin Conservation Department had organized the fisheries of Lake Superior for efficient management and partitioned northern Wisconsin for the same purpose. The NPS brought a similar management imperative to the landscapes of the Apostle Islands. From the earliest stages of planning, AINL rangers ordered and arranged the land under their control, specifying which kinds of activities could occur and how each area of the park should be valued. The result was a landscape classified for ecological study, recreation, and scenic beauty—a wilderness. The act of classifying, in turn, brought a management regime that further molded island landscapes to fit the wilderness ideal.

In the 1960s and 1970s, NPS leaders placed a new emphasis on land classification and zoning. Although the National Park System had grown significantly in the postwar years, the agency had faced sharp criticism from a variety of sources. The Outdoor Recreation Resources Review Commission (ORRRC) published a report in 1962 that criticized NPS management of recreational resources. Environmentalists complained that the NPS focused too much on recreational development, at the expense of nature protection. Agency planners hoped zoning would allow for more precise management of all kinds of resources—natural, cultural, and recreational. "In the master plan," one NPS official explained, "the best useful purpose for each portion of land is established. Some lands or waters are suitable and absolutely needed for intensive public use; others may accommodate only moderate use without damage and must be used cautiously, if at all." Through such planning and zoning measures, "the paradox between public use and preservation is resolved." To further this purpose, the NPS adopted a land classification system recommended by the ORRRC.[30]

Planning for Apostle Islands National Lakeshore reflected the new emphasis. In accordance with NPS policies, the 1971 master plan divided the islands into management zones. All but three of the islands were designated "primitive," which meant that they would receive no development whatsoever. Sand, Rocky, and South Twin islands were excluded from this category, ostensibly because they had the most clearly visible human impact. These islands, as well as Presque Isle Point on Stockton Island and the entire mainland unit, were designated as "natural environment," a category that permitted "trails, interpretive devices, an occasional picnic table, and other such low-key developments." The only exceptions to these two classifications were the quarry sites on Stockton and Basswood islands and the five lighthouses, all designated in the "historical and cultural" category, and small enclaves on several islands set aside for "essential public use and development"—ranger stations, campgrounds, and other facilities. More than 90 percent of the park fell into the primitive or natural environment categories.[31]

Nowhere does the master plan mention "wilderness management" or a "wilderness designation." The omission resulted in part from confusion about the statutory requirements of the National Park Service under the Wilderness Act of 1964. The act required that the Department of the Interior evaluate roadless areas under its jurisdiction for wilderness suitability. It remained unclear, however, whether this stipulation applied to lands acquired after 1964. The language of classification had vital implications; special management guidelines applied to areas formally recognized as designated or potential wilderness.[32]

Gaylord Nelson and other wilderness advocates insisted that the NPS move forward with plans to designate wilderness in the Apostles. During the first hearings on the lakeshore proposal in 1967, Wilderness Society spokesman M. Rupert Cutler urged Congress to designate the islands as a part of the National Wilderness Preservation System: "Such action would be in line with the bill's objective, namely, to preserve this archipelago as an unspoiled area of great natural beauty." Others offered similar testimony. When Congress created the lakeshore without the wilderness designation, Nelson pressed NPS leaders to move in this direction. "The legislative history of the Lakeshore's Organic Act makes clear Congress's intent to have this unit of the NPS managed as a wilderness park," he explained to one agency official in 1975. "In my judgment many of the islands meet and exceed the criteria established in the 1964 Wilderness Act for designation as wilderness." The NPS had not pursued wilderness designation in the five years since the creation of the park, and Nelson wanted to push the process forward.[33]

Park Service leaders had a different analysis of their responsibilities under the Wilderness Act. Many NPS officials regarded the Wilderness Act as a threat to their ability to manage lands as they saw fit. In addition, they did not necessarily see the construction and development goals of Mission 66 as compatible with the wilderness movement's definition of the term. The Wilderness Act required the NPS to survey its holdings within ten years to determine which areas qualified for designation. Many of these studies occurred well past the ten-year deadline, or never occurred at all. When NPS planners did complete these studies, they often excluded a great deal of wilderness-qualifying lands. The lukewarm support from NPS leaders guaranteed that the formal wilderness study would not take place at AINL for another three decades.[34]

Although NPS officials refused Nelson's demand for formal wilderness designation in the Apostles, NPS policies stipulated that, in the interim, the islands be treated as wilderness. The lakeshore's second management document, published in 1977, placed the vast majority of the park within a Wilderness Study Subzone. Identifying the islands as a potential wilderness obligated NPS officials to manage the islands in a way that preserved their wilderness character. The 1978 NPS *Management Policies* manual directed that areas considered for wilderness study "will be protected from activities which would endanger or alter their natural, primitive character until administrative study or the legislative process determine their suitability for wilderness designation." This meant de facto wilderness management in the vast majority of the lakeshore. Small parcels of land were placed in a Development Zone (a mainland administrative area and campgrounds on Rocky and Stockton islands) or a Historic Zone (the quarries and lighthouses). Lands still the subject of condemnation proceedings and not yet under NPS control were labeled Special Use Zones. Fully 97 percent of the park fell into the category of potential wilderness. The goal of this policy was to protect areas that might be designated as wilderness from potential development and also to provide management guidance during the decades-long process of wilderness designation. The decision to manage the lakeshore in this way committed the NPS to a management paradigm that hastened the rewilding of the islands.[35]

A wilderness ideal particular to the 1960s and 1970s informed these land classification decisions. Wilderness advocates of the early twentieth century fought for the preservation of places unsullied by an increasingly modern consumer culture. Wilderness, they believed, should be reserved for those with the skills and enthusiasm to enjoy it. Consumer society—symbolized by tourists and their gadgets—represented a greater threat than extractive industries like mining or logging. Aldo Leopold stated just this perspective in 1925: "Generally speaking, it is not timber, and certainly not agriculture, which is causing the decimation of wild areas, but rather the desire to attract tourists." Some of Leopold's early writings make quite clear that activities like logging and grazing were not incompatible with his proposals for wilderness protection. Leopold recognized, as well, that wilderness areas in long-settled regions like the northern Great Lakes would inevitably bear the mark of human activity. This did not stop him or his colleagues from calling for the protection of such places as wilderness.[36]

But wilderness advocacy and the wilderness ideal underwent a subtle shift in the years after World War II. As wilderness became an ever more popular destination—in part because of the success of wilderness activism—the wilderness ideal shifted to one that valued pristine nature, nature untouched by the human hand. The increasing numbers of people visiting wild areas ensured that even woodcraft—wilderness survival skills such as cutting firewood and building lean-tos—would cause unacceptable damage. Instead, wilderness users and advocates embraced an ethic of "Leave No Trace," with its high-tech camping gear, as a way to mitigate the potential damage caused by wilderness recreation. Wilderness became a haven for a brand of outdoor recreation fueled by consumer culture, not a retreat from it. As this type of outdoor recreation became more popular, the wilderness ideal that emerged in the 1960s became more rigid in its exclusion of signs of human activity.[37]

The creation of Apostle Islands National Lakeshore—which tied the goal of nature protection to economic stimulation and outdoor recreation—had been informed by this new wilderness ideal, not by the antimodern social critique of Leopold and other early wilderness advocates. A guidebook for the Apostle Islands and the Bayfield Peninsula published a few years after the creation of the park embraced the new ethic: "The Apostle Islands are undoubtedly an exceptional natural area that deserves your attention and respect. Use them and enjoy them, but remember that their charm is a fragile beauty, so please do nothing that might diminish their romantic appeal or disturb their natural conditions." The guidebook authors intended these words for visitors to the Apostles, but NPS officials used the same philosophy as they planned the new lakeshore.[38]

Changing NPS resource management goals reinforced the postwar wilderness ideal. As the environmental movement gained strength, the NPS faced criticism for its focus on recreation and its management of natural resources. One result of this criticism was the creation of the Leopold Committee in 1962, a panel of distinguished scientists chaired by A. Starker Leopold and charged with evaluating wildlife management in the parks. The committee lambasted the NPS for its lack of attention to ecological science and nature preservation. It suggested a new direction for NPS management: "As a primary goal, we would recommend that the biotic associations within each park be maintained, or where necessary recreated, as nearly as possible in the condition that prevailed when the area was first visited by the white man. A national park should represent a vignette of primitive America." The committee urged the NPS to move away from its focus on recreation and to adopt a more "natural" approach to management: "Above all other policies, the maintenance of naturalness should prevail." Within two months of publication, Secretary of the Interior Stewart Udall declared the Leopold Report's findings official NPS policy.[39]

The Leopold Report coincided with an emerging focus within the agency on the restoration of wilderness characteristics within the parks. Although many NPS officials viewed the Wilderness Act as an unwelcome intrusion on their management authority, they continued to regard the protection of the wilderness itself as a priority—so long as they could determine which areas qualified for this status. After all, the NPS—alone among federal land management agencies—had the mandate to preserve land "unimpaired for the enjoyment of future generations." Wilderness restoration became an important part of the agency's approach to meeting the terms of this mandate. Associate Director Eivind Scoyen explained in 1961 that the NPS definition of wilderness "recognizes that natural processes, in time, can restore to wilderness, areas previously abused and impaired." He cited examples from around the country to underscore the ability of the NPS to manage for this goal, among them King's Canyon, Big Bend, Great Smoky Mountains, and Shenandoah national parks. NPS director George Hartzog agreed: "Today's traveler to [Shenandoah and Great Smoky Mountains] sees little evidence of their harsh past. Tomorrow's visitor will have a keen reminder of the unbelievably rich and varied eastern hardwood forests that once stood as a wilderness barrier to the seaboard colonists." Part of the agency's resistance to the Wilderness Act stemmed from the belief of many NPS officials that existing wilderness management procedures had proven quite effective. The embrace of the potential for restoration, in particular, distinguished the NPS from other federal land management agencies, which were often hostile to this possibility. There was thus a strong record of restoration and an emerging sense within the NPS that places like the Apostle Islands should be managed to restore their wilderness characteristics.[40]

The staff at AINL translated these servicewide concerns for wilderness, recreation, and nature protection into concrete resource management plans. NPS guidelines for natural zones—the vast majority of the lakeshore—called for the restoration of ecological processes altered by humans. For the Apostles, this meant a goal of establishing prelogging environmental conditions. "The National Park Service believes that it is important for the Park visitor to have some insight as to how the islands looked prior to the logging era," explained Superintendent Miller. This policy put the lakeshore in line with the suggestions of the Leopold Report and reinforced the decision to manage the islands as wilderness. Miller summarized the lakeshore's goals in 1977: "We feel that we can conserve the islands' historic and cultural resources, make the islands available and accessible to the visiting public, and manage the natural resources in such a manner as to preserve—in some cases even reestablish—their wilderness character."[41]

To help meet these goals, Miller placed a premium on gathering information about the environments of the new park. He hired contractors to perform ecological assessments and inventories and added ecologist Robert Brander to the park staff. Miller and Brander wanted ecological research to provide a baseline with which they could measure the status of island environments against historical conditions. As Brander explained to one prospective researcher, "this means that we must know a great deal about the history of disturbances, natural and man-caused, that have caused the system to deviate from the path it was on in the mid-1800's." Over the next twenty years, the park sponsored dozens of studies on such topics as vegetation ecology, wildlife habits, dune formation patterns, the impact of deer, and fire history. By the late 1970s, the park hosted an annual research conference to share and publicize the results of these studies. Ecological value had contributed to the appeal of the islands as a potential park, and the prioritization of research reinforced this value.[42]

The wilderness ideal and the focus on primitive America also informed the park's recreational management plans. The park's 1971 master plan and other management documents called for campgrounds and trails at various points around the archipelago. Little Sand Bay, in the mainland unit, would house a visitor center, marina, and small concession station, but no overnight accommodations. On Stockton Island—a destination for campers and boaters since 1956—AINL managers planned large campsites at Presque Isle Bay and Quarry Bay. Sand Island would also receive two campgrounds, one designed especially for large groups. The campgrounds would be equipped with picnic tables, fire grates, and vault toilets. NPS officials had few plans for the other islands. They installed "primitive campsites . . . for those wishing a primitive camping experience." The desire to protect the wilderness character of the islands motivated these plans. "The wild beauty and appeal of the marshes and the remote beach areas will be lost with over-development," explained the master plan. By concentrating campgrounds in a few places and leaving the rest of the lakeshore with minimal facilities, NPS planners hoped to structure the lakeshore in a way that both maximized the wilderness experience for visitors and observed the management demands of legibility.[43]

Managing a Rewilding Landscape

Superintendent Miller's goal of reestablishing "wilderness character" reveals the central paradox of the politics and management of wilderness. If wilderness meant pristine nature, then what exactly did it mean to reestablish wilderness? The rewilding landscapes of the Apostles made this a particularly difficult question to answer. In some places, the human impacts were easy to see—at the quarries, for example, or where summer homes and fishermen's cabins still stood. Human influence elsewhere was more subtle but no less profound. The decisions of lumberjacks, fishermen, farmers, and state conservation managers had shaped the island environments, and their legacy remained in the clearings that once housed logging camps or hayfields and in the composition of island forests. NPS officials found in the rewilding islands a landscape ill suited to bureaucratic state management. They wanted legible landscapes with strict boundaries that separated island landscapes by use and value. NPS personnel accomplished this by segregating natural and cultural resources. They tried to make island environments conform to the dehumanized wilderness ideal, disguising or removing evidence of the islands' human past to create the appearance of pristine nature. The American wilderness ideal—and especially the articulation of this ideal in NPS policy—segregated nature and culture, wilderness and history.

The Wilderness Act of 1964 defines wilderness as a place where "the earth and its community of life are untrammeled by man, where man himself is a visitor who does not remain." The act further stipulates that wilderness should retain "its primeval natural character and influence, without permanent improvements or human habitation." The rewilding environments of the islands, with their fishing shacks, logging camps, and second-growth forests, might seem poor candidates for wilderness. Early debates over wilderness classification focused on what it meant for a place to be "untrammeled." A number of industry groups, as well as the U.S. Forest Service, argued for the strictest possible interpretation of this term as a way to limit the number of acres that might qualify for designation. They advanced what became known as the "purity" standard, arguing that only pristine lands could qualify for wilderness designation.[44]

Wilderness advocates demanded a looser interpretation. The 1964 legislation specified that wilderness included land "which generally *appears* to have been affected primarily by the forces of nature, with the imprint of man's work *substantially* unnoticeable." This language, environmentalists argued, provided room for land affected by human actions, and the 1964 act had designated two eastern wilderness areas with a history of rewilding. Congress reiterated the potential place for history in wilderness when it passed the Eastern Wilderness Areas Act of 1975. By designating sixteen wilderness areas east of the Mississippi River, the law affirmed the less restrictive definition and underscored the need to identify and protect places where wilderness characteristics had returned after disruptive human use. This had an important consequence: it elevated the importance of appearance over the history of use in determinations of wilderness designation. It also allowed the assignment of wilderness value to places that would become more wild in the future, even if they might be less wild in the present. The Apostles more easily qualified for wilderness designation under this broader definition.[45]

In 1977, most of the islands were placed in a Wilderness Study Subzone. NPS policy required the agency to manage areas like this to preserve their wilderness character and even to take active steps to restore wilderness. These requirements applied, in particular, to areas with long histories of human use. The 1975 edition of the Park Service's *Management Policies* provided guidance for the administration of areas with evidence of logging, grazing, and farming: "Where such uses have impaired wilderness qualities, management will be directed toward restoration of wilderness character." Later versions of the policy manual used more bureaucratic language, employing the term "nonconforming conditions" to refer to evidence of past human use: "The National Park Service will seek to remove from potential wilderness areas the temporary, non-conforming conditions that preclude wilderness designation." Many NPS officials have read this as a requirement that they remove evidence of history to encourage the appearance of wilderness unsullied by humans.[46]

The agency's tradition of protecting and restoring wilderness has thus had an important and ironic consequence for the management of rewilding landscapes: the oft-held view that history intrudes on the ecological integrity and significance

of places valued for their natural characteristics. This is particularly true in designated wilderness areas. The NPS has a long record of removing cultural resources
from natural areas in the name of nature protection. Parks as widely dispersed as
Shenandoah National Park in Virginia, Point Reyes National Seashore in California, and Sleeping Bear Dunes National Lakeshore in Michigan have all followed
this course. In many cases, NPS officials have used wilderness status as a mandate
to remove shelters, cabins, or other artifacts without regard for their significance
as historical resources. Or, they have simply allowed historical resources to fall
into such disrepair that they are removed as safety hazards. In managing for a
wilderness ideal that excludes humans, the NPS has removed evidence of human
history from wilderness areas.[47]

Shifting definitions of wilderness and the bureaucratic language of nonconforming conditions might seem abstract. But as in other wild places around
the country, these concepts had on-the-ground consequences for the Apostle
Islands. The wilderness ideal that emerged in the 1960s became embedded in
NPS management policies. As NPS personnel applied guidelines designed to
follow the twin imperatives of legibility and a dehumanized wilderness ideal,
they altered island landscapes. By confining recreational developments to small
areas of the park and removing nonconforming conditions, they created the
appearance of pristine wilderness.[48]

When the NPS assumed control of the Apostle Islands, it inherited almost
two hundred structures—net reels, ruined logging camps, summer cottages,
and other remnants of more than a century of human use. Under wilderness
management, these structures became nonconforming conditions. Property
owners retained use-and-occupancy rights in some of these buildings, but
maintenance crews razed many of the structures controlled by the NPS. The
agency removed eleven buildings from Rocky Island in 1975 and most of the
buildings that had once made up the Troller's Home Resort on South Twin
Island in 1977. The Rocky Island Air Haven followed in 1982. Dozens of buildings on other islands and the mainland received the same treatment. AINL staff
seeded most of these sites with native plants. One AINL official explained the
policy toward old cabins and other structures: "[The] National Park Service
will remove them and allow the natural vegetation to return. . . . The plans of
Apostle Islands National Lakeshore are to maintain the area in a near natural
state." Tearing down a fishing shack, planting native vegetation, and installing a rustic campsite enhanced the wilderness experience for visitors. Campers

6.1 and 6.2 In 2007, the NPS removed the Visitor Center from South Twin Island and planted native vegetation in its place. The visitor center had once been the Troller's Home Resort, a cabin rental service that catered to sport fishermen in the 1940s. The boardwalk that remains ensures that today's visitors do not trample the fragile dune vegetation, a testament to the need for a continued human role in protecting island environments. Courtesy of the National Park Service.

could stay on the islands, camp in clearings created by farmers and fishermen, but believe that they were exploring pristine nature.[49]

The removal of nonconforming conditions both supported the wilderness ideal and met the demands of legibility. The NPS specified how a wilderness should look and feel so that wilderness management could be consistent across federal lands, no matter the local conditions. A legible landscape like wilderness is easier to manage than messy, illegible reality, where every individual landscape is the product of an intricate blend of natural and cultural history that necessarily varies by site. Indeed, NPS policy specifies that the agency "will seek to achieve consistency in wilderness management objectives, techniques, and practices on both a servicewide and an interagency basis." The demand for simplified management motivated federal acquisition of the Apostles as well as the subsequent decisions about how to administer them. First by classifying lands as potential wilderness, and then by managing to ensure that those lands met a statutory definition, state authority played an essential role in the rewilding of the islands. Wilderness was at once a motivation for state management as well as an artifact of it.[50]

The NPS does protect and interpret history at AINL, and it does so well. The lighthouses remain showpieces. Visitors tour the buildings, climb the towers, play croquet on the lawns, and imagine the lonely lives of the keepers. In 2003, the NPS completed a comprehensive renovation of the Raspberry Island lighthouse, which serves as the center of the park's interpretive efforts. Restoration work is planned for several other light stations. The NPS has restored the Hokenson fishery, on the mainland at Little Sand Bay, to represent the family-managed fishing operations that persisted for much of the twentieth century. At Manitou Island, the NPS interprets the lives of poor, itinerant fishermen. AINL staff are developing a plan to manage and interpret the Hansen home on Sand Island as well. At these sites, visitors learn about an era when resource extraction drove the island economy. The NPS also provides information for visitors curious about the quarries, farms, and logging camps.[51]

The park's management of historical resources, however, reinforces the segregation of nature and culture. The interpretation of history is confined to small, isolated enclaves—the light stations and the fish camps—designated specifically for the management of cultural resources. This segregation occurred immediately after the creation of the park. The 1971 master plan classified the lighthouses and quarry sites as Historic and Cultural Zones, and this division

6.3 and 6.4 The abandoned cook shack and rusting trucks at the Lullabye Lumber Company camp on Outer Island, photographed in the late 1970s, became "nonconforming conditions" when the NPS began managing the Apostles as wilderness. The cook shack will molder into the ground, but the trucks will remain as evidence of the human role in creating today's Outer Island wilderness landscape. Courtesy of the National Park Service.

has persisted. Historical sites that meet the criteria for listing on the National Register of Historic Places typically—although not necessarily—qualify for continued preservation within a wilderness area; those that do not are classified as nonconforming conditions and targeted for removal. The Apostle

Islands have several sites on the national register: the lighthouse complexes, the Basswood Island quarry, the fish camps on Rocky Island, the Sevona cabin and Shaw farm on Sand Island, and the Hokenson fishing dock on the mainland. Of these, only the Basswood Island quarry lies within the potential wilderness area mapped out in 1977. None falls within today's designated wilderness area. NPS managers zoned the park for simpler management, strictly dividing the park's historical and natural resources.[52]

The segregation of natural and cultural resources leads to the concentration of camping and visitor facilities in areas with past human use. The NPS located campgrounds, hiking trails, and other facilities in previously "disturbed" areas. For example, planners typically avoided creating beachside campsites because of the potential damage to fragile dune vegetation. "The one campsite which was established on the beach was located because of previous use patterns which did make it a disturbed site already," explained Superintendent Miller. Modern campgrounds inhabit old logging camps on Oak Island and at Stockton Island's Quarry Bay, several Rocky Island fish camps, and the site of Sand Island fisherman-farmer Herman Johnson's home. In many cases, the NPS removed existing buildings to create the needed space. On Sand, Rocky, South Twin, and Stockton islands, old fishing cabins or summer homes became visitor contact stations or housing for park employees. Logging roads and railroad grades became hiking trails. By channeling modern visitor activity to previously used locations, the NPS maintained the boundary between the human and the natural.[53]

In many ways, the NPS has simply continued a tradition of reusing the most accessible and resource-rich locations. For example, today's group campsite at the Oak Island sandspit inhabits a clearing with a history of use as deep as any spot in the islands. Benjamin Armstrong established a homestead at the spot in the mid-1850s, the first in the islands other than Madeline. Armstrong was followed at the Oak Island sandspit by the first known logging operation in the islands (1865–71), William Knight and James Chapman's fuelwood station (1870s), and the logging camps of R. D. Pike (early 1900s) and the John Schroeder Logging Company (1919–28). In 1909 and 1910, several construction companies excavated sand. For twenty-five years in the early twentieth century, a reclusive fisherman and moonshine distiller named Martin Kane lived there too. Little remains to indicate this remarkably diverse history. If one knows where to look, the berms and depressions left by old buildings and barns are

6.5 This 1990 photograph of the National Park Service dock at Stockton Island's Presque Isle Bay demonstrates the high level of boat traffic experienced in some parts of the park. Due to this heavy traffic, the area remains outside of the designated wilderness area. Courtesy of the National Park Service.

still visible. A few rusting artifacts lie scattered in the resurgent woods. There is little in the way of active interpretation or protection of the site, and few visitors recognize the rich history that surrounds them.[54]

But removing or hiding the evidence does not change the past. Forests have regenerated after logging followed by fire, and the dates and methods of logging have shaped the composition of the modern forest. "Many of the existing forest associations are sere stages of secondary succession, created by temporal differences of logging disturbance, and further influenced by soil variations," succinctly concludes one study. The lighthouses still guard some of the most valuable old-growth forests in the western Great Lakes, complicating and enriching the forest mosaic. The lake trout that sport fishermen chase among the islands trace their ancestry to stocked fish released after fisheries managers brought the sea lamprey under control.[55]

Even the islands' wildness derives in part from deliberate human choice. The Norings, Hills, and other Sand Island families made choices to leave their homes, to let the forests reclaim their farms and fields. When the State of Wisconsin first adopted its acquisition policy for Stockton Island, state officials considered harvesting the timber on the island to help pay the purchase cost; they chose, instead, to manage it as a wilderness. When NPS planners put together their initial proposal in 1965, they included a section titled "Alternatives." In it, they explained what they expected would transpire in the islands without federal action: "In the absence of a National Lakeshore, many of the amenities in this region will eventually become private developments. Although they may be orderly and well-planned, the history for comparable parts of the Great Lakes region provides ample evidence to the contrary." Creating the lakeshore ensured that the islands would become a wilderness.[56]

Of course, the rewilding of the islands is not solely an artifact of human history and NPS policy. Few who visit the islands today doubt their wildness. Parts of the archipelago rarely receive human visitors, protected by impenetrable forests and the threat of a Lake Superior storm. More than one hundred years have passed since the last quarrying, more than sixty years since the last farming, more than thirty years since the last logging. There has been little or no active management of the places where these activities once occurred. The Apostles are untrammeled, uncontrolled, and wild. Traces of the logging and farming of the past are getting harder to find. Each year the forest creeps farther into the old fields, the undergrowth buries the ruined houses still deeper, and Lake Superior carries away the remnants of another dock. The islands' human past is being obscured by the power of wild nature as well as by the modern wilderness ideal.

Wilderness has brought many benefits to the Apostle Islands and the Chequamegon Bay region. The island environments are diverse, healthy, and thriving. Park biologists conduct effective programs to monitor exotic species and to protect the archipelago's threatened plants and animals and its vulnerable bogs and sandscapes. Visitors enjoy the combination of Bayfield's rustic charm and the islands' rugged beauty. Hikers, boaters, and kayakers find in the islands the peace and spirituality they often seek in wilderness areas. The national lakeshore has been a boon to the local economy. Tourism has provided a far more stable economic base than did the boom-and-bust extractive industries like logging, quarrying, and fishing.

6.6 Kayaking has grown in popularity since the 1980s, and has become one of the most desirable ways to experience the island wilderness. These kayakers enjoy smooth paddling off the shore of Sand Island. Photograph by William Cronon.

At the same time, wilderness management has changed, in fundamental ways, the interactions that people can have with island environments. It has severed the rich connections between islanders and their homes, particularly on Sand and Rocky islands. These changes have been equally profound for those without such historical ties to the islands. The NPS now delineates what kind of experiences we can have in the islands—determining where we go to find the solitude of wilderness or the insights of history. Opportunities for wilderness recreation have come at the expense of other activities based on such amenities as lodges, restaurants, and scenic roads. Without doubt, many people far prefer the modern wilderness landscapes to what might have been had the park never been created or had the NPS pursued its initial plans for more commercial development. But wilderness management has prescribed our interactions with island environments and has led to their use in a far more restrictive way than had been the case in an earlier era. It has created the appearance of unfettered wild nature in the islands and encouraged us to value the islands precisely because they have no apparent human history.

Clearings in the Wilderness

There are places in the Apostles that symbolize both the dilemma of rewilding and the potential for helping us rethink the relationships between wilderness and history. Early NPS surveys identified twenty-eight forest clearings, ranging in size from one to twenty acres, where logging, farming, or some other activity had left an opening in the woods. These clearings contained historical resources, but also exotic species—themselves the product of the islands' history, but in some cases threats to the health of island ecosystems. These places were at once natural and cultural landscapes, and constantly changing ones at that.

Park Service officials had to decide if these clearings would be preserved for their historical and interpretive value, actively reforested, or left alone. Maintaining the clearings risked compromising a central goal of natural resource management. Park ecologist Robert Brander explained the dilemma in 1981: "It will be impossible to achieve the managerial objective of returning forest vegetation to its pristine aspect because many historically important cultural sites will be maintained in their current unnatural state. Evidence of Man's exploitation of the Apostle Islands will abound." In addition, NPS ecologists expected that maintaining the clearings would benefit the island deer populations, which would in turn retard their ability to regenerate pine, hemlock, and other vegetation sensitive to deer browse.[57]

At the opposite end of the management spectrum, NPS planners considered removing "cultural vegetation" such as apple orchards or ornamental plants—species not native to the islands—and actively restoring the clearings with native plants. They recognized, however, that such features as soil, topography, and accessibility to landing sites made these locations "attractive habitats for humans in the past—for the same reasons they remain attractive today" as potential campgrounds and as interpretive sites. The Oak Island sandspit proves the truth of this statement. Reforestation of the island clearings would mean the further concentration of visitor use in otherwise "disturbed" areas. This meant a greater threat to the park's cultural resources.[58]

Ultimately, lakeshore officials decided on a middle path, proposing as their preferred alternative the management of a few clearings for their cultural value while allowing the forest to reclaim the rest: "[It] may not be desirable to manage or to keep clear all of these sites, however, in the interest of preserving the cultural resources of the lakeshore, it maybe desirable to retain a few as open spaces rather then let the forest displace them." A lack of funds, labor, and inclination ensured that this has not happened. The historical significance of the clearings has suffered from the relatively lower priority assigned to cultural resources within the NPS management structure. Other than the occasional vegetation removal at some of the quarries in the 1970s, the NPS has not maintained any of the clearings. The only exceptions to this rule reiterate the segregation of nature and culture: campgrounds needed as recreational facilities and lighthouses managed as explicitly historical landscapes. Today, only the clearings at one or two old farmsteads on Basswood and Sand islands can still be easily identified.[59]

Exotic species presented a different problem, one that underscores the necessity of a continuing human role in the maintenance of wild and healthy island environments. Particularly aggressive invaders threaten the ecological and evolutionary integrity of the lakeshore; they can wipe out local species and endanger entire ecosystems. Purple loosestrife, for example, has no natural predators and can quickly take over wetland habitats, affecting the abundance of the insects that pollinate native plants. AINL personnel have for years tried to control a loosestrife infestation on Long Island. Spotted knapweed has been found on sandscapes on several of the islands and on the mainland. Garlic mustard, one of the most aggressive invasives, also threatens to disrupt park ecosystems. In the designated wilderness at Shenandoah National Park, garlic mustard is so widespread that it cannot be treated or even monitored. The plant has been seen on the Bayfield Peninsula, although not yet within the boundaries of AINL. The park's mainland unit remains vulnerable because the roads and old railroad grades that cross it provide a vector for the spread of exotics. AINL staff remain on the lookout for signs of this dangerous plant. Despite these threats and its long history of logging, farming, and fire, the lakeshore ranks as among the "cleanest" public lands in the Great Lakes, with a remarkably low number of exotic species. This raises the stakes for efforts to control those that do exist.[60]

Exotic species are not new to the Apostles. The introduction of new species served as one of the earliest and most lasting changes wrought by human use of the islands. The farmers on Basswood, Michigan, Oak, and Sand islands introduced crop plants and orchard trees. The cattle released on Stockton Island to provide food for lumberjacks surely contributed to the spread of forage plants. When Harlan Kelsey visited Oak Island in 1930—to gather evidence for the

6.7 The National Park Service has removed many buildings from the islands to foster their appearance as a wilderness. Many structures remain, however, including this outhouse on Otter Island. There is no information to indicate the history of sites like this; visitors discover it for themselves. Photograph by James Feldman.

report that seemed to foreclose any chance of creating a national park in the Apostles—he reported walking through a field filled with "Timothy 4–5 ft. high, Red Clover and Redtop grass 3–4 ft. high and White Clover 2 ft. high." Exotic species all, they were likely introduced to feed the horses and cattle that helped clear the island of its timber.[61]

Most of the exotic species in the park pose no threat whatsoever. One 1993 survey found 160 exotic species, or 21 percent of all recorded plants. Only two—purple loosestrife and spotted knapweed—are considered "very threatening," while fifteen others are considered "moderately threatening." Predictably, the areas of the park with the most extensive human history have the most exotics: the mainland unit and Sand, Michigan, Raspberry, and Rocky islands. Sheep sorrel, orange hawkweed, Canada bluegrass, oxeye daisy, and white clover are the most common. Most of these plants inhabit the cultural landscapes of the lighthouse clearings, cabins, and farm fields—exotic they might be, but these plants are also historical. Only experts will recognize some of them as nonnative. The periwinkles that line the trail to the Sand Island lighthouse—escapees from a long-ago garden—seem to most visitors like nothing more than pretty wildflowers. These plants do not threaten to disrupt native ecosystems—they are exotic species but not invasive ones, and they are likely never to be eradicated. They have become native, or are in the process of becoming so. They provide further evidence of the continuing presence of human history in the wilderness.[62]

One might argue that the history of human use tarnishes the wilderness, that the Apostles would have been more valuable had they never been logged and farmed. Certainly, the old-growth stands on Outer, Raspberry, and elsewhere are among the park's most prized and important ecosystems. And it remains vitally important to protect island ecosystems from destructive invasive species like purple loosestrife or garlic mustard. But the relative value of more- and less-pristine landscapes is beside the point. The islands *were* logged and farmed. This history cannot be changed, despite the attempts of NPS managers to create the appearance of pristine wilderness. Devaluing wild places because of their human pasts risks falling into the paradox of wilderness that lies at the center of the wilderness debates.

Recognizing the history embedded in the island environments does not detract from their value. Rather, it deepens and enriches this value. The Apostle Islands should be treasured as a wild place, and particularly as a rewilding place.

Doing so will let us see in such places the consequences of human interactions with the world that surrounds us. As we rethink the wilderness idea—and the wilderness debates of the past twenty years indicate that we are doing just this—we also need to rethink the way that we manage wild places with human pasts. The forest clearings of the Apostles provide an opportunity to do so. They provide examples of how nature and history, working together, created a treasured wild place. ✒

Epilogue

READING LEGIBLE LANDSCAPES

IN NOVEMBER 2004, CONGRESS DESIGNATED NEARLY 80 PERCENT OF Apostle Islands National Lakeshore as the Gaylord Nelson Wilderness. The name of the new wilderness area recognized Nelson's crucial role in the establishment of the lakeshore and the protection of the islands' environments. Congress reiterated the preeminent ecological and recreational value of the islands—designation of wilderness is reserved for the nation's most cherished environments. The challenge for the NPS became one of how to manage this landscape in a way that maximized its value as both a wild and historical landscape—as a storied wilderness.

In 2001, NPS planners initiated a wilderness suitability study for Apostle Islands National Lakeshore. The importance of outdoor recreation resurfaced in decisions about where to draw boundaries of the potential wilderness. NPS planners agreed not to consider wilderness designation on Lake Superior itself or near any of the public docks that provide access to the islands. The water between the islands lies outside of the boundaries of AINL; the State of Wisconsin still holds this jurisdiction. Although the NPS does own the surface water one-quarter mile from the island shorelines, planners decided that managing this narrow stretch of water as wilderness was not practical. NPS planners likened the docks to mainland parking lots and excluded them from consideration. These decisions reflected the history of the islands as a destination for outdoor recreation, whether people traveled there by motor, sail, or kayak.[1]

The demands of legibility, too, determined prospective boundaries. NPS administrators wanted clearly identified lines between wilderness and nonwilderness. AINL superintendent Bob Krumenaker explained that "boundaries had to be defensible both on the map and findable on the ground." The lighthouses and their adjoining cultural landscapes, the administrative areas on several islands, and the interpretive fish camp on Manitou Island were excluded from wilderness study. The environmental impact statement explained that the fish camp "is a major visitor attraction, which under NPS policies should not be recommended for wilderness designation. The area is being managed to preserve human activities." Planners also removed two important Sand Island sites from wilderness consideration: the Shaw/Hill farmstead and the West Bay Club. The Shaw/Hill site contained many historical structures, and the Anderson/Rice family maintained a lifetime lease on the property that would keep the site out of NPS control for several decades at least. As for the West Bay Club, the NPS declared it "clearly a sign of past human activity." By excluding these areas from consideration, NPS officials gave the zoning decisions of the previous thirty years the force of law. They further specified which areas of the park would be valued for history and which for wilderness.[2]

The NPS study team conducted the wilderness suitability study in the shadow of ongoing servicewide debates about wilderness management. Park Service leaders recognized that their agency's initial hesitance about the Wilderness Act had translated into years of apathy and poor leadership in wilderness management. The agency had failed to respond to challenges posed by issues like invasive species, changing fire regimes, and the management of cultural resources in wilderness. A series of high-profile task forces and management groups attempted to resolve these problems, publishing policy papers to help guide land managers. In 2002, the National Wilderness Steering Committee specifically addressed the place of cultural resources in designated wilderness areas: "A landscape can have hundreds of prehistoric and historic archeological sites on it and still appear to have been affected primarily by the forces of nature. Even a maintained historic structure could be substantially unnoticeable if it were surrounded by many acres of land that did not contain other structures." Laws like the Wilderness Act and the National Historic Preservation Act did not give priority to either natural or cultural resources. The NPS was obligated to meet the regulatory demands of both laws, simultaneously. The problem, the steering committee believed, lay in the way that individual managers had interpreted NPS policies: "[Not] all wilderness managers understand or appreciate cultural resource laws, policies, and values."[3]

These concerns shaped the resulting three-year wilderness suitability study at AINL. Park planners identified four alternatives for wilderness designation. Alternative A recommended no wilderness whatsoever. Alternative B maximized wilderness by declaring 94 percent of the park's land base as wilderness. Alternative C recommended that 80 percent of the land base be declared wilderness, leaving out Sand, Basswood, Long, and portions of Stockton and Rocky islands. Alternative D recommended 55 percent of the land base for designation, limiting wilderness to the most remote, least visited parts of the park.[4]

In early 2004, after extensive public comment, the study team declared alternative C as its preferred alternative. The intention was to give the NPS flexibility in managing for the park's intermingled natural and cultural resources and to address the potential conflict between the two: "This alternative . . . is intended to ensure that there will be outstanding opportunities for people to learn both the stories of the people who settled and altered these islands and the story of the 'rewilding' of the park . . . the process whereby the park's historical 'wilderness' qualities are gradually returning." Alternative C excluded Sand and Basswood islands, Krumenaker explained, "because of the density of cultural sites and our commitment to actively managing and interpreting them." The inclusion of these islands would require the NPS to remove so-called nonconforming conditions from long-inhabited landscapes. Their exclusion meant that these resources could remain and serve as the center of interpretative efforts. NPS planners also worried that designating the maximum amount of wilderness would concentrate future development in the limited nonwilderness portions of the park, places that had been excluded largely for their cultural value. Alternative C thus gave AINL staff flexibility in planning for future development and in interpreting the rewilding of the park.[5]

The decision to exclude nearly six thousand acres from the designation did not please many wilderness advocates. To some, the Park Service's preferred alternative realized the worst possible outcome of the wilderness debates that had swirled within academia since the 1990s: the attempt to recognize the role of history in wilderness threatened to decrease the number of acres protected

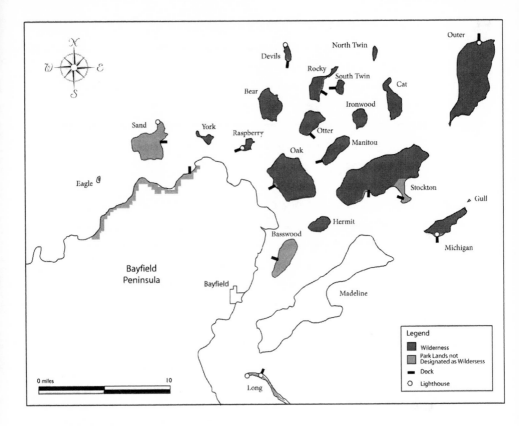

Map 4 The Gaylord Nelson Wilderness at Apostle Islands National Lakeshore

as wilderness. Others worried that leaving so much land outside the wilderness boundary raised the specter of future development. Community leaders and wilderness advocates together proposed a compromise alternative, one that would include most of Basswood Island in the wilderness but leave Sand Island outside the boundary to serve as the showpiece of the park's interpretation of rewilding. This "Shared Vision" compromise garnered broad public support.[6]

In May 2004, after three years of planning and public meetings and thousands of public comments, the NPS recommended its originally preferred alternative, citing the promised management flexibility as its greatest attribute. The formal designation process then moved with remarkable speed. Congress established the Gaylord Nelson Wilderness in November 2004, and President George W. Bush signed the law one month later. For NPS planners, the attempt to balance nature and history in wilderness planning served as one of the most significant achievements of the process. "[The] park's embrace of its human history as a complement, rather than a competitor, to wilderness may be unique and hopefully heralds a new era in celebrating the integration of natural and cultural resource preservation in the national park system," explained Superintendent Krumenaker.[7]

Congress affirmed the importance of outdoor recreation to the past and future of the islands when it stated that wilderness status should not "be construed to modify, limit, or in any way affect the use of motors on the lake waters, including . . . the beaching of motorboats adjacent to wilderness areas." This language would certainly have surprised early wilderness advocates who fought for wilderness as a place to escape from the impact of automobiles and other signs of modern society. The provision for motorboat access provides a telling commentary on the motivations for wilderness protection in the Apostles. This wilderness was not established as a part of a critique of modern consumer society. It was a creation of that society.[8]

The boundaries of the wilderness area further testify to this point. Although NPS planners had crafted their preferred alternative to reconcile the tensions between wilderness and history embedded within NPS management, they had in fact sidestepped the issue. As with outdoor recreation, the demand for legibility helped to restore wilderness characteristics to the islands and also played a central role in the formal wilderness designation. NPS planners kept Sand and Basswood islands—the two islands with the richest human history and the most evocative rewilding landscapes—outside of the wilderness. NPS managers would not have to wrestle with the question of how to manage the nonconforming conditions and other marks of human history in a wilderness area. Lands valuable as cultural resources were zoned out of the wilderness. The result is a wilderness boundary created for management, one with boundaries that do not blur the lines between nature and culture—a legible wilderness.

The NPS planners who conducted the suitability study and the AINL rangers who will manage the Gaylord Nelson Wilderness wrestled with the same question as the academics and environmentalists who have been embroiled in the wilderness debates for the past two decades: what is the role of history in the wilderness? For the manager, however, these debates are much less abstract. The decision to designate certain islands wilderness—but not others—has on-the-ground consequences for how these lands will be managed and how visitors will experience them. When viewed in such concrete terms, separating wilderness and history becomes much more difficult. Both defy the categorization suggested in lines neatly drawn on a map.

Rewilding landscapes deserve continued management and the protection of both their natural and historical resources. This management should be an active one. AINL staff must determine how the park will respond to threats such as those posed by a surging deer herd and a warming climate. These problems have roots in historical processes as well as ecological ones and threaten both the natural and cultural landscapes of the lakeshore. Human choices have shaped the rewilding of the Apostle Islands for decades, and this role should continue. This might mean the monitoring and removal of exotic species that threaten island environments or the stabilization and interpretation of ruins that reveal island history.[9]

Nothing in the formal designation of wilderness precludes such management. The Wilderness Act itself specifies that wilderness areas may contain "features of scientific, educational, scenic, or historical value." It is the way that NPS policies have interpreted the wilderness ideal that has created the apparent conflict between wilderness and history. Wilderness might even be a vehicle for protecting historical resources, and protecting them in a way that helps explain not just human history but also the way that the natural world framed and informed this history. Historical resources would thus be a part of the wilderness landscape, not an intrusion upon it.[10]

Staff at AINL now face the challenge of managing the rewilding landscapes of the islands. This entails building on the NPS's strong and underappreciated tradition of protecting and restoring wilderness characteristics but also determining how to preserve buildings, stabilize ruins, and protect ecosystems in a way that evokes for visitors the complicated interactions between nature and history that have created these places. It means figuring out where to put signs and interpretive exhibits — and where not to. But most importantly, it means celebrating the Apostle Islands as a storied wilderness. If NPS management demands categorization, then perhaps AINL planners will pioneer a new category for the administration of such places, one that recognizes both natural and cultural history. A category that allows for shades of gray will be difficult to conceive but might be necessary for a management regime that is historically accurate, ecologically sound, and responsive to the richness of rewilding landscapes. These decisions will be made as a part of the park's general management procedures. Superintendent Krumenaker sees the challenge as an opportunity:

"I don't think, if we do it right . . . that wilderness has to entail either balancing nature and culture—which suggests one gains while the other loses—or sacrificing one at the expense of the other. We can preserve both nature and culture at the Apostle Islands and should embrace the chance to do so."[11]

The NPS can best meet this challenge by creating legible landscapes—but landscapes that are legible to the visitor, not the manager. The demands of management have required the strict segregation of nature and culture. This has led the NPS to create an illusion—the appearance of untouched nature. This is what many visitors expect to find in the islands and in other wilderness areas, an expectation reinforced by both the dominant wilderness ideal and past NPS management. The segregation of natural and cultural landscapes obscures the human stories buried in the wilderness, making it much harder to see the connections between nature and culture that created so many wild places. In so doing, it hides the most important lessons that rewilding places can teach. A wilderness legible to visitors would reveal these connections and would open for visitors a new way of thinking about the relationship between humans and nature. NPS interpretative and management efforts can inform visitors about the rich histories of the islands, their vibrant environments, and the ways that these two seemingly distinct categories overlap. Visitors would enter the wilderness armed with the ability to see its history and would emerge from it more able to recognize the consequences of human habitation in nature.

Visitors equipped with such information would not expect to find pristine wilderness, and they would be better able to understand the landscapes that they encounter. The forest clearing that once housed the Moes' Sand Island farm would no longer appear to be a field of wildflowers or pristine wild nature, but rather a rich historical landscape *and* a wilderness. The commercial fishing nets that still float in the channels between the islands would no longer be a commercial and extractive intrusion into the purity of the wilderness, but instead a clue about past and ongoing interactions with nature. The revegetation of disturbed landscapes in the wilderness would no longer seem like a paradox of management, but rather evidence of the continuing human role in the rewilding of the islands and the necessity of intervention to protect the places we value most. What seems a pristine wilderness would become a storied one.

Many other places teach the same lessons, especially areas east of the Mississippi River, places where wildness has returned after long periods of human use. But stories of nature and history inhabiting the same landscapes emerge in the

E.1 A solitary beach walker on the East side of the Stockton Island tombolo. Photograph by William Cronon.

West too, as they do in the Phillip Burton Wilderness, located forty miles north of San Francisco at Point Reyes National Seashore. Congress created the park in 1962, in response to the same surging demand for outdoor recreation that led the establishment of AINL, and it designated over twenty-five thousand acres of the park as wilderness in 1976. The park is a favored destination for those seeking to escape the crowds and congestion of San Francisco. Visitors can hike over 140 miles of trails and explore "a serene and sternly beautiful expanse of rock-lined beaches and a forest of fir and pine broken by meadowlands." As at AINL, this wilderness was created out of a historical landscape—those forests and meadowlands once housed dairy farms. Wilderness designation depended on an NPS policy of removing buildings, roads, and other structures, and even on minimizing knowledge and interpretation of the park's human history, to foster the appearance of pristine nature.[12]

Even at the Grand Canyon, one of the crown jewels of the National Park System and one of the places most celebrated for its wilderness, historical and wild landscapes overlap. Over five million people visit the Grand Canyon each year, but the vast majority of them stay at the visitor complex on the South Rim. Three visitor centers, hotels, restaurants, and other services cater to the needs of tourists and a scenic road offers stunning views of the canyon. Hikers who descend below the rim typically use the Kaibab and Bright Angel trails, both easily accessed from the visitor center and rim drive. Few would consider the crowded South Rim or the popular trails a wilderness. Those in search of a wilderness experience choose the other trails like the Grandview, the South Bass, or the Tanner. Yet these trails have a history not readily apparent to today's hikers. Many of the trails carried Hopi and Havasupai Indians on trade routes; others were constructed by miners seeking a way to pack copper ore or asbestos out of mines located deep in the canyon. Hikers who follow the 3.2 steep and winding miles of the Grandview trail to Horseshoe Mesa encounter the remains of the Last Chance mine—mining pits, ore cars, and other industrial machinery, surely an unexpected find in the middle of the Grand Canyon. On the Grandview and the other trails, the miners eventually realized that it would be more lucrative to load their mules with tourists rather than ore. As in the Apostle Islands, wilderness at the Grand Canyon is layered with stories. So, too, are the designated wilderness areas at Yellowstone and Yosemite national parks. Even the deepest wilderness areas are riddled with history.[13]

Recognizing these stories will not compromise the value of the Grand Canyon or the Apostle Islands as wild places, or as wilderness. These places tell stories about past human choices and their consequences—stories about the destruction caused by logging and mining, but also tales of making a home and of protecting and restoring nature. In the Apostles, the actions of the fishermen, lumberjacks, and land managers of a century ago are imprinted on island landscapes and will remain so deep into the future. As we come to recognize the long-term consequences of those actions, we can better predict the legacies that our own choices will leave and better protect the wild places that we cherish. ✎

Notes

Introduction

1   Jonathan B. Tourtellot, "National Park Destinations Rated," *National Geographic Traveler* (July/August 2005); http://traveler.nationalgeographic.com/2005/07/destinations-rated/central-text (accessed June 16, 2009). (The first and last quotes are in the print version; the middle two quotes are in the online version only.)

2   Emmet J. Judziewicz and Rudy G. Koch, "Flora and Vegetation of the Apostle Islands National Lakeshore and Madeline Island, Ashland and Bayfield Counties, Wisconsin," *The Michigan Botanist* 32 (March 1993): 43–189; Bob Krumenaker, "An Ecological Disaster in the Making," *Around the Archipelago* (2009): 2.

3   Jeff Rennicke, *Jewels on the Water: Lake Superior's Apostle Islands* (Bayfield, WI: Friends of the Apostle Islands, 2005), 98.

4   Michael Van Stappen, *Northern Passages: Reflections from Lake Superior Country* (Madison, WI: Prairie Oak Press, 2003), 26; Tourtellot, "National Park Destinations Rated," 83.

5   Harlan P. Kelsey, "Report on Apostle Islands National Park Project," January 20, 1931, RG 79, Box 634, National Park Service, General Classified Files, 1907–32, Proposed National Parks, 0–32 (hereafter cited as First Park Proposal Files), National Archives, College Park, MD (hereafter, NA MD).

6   Apostle Islands National Lakeshore, Wisconsin, *General Management Plan: Apostle Islands National Lakeshore, Wisconsin* (Denver: U.S. Department of the Interior, National Park Service, 1989).

7   Others use this term differently. For the Rewilding Institute, the term connotes the plan for large-scale wilderness restoration built around the conservation of large predators like wolves and bears. For other scholars, it means the introduction of African megafauna as proxies for the animals that disappeared from North America during the Pleistocene extinctions. For still others, it simply means the reintroduction of extirpated animals to a part of their former range. Dave Foreman, *Rewilding North America: A Vision for Conservation in the 21st Century* (Washington, D.C.: Island Press, 2004); Reed Noss and Michael Soulé, "Rewilding and Biodiversity: Complimentary Goals for Continental Conservation," *Wild Earth* 3 (Fall 1998): 22–43; Josh Donlan et al., "Rewilding North America," *Nature* 436 (August 2005): 913–14; Paul S. Martin, *Twilight of the Mammoths: Ice Age Extinctions and the Rewilding of America* (Berkeley: University of California Press, 2005).

8   Richard White, "'Are You an Environmentalist, or Do You Work for a Living': Work and Nature," in *Uncommon Ground: Rethinking the Human Place in Nature*, ed. William Cronon (New York: W. W. Norton, 1995), 171–85.

9   Paul S. Sutter, *Driven Wild: How the Fight against Automobiles Launched the Modern Wilderness Movement* (Seattle: University of Washington Press, 2002), and "'A Blank Spot on the Map': Aldo Leopold, Wilderness, and U.S. Forest Service Recreational Policy, 1909–1924," *Western Historical Quarterly* 29 (Summer 1998): 187–214.

10 James Morton Turner, "From Woodcraft to 'Leave No Trace': Wilderness, Consumerism, and Environmentalism in Twentieth-Century America," *Environmental History* 7 (July 2002): 462–84.

11 James C. Scott, *Seeing Like a State: How Certain Schemes to Improve the Human Condition Have Failed* (New Haven, CT: Yale University Press, 1998), 2.

12 There is a vibrant literature on the role of the state in promoting both economic development and the protection of nature. Most of these studies assess the federal government and its land management agencies—especially the National Park Service and the Forest Service. But a narrow focus on federal agencies misses essential elements of the expansion of state authority. For discussions of the role of the state in domestic economic development, see Richard White, *"It's Your Misfortune and None of My Own": A New History of the American West* (Norman: University of Oklahoma Press, 1991); and William G. Robbins, *Colony and Empire: The Capitalist Transformation of the American West* (Lawrence:

University Press of Kansas, 1994). Studies of the role of the federal government in nature protection include Richard West Sellars, *Preserving Nature in the National Parks: A History* (New Haven, CT: Yale University Press, 1997); Ronald A. Foresta, *America's National Parks and Their Keepers* (Washington, D.C.: Resources for the Future, 1984); Alfred Runte, *National Parks: The American Experience*, 2d ed. (Lincoln: University of Nebraska Press, 1987); Paul W. Hirt, *A Conspiracy of Optimism: Management of the National Forests Since World War Two* (Lincoln: University of Nebraska Press, 1996); and Nancy Langston, *Forest Dreams, Forest Nightmares: The Paradox of Old Growth in the Inland West* (Seattle: University of Washington Press, 1995).

13 In this book, I use the term *state* to discuss these trends, and I use the specific names of the various agencies that carried state authority (like the National Park Service or the Wisconsin Conservation Department). On the role of federalism in shaping environmental politics and policy, see Scott Hamilton Dewey, *Don't Breathe the Air: Air Pollution and U.S. Environmental Politics, 1945–1970* (College Station: Texas A&M University Press, 2000).

14 Multiple perspectives on the wilderness debate are included in J. Baird Callicott and Michael P. Nelson, eds., *The Great New Wilderness Debate: An Expansive Collection of Writings Defining Wilderness from John Muir to Gary Snyder* (Athens: University of Georgia Press, 1998), as well as in the citations listed through note 19.

15 See, for example, Richard White, *The Roots of Dependency: Subsistence, Environment, and Social Change among the Choctaws, Pawnees, and Navajos* (Lincoln: University of Nebraska Press, 1983); Theodore Catton, *Inhabited Wilderness: Indians, Eskimos, and National Parks in Alaska* (Albuquerque: University of New Mexico Press, 1997); Mark David Spence, *Dispossessing the Wilderness: Indian Removal and the Making of the National Parks* (New York: Oxford University Press, 1999); William M. Denevan, "The Pristine Myth: The Landscape of the Americas in 1492," *Annals of the Association of American Geographers* 82 (September 1992): 369–85; and Shepard Krech III, *The Ecological Indian: Myth and History* (New York: W. W. Norton, 1999). For a critique of the studies that assert widespread Native influence, see Dave Foreman, "The Pristine Myths," *Wild Earth* 11 (Spring 2001): 1–5.

16 William Cronon, "The Trouble with Wilderness, or, Getting Back to the Wrong Nature," in *Uncommon Ground*, ed. Cronon, 69–90; J. Baird Callicott, "The Wilderness Idea Revisited: The Sustainable Development Alternative," in *Great New Wilderness Debate*, ed. Callicott and Nelson, 353–54.

17 Daniel B. Botkin, *Discordant Harmonies: A New Ecology for the Twenty-first*

Century (New York: Oxford University Press, 1990), 62; Donald Worster, "The Ecology of Order and Chaos," in *The Wealth of Nature: Environmental History and the Ecological Imagination* (New York: Oxford University Press, 1993), 156–170, and "Nature and the Disorder of History," in *Reinventing Nature? Responses to Postmodern Deconstruction*, ed. Michael E. Soulé and Gary Lease (Washington, D.C.: Island Press, 1995), 65–85; Stephen Budiansky, *Nature's Keepers: The New Science of Nature Management* (New York: Free Press, 1995); Callicott, "Wilderness Idea Revisited," 353–54; William Holland Drury Jr., *Chance and Change: Ecology for Conservationists* (Berkeley: University of California Press, 1998).

18   Dave Foreman, "Wilderness Areas for Real," in *Great New Wilderness Debate*, ed. Callicott and Nelson, 396; Michael E. Soulé, "The Social Siege of Nature," 137–70, and Worster, "Nature and the Disorder of History," in *Reinventing Nature?* ed. Soulé and Lease; Michael Pollan, ed., "Only Man's Presence Can Save Nature: Beyond the Wilderness," *Harper's Magazine* (April 1990): 37–48; Gary Snyder, "Nature as Seen from Kitkitdizze Is No 'Social Construction,' " *Wild Earth* 6 (Winter 1996–97), 9; Donald M. Waller, "Wilderness Redux: Can Biodiversity Play a Role?" *Wild Earth* 6 (Winter 1996–97): 36–45; Susan Zakin, "Shake Up: Greens inside the Beltway," *High Country News*, November 11, 1996.

19   See Roderick F. Nash, *Wilderness and the American Mind*, 3d ed. (New Haven, CT: Yale University Press, 1982); Cronon, "Trouble with Wilderness"; Sutter, *Driven Wild*; and *Wilderness Act of 1964*, Public Law 88–577, 16 U.S.C. 1131 (1964).

20   J. A. Simpson and E. S. C. Weiner, preparers, *The Oxford English Dictionary*, 2d ed. (Oxford: Clarendon Press, 1989), 330–34; Gary Snyder, *The Practice of the Wild: Essays* (San Francisco: North Point Press, 1990), 9–10. See also Jack Turner, *The Abstract Wild* (Tucson: University of Arizona Press, 1996).

21   *Bayfield Press* (hereafter, *BP*), March 9, 1872; Kathryn Bishop Eckert, *The Sandstone Architecture of the Lake Superior Region* (Detroit: Wayne State University Press, 2000), 35.

22   *Ashland Press* (hereafter, *AP*), October 18 and 25, 1873; *Bayfield County Press* (hereafter, *BCP*), December 12, 1885; Eckert, *Sandstone Architecture*, 18, 20, 86–87, 223.

23   Kathleen Lidfors, "Sandstone Quarries of the Apostle Islands: A Resource Management Plan" (Bayfield, WI: Apostle Islands National Lakeshore, Apostle Islands National Lakeshore Library, Bayfield, WI) (hereafter cited as AINL Library), 73.

24   Ibid., 74.

25   K. A. Ursic, N. C. Kenkel, and D. W. Larson, "Revegetation Dynamics of Cliff Faces in Abandoned Limestone Quarries," *Journal of Applied Ecology* 34 (April 1997): 289–303; M. B. Usher, "Natural Communities of Plants and Animals

in Disused Quarries," *Journal of Environmental Management* 8, no 2 (1979): 223–36; Julie Van Stappen, personal communication, August 14, 2006; Clifford M. Wetmore, "Lichens and Air Quality at Apostle Islands National Lakeshore: Final Report" (St. Paul, MN: National Park Service, Midwest Region, 1988), AINL Library.

26   John Elder, "Inheriting Mt. Tom," *Orion* 16 (Spring 1997): 28, and *Reading the Mountains of Home* (Cambridge, MA: Harvard University Press, 1998).

27   Karl Jacoby, *Crimes against Nature: Squatters, Poachers, Thieves, and the Hidden History of American Conservation* (Berkeley: University of California Press, 2001); Philip G. Terrie, *Forever Wild: A Cultural History of Wilderness in the Adirondacks* (Syracuse, NY: Syracuse University Press, 1994).

28   Justin Reich, "Re-Creating the Wilderness: Shaping Narratives and Landscapes in Shenandoah National Park," *Environmental History* 6 (January 2001): 95–117; *Cultural Resource Management* 21, no. 1 (1998), special issue on Shenandoah National Park, especially Bob Krumenaker, "Cultural Resource Management at Shenandoah: It Didn't Come Naturally," 4–6, and Audrey Horning, "'Almost Untouched': Recognizing, Recording, and Preserving the Archeological Heritage of a Natural Park," 31–33. Other eastern parks have histories of eviction and the subsequent challenges of balancing natural and cultural resource management. See T. Young, "False, Cheap and Degraded: When History, Economy and Environment Collided at Cade's Cove, Great Smoky Mountains National Park," *Journal of Historical Geography* 32 (2006): 169–89; and Durwood Dunn, *Cade's Cove: The Life and Death of a Southern Appalachian Community, 1817-1937* (Knoxville: University of Tennessee Press, 1988).

29   Public Employees for Environmental Responsibility, "Olympic Park Associates, Wilderness Watch, and Public Employees for Environmental Responsibility, Plaintiffs v. Fran Manella, Jonathan B. Jarvis, and William G. Laitner, Defendants," Case no. C04-5732FDB, http://www.peer.org/docs/wa/05_3_8_shelters.pdf (accessed August 3, 2006); Public Employees for Environmental Responsibility, "U.S. District Court Upholds Wilderness Act—Olympic National Park's Shelters Are in Violation of Act," August 4, 2005, http://www.peer.org/news/news_id.php?row_id=562 (accessed August 3, 2006).

1 | Lines in the Forest

1   Rennicke, *Jewels on the Water*, 67.

2   "Apostle Islands Fact Book" (Apostle Islands National Lakeshore, Bayfield, WI; copy in author's files); *Duluth News Tribune*, September 5, 1905.

3   Douglas J. Frederick and Lawrence Rakestraw, *A Forest Type Map of Apostle Islands and Pictured Rocks National Lakeshores, from the Original General Land Office Survey Records* (National Park Service, 1976), AINL Library; Mary T. Bell, *Cutting across Time: Logging, Rafting, and Milling the Forests of Lake Superior* (Schroeder, MN: Schroeder Area Historical Society, 1999), 78; Angus White, *A History of John Schroeder and the John Schroeder Lumber Company, Milwaukee, Wisconsin* (Lanesboro, MN: Forest Resource Center, 1991), 36.

4   *BCP*, August 20, 1936.

5   Judziewicz and Koch, "Flora and Vegetation of the Apostle Islands National Lakeshore," 102; R. K. Anderson et al., *Basic Ecological Study of Outer Island, at Apostle Islands National Lakeshore* (Stevens Point: University of Wisconsin–Stevens Point, 1979), 73, 79; Douglas W. Smith and Rolf O. Peterson, "Beaver Ecology in Apostle Islands National Lakeshore," in *Twelfth Research Conference, Apostle Islands National Lakeshore*, ed. Robert B. Brander and Margaret D. Ludwig (Omaha, NE: National Park Service, Midwest Regional Office, 1990), 17–18.

6   *Apostle Islands Fact Book.*

7   National Park Service, *Apostle Islands National Lakeshore: Statement for Management* (Washington, D.C.: U.S. Department of the Interior, National Park Service, 1977), 18.

8   Robert B. Brander, "Environmental Assessment: Natural Resources Inventory and Management, Apostle Islands National Lakeshore" (National Park Service, Apostle Islands National Lakeshore, Bayfield, WI, 1981).

9   Julie Van Stappen, personal communication, January 25, 2007; Lucy Tyrrell, "An Inventory of Old-Growth Forests on Lands of the National Park Service" (Department of Botany, University of Wisconsin–Madison, ca. 1990), 32.

10   Robert F. Fries, *Empire in Pine: The Story of Lumbering in Wisconsin, 1830–1900.* Rev. ed. (Sister Bay, WI: William Caxton Ltd., 1989), 6; John T. Curtis, *The Vegetation of Wisconsin: An Ordination of Plant Communities* (Madison: University of Wisconsin Press, 1979), 200.

11   Frederick and Rakestraw, *Forest Type Map of Pictured Rocks and Apostle Islands National Lakeshore*; Judziewicz and Koch, "Flora and Vegetation of the Apostle Islands," 53; Curtis, *Vegetation of Wisconsin*, 171, 246; Filibert Roth, *On the Forestry Conditions of Northern Wisconsin* (Madison: Wisconsin Geological and Natural History Survey, 1898), 3; Eric A. Bourdo Jr., "The Forest the Settlers Saw," in *The Great Lakes Forest: An Environmental and Social History*, ed. Susan A. Flader (Minneapolis: University of Minnesota Press, 1983), 3–16,

12   *Bayfield Mercury* (hereafter, *BM*), April 18, 1857; Charles E. Twining, "Logging

on the Apostle Islands: A 19th Century Overview," Northland College Report, 1981, AINL Library, and "A Brief Look at a Brief Experience: Early Logging on the Apostle Islands," in *Third Annual Research Conference, Apostle Islands National Lakeshore*, ed. Jim Wood (Bayfield, WI: U.S. Department of the Interior, National Park Service, Midwest Regional Office, 1981), 18–20.

13   Fries, *Empire in Pine*, 18–20, 29.

14   Twining, "Logging on the Apostle Islands," 16, AINL Library; William F. Raney, "Pine Lumbering in Wisconsin," *Wisconsin Magazine of History* 19 (September 1935): 71–90; William Cronon, *Nature's Metropolis: Chicago and the Great West* (New York: W. W. Norton, 1991), 148–207.

15   Andrew Tate to William F. Dalrymple, April 12, 1870, Box 3, Folder 4, William F. Dalrymple Papers (hereafter, Dalrymple Papers), Wisconsin Historical Society Archives, Madison, WI (hereafter, WHS).

16   *BP*, October 13, 1870; *Ashland Daily Press* (hereafter, *ADP*), May 6 and 13, 1871; George W. Hotchkiss, *History of the Lumber and Forest Industry of the Northwest* (Chicago: George W. Hotchkiss & Co., 1898), 752.

17   Hotchkiss, *History of the Lumber and Forest Industry*, 752; Guy M. Burnham, *The Lake Superior Country in History and Story* (Ashland, WI: Ashland Daily Press/R. Browzer Books, 1939), 255; *ADP*, July 20 and September 21, 1872.

18   James Peet Diary, July 6, 1857, WHS; *BP*, October 27, 1870; *ADP*, July 27, 1872.

19   Charles E. Schefft, "The Tanning Industry in Wisconsin: A History of Its Frontier Origins and Its Development" (master's thesis, University of Wisconsin, 1938), 7–22, 33, 51.

20   George Corrigan, "Tanneries and the Hemlock Bark Industry in Wisconsin," in *Some Historic Events in Wisconsin's Logging History: Proceedings of the Third Annual Meeting of the Forest History Association of Wisconsin*, ed. Ramon R. Hernandez (Wausau, WI: Forest History Association , 1978), 25–27; *BP*, July 22, 1871; *BCP*, July 3, 1880, and September 26, 1885.

21   Michael Williams, *Americans and Their Forests: A Historical Geography* (New York: Cambridge University Press, 1989), 211–16; Fries, *Empire in Pine*, 34, 88; Cronon, *Nature's Metropolis*, 148–206; James P. Kaysen, "Railroad Logging in Wisconsin," in *Some Historic Events in Wisconsin's Logging History*, ed. Hernandez, 39–44.

22   David R. Foster and John D. Aber, eds., *Forests in Time: The Environmental Consequences of 1000 Years of Change in New England* (New Haven, CT: Yale University Press, 2004), xi; Clifford E. Ahlgren and Isabel F. Ahlgren, "The Human Impact on Northern Forest Ecosystems," in *Great Lakes Forest*, ed. Flader, 33–51; Forest Stearns and Gene E. Likens, "One Hundred Years of Recov-

ery of a Pine Forest in Northern Wisconsin," *American Midland Naturalist* 148 (July 1992): 2-19; D. A. Orwig and M. D. Abrams, "Impacts of Early Selective Logging on the Dendroecology of an Old Growth, Bottomland Hemlock-White Pine-Northern Hardwood Forest on the Allegheny Plateau," *Journal of the Torrey Botanical Society* 126 (July-September 1999): 234-44.

23 Quote from Foster and Aber, *Forests in Time*, xii. See also David R. Foster, "Insights from Historical Geography to Ecology and Conservation: Lessons from the New England Landscape," *Journal of Biogeography* 29 (October 2002): 1269-75; David R. Foster et al., "The Importance of Land-Use Legacies to Ecology and Conservation," *Bioscience* 53 (January 2003): 77-88.

24 Anderson et al., *Basic Ecological Study of Outer Island*; William J. Fraundorf, "Forest Vegetation: Inventory and Management Recommendations, Outer Island, Apostle Islands National Lakeshore, Wisconsin" (master's thesis, University of Wisconsin-Stevens Point, 1984), 13-14, 20, 27.

25 Margaret B. Davis et al., "3,000 Years of Abundant Hemlock in Upper Michigan," in *Hemlock Ecology and Management: Proceedings of a Regional Conference on Ecology and Management of Eastern Hemlock*, ed. Glenn Mroz and Jeff Martin (Madison: Department of Forestry, University of Wisconsin-Madison, 1995), 19-27; Daniel L. Goerlich and Ralph D. Nyland, "Natural Regeneration of Eastern Hemlock: A Review," in *Proceedings: Symposium on Sustainable Management of Eastern Hemlock Ecosystems in North America*, ed. Katherine A. McManus, Kathleen S. Shields, and Dennis R. Souto (Newtown Square, PA: U.S. Department of Agriculture, 1999), 14-23.

26 Superintendent, Apostle Islands National Lakeshore, to Regional Director, Midwest Region, June 8, 1981, Subject: Environmental Assessment, AINL Library correspondence files; Kathi Borgmann, Donald M. Waller, and Thomas P. Rooney, "Does Balsam Fir (*Abies balsamea*) Facilitate the Recruitment of Eastern Hemlock (*Tsuaga canadensis*)," *American Midland Naturalist* 141 (April 1999): 391.

27 Fraundorf, "Forest Vegetation," 44, 51-71.

28 Wisconsin Board of Commissioners of Public Lands, Surveyors Field Notes, 1832-1865, notes for T52N, R2W and T51N, R2W, Series 701, Reel 2, vol., 19, WHS; Frederick and Rakestraw, *Forest Type Map of Pictured Rocks and Apostle Islands National Lakeshore*, 24; Judziewicz and Koch, "Flora and Vegetation of the Apostle Islands," 112; Raymond Kenneth Anderson and C. J. Milfred, *Inventory of Select Stockton Island Resources for Recreational Planning* (Stevens Point: University of Wisconsin-Stevens Point, 1980), 66-69; Albert M. Swain and Marjorie Winkler, "Forest and Disturbance History at Apostle Islands National Lakeshore Park," *Park Science* 3 (Summer 1983): 3-5.

29 Tax rolls from 1859 to 1870 have no information on Stockton Island landownership; presumably no individual owned or paid taxes on the land. After 1870,
records only exist for every tenth year. The 1880 tax rolls show taxes levied but
not paid on Stockton Island and do not list the names of landowners. Ashland
County Tax Rolls, 1880, 1890, 1900, Ashland County Series 4, WHS; *BCP*, June
7, 1884, November 7, 1885, and March 20, 1886.

30 Vilas became the national chairman of the Democratic Party in 1886, postmas-
ter general in 1885, and secretary of the interior in 1888. He also served as a
Wisconsin senator in 1885 and from 1890 to 1897. Horace Samuel Merrill, *William Freeman Vilas: Doctrinaire Democrat* (Madison: State Historical Society of
Wisconsin, 1991), 11, 27–29; Lars Larson, *Chequamegon Bay and Its Communities: A Brief History, 1659–1883* (Whitewater, WI: privately printed, 2001), 216.

31 Knight and Vilas's investments became the subject of intense investigation by
Wisconsin newspapers, led by the *Milwaukee Sentinel*. Registrars could legally
purchase public lands until 1892, but Knight almost always purchased lands in
Vilas's name. Knight paid the taxes on these investments, using money provided
by Vilas. Vilas's political enemies tried to use these suspicious arrangements to
political advantage, and scandal dogged the partners throughout the rest of the
century. Merrill, *William Freeman Vilas*, 11, 27–29; *BCP*, January 16, 1886; G.
Burnham, *Lake Superior Country*, 226; Ashland County Tax Rolls, 1900, WHS.

32 John H. Knight to William F. Vilas, June 6, 1889, Box 9, and July 25, 1891, Box
11, William F. Vilas Papers, (hereafter, Vilas Papers), WHS; Eckert, *Sandstone
Architecture*, 204, 223; *BCP*, January 7, 1888.

33 John H. Knight to William F. Vilas, July 25, 1891, and August 5, 1891, Box 11, Vilas
Papers, WHS.

34 James Willard Hurst, *Law and Economic Growth: The Legal History of the
Lumber Industry in Wisconsin, 1836–1915* (Cambridge, MA: Belknap Press of
Harvard University Press, 1964).

35 John H. Knight to William K. Vilas, January 28, 1895, Box 23, Vilas Papers,
WHS; Ashland County Tax Rolls, 1890 and 1900, WHS. The tax figures were
arrived at as follows: In 1890 Knight and Vilas owned 6,015.46 acres, valued at
$6,610, on which they paid $308.60 in taxes (average value of $1.10/acre, aver-
age tax of $0.051/acre). In 1900, they owned 7,739.48 acres, valued at $7,650.60,
on which they paid $520.61 in taxes (average value of $0.99/acre, average tax
of $0.067/acre). The average annual value ($1.045/acre) and tax rates ($0.059/
acre) were applied to the average number of acres (6,877.47).

36 Hotchkiss, *History of the Lumber and Forest Industry*, 641; Fries, *Empire in Pine*,
105, 247.

37 John H. Knight to William F. Vilas, September 21, 1891, Box 12, Vilas Papers, WHS.

38 Knight to Vilas, May 13, 1895, Box 24, Vilas Papers, WHS.

39 Knight to Vilas, May 22, 1895, Box 24, and July 31, 1896, Box 29, Vilas Papers, WHS.

40 J. F. Van Dooser to William F. Vilas, December 9, 1896, Box 31, and September 16, 1897, Box 33, Vilas Papers, WHS.

41 Bell, *Cutting across Time*, 1–10, 54, 65–78; White, *History of John Schroeder and the John Schroeder Lumber Company*, 1–8, 13, 16–17; W. G. Nohl and H. Rettinghouse, comps., *Map of Ashland County, Wisconsin, 1905* (New York: W. G. Nohl, 1905).

42 *BCP*, October 6, 1911 and March 12, 1915; *AP*, February 17, 1914; Jeffrey J. Richner, "An Archeological Evaluation of the Trout Point Logging Camp" (Lincoln, NE: National Park Service, Midwest Archeological Center, 1986), 8, 10.

43 Lynn Sandberg, "The Response of Forest Industries to a Changing Environment," in *Great Lakes Forest*, ed. Flader, 195–219.

44 Bell, *Cutting across Time*, 59–61; White, *History of John Schroeder and the John Schroeder Lumber Company*, 12–15; *BCP*, June 6, 1919.

45 *BCP*, February 27, 1920.

46 Albert M. Swain, "Final Report to the National Park Service on Forest and Disturbance History of the Apostle Islands" (University of Wisconsin Center for Climatic Research, 1981), 5–6, AINL Library; Swain and Winkler, "Forest and Disturbance History at Apostle Islands National Lakeshore Park," 3–4; Carol A. Jefferson, "Ecology of the Sand Vegetation of the Apostle Islands," in *Proceedings of the First Conference on Scientific Research in the National Parks*, ed. Robert M. Linn (New Orleans: Government Printing Office, 1976), 115–16; Anderson and Milfred, *Inventory of Select Stockton Island Resources*, 93; Brander, *Environmental Assessment*, 50.

47 Anderson and Milfred, *Inventory of Select Stockton Island Resources*, 71–72, 93; National Park Service, *Final Fire Management Plan for Apostle Islands National Lakeshore* (Bayfield, WI: U.S. Department of the Interior, National Park Service, 2005), 26.

48 Jefferson, "Ecology of the Sand Vegetation of the Apostle Islands," 116; *BCP*, August 16, 1934, and August 20, 1936; Brander, *Environmental Assessment*, 146; National Park Service, *Final Fire Management Plan*, 2; *BCP*, August 16, 1934.

49 Brander, *Environmental Assessment*, 147.

50 National Park Service, *Final Fire Management Plan*, 8, 9, 10.

51 Ronald N. Satz, "Chippewa Treaty Rights: The Reserved Rights of Wisconsin's

Chippewa Indians in Historical Perspective," Special Issue, *Transactions of the Wisconsin Academy of Sciences, Arts, and Letters* 79, no. 1 (1991): 1–128, 199–251.

52 U.S. Congress, House, *Message of President on Allotment of Lands in Severalty to Lake Superior Chippewa Indians*, 48th Cong., 1st sess., 1883, H. Exec. Doc. 12, serial 2193.

53 Originally called the Office of Indian Affairs or the Indian Office, I refer to the agency by its modern name, the Bureau of Indian Affairs, or the BIA.

54 Anthony Godfrey, *A Forestry History of Ten Wisconsin Indian Reservations under the Great Lakes Agency* (Minneapolis: U.S. Department of the Interior, Bureau of Indian Affairs, 1996), 24–25.

55 For a similar case, see Melissa L. Meyer, *The White Earth Tragedy: Ethnicity and Dispossession at a Minnesota Anishinaabe Reservation, 1889–1920* (Lincoln: University of Nebraska Press, 1994).

56 U.S. Commissioner of Indian Affairs, *Annual Report of the Commissioner of Indian Affairs* (Washington, D.C.: Government Printing Office, 1871) (hereafter, BIA [year] Report), 600–601; BIA 1874 Report, 26–27, 188; *BP*, August 12 and October 21, 1871.

57 BIA 1881 Report, 180; BIA 1876 Report, 140; Godfrey, *Forestry History of Ten Wisconsin Indian Reservations*, 28.

58 BIA 1884 Report, liii–liv; U.S. Congress, Senate, Select Committee on Indian Traders, *Chippewa Allotments of Lands and Timber Contracts*, 50th Cong., 2nd sess., 1889, S. Rept. 2710, serial 2624, 1007–11.

59 BIA 1887 Report, 229; BIA 1888 Report, xli–xlii; U.S. Congress, Senate, Select Committee on Indian Traders, *Chippewa Allotments of Lands and Timber Contracts*, iii; Godfrey, *Forestry History of Ten Wisconsin Indian Reservations*, iii, 34. These statistics cover all of the reservations under the La Pointe Agency, including Red Cliff, Bad River, Lac Court Oreilles, Lac du Flambeau, and Fond du Lac (in Minnesota).

60 U.S. Congress, Senate, Select Committee on Indian Traders, *Chippewa Allotments of Lands and Timber Contracts*, v–vi; Merrill, *William Freeman Vilas*, 141–44; John H. Knight to William F. Vilas, September 26, 1887, Box 9, Vilas Papers, WHS.

61 U.S. Congress, Senate, Select Committee on Indian Traders, *Chippewa Allotments of Lands and Timber Contracts*, i, vi–vii, 256.

62 Merrill, *William Freeman Vilas*, 144–45; J. P. Kinney, *Indian Forest and Range: A History of the Administration and Conservation of the Redman's Heritage* (Washington, D.C.: Forestry Enterprises, 1950), 23–24.

63   BIA 1884 Report, lv; *BCP*, April 17, 1886.

64   J. A. Davis to William F. Dalrymple, September 17, 1874, Box 3, Folder 5, Dalrymple Papers, WHS; Roth, *On the Forestry Conditions of Northern Wisconsin*, 57.

65   BIA 1889 Report, 303; BIA 1890 Report, xlix, 239; Godfrey, *Forestry History of Ten Wisconsin Indian Reservations*, 61; Kinney, *Indian Forest and Range*, 76.

66   BIA 1889 Report, 303; W. A. Mercer to Hon. Commissioner of Indian Affairs, December 7, 1896, Records of the Bureau of Indian Affairs, Special Cases 1821–1907 (hereafter, BIA Archives), Special Case 32, RG 75, Box 33, National Archives, Washington, D.C. (hereafter, NA DC); BIA 1897 Report, 45–46.

67   Mercer to Commissioner of Indian Affairs, BIA Archives, NA DC; BIA 1897 Report, 45–47, 313; *BCP*, January 13, and February 6, 1897. Godfrey, *Forestry History of Ten Wisconsin Indian Reservations*, 61–62. In 1909–10, the Senate again investigated charges of corruption and the misuse of power at the La Pointe Agency and the logging of the Bad River Reservation by the Stearns Lumber Company. See Patty Loew, "Newspapers and the Lake Superior Chippewa in the 'Unprogressive' Era" (Ph.D. diss., University of Wisconsin–Madison, 1998), 29–37.

68   G. L. Scott to W. A. Jones, September 7, 1897, and E. T. Buxton to W. A. Jones, June 14, 1898, BIA Archives, Special Case 32, Box 34, File number 1897: 37057, NA DC; BIA 1896–1905 Reports; Godfrey, *Forestry History of Ten Wisconsin Indian Reservations*, 63–64.

69   Godfrey, *Forestry History of Ten Wisconsin Indian Reservations*, 64, 103–7.

70   J. W. Dady to Dr. A. N. Bessesen, November 26, 1913, Box "Records Relating to the Sale of Indian Lands 1913–1917," Folder "Sale of Non-Competent Indian Lands, 1913," Records of the Red Cliff Agency, RG 75, National Archives, Great Lakes Region, Chicago (hereafter, NA GL); Godfrey, *Forestry History of Ten Wisconsin Indian Reservations*, 107, 158.

71   "In re the cutting of the timber on the Red Cliff Reservation," ca. 1910, Box "Records Relating to Timber Operations, 1901–1920," Folder "Timber Matters, Correspondence, 1908–1911," Records of the Red Cliff Agency, RG 75, NA GL.

72   Francis Paul Prucha, *The Great Father: The Untied States Government and the American Indians*, abr. ed. (Lincoln: University of Nebraska Press, 1984), 311–25.

73   "First of the Chippewas to Vote on Constitution and By-Laws," *Indians at Work* 3 (May 15, 1936): 46; Godfrey, *Forestry History of Ten Wisconsin Indian Reservations*, 158; "Annual Forestry and Grazing Report, Great Lakes Indian Agency," June 30, 1939, General Correspondence Files, Annual Reports, 1939–42, Records of the Great Lakes Agency, RG 75, NA GL.

74   Michelle Steen-Adams, "Change on a Northern Wisconsin Landscape: Legacies of Human History" (Ph.D. diss., University of Wisconsin–Madison, 2005), 222, 226, 243.

75   Amanda Wegner, "Spirit to Save," *Gumee* 1 (Summer 2005): 37–43.

76   National Park Service, *Apostle Islands National Lakeshore: Statement for Management* (1977), 28, and *Final Fire Management Plan*, 33.

77   Twining, "Brief Look at a Brief Experience," 18; *BCP*, August 27, and September 10, 1924.

78   Bell, *Cutting across Time*, 78; White, *History of John Schroeder and the John Schroeder Lumber Company*, 36.

79   James Kates, *Planning a Wilderness: Regenerating the Great Lakes Cutover Region* (Minneapolis: University of Minnesota Press, 2001); Robert Gough, *Farming the Cutover: A Social History of Northern Wisconsin, 1900–1940* (Lawrence: University Press of Kansas, 1997).

80   The lighthouse erected on Michigan Island in 1856 was intended for Long Island. The contractors were forced to build another lighthouse, at their own expense, at the correct location. The Michigan Island light was relit in 1869. *Apostle Islands Fact Book*.

81   National Park Service, *Final Fire Management Plan*, 13.

2 | Creating a Legible Fishery

1   *Madison Wisconsin State Journal*, April 17, 1997; Stephen Schram, personal communication, April 23, 2007.

2   The name of the Wisconsin Fish Commission changed in 1899 to the Wisconsin Fisheries Commission; I will refer to it by this later name.

3   Scott, *Seeing Like a State*, 2.

4   *Dictionary of Wisconsin Biography* (Madison: State Historical Society of Wisconsin, 1960), 266; Fish Commissioners of the State of Wisconsin, *Fifth Annual Report of the Fish Commissioners of the State of Wisconsin for the Year Ending December 31, 1878* (Madison: David Atwood, 1878) (hereafter cited as WFC Year Report), 7.

5   *BM*, August 22 1857; *BP*, October 13, 1870, and April 4 and May 5, 1871; U.S. Department of the Interior, National Park Service, *Family-Managed Commercial Fishing in the Apostle Islands during the 20th Century, with Background Information on Commercial Fishing in Lake Superior* (Bayfield, WI: Apostle Islands National Lakeshore, 1985), 13–15.

6   A. H. Lawrie and Jerold F. Rahrer, *Lake Superior: A Case History of the Lake*

and Its Fisheries (Ann Arbor, MI: Great Lakes Fishery Commission, 1973), 44; George C. Becker, *Fishes of Wisconsin* (Madison: University of Wisconsin Press, 1983), 323–29, 335–40; "Whitefish—Distribution—Abundance in Places, Lake Superior," Notes and Files of the Joint Commission Relative to the Preservation of the Fisheries in Waters Contiguous to Canada and the United States (hereafter, IJC Notes), Notes by Subject, Lake Superior, 1894, Box 10, vol. C, 45, RG 22, NA MD.

7   Lawrie and Rahrer, *Lake Superior*, 34; "Whitefish—Distribution—Abundance in Places, Lake Superior," IJC Notes, NA MD; U.S. Department of the Interior, National Park Service, *Family-Managed Commercial Fishing*, 13.

8   Hugh M. Smith and Merwin-Marie Snell, comps., "Review of the Fisheries of the Great Lakes in 1885," in U.S. Commission of Fish and Fisheries, *Report of the Commissioner for 1887* (Washington, D.C.: Government Printing Office, 1891) (hereafter, annual reports of the U.S. Commission of Fish and Fisheries and its successor, the U.S. Bureau of Fisheries, are cited as USFC Year Report); George Brown Goode, "History and Methods of the Fisheries," part 5 of *The Fisheries and Fishery Industries of the United States* (Washington, D.C.: Government Printing Office, 1887), 757.

9   USFC 1887 Report.

10 Ibid., 50–52; James W. Milner, "Report on the Fisheries of the Great Lakes: The Result of Inquiries Prosecuted in 1871 and 1872," in USFC 1872–73 Report, 34; Margaret Beattie Bogue, *Fishing the Great Lakes: An Environmental History* (Madison: University of Wisconsin Press, 2000), 39–40.

11 Bogue, *Fishing the Great Lakes*, 38; Smith and Snell, "Review of the Fisheries of the Great Lakes in 1885," 53.

12 Bogue, *Fishing the Great Lakes*, 85; M. F. Kalmbach, interview by Richard Rathbun, July 5, 1894, Duluth, MN, IJC Notes, Box 7, vol. II.

13 *BP*, February 25, 1871; *BCP*, April 23 and November 15, 1879; Smith and Snell, "Review of the Fisheries of the Great Lakes in 1885," 52; Martha Neuman, *Special History Study: Rocky and South Twin Islands; A History of Commercial Fishing Camps and Resorts* (Bayfield, WI: National Park Service, Apostle Islands National Lakeshore, 1992), Rocky Island File, AINL Library.

14 A. J. Woolman, "Notes to Accompany Chart No.3, Lake Superior (South Shore)," 1894, IJC Notes, Box 9, vol. I, NA MD; *BP*, November 12, 1870, and February 11, 1871; Smith and Snell, "Review of the Fisheries of the Great Lakes in 1885," 45; U.S. Department of the Interior, National Park Service, *Family-Managed Commercial Fishing*, 62.

15 Smith and Snell, "Review of the Fisheries of the Great Lakes in 1885," 35, 49; Goode, "The Fishermen of the United States," part 4 of *Fisheries and Fishery Industries of the United States*, 45; U.S. Bureau of the Census, *Tenth Census, 1880*, Manuscript Census, Bayfield and Ashland counties, WI.

16 Grace Lee Nute, "American Fur Company's Fishing Enterprises on Lake Superior," *Mississippi Valley Historical Review* 12 (March 1926): 483–503; Goode, "Fishermen of the United States," 45, 49; BIA 1875 Report, 371; BIA 1882 Report, 173; BIA 1891 Report, 468.

17 Smith and Snell, "Review of the Fisheries of the Great Lakes in 1885," 55; USFC 1892 Report; M. B. Johnson, interview by Richard Rathbun, July 10, 1894, Bayfield, WI, and Irving Chafe, interview by Richard Rathbun, July 10, 1894, Bayfield, WI, both in IJC Notes, Box 8, vol. III, NA MD; BIA 1850 Report, 53; BIA 1881 Report, 180; Patricia A. Shifferd, "A Study in Economic Change: The Chippewa of Northern Wisconsin: 1854–1900," *Western Canadian Journal of Anthropology* 6, no. 4 (1976): 16–41

18 *BCP*, November 24, 1883, and January 17, 1885.

19 Lawrie and Rahrer, *Lake Superior*, 31; Smith and Snell, "Review of the Fisheries of the Great Lakes in 1885," 49; *BCP*, April 16, 1879; Bogue, *Fishing the Great Lakes*, 49; Frank Prothero, *The Good Years: A History of the Commercial Fishing Industry on Lake Erie* (Belleville, Ontario: Mika Publishing, 1973), 95; January 9, 1886.

20 Bogue, *Fishing the Great Lakes*, 59–73; *BCP*, March 1, 1884, December 12, 1885, and June 21, 1889.

21 Justin Walsted, interview by Roy Tull, 1979, Bayfield, WI, transcript, AINL Library; *BCP*, June 21, 1889; U.S. Department of the Interior, National Park Service, *Family-Managed Commercial Fishing*, 60.

22 Fred Benson, interviewer unidentified, Rocky Island, WI, August 30, 1979, tape recording, AINL Library; M. B. Johnson interview, IJC Notes, NA MD.

23 Bogue, *Fishing the Great Lakes*, 97; Chas W. Smiley, "Changes in the Fisheries of the Great Lakes during the Decade, 1870–1880," *Bulletin of the United States Fish Commission* 1 (1882): 252–58; USFC 1904 Report, 649–61; Notes of Richard Rathbun, IJC Notes, Box 10, vol. B, 43, NA MD.

There are too many variables to quantify the increase in fishing intensity. Nineteenth-century statistics are often quite suspect, varying widely from year to year. Different investigators assessed the fisheries in different ways. There were no standard lengths or mesh sizes for gill nets and no system of reporting the size of the harvest. Fishermen did not always provide truthful information to investigators. Not until the 1930s did fisheries experts devise a standardized method for assessing the fisheries. See Ralph Hile, *Collection and Analysis of Commercial Fishery Statistics in the Great Lakes* (Ann Arbor, MI: Great Lakes Fishery Commission, 1962).

24 USFC 1904 Report, 649–61, and 1885, 37–40; *BCP*, January 9, 1886.

25 USFC 1887 Report, 37–40.

26 USFC 1904 Report, 650; Arthur F. McEvoy, *The Fisherman's Problem: Ecology and Law in the California Fisheries, 1850-1950* (New York: Cambridge University Press, 1986); Lawrie and Rahrer, *Lake Superior*, 44–48.

27 Milner, "Report on the Fisheries of the Great Lakes," 14, 17; Smiley, "Changes in the Fisheries of the Great Lakes," 252; W. D. Tomlin, "Migration of Lake Superior Fish," *Transactions of the American Fisheries Society* 16 (1887): 60; WFC 1884 Report, 8.

28 Catch statistics for specific places fluctuated wildly from year to year, for reasons unrelated to the health of the fish populations or fishing intensity. Storms, early thaws or late freezes, and water temperature variations influenced the size of the harvest, and the addition of a single large ship—such as when the Booth Company stationed a steamer at Rocky Island in 1888—could dramatically alter the size of the catch.

29 Goode, "A Geographical Review of the Fisheries Industries and Fishing Communities for the Year 1880," part 2 of *Fisheries and Fishery Industries of the United States*, 636; WFC 1887–88 Report; *BCP*, January 15, 1887.

30 USFC 1887, 1892, 1902 Reports, 1904; James Smith, interview by A. J. Woolman, July 12, 1894, Rice or Rocky Island, WI, IJC Notes, Box 8 vol. III, NA MD.

31 IJC Notes, Box 11, vol. E, 74, 105; M. F. Kalmbach interview, IJC Notes, NA MD.

32 James Smith interview, IJC Notes, NA MD; Becker, *Fishes of Wisconsin*, 335; Lawrie and Rahrer, *Lake Superior*, 44–48. In some cases, competition between poundnetters and gillnetters can break down along racial, ethnic, or economic divides. This does not appear to be the case in the Chequamegon Bay. The use of steam tugs and mechanical net lifters had increased the capital investment required in gillnet fishing and decreased the cost differences between pound and gill nets. Even the poundnet fishermen generally agreed that their apparatus caused more harm to young fish. Joseph E. Taylor III, *Making Salmon: An Environmental History of the Northwest Fisheries Crisis* (Seattle: University of Washington Press, 1999), 141–47; Bogue, *Fishing the Great Lakes*, 101.

33 M. F. Kalmbach interview, IJC Notes, NA MD; Lawrie and Rahrer, *Lake Superior*, 48; Bogue, *Fishing the Great Lakes*, 120–128.

34 John D. Buenker, *The Progressive Era: 1893-1914*, vol. 4 of *The History of Wisconsin Series*, ed. William Fletcher Thompson (Madison: State Historical Society of

Wisconsin Press, 1998); Robert H. Wiebe, *The Search for Order, 1877-1920* (New York: Hill & Wang, 1967); Samuel P. Hays, *Conservation and the Gospel of Efficiency: The Progressive Conservation Movement, 1890-1920* (Cambridge, MA: Harvard University Press, 1959); David Stradling, *Smokestacks and Progressives: Environmentalists, Engineers, and Air Quality in America, 1881-1951* (Baltimore, MD: Johns Hopkins University Press, 1999).

35 WFC 1905-6 Report, 2518.

36 Wisconsin Conservation Commission, *Biennial Report of the State Conservation Commission of Wisconsin for the Years 1915-1916* (Madison: State Conservation Commission, 1917) (hereafter, CC Year Report), 18.

37 Walter E. Scott and Thomas Reitz, *The Wisconsin Warden: Wisconsin Conservation Law Enforcement; A Centennial Chronology (1879-1979)* (Madison: Wisconsin Department of Natural Resources, 1979), i, 1-5; WFC 1874 Report.

38 Ron Poff, *From Milk Can to Ecosystem Management: A Historical Perspective on Wisconsin's Fisheries Management Program, 1830s-1990s* (Madison: Bureau of Fisheries Management and Habitat Protection, Wisconsin Department of Natural Resources, 1996), 3; WFC 1874 Report; WFC 1876 Report, 5; WFC 1885-86 Report, 19; USFC 1885 Report, ix; Madison *Wisconsin State Journal*, July 2, 1922.

39 WFC 1895-96 Report, 1-10, 20; 1899-1900, 99; and 1901-2, 94-95.

40 USFC 1892 Report, 372; M. B. Johnson interview, IJC Notes, 17, NA MD; IJC Notes, Box 11, vol. D, 220, 226-27, 234, NA MD.

41 James Nevin, "Artificial Propagation versus a Close Season for the Great Lakes," *Transactions of the American Fisheries Society* 27 (1898): 25; Taylor, *Making Salmon*, 100, 109. The actual impact of stocking fish remains unclear. It did little to arrest the collapse of the whitefish population in the 1890s. Not until the 1920s did a few scientists begin to question the efficiency and cost of the programs, and even then the clear majority continued to support them. Twentieth-century propagation programs have been more successful, such as the rehabilitation of the Lake Superior lake trout population since the 1960s. Lawrie and Rahrer, *Lake Superior*, 3; J. R. Fymond, "Artificial Propagation in the Management of Great Lakes Fisheries," *Transactions of the American Fisheries Society* 86 (1956): 384-92; McEvoy, *Fisherman's Problem*, 105-8.

42 Nevin, "Artificial Propagation versus a Close Season," 25; Scott and Reitz, *Wisconsin Warden*, i, 1-5; WFC 1885-86 Report, 6 (second Nevin quote).

43 Scott and Reitz, *Wisconsin Warden*, 1; WFC 1889-90 Report, 56, 60, and WFC 1885-86 Report (published in 1887), 5.

44 McEvoy, *Fisherman's Problem*, 100-101; Bogue, *Fishing the Great Lakes*, 238-43.

45 *Laws of Wisconsin, 1887* (Madison: Democrat Printing Co., 1887), ch. 520, sec. 2;

Secretary of State, *Fish and Game Laws of the State of Wisconsin, 1891* (Madison: Democrat Printing Co., State Printers, 1891); WFC 1891–92 Report, 24 (Nevin quote); Scott and Reitz, *Wisconsin Warden*, 6–8; *BCP*, January 15, 1887, and January 21, 1899; "Statistics of the Fisheries of the Great Lakes," in USFC 1901 Report, 585; U.S. Department of the Interior, National Park Service, *Family-Managed Commercial Fishing*, 25.

46 *Fish and Game Laws of the State of Wisconsin, 1891, 1895, 1897* (Madison, WI). (The volumes for the 1887–1894 reports were issued by the Secretary of State; for 1895, by the State Fish Commission; for 1897–1913, by the State Fish and Game Warden.)

47 WFC 1887–88 Report; *Laws of Wisconsin, 1905* (Madison: Democrat Printing Co., 1905), ch. 489, sec. 3–4; *Laws of Wisconsin, 1909* (Madison: Democrat Printing Co., 1909), ch. 357, sec. 1.

48 Jacoby, *Crimes against Nature*, and "Class and Environmental History," *Environmental History* 2 (July 1997): 324--2; Benjamin Heber Johnson, "Subsistence, Class and Conservation at the Birth of Superior National Forest," *Environmental History* 4 (January 1999): 80–99; Louis Warren, *The Hunters' Game: Poachers and Conservationists in Twentieth-Century America* (New Haven, CT: Yale University Press, 1999); Steven Hahn, "Hunting, Fishing, and Foraging: Common Rights and Class Relations in the Postbellum South," *Radical History Review* 26 (October 1982): 37–64.

49 Smith and Snell, "Review of the Fisheries of the Great Lakes in 1885," 36; F. W. Roach, IJC Notes, Box 11, vol. D, 147, NA MD.

50 *BCP*, October 20, 1983.

51 IJC Notes, especially Box 11, vol. D., 145–47, 174–97, NA MD; Nevin, "Artificial Propagation versus a Close Season," 25.

52 WFC 1895–96 Report, 35, and 1897–98, 86; Scott and Reitz, *Wisconsin Warden*, 6, 8.

53 Shifferd, "Study in Economic Change"; Edmund Jefferson Danziger, *The Chippewas of Lake Superior* (Norman: University of Oklahoma Press, 1979); Satz, "Chippewa Treaty Rights," 79.

54 D. M. Browning, Commissioner, to Lieut. W. A. Mercer, June 25, 1894 (Ojibwe quote), and W. A. Mercer to H. E. Briggs, June 6, 1896, both in Wisconsin Department of Justice, Closed Case Files, Series 644 (hereafter, WDOJ Files), Box 2, Folder 5 (36), WHS; Lieut. W. A. Mercer to Commissioner of IA, June 12, 1894, Records of the Bureau of Indian Affairs, RG 75, Box 1096, LR 1894: 22633, NA DC.

55 M. B. Johnson interview, IJC Notes, 18, 19–20, NA MD.

56 WFC 1878 Report, 24.

57 W. H. Mylrea to G. H. McCloud, June 26, 1896, WDOJ Files, Box 2, Folder 5 (36), WHS.

58 *In re. Blackbird, No. 602*, 109 F. 139 (W.D. Wis. 1901). See also Charles F. Wilkinson, *To Feel the Summer for the Spring: The Treaty Fishing Rights of the Wisconsin Chippewa* (Madison: University of Wisconsin Law School, 1990), 20; and Steven Eric Silvern, "Nature, Territory, and Identity in the Wisconsin Ojibwe Treaty Rights Conflict" (Ph.D. diss., University of Wisconsin–Madison, 1993), 139.

59 *State v. Morrin*, 136 Wis. 552 (Wis. S. Ct. 1908), 559; F. L. Gilbert and A. C. Titus, Attorneys for Plaintiff, and W. M. Tomkins and M. E. Dillon, Attorneys for Defendant, "State of Wisconsin vs. Michael Morrin, Wisconsin Supreme Court," *Wisconsin Reports Cases and Briefs* 136 (Book 12): 552; Victor T. Pierrelee to F. L. Gilbert, July 13, 1907, WDOJ Files, Box 8, Folder 36; Wilkinson, *To Feel the Summer for the Spring*, 21; Silvern, "Nature, Territory, and Identity," 140–41.

60 Satz, "Chippewa Treaty Rights," 87–90; Silvern, "Nature, Territory, and Identity," 141–44; Patty Loew, "Hidden Transcripts in the Chippewa Treaty Rights Struggle: A Twice Told Story of Race, Resistance, and the Politics of Power," *American Indian Quarterly* 21 (Fall 1997): 713–19; Larry Nesper, *The Walleye War: The Struggle for Ojibwe Spearfishing and Treaty Rights* (Lincoln: University of Nebraska Press, 2002).

61 Scott, *Seeing Like a State*, 2–3.

62 USFC 1887, 1892, 1902, and 1904 Reports; M. B. Johnson interview, IJC Notes, NA MD.

63 Edward S. Smith, interview by Richard Rathbun, July 5, 1894, Duluth, MN, IJC Notes, Box 7, vol. II, NA MD.

64 USFC 1894, 1902, 1904 Reports.

65 A. C. Dunn, "The Lake Superior Herring," *Transactions of the American Fisheries Society* 47 (1917–18): 92–95; Rahrer and Lawrie, *Lake Superior*, 52; Becker, *Fishes of Wisconsin*, 341–45; Woolman, "Notes to Accompany Chart No. 3," IJC Notes, NA MD.

66 Bogue, *Fishing the Great Lakes*, 155–56; USFC 1892 Report, 370, and USFC 1904 Report, 652.

67 Statistics compiled from USFC, 1887, 1892, 1902, and 1904 Reports; Woolman, "Notes to Accompany Chart No. 3," IJC Notes, NA MD.

68 Bogue, *Fishing the Great Lakes*, 264–72; John L. Goodier, "Fishermen on Canadian Lake Superior: One Hundred Years," *Inland Seas* 45 (Fall 1989): 289; WFC 1905–6 Report, 22; Fred Benson interview, AINL Library.

69 Neuman, *Special History Study*; Fred Benson interview, AINL Library.

70   U.S. Lighthouse Service, Sand Island Keeper's Log (hereafter, SI Keeper's Log),
      August 25, 1904, AINL Library; USFC 1901 Report, 589, 1904, 647, 655, and
      USFC 1925 Report, 555–56; Bogue, *Fishing the Great Lakes*, 258; Martha Neu-
      man, "What Are Those Cabins Doing There?" (master's thesis, University of
      Wisconsin, 1991), 34, 36.

71   Gregory Summers, *Consuming Nature: Environmentalism in the Fox River Val-
      ley, 1850–1950* (Lawrence: University Press of Kansas, 2006), 155–58; CC 1912
      Report, 2; *Laws of Wisconsin, 1927* (Madison: State Printer, 1927), ch. 426.

72   CC 1927–28 Report, 9; CC 1929–30 Report, 102.

73   "Commercial Fish Product," *Wisconsin Conservationist* 1, no. 6 (January 1920):
      3; James Nevin, "Fifty Years Experience in Fish Culture," *Wisconsin Conserva-
      tionist* 2, no. 5 (November 1920): 7.

74   Ralph Hile, Paul H. Eschmeyer, and George F. Lunger, "Status of the Lake Trout
      Fishery in Lake Superior," *Transactions of the American Fisheries Society* 80
      (1951): 278–312.

75   Lawrie and Rahrer, *Lake Superior*, 48; Norman S. Baldwin and Robert W. Saa-
      lfield, *Commercial Fish Production in the Great Lakes, 1867–1960* (Ann Arbor,
      MI: Great Lakes Fishery Commission, 1962), 150.

76   Lawrie and Rahrer, *Lake Superior*, 49; Bogue, *Fishing the Great Lakes*, 156; Hile,
      Eschmeyer, and Lunger, "Status of the Lake Trout Fishery in Lake Superior,"
      308–9; William R. Dryer, "Age and Growth of Whitefish in Lake Superior," *Fish-
      ery Bulletin* 63, no. 1 (1963): 78.

77   Satz, "Chippewa Treaty Rights," 85, 87; Anthony D. Gulig, "In Whose Interest?
      Government-Indian Relations in Northern Saskatchewan and Wisconsin, 1900–
      1940," (Ph.D. diss., University of Saskatchewan, Canada, 1997), 121, 127–31, 154.

3 | Consuming the Islands

1   Grace Nourse, interview by Greta Swenson, 1981, Bayfield, WI, transcript, AINL
     Library ; Neuman, "What Are Those Cabins Doing There?" 96–99, 101–7.

2   Grace Nourse interview, AINL Library; Burton L. Dahlberg and Ralph C.
     Guettinger, *The White-Tailed Deer in Wisconsin* (Madison: Wisconsin Conser-
     vation Department, 1956), 14–16, 39–42.

3   Grace Nourse interview, AINL Library.

4   In focusing on tourism as a cultural activity, historians have explored the mean-
     ing of the tourist trade rather than its impact. Tourism has been used as vehicle
     to study emerging regional and national identity, class structure, or changing
     ideas about nature, work, and leisure. For tourism and the emergence of national

and regional (usually western) identity, see Marguerite S. Shaffer, *See America First: Tourism and National Identity, 1880–1940* (Washington, D.C.: Smithsonian Institution Press, 2001); Anne Farrar Hyde, *An American Vision: Far Western Landscape and National Culture, 1820–1920* (New York: New York University Press, 1990); Scott Norris, ed., *Discovered Country: Tourism and Survival in the American West* (Albuquerque, NM: Stone Ladder Press, 1994); and Hal K. Rothman, *Devil's Bargains: Tourism in the Twentieth-Century West* (Lawrence: University Press of Kansas, 1998). For tourism as a form of consumption, see Shaffer, *See America First*; and Orvar Löfgren, *On Holiday: A History of Vacationing* (Berkeley: University of California Press, 1999). For tourism and class identity, see Cindy S. Aron, *Working at Play: A History of Vacations in the United States* (New York: Oxford University Press, 1999); and Warren James Belasco, *Americans on the Road: From Autocamp to Motel, 1910–1945* (Cambridge, MA: MIT Press, 1979). For tourism and changing ideas of nature and wilderness, see David Louter, *Windshield Wilderness: Cars, Roads, and Nature in Washington's National Parks* (Seattle: University of Washington Press, 2006); John F. Sears, *Sacred Places: American Tourist Attractions in the Nineteenth Century* (New York: Oxford University Press, 1989); Nash, *Wilderness and the American Mind*; Patricia Jasen, *Wild Things: Nature, Culture, and Tourism in Ontario, 1790–1914* (Toronto: University of Toronto Press, 1995); and especially Sutter, *Driven Wild*.

5   Wisconsin Central Railroad, *Famous Resorts of the Northwest, Summer of 1887* (Chicago: Poole Bros., 1887), 7, WHS; Wisconsin Central Railroad Company, *Summer Resorts of the Wisconsin Central Railroad, Lake Superior Line* (Milwaukee: Cramer, Aikens, and Cramer, 1879), 19, WHS; Island View Hotel Company, *Bayfield Wisconsin: The Most Famous Health and Pleasure Resort in Northern Wisconsin* (Bayfield, WI: Bayfield County Press, 1890), WHS.

6   Gregg Mitman, *Breathing Space: How Allergies Shape our Lives and Landscapes* (New Haven, CT: Yale University Press, 2007); Hyde, *American Vision*, 150; Aron, *Working at Play*, 15–44.

7   Island View Hotel Company, *Bayfield Wisconsin*, 1, 4, 9, WHS; G. Burnham, *Lake Superior Country*, 281–82; BP, December 18, 1878; Wisconsin Central Railroad Company, *Summer Resorts of the Wisconsin Central Railroad*, 31, WHS.

8   Nash, *Wilderness and the American Mind*; Barbara Novak, *Nature and Culture: American Landscape Painting, 1825–1875* (New York: Oxford University Press, 1980).

9   Chicago, St. Paul, Minneapolis, & Omaha Railway, *Health and Pleasure Midst the Pines, Northwest Wisconsin and the Shores of Lake Superior* (St. Paul, MN:

Pioneer Press, 1885), 37, WHS; *The Apostle Islands and Lake Superior* (Milwaukee, WI: Cramer, Aikens, and Cramer, 1884), 35, WHS.

10 *ADP*, December 21, 1895.

11 Colleen J. Sheehy, "American Angling: The Rise of Urbanism and the Romance of the Rod and Reel," and Russell S. Gilmore, " 'Another Branch of Manly Sport': American Rifle Games, 1840–1900," in *Hard at Play: Leisure in America, 1840–1940*, ed. Kathryn Grover (Amherst: University of Massachusetts Press, 1992), 77–92 and 93–112; Gail Bederman, *Manliness and Civilization: A Cultural History of Gender and Race in the United States, 1880–1917* (Chicago: University of Chicago Press, 1995), 170–216; Aron, *Working at Play*, 156–77.

12 Wisconsin Central Railroad, *Famous Resorts of the Northwest*, 9, WHS; *Apostle Islands and Lake Superior*, 31, WHS; *BCP*, May 26, 1900.

13 Island View Hotel Company, *Bayfield Wisconsin*, 1, WHS; *Apostle Islands and Lake Superior*, 11, WHS.

14 Jasen, *Wild Things*, 80–88; Shaffer, *See America First*, 280–82; Eric D. Olmanson, *The Future City on the Inland Sea: A History of Imaginative Geographies of Lake Superior* (Athens: Ohio University Press, 2007), 211–12.

15 Edwards Roberts, *Gogebic, Eagle River, Ashland, and the Resorts in Northern Michigan and Wisconsin Reached by the Milwaukee, Lake Shore & Western Railway* (Chicago: Poole Bros., 1886), 48, WHS; *Apostle Islands and Lake Superior*, 9, 31, WHS; Arthur Tenney Holbrook, *From the Log of a Trout Fisherman* (Norwood, MA: Plimpton Press, 1949), 25; Jasen, *Wild Things*, 133.

16 Chicago, St. Paul, Minneapolis & Omaha Railway, *Health and Pleasure Midst the Pines*, 3, WHS.

17 *BCP*, June 20, 1911, July 2 and December 31, 1915, and May 23, 1919; Donald G. Albrecht, ed., *The Chequamegon Bay Apostle Islands Fishery* (Ashland, WI: Northland College, 1975), 25; *BP*, August 21, 1878.

18 Wisconsin Central Railroad Company, *Summer Resorts of the Wisconsin Central Railroad*, 19, WHS; G. Burnham, *Lake Superior Country*, 225; Island View Hotel Company, *Bayfield Wisconsin*, 11–12, WHS; *BP*, August 19, 1871, July 31, 1878, July 29, 1882, and August 18, 1883; Jasen, *Wild Things*, 97, 135–36.

19 WFC 1879 Report, 11; 1884, 6; and 1889–90, 4.

20 WFC 1880 Report, 8, and 1907–8, 13; Poff, *From Milk Can to Ecosystem Management*, 3–5.

21 Becker, *Fishes of Wisconsin*, 291–92, 295, 299, 302; Poff, *From Milk Can to Ecosystem Management*, 4.

22   WFC 1895–96 Report, 9–12.

23   D. John O'Donnell, "A History of Fishing in the Brule River," *Transactions of the Wisconsin Academy of Sciences, Arts, and Letters* 36 (1944): 24, 28; G. Burnham, *Lake Superior Country*, 318.

24   Holbrook, *From the Log of a Trout Fisherman*, 73–74.

25   G. Burnham, *Lake Superior Country*, 316–19; Albert M. Marshall, *Brule Country* (St. Paul, MN: North Central Publishing Co., 1954), 167–79; James Nevin, "Fish in the Brule River," *Wisconsin Conservationist* 3 (March 1921): 2.

26   Joseph F. Cullon, "Landscapes of Labor and Leisure: Common Rights, Private Property and Class Relations along the Bois Brule River, 1870–1940" (master's thesis, University of Wisconsin–Madison, 1995).

27   Cullon, "Landscapes of Labor and Leisure," 122–26, quote on 124.

28   D. John O'Donnell, "A Four-Year Creel Census on the Brule River, Douglas County, Wisconsin," *Transactions of the Wisconsin Academy of Sciences, Arts, and Letters* 37 (1945): 279, and "History of Fishing on the Brule River," 27; Marshall, *Brule Country*, 204.

29   Becker, *Fishes of Wisconsin*, 291–92, 321–22; Cullon, "Landscapes of Labor and Leisure"; Holbrook, *From the Log of a Trout Fisherman*, 124–37.

30   U.S. Department of Commerce, Bureau of the Census, *Eighth Census, 1860*, Manuscript Census and Agricultural Schedule, Ashland County, WI; Smith and Snell, "Review of the Fisheries of the Great Lakes in 1885," 48; *BP*, May 4, 1872, and December 10 and 24, 1870; *BCP*, July 23 and October 22, 1881, April 7, 1883, and January 29, 1887; Hamilton Nelson Ross, *La Pointe: Village Outpost on Madeline Island* (1960; repr., Madison: State Historical Society of Wisconsin, 2000), 120; Island View Hotel Company, *Bayfield Wisconsin*, 1, WHS; *Apostle Islands and Lake Superior*, 11, WHS; *BCP*, August 26, 1893; George F. Thomas, *"Tourist Supplement": Specimen Pages from Lake Superior Souvenir* (Ashland, WI, 1891), WHS pamphlet collection.

31   Wilfrid A. Rowell, "The Story of the Old Mission," 1932, WHS pamphlet collection; Vickie Lock, "A Summer Place: Elizabeth Hull's Madeline Island Photo Album," *Wisconsin Magazine of History* 85 (Summer 2002): 32–39; Ross, *La Pointe*, 158–60; Madeline Island Historical Preservation Association Inc., *On the Rock: The History of Madeline Island Told through Its Families* (Friendship, WI: New Past Press, 1997), 340.

32   *BCP*, July 12 and September 13, 1912; Madeline Island Historical Preservation Association, *On the Rock*, 18–19, 20, 25, 30–31; Anton H. Turrittin, "Social Change in an Isolated Community: A Study of the Transformation of Mad-

eline Island, Wisconsin" (master's thesis, University of Minnesota, 1960), 104; John O. Holzhueter, *Madeline Island and the Chequamegon Region* (Madison: State Historical Society of Wisconsin Press, 1974), 57.

33 Ross, *La Pointe*, 166–67.

34 "Hermit Island: Near Bayfield Peninsula, Lake Superior," n.d., Hermit Island File, AINL Library; Holzhueter, *Madeline Island and the Chequamegon Bay Region*, 52.

35 U.S. Department of Commerce, Bureau of the Census, *Twelfth Census of the United States, 1900*, Manuscript Census, Ashland County, WI; U.S. Department of Commerce, Bureau of the Census, *Fifteenth Census of the United States, 1930*, Manuscript Census, Ashland County, WI; Rebecca Sample Bernstein and Tricia L. Canaday, "Madeline Island Intensive Architectural and Historical Survey," Report Prepared for Town of La Pointe (1993), 21, WHS; Madeline Island Historical Preservation Association, *On the Rock*, 40, 122; Turrittin, "Social Change in an Isolated Community," 23.

36 Hamilton Nelson Ross, "The Great La Pointe Fire of 1869," n.d., Box 5, Folder 7, Hamilton Nelson Ross Papers, WHS; Lock, "Summer Place," 33; Bernstein and Canaday, "Madeline Island Intensive Architectural and Historical Survey," 25, WHS; Ross, *La Pointe*, 123, 159.

37 Dredging the lagoon and expanding the marina proved quite controversial, for in doing so developers intruded on a historical Ojibwe burial ground. Edward Salmon, " 'Old Mission': Madeline Island, Wisconsin," n.d., WHS pamphlet collection; Holzhueter, *Madeline Island and the Chequamegon Region*, 59; W. F. Pett, "A Forgotten Village," *Wisconsin Magazine of History* 12 (September, 1928): 18; Madeline Island Historical Preservation Association, *On the Rock*, 81, 97, 98; BCP, May 29, 1908.

38 Madeline Island Historical Preservation Association, *On the Rock*, 40, 43, 58, 63, 65; Turrittin, "Social Change in an Isolated Community," 86, 94.

39 Olmanson, *Future City on the Inland Sea*, 205–10; Kenneth M. Ellis, "Ke-wa-de-no-kwa: First Annual Apostle Islands Indian Pageant, 1924," WHS pamphlet collection; BCP, July 20, 1923.

40 BCP, July 20 and August 10, 1923, and June 25, 1924; David Glassberg, *American Historical Pageantry: The Uses of Tradition in the Early Twentieth Century* (Chapel Hill: University of North Carolina Press, 1990).

41 "Apostle Islands Indian Pageant: America's Super Indian Classic" (ca. 1925), WHS pamphlet collection.

42 Paul W. Glad, *War, a New Era, and Depression, 1914-1940*, vol. 5 of *The History of Wisconsin Series*, ed. William Fletcher Thompson (Madison: State Historical

Society of Wisconsin Press, 1990), 215; Shaffer, *See America First*, 132; Sutter, *Driven Wild*, 24–44; Belasco, *Americans on the Road*, 71–79.

43 Ballard Campbell, "The Good Roads Movement in Wisconsin, 1890–1911," *Wisconsin Magazine of History* 40 (Summer 1966): 273–94; Glad, *War, a New Era, and Depression, 1914–1940*, 155–62; State Highway Commission of Wisconsin and the U.S. Public Roads Administration, *A History of Wisconsin Highway Development, 1935–1945* (Madison: State-Wide Highway Planning Survey, 1947), 35–43, 77–78.

44 Campbell, "Good Roads Movement in Wisconsin"; Glad, *War, a New Era, and Depression, 1914–1940*, 155–62; Belasco, *Americans on the Road*, 72, 76; Sutter, *Driven Wild*, 25.

45 BCP, August 10, 1923, and June 25, 1924 (McKenzie quote); *Wisconsin Up-to-Date Road Map and Tourists' Guide* (Portage, WI: Columbia Novelty Co., 1922), WHS; State Printing Board, comp., "Official Highway Map of Wisconsin," in *1925 Wisconsin Blue Book* (Madison: State Printing Board, 1925).

46 Glad, *War, a New Era, and Depression, 1914–1940*, 214; "Apostle Islands Indian Pageant" and "Wisconsin State Tourist Bureau," 1928, WHS; *Wisconsin Land of Lakes Magazine* 1–5 (1925–29).

47 BCP, August 13 and 20, 1924, August 20 and 27, 1925, and July 15, 1926.

48 Aaron Shapiro, " 'One Crop Worth Cultivating': Tourism in the Upper Great Lakes, 1910–1965" (Ph.D. diss., University of Chicago, 2005), 70.

49 Gough, *Farming the Cutover*, 162–67.

50 Kates, *Planning a Wilderness*, 15–51.

51 Shapiro, " 'One Crop Worth Cultivating,' " 135; George S. Wehrwein and Kenneth H. Parsons, *Recreation as Land Use*, Bulletin 422 (Madison: Madison: University of Wisconsin Agricultural Experiment Station,, 1932), 3.

52 Wehrwein and Parsons, *Recreation as Land Use*, 29.

53 Early wilderness regulations pioneered by the U.S. Forest Service emerged from similar discussions about zoning and the segregation of different land uses. Walter A. Rowlands and Fred B. Trenk, *Rural Zoning Ordinances in Wisconsin*, Circular No. 281 (Madison: University of Wisconsin Agricultural Experiment Station, 1936); Walter Rowlands, Fred Trenk, and Raymond Penn, *Rural Zoning in Wisconsin*, Bulletin 479 (Madison: University of Wisconsin Agricultural Experiment Station, 1948); F. G. Wilson, "Zoning for Forestry and Recreation: Wisconsin's Pioneer Role," *Wisconsin Magazine of History* 41 (Winter 1957–58): 102–6; Kates, *Planning a Wilderness*, 146–60.

54 Rowlands and Trenk, *Rural Zoning Ordinances in Wisconsin*, 13; Rowlands, Trenk, and Penn, *Rural Zoning in Wisconsin*, 8.

55 *Making the Most of Ashland County Land*, Special Circular (Madison: Extension Service of the College of Agriculture, University of Wisconsin, October 1930), 7, 27, WHS.

56 Ashland County Land Use Planning Committee, *Ashland County Intensive Land Use Planning Report* (Ashland, WI: Ashland County Land Use Planning Committee, May 1, 1941), 21, 25.

4 | Sand Island Stories

1 "Summary of Written Scoping Comments," AINL Wilderness Suitability Study, March 11, 2002, copy in author's files; National Park Service, *Apostle Islands National Lakeshore, Wisconsin: Draft Wilderness Study/Environmental Impact Statement* (Washington, D.C.: U.S. *Department* of the Interior, National Park Service, 2003), 33; National Park Service, *Apostle Islands National Lakeshore, Wisconsin: Final Wilderness Study/Environmental Impact Statement* (Washington, D.C.: U.S. Department of the Interior, National Park Service, 2004), 112.

2 National Park Service, *National Park Service Management Policies* (Washington, D.C.: U.S. Department of the Interior, National Park Service, 1988), secs. 6.3.1, 6.3.10.4; National Park Service, "Draft Wilderness Study," 33.

3 William Cronon, "Protecting and Interpreting a Storied Wilderness," Apostle Islands Wilderness Comment, ca. 2003, copy in author's files, emphasis in original.

4 Martin Hanson et al., "A Shared Vision for Protecting the Rich Cultural Heritage and Remarkable Natural Features of the Apostle Islands," 2003, manuscript, copy in author's files.

5 Laura A. Watt, "The Trouble with Preservation, or, Getting Back to the Wrong Term for Wilderness Protection: A Case Study at Point Reyes National Seashore," *The Yearbook of the Association of Pacific Coast Geographers* 64 (2002), 55–72; Matthew A. Lockhart, " 'The Trouble with Wilderness' Education in the National Park Service: The Case for the Lost Cattle Mounts of Congaree," *Public Historian* 28 (Spring 2006): 11–30; "DEC Issues Draft UMP for Blue Ridge Wilderness and Wakely Mountain Area," *Environment DEC*, January 2006, www.dec.ny.gov/environmentdec/18977.html (accessed August 17, 2007); Yosemite National Park, National Park Service, U.S. Department of the Interior, *Cascades Diversion Dam Removal Project: Environmental Assessment*, 2003, /www.nps.gov/archive/yose/planning/cascades/cascades_ch1.htm (accessed August 23, 2009).

6 Robert J. Salzer and David F. Overstreet, *Summary Report: Apostle Island Project; Inventory and Evaluation of Cultural Resources within the Apostle Islands National*

Lakeshore, Wisconsin (Bayfield, WI: Apostle Islands National Lakeshore, 1976), 65, 68; Wisconsin Board of Commissioners of Public Lands, Surveyors Field Notes, 1832–65, notes for T52N, R5W, series 701, vol. 50, reel 8, WHS.

7   Arnold R. Alanen, *The Shaw-Hill Farm Site on Sand Island (Apostle Islands National Lakeshore): Biographical and Site-Related Information* (1990), 4–8, AINL Library; F.W. Shaw, interviewed by A. J. Woolman, Sand Island, July 12, 1894, IJC Notes, Box 7, Volume 2, NA MD; U.S. Department of Commerce, Bureau of the Census, *Tenth Census, 1880*, Manuscript Census, La Pointe Township, Ashland County, WI; Wisconsin Department of State, *1885 Wisconsin State Census*, Town of Bayfield, Bayfield County.

8   *BCP*, July 31, 1897; William H. Tishler, Arnold R. Alanen, and George Thompson, *Early Agricultural Development on the Apostle Islands* (Madison: Apostle Islands National Lakeshore and Department of Landscape Architecture, University of Wisconsin, 1984), 31–32, AINL Library.

9   Smith and Snell, "Review of the Fisheries of the Great Lakes in 1885," 45; *BCP*, November 12, 1870, and December 6, 1884.

10 *BCP*, December 12 and 20, 1884, and February 14, June 27, and December 28, 1885.

11 *BCP*, July 2 (quote), and September 17, 1881.

12 Sheree L. Peterson, "Camp Stella: Meeting Place of Kindred Souls" (Bayfield, WI: Eastern National Park and Monument Association, Apostle Islands National Lakeshore, 1997), 22–37, AINL Library.

13 Peterson, "Camp Stella," 53; Samuel S. Fifield, "Among the Historic Apostle Islands," *National Magazine* 8 (July 1898), 364.

14 Tishler, Alanen, and Thompson, *Early Agricultural Development*, 34; Alma Dahl, Carl Dahl, and Bill Noring, interview by Norma Lien and Jan Moran, February 2, 1981, transcript, AINL Library; Jon Gjerde, *From Peasants to Farmers: The Migration from Balestrand, Norway to the Upper Middle West* (New York: Cambridge University Press, 1985); Wisconsin Department of State, *Wisconsin State Census, 1895*, Township of Bayfield, Bayfield County; *ADP*, December 21, 1895; *BCP*, January 13, 1911; Frederick H. Dahl, ed., *Diary of a Norwegian Fisherman: The Collected Diaries of Frederick A. Hansen* (Jacksonville, FL: Paramount Press, 1989) (hereafter, Hansen Diary), v; U.S. Department of Commerce, Bureau of the Census, *Twelfth Census of the United States, 1900, Thirteenth Census of the United States, 1910*, and *Fourteenth Census of the United States, 1920*, Manuscript Census, Bayfield Township, Bayfield County, WI.

15 Arnold R. Alanen and William H. Tishler, "Farming the Lake Superior Shore: Agriculture and Horticulture on the Apostle Islands, 1840–1940," *Wisconsin*

Magazine of History 79 (Spring 1996): 195–96; Burt Hill Memoir, ca. 1941, 3, 5, 7, AINL Library name file.

16 Hansen Diary; SI Keeper's Log, AINL Library.

17 Bill Noring, interview by William Tishler, September 14, 1981, tape recording, Sand Island File, AINL Library; Bill Noring, interview by Norma Lien and Jan Moran, December 16, 1980, transcript, AINL Library name file; *BCP*, July 5, 1912; Harold Palm, interview by Carol Ahlgren, October 17, 1987, White Bear Lake, MN, transcript, AINL Library name file; Melvin Dahl, interview by Carol Ahlgren, November 12, 1987, Minneapolis, transcript, AINL Library name file; Alanen and Tishler, "Farming the Lake Superior Shore," 185–95.

18 Alanen, *Shaw-Hill Farm Site on Sand Island*, 12–15; Hill Memoir, AINL Library; Burt Hill Account Books, 1914–44, AINL Library. Whether in fishing or farming, women played an essential role in family economic life, although their labor is hard to trace. It is not clear who worked in the gardens and tended the dairy cows on Sand Island—two areas traditionally considered women's work on midwestern farms but undergoing changes as farms became more specialized. Burt Hill cared for his small dairy herd, but traditional Norwegian families considered tending dairy cows women's work. There is no evidence of Sand Island wives or daughters working on the fish boats, although they might have, as women did in fishing families elsewhere on the Great Lakes. See Gjerde, *From Peasants to Farmers*; Mary Neth, *Preserving the Family Farm: Women, Community and the Foundations of Agribusiness* (Baltimore, MD: Johns Hopkins University Press, 1985), 30; and Bogue, *Fishing the Great Lakes*, 75–76. On women's work on the family farm, see Joan M. Jensen, *Loosening the Bonds: Mid-Atlantic Farm Women, 1750–1850* (New Haven, CT: Yale University Press, 1986); and Katherine Jellison, *Entitled to Power: Farm Women and Technology, 1913–1963* (Chapel Hill: University of North Carolina Press, 1993).

19 Bayfield County Tax Rolls, 1925, Bayfield County Courthouse, Washburn, WI; Bill Noring, interview by Lien and Moran, AINL Library; Bill Noring, interview by Tishler, AINL Library; Tishler, Alanen, and Thompson, *Early Agricultural Development on the Apostle Islands*, 40, 42.

20 Historians and other scholars typically isolate and abstract individual industries for analysis. This abstraction renders persuasive analyses but also hides local details and conditions and draws attention away from the point of production. See, for example, McEvoy, *Fisherman's Problem*; Taylor, *Making Salmon*; Williams, *Americans and Their Forests*; William G. Robbins, *Hard Times in*

Paradise: Coos Bay, Oregon, 1850–1986 (Seattle: University of Washington Press, 1988); Fries, *Empire in Pine*.

21 Hill Account Books, 1915, 1933, 1936, AINL Library; Hansen Diary, June 2, 1914, July 5, 1915, and August 21, 1924.

22 Hansen Diary, July 2 and 8, 1923, May 26, 1934, October 26, 1933, and October 27, 1934

23 Hansen Diary, December 27, 1916, November 7, 1929, December 1932, and December 1933; Bill Noring, interview by Tishler, AINL Library; SI Keeper's Log, September 5, 1917, AINL Library.

24 Hansen Diary; Alma Dahl, Carl Dahl, and Bill Noring interview, AINL Library.

25 Bill Noring, interview by Lien and Moran, AINL Library; Hill Memoir, 8, AINL Library; Hansen Diary, August 1919.

26 Tishler, Alanen, and Thompson, *Early Agricultural Development*, 35; BCP, March 13, 1897, May 28, 1898, and April 12, 1924; Register of Deeds Office, Bayfield County Courthouse, Washburn, WI, Volume 63 Deeds, 18.

27 Tishler, Alanen, and Thompson, *Early Agricultural Development*, 35; Alma Dahl, Carl Dahl, and Bill Noring interview, AINL Library; BCP, January 21, 1916.

28 Fries, *Empire in Pine*, 28; A. R. Reynolds, *The Daniel E. Shaw Lumber Company: A Case Study of the Wisconsin Lumbering Frontier* (New York: New York University Press, 1957), 10, 27; BCP, September 21, 1895.

29 Alma Dahl, Carl Dahl, and Bill Noring interview, AINL Library; Melvin Dahl interview, AINL Library; Elizabeth (Anderson) Hulings, interview by Arnold Alanen, October 27, 1988, Bayport, MN, tape recording, AINL Library.

30 Kerlin M. Seitz, "Types of Part-Time Farming in Northern Wisconsin," *Transactions of the Wisconsin Academy of Sciences, Arts, and Letters* 49 (1958): 161–71; Mark Davis, "Northern Choices: Rural Forest County in the 1920s, Part 1," *Wisconsin Magazine of History* 79 (Autumn 1995): 31; Neth, *Preserving the Family Farm*, 30, 60. On the debates over the origins of market-focused agriculture, see Steven Hahn and Jonathan Prude, eds., *The Countryside in the Age of Capitalist Transformation* (Chapel Hill: University of North Carolina Press, 1985).

31 Hansen Diary, 181; USFC 1928 Report, 607, 610; Reynolds, *Daniel Shaw Lumber Company*, 158–61; Bayfield County Tax Rolls, 1880–1915, Bayfield County Courthouse, Washburn, WI (Moe paid half the taxes on a plot of land owned by Knight in 1915, suggesting a stumpage-rights agreement); William Knight, "Fruit in the Bayfield District: Apples, Cherries, and Other Fruits Discussed," speech before the Wisconsin State Horticultural Society, Madison, 1908, Box 28, Folder 1, Dalrymple Papers, WHS.

32   *BCP*, August 22, 1913; Samuel S. Fifield, "The Story of the Apostles," *Picturesque Wisconsin* 1 (July 1899): 70; Wisconsin Central Railroad Company, *Summer Resorts of the Wisconsin Central Railroad*, 19, WHS.

33   WFC 1903–4 Report, 59.

34   *BCP*, August 13, 1915; Hill Memoir, 6, AINL Library; Hulings interview, AINL Library; Peterson, "Camp Stella," 104, 109.

35   Thomas Gerstenberger, "Island Hideaway: The West Bay Club," *Lake Superior Magazine* 14 (December/January 1992): 50–53; Bayfield County Tax Rolls, 1915–40, Bayfield County Courthouse, Washburn, WI.

36   Bayfield County Tax Rolls, 1914–15, Bayfield County Courthouse, Washburn, WI; Harold Palm interview, AINL Library.

37   Mark Davis, "Northern Choices: Rural Forest County in the 1920s, Part 2," *Wisconsin Magazine of History* 79 (Winter 1995–96): 109–38; Aaron Shapiro, "Up North on Vacation," *Wisconsin Magazine of History* 89 (Summer 2006): 2–13; Kates, *Planning a Wilderness*.

38   Hill Account Books, AINL Library; Helen Hillstrom, interview by Susan Monk, July 1985, Sand Island, WI, transcript, AINL Library name file; Harold Palm, interview by Carol Ahlgren, October 17, 1987, White Bear Lake, MN, transcript, AINL Library name file.

39   Hill Account Books, AINL Library; Helen Hillstrom, "My Recollections of Sand Island, 1926–1984," n.d., AINL Library name file.

40   *BCP*, July 31, 1897; Grace Lee Nute, *Lake Superior* (Indianapolis, IN: Bobbs-Merrill, 1944), 265.

41   David Danbom, *Born in the Country: A History of Rural America* (Baltimore, MD: Johns Hopkins University Press, 1995), 196–97; Neth, *Preserving the Family Farm*, 251; White, *"It's Your Misfortune and None of My Own,"* 431–32, 464–65.

42   Alanen and Tishler, "Farming the Lake Superior Shore," 194, 199; Tishler, Alanen, and Thompson, *Early Agricultural Development*, 38–39; Hansen Diary, July 16, 1930; Hill Memoir; Bill Noring interview, AINL Library; Bob Mackreth, personal communication, September 8, 2009; Harold Palm interview, AINL Library (islander quote).

43   "Sand Island Utterly Deserted, 1st Time in Half a Century," *ADP*, October 17, 1944.

44   Hill Memoir, 26; John Harrington, "Shaw Farm Vegetation Survey," University of Wisconsin–Madison, 1982, 7, AINL Library; Judziewicz and Koch, "Flora and Vegetation of the Apostle Islands National Lakeshore," 110.

45   Harrington, "Shaw Farm Vegetation Survey," 4, 8–10; Judziewicz and Koch,

"Flora and Vegetation of the Apostle Islands National Lakeshore," 110; Aerial photographs, 1938, 1963, 1973, 1978, 1988, AINL Library.

46 Harrington, "Shaw Farm Vegetation Survey," 4; Raymond Kenneth Anderson, *Basic Ecological and Recreational Resources Inventory of Sand Island, at Apostle Islands National Lakeshore* (Stevens Point: University of Wisconsin–Stevens Point, 1982), 57–58, 64.

47 Judziewicz and Koch, "Flora and Vegetation of the Apostle Islands National Lakeshore," 110; Tishler, Alanen, and Thompson, *Early Agricultural Development,* 42.

48 Anderson, *Basic Ecological and Recreational Resources Inventory of Sand Island,* 95, 106; Judziewicz and Koch, "Flora and Vegetation of the Apostle Islands National Lakeshore," 110; Wisconsin Department of Natural Resources, State Natural Areas Program, www.dnr.state.wi.us/org/land/er/sna/sna266.htm (accessed August 21, 2007).

49 Anderson, *Basic Ecological and Recreational Resources Inventory of Sand Island,* 41–51.

50 Bayfield County Tax Rolls, 1920–45, Bayfield County Courthouse, Washburn, WI; *BCP,* May 18, 1929; Anderson, *Basic Recreational and Ecological Resources Inventory of Sand Island,* 57–58, 90, 95, 99, 106, 111; *Plat Book of Wisconsin* (Rockford, IL: W. W. Hixson & Co., 1923); *Plat Book of Bayfield County, Wisconsin* (Rockford, IL: W. W. Hixson & Co., 1931); *Plat Book with Index to Owners* (Rockford, IL: Rockford Map Publishers, 1954); *Plat Book with Index to Owners, Bayfield County* (Rockford, IL: Rockford Map Publishers, 1967); Gerstenberger, "Island Hideaway," 50.

51 William Cronon, "A Place for Stories: Nature, History, and Narrative," *Journal of American History* 78 (March 1992), 1369–70, 1375.

5 | A Tale of Two Parks

1 *New York Times,* August 23, 1970, E13.

2 Historians and other scholars have documented countless examples of controversies between locals and outsiders over control of land and resources, from around the country and around the world. A common pattern of conflict over nature protection in Africa and elsewhere in the developing world involves outsiders—international conservation groups, tourist operators, and governmental elites—protecting wildlife at the expense of the subsistence needs of local indigenous peoples. In these conflicts, the group that most successfully

wields state authority can ensure that its own needs are protected. See Jacoby, *Crimes against Nature*; Warren, *Hunters' Game*; Robert W. Righter, *Crucible for Conservation: The Creation of Grand Teton National Park* (Boulder: Colorado Associated University Press, 1982); Ramachandra Guha, "Radical American Environmentalism and Wilderness Preservation: A Third World Critique," *Environmental Ethics* 11 (Spring 1989): 71–83; David Harmon, "Cultural Diversity, Human Subsistence, and the National Park Ideal," *Environmental Ethics* 9 (Summer 1987): 71–83; and Roderick P. Neumann, *Imposing Wilderness: Struggles over Livelihood and Nature Preservation in Africa* (Berkeley: University of California Press, 1998).

3   *BCP*, March 20, 1930; Charles M. Sheridan, interview by Lawrence Rakestraw, 1975, in Lawrence Rakestraw, "Forest and Cultural History in Apostle Islands and Pictured Rocks National Lakeshores, Lake Superior" (Michigan Technological University, Houghton, 1975), 71, AINL Library; G. Burnham, *Lake Superior Country*, 316.

4   G. Burnham, *Lake Superior Country*, 347–48.

5   *BCP*, February 7 and December 12, 1929, and January 30 and May 15, 1930 ("National Park Looks Certain"); Arno B. Cammerer to Hubert H. Peavey, January 19, 1929, First Park Proposal Files, NA MD.

6   W. B. Lewis to Mr. Albright, November 26, 1929, First Park Proposal Files, NA MD; *BCP*, January 31 and February 14, 1929.

7   Kelsey, "Report on Apostle Islands National Park Project," NA MD.

8   Ibid., 3, 4, 8.

9   Harlan Kelsey visited Shenandoah in 1936 and spoke enthusiastically about the prospects of restoring "natural conditions" in the park. His belief that the humanized landscapes of Shenandoah could be restored, while those of the Apostles evidently could not, is hard to explain. In the six years between his visit to the islands and his comments about Shenandoah, however, Kelsey had witnessed the ability of the Civilian Conservation Corps and other federal works projects to radically alter landscapes through reforestation and the construction of recreational facilities. Also, when given his tour of Shenandoah, park supporters carefully shepherded Kelsey to the most natural, least disturbed areas. On the other hand, Apostle Islands promoters brought him to an active logging camp on Outer Island. Sellars, *Preserving Nature in the National Parks*, 67–68; Foresta, *America's National Parks and Their Keepers*, 33–36; Arno Cammerer, "Memorandum for Director Albright covering report on inspection of the Apostle Islands (Wisconsin) project," September 4, 1931, First Park Proposal Files, NA MD; Reich, "Re-Creating the Wilderness," 96.

10   Kelsey, "Report on Apostle Islands National Park Project," 9, NA MD; Cammerer, "Memorandum for Director Albright," 5, NA MD.

11   Hile, Eschmeyer, and Lunger, "Status of the Lake Trout Fishery in Lake Superior," 310–11; Richard L. Pycha and George R. King, *Changes in the Lake Trout Population of Southern Lake Superior in Relation to the Fishery, the Sea Lamprey, and Stocking, 1950–1970* (Ann Arbor, MI: Great Lakes Fishery Commission, 1975), 7, 11.

12   *BCP*, October 1, 1936, July 27, 1939, and April 30, 1942; Nute, *Lake Superior*, 265; Ronald W. Johnson, *The Manitou Island Fish Camp: A Special Study* (Denver: Denver Service Center, National Park Service, 1983), 21, AINL Library; Cliff and Harvey Hadland, interview by author, November 8, 2001, Bayfield, WI; "Alex Kirschling, President of Lullabye Furniture Co.," n.d., AINL Library name file; Anderson, *Basic Ecological and Recreational Resources Inventory of Sand Island*, 56.

13   Grace Nourse interview, AINL Library; Neuman, "What Are Those Cabins Doing There?" 96–99, 101–7; Ben F. Waskow and George A. Curran, "Deer Hunting on the Apostle Islands," *Wisconsin Conservation Bulletin* 19 (October 1954): 3–7; *BCP*, October 11, 1945; Loel Tiffany and Hanford Tiffany, "One of the Apostles," *The Chicago Naturalist* 7, no. 4 (1944), 80; Turrittin, "Social Change in an Isolated Community," 109.

14   Dahlberg and Guettinger, *White-Tailed Deer in Wisconsin*, 14–16, 39–42; Susan L. Flader, *Thinking Like a Mountain: Aldo Leopold and the Evolution of an Ecological Attitude toward Deer, Wolves, and Forests* (Madison: University of Wisconsin Press, 1974); Keith R. McCaffery, "History of Deer Populations in Northern Wisconsin," in *Hemlock Ecology and Management*, ed. Mroz and Martin, 109–12.

15   Brander, *Environmental Assessment*, 99–103 (quote from state deer ecologist on 99); Fred Benson interview, AINL Library; G. N. Lamb, "Report of Investigation of Proposed National Parks," Apostle Islands National Park, 1936, p. 2, First Park Proposal Files, NA MD.

16   *BCP*, August 16, 1934; Anderson and Milfred, *Inventory of Select Stockton Island Resources*, 70–72; Jefferson, "Ecology of the Sand Vegetation of the Apostle Islands," 115; Tiffany and Tiffany, "One of the Apostles," 80; Burton L. Dahlberg to L. P. Voigt, May 17, 1955, Box 453, Folder 39, Wisconsin Conservation Department, Subject Files, 1917–68 (hereafter, WCD Files), WHS.

17   Waskow and Curran, "Deer Hunting on the Apostle Islands," 3; Brander, *Environmental Assessment*, 102–3; *Milwaukee Journal*, November 21, 1950.

18   Brander, *Environmental Assessment*, 102–3; Lelyn Standyk, Richard L. Verch,

and Bruce A. Goetz, *Stockton Island Survey: An Ecological Survey and Environmental Impact Study of Stockton Island, Apostle Islands National Lakeshore* (Ashland, WI: Northland College, 1974), 22. Deer fluctuations continue to cause problems in the islands. In September 2009, AINL officials closed Sand and York islands to all public visits while sharpshooters sought to reduce or eliminate the deer herd, an effort to protect the islands' fragile environments from overgrazing. Apostle Islands National Lakeshore, "Sand and York Islands to Be Closed This Fall," press release, September 15, 2009, www.nps.gov/apis/parknews/upload/2009-2010%20Sand%20York%20Closure.pdf (accessed January 15, 2010).

19 Emory D. Anderson and Lloyd L. Smith Jr., "Factors Affecting Abundance of Lake Herring (*Coregonus artedii* Lesueur) in Western Lake Superior," *Transactions of the American Fisheries Society* 100 (1971): 691–707; John Van Oosten, "The Dispersal of Smelt, *Osmerus mordax* (Mitchill), in the Great Lakes Region," *Transactions of the American Fisheries Society* 66 (1936): 160–71; Lawrie and Rahrer, *Lake Superior*, 55.

20 Recent research has questioned the role of the lamprey in the destruction of the Great Lakes lake trout fishery. Contemporary observers of the collapsing fisheries universally blamed the sea lamprey, often in combination with overfishing. More recent studies have suggested that dioxins—chemical by-products of papermaking and other industrial processes—polluted the Great Lakes and offer a more likely explanation. This analysis applies more to the lower Great Lakes than to Lake Superior, where dioxin levels remained low. Daniel W. Coble et al., "Lake Trout, Sea Lampreys, and Overfishing in the Upper Great Lakes: A Review and Reanalysis," *Transactions of the American Fisheries Society* 119 (1990): 985–95.

21 Pycha and King, *Changes in the Lake Trout Population of Southern Lake Superior*, 2; Bernard R. Smith, J. James Tibbles, and B. G. H. Johnson, *Control of the Sea Lamprey* (Petromyzon marinus) *in Lake Superior, 1953–1970* (Ann Arbor, MI: Great Lakes Fishery Commission, 1974), 2; Carl L. Hubbs and T. E. B. Pope, "The Spread of the Sea Lamprey through the Great Lakes," *Transactions of the American Fisheries Society* 66 (1936): 172–76; John Boehme, interview by Phil Peterson, 1983, Bayfield, WI, AINL Library name file.

22 Pycha and King, *Changes in the Lake Trout Population in Southern Lake Superior*, 2; Lawrie and Rahrer, *Lake Superior*, 40; "Summary of Accomplishments in the Fish Management Division During 1956," Box 780, Folder 6, WCD Files, WHS; "Summary of Accomplishments in the Fish Management Division Dur-

ing 1957," Box 780, Folder 5, WCD Files, WHS; "Annual Report for 1960, Fish Management Division," Box 781, Folder 2, WCD Files, WHS.

23   Quote from Julian Nelson, interview by author, November 12, 2001, Bayfield, WI. Roy and Irene Hokenson, interview by S. L. Fisher, December 9, 1981, AINL Library name file; David Nourse, interview by Greta Swenson, 1981, Bayfield, WI; AINL Library name file; Cliff and Harvey Hadland, interview by Martha Neuman, July 25, 1992, Rocky Island, WI, tape recording, AINL Library.

24   James Napoli, *The Coasts of Wisconsin* (Madison: Wisconsin Sea Grant College Program, 1975), 10; Wisconsin Department of Resource Development, *Recreational Potential of the Lake Superior South Shore Area* (Madison: Wisconsin Department of Resource Development, 1964), 5, and *Economy of Northwest Wisconsin: State Planning Area VI; Population Analysis, Economic Analysis, Program for Economic Development* (Madison: Wisconsin, Department of Resource Development, 1967).

25   David Snyder, "Sand Island," n.d., Sand Island File, AINL Library; Johnson, *Manitou Island Fish Camp*, 8, AINL Library; Madeline Island Historical Preservation Association, *On the Rock*, 137; Turrittin, "Social Change in an Isolated Community," 94.

26   Foresta, *America's National Parks and Their Keepers*, 62–64; Sellars, *Preserving Nature in the National Parks*, 173–91; Outdoor Recreation Resources Review Commission, *Outdoor Recreation for America* (Washington, D.C.: Government Printing Office, 1962), 35.

27   Sutter, *Driven Wild*, 255–61; J. M. Turner, "From Woodcraft to 'Leave No Trace' "; Outdoor Recreation Resources Review Commission, *Outdoor Recreation for America*.

28   E. J. Vanderwall, *Historical Background of the Wisconsin State Park System* (Madison: Wisconsin Conservation Department, 1953); Roman H. Koenings, "The Status of the State Parks in Wisconsin," speech delivered at the National Conference on State Parks, September 1960, Box 815, Folder 6, WCD Files, WHS; Leonard J. Seyberth, "Wisconsin State Parks Going Down Hill; Why?" 1962, Box 871, Folder A, WCD Files, WHS; quote from "Annual report to the Conservation Commission, Forests and Parks Division," 1959, Box 781, Folder 1, pp. 3, 4, WCD Files, WHS.

29   I. V. Fine, Ralph B. Hovind, and Philip H. Lewis Jr., *The Lake Superior Region Recreational Potential: Preliminary Report* (Madison: Wisconsin Department of Resource Development, 1962); I. V. Fine, *Apostle Islands: Some of the Economic Implications of the Proposed Apostle Islands National Lakeshore* (Madison: Uni-

versity of Wisconsin, School of Commerce, Bureau of Business Research &
Service, and Center for Research on Tourism, 1965), 3.

30 Thomas R. Huffman, *Protectors of the Land and Water: Environmentalism in Wisconsin, 1961–1968* (Chapel Hill: University of North Carolina Press, 1994), 9–35.

31 Wisconsin Conservation Commission, Minutes (hereafter, CC Minutes),
May 12 and November 10, 1950, Wisconsin Natural Resources Board, WHS;
John Borkenhagen to C. L. Harrington, June 5, 1935, and Paul J. Houfek, "A
Report on The Apostle Islands of Lake Superior," May 1935, both in Box 453,
Folder 38, WCD Files, WHS; Harold C. Jordahl Jr., *A Unique Collection of
Islands: The Influence of History, Politics, Policy and Planning on the Establishment of Apostle Islands National Lakeshore* (Madison: Department of Urban
and Regional Planning, University of Wisconsin–Extension, 1994), 101–3.

32 CC Minutes, July 11, 1952, WHS.

33 Tiffany and Tiffany, "One of the Apostles," 76; Swain and Winkler, "Forest and
Disturbance History at Apostle Islands National Lakeshore Park," 3; Anderson,
Basic Ecological and Recreational Resources Inventory of Sand Island, 70; Wisconsin Legislative Council, Conservation Committee, Minutes, January 9, 1956,
Box 453, Folder 39, WCD Files, WHS. On climax theory, see Donald Worster,
Nature's Economy: A History of Ecological Ideas, 2d ed. (New York: Cambridge
University Press, 1994), 235–52.

34 Ahlgren and Ahlgren, "Human Impact on Northern Forest Ecosystems," 39; E.
W. Beals and G. Cottam, "The Forest Vegetation of the Apostle Islands, Wisconsin," *Ecology* 41 (October 1960): 743–51; Judziewicz and Koch, "Flora and
Vegetation of the Apostle Islands," 53; Albert M. Swain, "The Role of White
Pine and Hemlock in the Forests of the Apostle Islands National Lakeshore:
Past, Present, and Future," in *Fifth Annual Research Conference, Apostle Islands
National Lakeshore*, ed. Merryll M. Bailey (Omaha, NE: U.S. Department of
the Interior, National Park Service, Midwest Regional Office, 1983); Davis et al.,
"3,000 Years of Abundant Hemlock in Upper Michigan," 22.

35 Beals and Cottam, "Forest Vegetation of the Apostle Islands," 743; "Report of
the Committee Investigating Stockton Island, Ashland County, Wisconsin,"
1955, Box 453, Folder 39, WCD Files, WHS; John A. Beale to Allen T. Edmunds,
September 6, 1956, Box 426, Folder 7, WCD Files, WHS; E. W. Beals, G. Cottam,
and R. J. Vogl, "Influence of Deer on Vegetation of the Apostle Islands, Wisconsin," *Journal of Wildlife Management* 24 (January 1960): 68–80.

36 Burton L. Dahlberg to L. P. Voigt, May 17, 1955, WHS. See also, "Report of the
Committee Investigating Stockton Island," 3, WHS.

37 Mark W. T. Harvey, *A Symbol of Wilderness: Echo Park and the American Conservation Movement* (Albuquerque: University of New Mexico Press, 1994); Nash, *Wilderness and the American Mind*, 220-26.

38 CC Minutes, April 1 (Committee on Land, WHS), February 9, June 10, and August 12, 1955, WHS.

39 CC Minutes, February 9, 1955, and March 9, 1956 (Committee on Land), WHS; Ray M. Stroud to State Conservation Department, May 5, 1955, and L. P. Voigt to Conservation Commission, May 23, 1955, both in Box 453, Folder 39, WCD Files, WHS.

40 G. E. Sprecher to L.P. Voigt, July 6, 1954, Merv Clough to Victor Wallin, October 13, 1954, and Ludwig Trammal to Vic C. Wallin, January 6, 1955, all in Box 453, Folder 39, WCD Files, WHS; CC Minutes, April 1, 1955 (Committee on Land), and December 14, 1956, WHS; Jordahl, *Unique Collection of Islands*, 121-22, 131; Minutes of February 12, 1956, Meeting of the County Board, Box 9, and Minutes of November 13 and 14, 1956, Meeting of the County Board, Box 10, Ashland County Board of Supervisors, County Board Proceedings, 1914-64, (hereafter, ACB Proceedings), WHS.

41 Jordahl, *Unique Collection of Islands*, 91-101; E. J. Vanderwall to Ernest S. Griffith, November 30, 1948, Box 439, Folder 3, WCD Files, WHS; Wisconsin Legislative Reference Library, comp., *The Wisconsin Blue Book, 1958* (Madison: State of Wisconsin, 1958), 354-55.

42 Wisconsin Legislative Council, Conservation Committee, Minutes, August 24, 1956, in Box 453, Folder 39, WCD Files, WHS (Todd quote); Jordahl, *Unique Collection of Islands*, 108, 119.

43 Wisconsin Legislative Council, Conservation Committee, Minutes, August 24, 1956, WHS.

44 CC Minutes, January 9 and March 12, 1959, WHS; *Proceedings of the Ashland County Board of Supervisors, 1959-1960*, April 19, 1960, 50-51, ACB Proceedings, WHS.

45 "Apostle Islands State Forest Guidelines for Development and Management," ca. 1966, Box B, Folder "State of Wis: Re: APIS Proposal-1960s," Harold C. Jordahl Papers (hereafter, Jordahl Papers), AINL Library.

46 Frederick C. Goetz to Gaylord Nelson, December 1965, and Molly Sulewsky to D. J. Mackie, September 13, 1965, both in Box 633, Folder 8, WCD Files, WHS; D. J. Mackie to Elizabeth Hawkes, April 18, 1966, Box 451, Folder 5, WCD Files, WHS.

47 L. P. Voigt to Bernard Gehrmann, November 1, 1966, Box 633, Folder 9, WCD Files, WHS; Holzhueter, *Madeline Island and the Chequamegon Region*, 59;

Madeline Island Historical Preservation Association, *On the Rock*, 79–80; Jordahl, *Unique Collection of Islands*, 319–20.

48   *BCP*, September 29, 1966, clipping in Box 633, Folder 9, WCD Files, WHS; Robert J. Sneed to L. P. Voigt, December 9, 1966, and L. P. Voigt to Bernard Gehrmann, November 1, 1966, both in Folder 9, Box 633, WCD Files, WHS.

49   L. P. Voigt to D. K. Tyler, August 16, 1966, Box 451, Folder 5, WCD Files, WHS; Roman H. Koenings to James Crum, March 7, 1962, Box 441, Folder 4, WCD Files, WHS; CC Minutes, February 24, 1962, and November 6, 1964, WHS.

50   Koenings to Crum, March 7, 1962, WHS.

51   Brian Belonger, *Lake Trout Sport Fishing in the Wisconsin Waters of Lake Superior*, Management Report no. 20 (Madison: Wisconsin Department of Natural Resources, Division of Fish, Game and Enforcement, 1969); Albrecht, *Chequamegon Bay Apostle Islands Fishery*, 25; CC Minutes, June 9–10, 1950, and September 12, 1952, WHS; Wisconsin Federation of Conservation Clubs, "Recommendations to advance the cause of conservation," n.d., Box 1, Folder 1, Vic Wallin Papers, Northern Great Lakes Visitor Center, Ashland, WI (hereafter, NGLVC), WHS; Minutes of the November 15 and 16, 1960, Meeting of the County Board, Box 10, ACB Proceedings, WHS.

52   Michael J. Hansen et al., "Lake Trout (*Salvelinus namaycush*) Populations in Lake Superior and Their Restoration in 1959-1993," *Journal of Great Lakes Research* 21, suppl. 1 (1995), 153, 159–64; Ronald J. Poff, *Lake Superior Fisheries* (Madison: State of Wisconsin Department of Natural Resources, 1972); Tom Kuchenberg, *Reflections in a Tarnished Mirror: The Use and Abuse of the Great Lakes* (Sturgeon Bay, WI: Golden Glow Publishing, 1978), 60–63, 78.

53   Wisconsin Department of Resource Development, *Recreational Potential of the Lake Superior South Shore Area*, 82; Hansen, "Lake Trout Populations in Lake Superior," 162; CC Minutes, January 12, 1968, WHS; Albrecht, *Chequamegon Bay Apostle Islands Fishery*, 23–24; John G. Brasch, *Lake Superior Fisheries Management* (Madison: Wisconsin Department of Natural Resources, n.d.), 2, 11–13; *Department of Natural Resources, State of Wisconsin, 1967–69 Biennial Report* (Madison: Wisconsin Department of Natural Resources, 1969), 17 ("the greatest good"); Kuchenberg, *Reflections in a Tarnished Mirror*, 76–77, 104–9.

54   Outdoor Recreation Resources Review Commission, *Outdoor Recreation for America*, 4, 70, 173–79.

55   U.S. Department of the Interior, *Our Fourth Shore: Great Lakes Shoreline Recreation Area Survey* (Washington, D.C.: U.S. Department of the Interior, National Park Service, 1959); Runte, *National Parks*, 225–28; Sellars, *Preserving Nature in*

the National Parks, 205–6; Foresta, *America's National Parks and Their Keepers*, 62–64.

56 John F. Kennedy, "Remarks of President John F. Kennedy, Ashland Wisconsin, September 24, 1963," appendix B in North Central Field Committee, *Proposed Apostle Islands National Lakeshore, Bayfield and Ashland Counties, Wisconsin* (Washington, D.C.: United States Department of the Interior, 1965) (hereafter, 1965 AINL Working Proposal).

57 Jordahl, *Unique Collection of Islands*, 234–35; Bad River Tribal Council, Resolution no. 1326, May 10, 1962, appendix A in 1965 AINL Working Proposal.

58 Harold C. Jordahl Jr. to Director, Resources Program Staff, March 15, 1965, preface to 1965 AINL Working Proposal, 5.

59 North Central Field Committee, *Apostle Islands National Lakeshore: A Proposal* (Washington, D.C.: U.S. Department of the Interior, 1965), 15–25; 1965 AINL Working Proposal, xviii, 65–77; Jordahl, *Unique Collection of Islands*, 258–59, 405–8.

60 Jordahl, *Unique Collection of Islands*, 235, 293–97; Recreation Advisory Council, *Federal Executive Branch Policy Governing the Selection, Establishment and Administration of National Recreation Areas* (Circular no. 1), March 26, 1963, http://www.nps.gov/history/history/online_books/anps/anps_5g.htm (accessed August 27, 2008) (quote); Dwight F. Rettie, *Our National Park System: Caring for America's Greatest Natural and Historic Treasures* (Urbana: University of Illinois Press, 1995), 234–35; Harold C. Jordahl Jr. to Mrs. George L. McCormick, September 14, 1971, Folder "06-117, Jensch, Herman," Land Acquisition Files, AINL Library.

61 1965 AINL Working Proposal, 98–99; L. P. Voigt to Warren Knowles, May 29, 1967, Box E, Folder "Miscellaneous Correspondence," Jordahl Papers, AINL Library.

62 U.S. Congress, Senate, Committee on Interior and Insular Affairs, *Apostle Islands National Lakeshore: Hearings before the Subcommittee on Parks and Recreation*, 91st Cong., 1st sess., March 17, 1969 (hereafter, 1969 Senate Hearings), 129, 133; A. D. Hulings to Mrs. Tom Vennum, October 1, 1966, Box B, Folder "1966 Correspondence," Jordahl Papers, AINL Library; U.S. Congress, Senate, Committee on Interior and Insular Affairs, *Apostle Islands National Lakeshore: Hearings before the Subcommittee on Parks and Recreation*, 90th Cong., 1st sess., May 9, June 1–2, 1967 (hereafter, 1967 Senate Hearings), 39.

63 Minutes of the Third Meeting of the Apostle Islands Subcommittee, November 23–24, 1964, Curtis Hotel, Minneapolis, Box B, Folder "Archadol Research

Proposals," Jordahl Papers, AINL Library; 1965 AINL Working Proposal, 98–99.

64   Lakeshore supporters doubted the validity of the petition presented by the Ashland Rod and Gun Club, suggesting that dubious and deceitful measures had been used to gather the signatures. *ADP*, October 29, 1969; Memo, Harold C. Jordahl Jr., Regional Coordinator, to Director Resources Program Staff, September 9, 1965, Subject: "Apostle Islands Meetings," Box D, Folder "Correspondence 7/1965-9/1965," Jordahl Papers, AINL Library; Martin Hanson to Harold Jordahl, April 28, 1965, Box D, Folder "Correspondence 6/1965–6/1965," Jordahl Papers, AINL Library.

65   Some of the property owners within the boundaries did support the park proposal, but they were very much in the minority. 1967 Senate Hearings, 45–59, 83–87, 158, 168, 171; Robert Hokenson to Gaylord Nelson, April 10, 1965, Box 123, Folder 28, Gaylord Nelson Papers (hereafter, Nelson Papers), WHS.

66   1967 Senate Hearings, 35; U.S. Congress, House, Committee on Interior and Insular Affairs, *Apostle Islands National Lakeshore: Hearings before the Subcommittee on National Parks and Recreation*, 91st Cong., 1st sess., August 19, 1969 (hereafter, 1969 House Hearings), 156, 159; Apostle Islands Residents Committee, "Questions and Answers about the Proposed Apostle Islands National Lakeshore," 1969, Box B, Folder "1969 Correspondence," Jordahl Papers, AINL Library.

67   1967 Senate Hearings, 133–34; 1969 House Hearings, 26, 142.

68   1967 Senate Hearings, 93; Robert M. Spears to Gaylord Nelson, September 20, 1965, Box 89, Folder 7, Nelson Papers, WHS.

69   1969 House Hearings, 72.

70   1967 Senate Hearings, 120.

71   Ibid.; Harold Kruse to Gaylord Nelson, September 27, 1963, Box 89, Folder 6, Nelson Papers, WHS.

72   Gaylord Nelson to Harold Kruse, October 1, 1963, Box 89, Folder 6, and Box 123, Folder 26, and Box 124, Folders 1–6, all in Nelson Papers, WHS; 1969 House Hearings, 16–19.

73   1967 Senate Hearings, 2–5; Danziger, *Chippewas of Lake Superior*, 149, 168; Aguar, Jyring & Whiteman—Planning Associates, *Tourist and Recreational Resources: Red Cliff Indian Reservation, Wisconsin* (Duluth, MN: U.S. Department of the Interior, Bureau of Indian Affairs, 1965); Jordahl, *Unique Collection of Islands*, 509–17.

74   For studies that focus on the oppositional relationship between Native Americans and the national parks, see Carolyn Merchant, "Shades of Darkness: Race and Environmental History," *Environmental History* 8 (July 2003): 380–94;

Philip Burnham, *Indian Country, God's Country: Native Americans and the National Parks* (Washington, D.C.: Island Press, 2000); and Robert H. Keller and Michael F. Turek, *American Indians and National Parks* (Tucson: University of Arizona Press, 1998). For a more nuanced telling of this relationship, see Catton, *Inhabited Wilderness*.

75 Satz, *Chippewa Treaty Rights*, 89; Nesper, *Walleye War*, 52–53.

76 Albert L. Whitebird to Harold C. Jordahl, August 12, 1964, Box D, Folder "Correspondence, 8/1/1964–12/31/1964," Jordahl Papers, AINL Library; Martin Hanson to Gaylord Nelson, September 8, 1964, Box D, Folder "Louis Hanson 1964 Correspondence," Jordahl Papers, AINL Library; Memo, Harold C. Jordahl to Regional Coordinator, Upper Mississippi–Western Great Lakes Area, September 21, 1964, and George Thompson to L. P. Voigt, December 30, 1964, both in Box E, Folder "Wild Rice, Hunting & Fishing," Jordahl Papers, AINL Library.

77 Bad River Tribal Council, Resolution no. 1326, 1965 AINL Working Proposal; Minutes of the First Meeting of the North Central Field Committee—Subcommittee on the Proposed Apostle Islands Region National Lakeshore, June 24–26, 1964, Ashland, WI, Box B, Folder "Archadol Research Proposals," Jordahl Papers, AINL Library; Albert Whitebird to Gaylord Nelson, August 23, 1963, Box 89, Folder 15, Nelson Papers, WHS.

78 Memo, Harold C. Jordahl to Director, Resources Program Staff, September 21, 1964; Memo, Daniel S. Boos to Coordinator, Apostle Islands Sub-Committee, September 25, 1964; E. J. Riley to Martin Hanson, March 11, 1965, all in Box E, Folder "Wild Rice, Hunting & Fishing," Jordahl Papers, AINL Library.

79 1967 Senate Hearings, 75–77, 226, 245; 1969 House Hearings, 49.

80 Alexandra Harmon, *Indians in the Making: Ethnic Relations and Indian Identities around Puget Sound* (Berkeley: University of California Press, 1998), 218, 221, 224; Ward Churchill, "The Bloody Wake of Alcatraz: Political Repression of the American Indian Movement During the 1970s," in *American Nations: Encounters in Indian Country, 1850 to the Present*, ed. Frederick E. Hoxie, Peter C. Mancall, and James H. Merrell (New York: Routledge, 2001), 375; William R. Bechtel to Martin Hanson, October 21, 1966, Box D, Folder "Louis Hanson 1966 Correspondence," Jordahl Papers, AINL Library.

81 U.S. Congress, House, Committee on Interior and Insular Affairs, *Apostle Islands National Lakeshore: Hearings before the Subcommittee on National Parks and Recreation*, 91st Cong., 2nd sess., March 23, 24, and June 3, 1970 (hereafter, 1970 House Hearings), 258, 343–44, 396, 413.

82 1970 House Hearings, 431; U.S. Congress, House, Committee on Interior and Insular Affairs, *Providing for the Establishment of the Apostle Islands National*

Lakeshore in the State of Wisconsin and for Other Purposes, 91st Cong., 2d sess., 1970, H. Rep. 91–1230.

83 Keller and Turek, *American Indians and National Parks*, xiv, 16; Wilkinson, *To Feel the Summer for the Spring*, 24; Nesper, *Walleye War*, 3.

6 | Rewilding and the Manager's Dilemma

1 U.S. Department of the Interior, National Park Service, *Master Plan: Apostle Islands National Lakeshore, Wisconsin* (Washington, D.C.: U.S. Department of the Interior, 1971) (hereafter, 1971 Master Plan), 28; Runte, *National Parks*, 225; Foresta, *America's National Parks and Their Keepers*, 237; Sellars, *Preserving Nature in the National Parks*, 65–66.

2 1971 Master Plan, 17. NPS planners considered applying the "Cape Cod Formula" for land acquisition, which would have allowed inholdings if the local governments adopted acceptable zoning ordinances. They decided that outright federal ownership was preferable and that the limited number of properties and their relatively low value made acquisition feasible. Jordahl, *Unique Collection of Islands*, 370–71.

3 1971 Master Plan, 22–23; Pat H. Miller to Richard E. Cohen, April 28, 1981, Folder 06-143, Land Acquisition Files, AINL Library.

4 Eric Westhagen to Mr. Russell Dickenson, March 23, 1981, and John M. Vaudreuil and Frank M. Tuerkheimer to David Watts, June 17, 1981, both in Folder 06-102, Land Acquisition Files, AINL Library.

5 Vaudreuil and Tuerkheimer to Watts, June 17, 1981, AINL Library; Pat Miller to Eric P. Westhagen and Helen F. Westhagen, May 8, 1981, and *United States of America v. Eric Westhagen et al.*, Civil Action No. 76-C-178, Final Judgment (W.D. Wis. November 4, 1983), both in Folder 06-102, Land Acquisition Files, AINL Library.

6 1967 Senate Hearings, 87–91.

7 *ADP*, August 25, September 26, and November 9, 1973; Memo to William Bromberg, July 12, 1973, and Regional Director, Northeast Region to Associate Director, Operations, August 15, 1973, both in Folder "06-109 x112," Land Acquisition Files (hereafter, Budvic Timber File), AINL Library.

8 Memo, Supervisory Park Ranger, Apostle Islands NL to Superintendent, November 15, 1973, and photographs of August 15, 1973, visit to Sand Island, Budvic Timber File, AINL Library.

9 *ADP*, November 9, 1973; *Declaration of Taking* (W.D. Wis. September 28, 1973), AINL press release, November 8, 1973, *United States of America v. Budvic Timber*

Inc., Final Judgment (W.D. Wis. June 30, 1980), and Basil G. Kennedy to Pat H. Miller, March 27, 1982, all in Budvic Timber File, AINL Library; Memo, Superintendent to Regional Director, October 3, 1979, AINL Library reading files.

10   Acting Superintendent, Apostle Islands NL, to Regional Director, Midwest Region, May 31, 1974; Superintendent, Apostle Islands NL, to Regional Director, Midwest Region, March 9, 1977; and Superintendent to Regional Director, October 3, 1979, all in AINL Library reading files.

11   Frank M. Tuerkheimer to Peter R. Steenland, May 4, 1981, Folder 06-143, Land Acquisition Files, AINL Library.

12   U.S. Congress, House, Committee on Interior and Insular Affairs, Subcommittee on Public Lands and National Parks, *Land Acquisition Policy and Program of the National Park Service*, report prepared by the staff, 98th Cong., 2d sess., 1984, Committee Print, 7, 12. On the Reagan administration's environmental policies, see William L. Graf, *Wilderness Preservation and the Sagebrush Rebellions* (Savage, MD: Rowan & Littlefield, 1990); Jonathan Lash, Katherine Gillman, and David Sheridan, *A Season of Spoils: The Reagan Administration's Attack on the Environment* (New York: Pantheon Books, 1984); and C. Brant Short, *Ronald Reagan and the Public Lands: America's Conservation Debate, 1979–1984* (College Station: Texas A&M University Press, 1989).

13   Alanen, "Shaw-Hill Farm Site on Sand Island," 27; *United States v. Mary Elizabeth Rice et al.*, Civil Action No. 76-C-199 (W.D. Wisc., March 16, 1981), and Bradley G. Clary to Ric Davidge, November 11, 1982, both in Folder "06-143, Rice, Mary Elizabeth (Sand Island Exchange)," Land Acquisition Files (hereafter, Sand Island Exchange Files), AINL Library; U.S. Congress, House, Committee on Interior and Insular Affairs, Subcommittee on Public Lands and National Parks, *Public Land Management Policy, Part V: Impact of Acquisition Delays on the Lands and Resources of the National Park System*, 98th Cong., 1st sess., 1983, 180.

14   *ADP*, January 18, 1983; *Milwaukee Journal*, January 22, 1983; Shari Eggleson to Sierra Club Members, John Muir Chapter, n.d., Sand Island Exchange Files, AINL Library.

15   House Committee, *Public Land Management Policy*, 170; House Committee, *Land Acquisition Policy and Program of the National Park Service*.

16   In 1969, the State of Wisconsin had purchased most of Oak Island from Ashland County for inclusion in Apostle Islands State Forest. Newspaper clipping, June 25, 1969, Box 124, Folder 35, Nelson Papers, WHS.

17   1971 Master Plan, 26; Jordahl, *Unique Collection of Islands*, 599–615; Natural Resources Board Minutes, October 6, 1970, and July 15, 1971, Wisconsin Natural Resources Board, WHS.

18   John C. Miles, *Wilderness in National Parks: Playground or Preserve* (Seattle: University of Washington Press, 2009), 137–58; Jordahl, *Unique Collection of Islands*, 606; 1967 Senate Hearings, 126; *Wisconsin Statutes*, sec. 1.026 (1975).

19   Jordahl, *Unique Collection of Islands*, 619–21; Judziewicz and Koch, "Flora and Vegetation of the Apostle Islands," 84–85; *ADP*, June 4, 1985.

20   U.S. Congress, Senate, Committee on Energy and Natural Resources, Subcommittee on Public Lands, Reserved Water and Resource Conservation, *Additions to the Wild and Scenic Rivers System, Boundary Adjustments to Units of the National Park System, and Revision of a Ski Area Permit System on National Forest Lands*, 99th Cong., 2d sess., 1986 (hereafter, 1986 Senate Hearings), 330; Jordahl, *Unique Collection of Islands*, 632–33; *ADP*, June 4, 1985.

21   Jordahl, *Unique Collection of Islands*, 644–45.

22   1986 Senate Hearings, 461.

23   Ibid., 30.

24   1965 AINL Working Proposal, xviii; 1967 Senate Hearings, 93; 1969 House Hearings, 26.

25   *Recreational Potential of the Lake Superior South Shore Area*, 24, 25.

26   1967 Senate Hearings, 59–65, 173–74; 1969 House Hearings, 96, 171; 1970 House Hearings, 383; Edward Schneberger to H. C. Jordahl, October 16, 1967, Box D, Folder "1967 Correspondence," Jordahl Papers, AINL Library.

27   Harold C. Jordahl Jr. to Burton Dahlberg, September 20, 1965, Box D, Folder "Correspondence 1/65–4/65," Jordahl Papers, AINL Library; William Bechtel, interview by Kathleen Lidfors, March 4, 1985, and George Hartzog, interview by Kathleen Lidfors, March 7, 1985, Fairfax, VA, both transcripts in Box A, Jordahl Papers, AINL Library; Miles, *Wilderness in National Parks*, 165.

28   1971 Master Plan, 3, 23; William Bromberg to Mr. and Mrs. Laurie Nourse, December 13, 1973, AINL Library reading files.

29   Lee E. Anderson to Gaylord Nelson, June 18, 1975, AINL Library reading files; Apostle Islands National Lakeshore, *Annual Report, 1982* (Bayfield, WI: National Park Service/Apostle Islands National Lakeshore, 1982), AINL Library.

30   Sellars, *Preserving Nature in the National Parks*, 192; National Park Service, *The National Parks: Shaping the System* (Washington, D.C.: U.S. Department of the Interior, 2005), 88; Miles, *Wilderness in the National Parks*, 170; Lemuel A. Garrison, "Practical Experience in Standards, Policies, and Planning," in *First World Conference on National Parks*, ed. Alexander B. Adams, 191, 193 (Washington, D.C.: Government Printing Office, 1962) (quote from NPS official).

31   1971 Master Plan, 25, 27.

32   Gaylord Nelson to Nathaniel P. Reed, ca.1973, Box 156, Folder 16, Nelson Papers, WHS.

33   1967 Senate Hearings, 59–60; Gaylord Nelson to Merril Beal, September 24, 1975, Box 156, Folder 16,Nelson Papers, WHS.

34   Sellars, *Preserving Nature in the National Parks*, 191–94; Douglas W. Scott, *The Enduring Wilderness: Protecting Our Natural Heritage through the Wilderness Act* (Golden, CO: Fulcrum, 2004), 72–73; Craig W. Allin, *The Politics of Wilderness Preservation* (New York: Greenwood Press, 1982), 146–49, 196.

35   National Park Service, *Apostle Islands National Lakeshore: Statement for Management* (1977), 5–8, 24; National Park Service, *Management Policies* (Washington, D.C.: U.S. Department of the Interior/National Park Service, 1978), sec. VI, p. 2; National Park Service, *Apostle Islands National Lakeshore: Statement for Management* (Washington, D.C.: U.S. Department of the Interior, National Park Service, 1983), 18.

36   Aldo Leopold, "Wilderness as a Form of Land Use," in *Great New Wilderness Debate*, ed. Callicott and Nelson, 81, 82; Sutter, "'A Blank Spot on the Map,'" 211.

37   Sutter, *Driven Wild*; Turner, "From Woodcraft to 'Leave No Trace.'"

38   Michael E. Duncanson and Gilbert Tanner, *A Guide to the Apostle Islands and the Bayfield Peninsula* (Eau Claire, WI: Cartographic Institute, 1976), 1.

39   A. Starker Leopold et al., "Wildlife Management in the National Parks," in *Transactions of the Twenty-Eighth North American Wildlife and Natural Resources Conference*, ed. James B. Trefethen (Washington, D.C.: Wildlife Management Institute, 1963), 32, 35; Sellars, *Preserving Nature in the National Parks*, 243–44. In 1964, the NPS classified each unit within the system as natural, historical, or recreational, each with its own set of management guidelines. Environmentalists worried that the focus on recreation undermined environmental protection, and in response to this pressure the NPS replaced the separate administrative policies with a single set of guidelines in 1975 and abolished the area categories in 1977. Recreation still served as an important goal for places like AINL, but NPS staff had a clear imperative to protect natural resources. National Park Service, *Administrative Policies for Recreation Areas of the National Park System* (Washington, D.C.: U.S. Department of the Interior, 1968), 17; National Park Service, *National Parks: Shaping the System*, 88.

40   Sellars, *Preserving Nature in the National Parks*, 193–94; Eivind T. Scoyen, "Appendix: National Park Wilderness," in *Wilderness: America's Living Heritage*, ed. David Brower (San Francisco: Sierra Club, 1961), 186, 192; George Hartzog Jr., "The Impact of Recent Legislation on Administrative Agencies," in *Wilderness*

in Changing World, ed. Bruce M. Kilgore (San Francisco: Sierra Club, 1966), 174; Miles, *Wilderness and the National Parks*. The ability of the NPS to meet its seemingly contradictory mandate — "to provide for the enjoyment" of the parks while also leaving them "unimpaired" has been contested and debated almost since the founding of the agency. So has the definition of wilderness, and many people disagreed with Scoyen and Hartzog's claims that the NPS had restored wilderness to the lands under its control. *National Park Service Organic Act of 1916*, Public Law 64-235, 16 U.S.C. secs. 1–18f (YEAR).

41 *Management Policies, National Park Service* (Washington, D.C.: U.S. Department of the Interior, 1975), IV-16; Superintendent, Apostle Islands National Lakeshore, to Regional Director, Midwest Region, June 8, 1981, AINL Library reading files; National Park Service, *Apostle Islands National Lakeshore: Statement for Management* (1983), 18; Pat H. Miller to Charles Hansing, March 15, 1977, AINL Library reading files.

42 1971 Master Plan, 18; Pat Miller, interview by Kate Lidfors, December 2, 1987, tape 2, side 2, transcript, AINL Library name files; Robert B. Brander to Raymond K. Anderson, December 12, 1977, AINL Library reading files.

43 1971 Master Plan, 24, 25.

44 *Wilderness Act of 1964*, Public Law 88-577, 16 U.S.C. 1131–1136 (1964); Scott, *Enduring Wilderness*, 66–67; James Morton Turner, "Wilderness East: Reclaiming History," *Wild Earth* 11 (Spring 2001): 19–26.

45 *Wilderness Act of 1964* (emphasis added); *Eastern Wilderness Areas Act*, Public Law 93-622, 16 U.S.C. 1132 (1975). See also Watt, "Trouble with Preservation"; Mark Woods, "Federal Wilderness Preservation in the United States: The Preservation of Wilderness?" in *Great New Wilderness Debate*, ed. Callicott and Nelson, 131–53.

46 *Management Policies* (1975), VI-2; National Park Service, *National Park Service Management Policies* (Washington, D.C.: U.S. Department of the Interior, National Park Service, 2001), sec. 6.3.1; National Wilderness Steering Committee, "Guidance 'White Paper' Number 1: Cultural Resources and Wilderness," November 30, 2002,www.wilderness.net/NWPS/documents/NPS/NWSC_White_Paper_1_Cultural_Resources_final.doc.

47 Stephanie S. Toothman, "Cultural Resource Management in Natural Areas of the National Park System," *Public Historian* 9 (Spring 1987): 69; Arnold R. Alanen and Robert Z. Melnick, "Introduction: Why Cultural Landscape Preservation?" 20, and Arnold R. Alanen, "Considering the Ordinary: Vernacular Landscapes in Small Towns and Rural Areas," 22–43, both in *Preserving Cultural Landscapes in America*, ed. Arnold R. Alanen and Robert Z. Melnick (Baltimore,

MD: Johns Hopkins University Press, 2000); Watt, "Trouble with Preservation"; Melody Webb, "Cultural Landscapes in the National Park Service," *Public Historian* 9 (Spring 1987): 77–89; Rebecca Conard, "Applied Environmentalism, or Reconciliation among 'the Bios' and 'the Culturals,'" *Public Historian* 23 (Spring 2001): 9–18; "Shenandoah: Managing Cultural Resources in a Natural Park," *Cultural Resource Management* 21, no. 1 (1998).

48 There is no easy explanation for why the NPS resisted the Wilderness Act but then quickly embraced the postwar wilderness ideal in its management policies. The agency had struggled with defining a wilderness policy for decades, and there was internal dissension among its leaders in the 1960s as to how the agency should respond to the Wilderness Act. NPS officials faced criticism from the ORRRC for their management of recreational lands and from environmental advocates for not paying enough attention to ecological concerns. By the late 1970s, however, the NPS had embraced the dehumanized wilderness ideal, as demonstrated by its management of the vast Alaskan parks that came under its control 1980 even while it struggled with questions such as Native American subsistence use and prior rights. See Miles, *Wilderness in National Parks*, 159–82, 205–23; and Catton, *Inhabited Wilderness*.

49 1975, 1978, 1979 AINL ARs; Neuman, "What Are Those Cabins Doing There?" 128; Katy E. Holmer, "A Superior Summer: A Landscape History of Rocky Island, an Apostle Islands Fishing Community" (master's thesis, University of Wisconsin–Madison, 2003), 104; Warren E. Bielenberg to Janice Blades, February 25, 1974, AINL Library reading files (quote from AINL official).

50 National Park Service, *Management Policies* (1988), sec. 6, p. 4. Wilderness boundaries in the Pacific Northwest also resulted in part from bureaucratic demands for an ordered landscape. Kevin R. Marsh, *Drawing Lines in the Forest: Creating Wilderness Areas in the Pacific Northwest* (Seattle: University of Washington Press, 2007).

51 For an overview of the lakeshore's historical resources programs, see "Islands of History" on the park Web site at www.nps.gov/apis/history.htm.

52 The National Historic Preservation Act of 1966 requires all federal agencies to document the properties under their control for eligibility on the National Register of Historic Places. Listed properties receive special management consideration. Before taking any action that might affect a listed property, the NPS must follow a consultation process to determine appropriate mitigation options. Nothing prohibits the inclusion of listed properties within wilderness areas, and listed properties can still be torn down or altered—so long as the consultation process has been followed. One by-product of the listing process is that only

places and stories thought to be historically significant at the time of the review are listed, although understanding of what is significant can change with new information or new interpretation. The way that we value and understand both nature and history changes over time. David Louter, personal communication, September 10, 2009; James W. Feldman and Robert W. Mackreth, "Wasteland, Wonderland, or Workplace: Perceiving and Preserving the Apostle Islands," in *Protecting Our Diverse Heritage: The Role of Parks, Protected Areas, and Cultural Sites*, ed. David S. Harmon, Bruce M. Kilgore, and Gay E. Vietzke (Hancock, MI: George Wright Society, 2004).

53 Pat H. Miller to Jack Brunell, July 20, 1977, AINL Library reading files.

54 Kate Lidfors, "Historic Logging Sites in the Apostle Islands National Lakeshore—A Resource Management Plan," 1984, 34–40, AINL Library; *BCP*, May 14, 1909, and May 27, 1910.

55 R. K. Anderson and L. R. Stowell, *Wildlife Management Plan for Select Habitats and Species of the Apostle Islands National Lakeshore* (Stevens Point: University of Wisconsin–Stevens Point, 1985), 47.

56 CC Minutes, June 10, 1955 (Committee on Land), WHS; 1965 AINL Working Proposal, 116.

57 Brander, *Environmental Assessment*, 128.

58 Ibid., 127, 129.

59 Superintendent, Apostle Islands National Lakeshore, to Regional Director, Midwest Region, June 8, 1981, AINL Library reading files.

60 Elizabeth A. Chornesky and John M. Randall, "The Threat of Alien Invasive Species to Biological Diversity: Setting a Future Course," *Annals of the Missouri Botanical Garden* 69 (Winter 2003): 68–69; Emmet J. Judziewicz, "Survey of Non-native (Exotic) Vascular Plant Species of Campgrounds and Developed Areas, at Apostle Islands National Lakeshore," January 9, 2000, pp. 6, 8, 9, AINL Library; Marilyn Marler, "A Survey of Exotic Plants in Federal Wilderness Areas," in *Wilderness Science in a Time of Change Conference*, vol. 5, *Wilderness Ecosystems, Threats, and Management*, comp. David N. Cole et al. (Ogden, UT: U.S. Forest Service, Rocky Mountain Research Station, 2000), 323; National Parks Conservation Association, *State of the Parks: National Parks of the Great Lakes* (Washington, D.C.: National Parks Conservation Association, 2007), 33–34.

61 Judziewicz, "Survey of Non-native (Exotic) Vascular Plant Species," 41, AINL Library; Kelsey, "Report on Apostle Islands National Park Project," NA MD.

62 Judziewicz, "Survey of Non-native (Exotic) Vascular Plant Species," 7–8, 40, 41, AINL Library.

Epilogue

1   National Park Service, Apostle Islands National Lakeshore, Wisconsin, *Apostle Islands: Wilderness Study Workbook* (Washington, D.C.: National Park Service, 2002), 6–7; Bob Krumenaker, "New Wilderness Can Be Created: A Personal History of the Gaylord Nelson Wilderness at Apostle Islands National Lakeshore," *George Wright Forum* 22 (October 2005): 37.

2   Krumenaker, "New Wilderness Can Be Created," 39; National Park Service, *Apostle Islands National Lakeshore, Wisconsin: Final Wilderness Study*, 28.

3   National Wilderness Steering Committee, "Guidance 'White Paper' Number 1."

4   National Park Service, *Apostle Islands National Lakeshore, Wisconsin: Draft Wilderness Study*; U.S. Department of the Interior, National Park Service, *Record of Decision: Wilderness Study Final Environmental Impact Statement*, www.nps.gov/apis/finalrod.pdf.

5   National Park Service, *Apostle Islands National Lakeshore, Wisconsin: Final Wilderness Study*, 33; Krumenaker, "New Wilderness Can Be Created," 41.

6   Hanson et al., "A Shared Vision"; National Park Service, *Apostle Islands National Lakeshore, Wisconsin: Final Wilderness Study*, 112.

7   *Consolidated Appropriations Act, 2005*, Public Law 108-447, division E, sec. 140; Krumenaker, "New Wilderness Can Be Created," 35. Congress designated the wilderness area in 2004 as the "Gaylord A. Nelson Apostle Islands National Lakeshore Wilderness" but shortened the name in 2005.

8   *Consolidated Appropriations Act, 2005*, Public Law 108-447, division E, sec. 140(d)2(C).

9   Krumenaker, "Ecological Disaster in the Making"; *Minneapolis–St. Paul Star Tribune*, March 7, 2007.

10 *Wilderness Act of 1964*.

11 William Cronon, "The Riddle of the Apostle Islands," *Orion* 22 (May/June 2003): 42.

12 "Philip Burton Wilderness," August 4, 2009, www.wilderness.net/index.cfm?fuse=NWPS&sec=wildView&WID=455; Watt, "Trouble with Preservation."

13 Formal wilderness designation in the Grand Canyon has been held up by disputes over the management of motorized rafts on the Colorado River; 94 percent of the park is managed as potential wilderness. J. Donald Hughes, *In the House of Stone and Light: A Human History of the Grand Canyon* (Grand Canyon Natural History Association, 1978), 47, 54.

Selected Bibliography

Archive Abbreviations

AINL Library   Apostle Islands National Lakeshore Library, Bayfield, Wisconsin
NA DC   National Archives, Washington, D.C.
NA GL   National Archives, Great Lakes Region, Chicago, Illinois
NA MD   National Archives, College Park, Maryland
NGLVC   Northern Great Lakes Visitor Center, Ashland, Wisconsin
WHS   Wisconsin Historical Society Archives, Madison, Wisconsin

Sources

Alanen, Arnold R. "The Shaw-Hill Farm Site on Sand Island (Apostle Islands National Lakeshore): Biographical and Site-Related Information." 1990. AINL Library.

Alanen, Arnold R., and Robert Z. Melnick, eds. *Preserving Cultural Landscapes in America*. Baltimore, MD: Johns Hopkins University Press, 2000.

Alanen, Arnold R., and William Tishler. "Farming the Lake Superior Shore: Agriculture and Horticulture on the Apostle Islands, 1840–1940." *Wisconsin Magazine of History* 79 (Spring 1996): 162–203.

Albrecht, Donald G., ed. *The Chequamegon Bay Apostle Islands Fishery*. Ashland, WI: Northland College, 1975.

Allin, Craig W. *The Politics of Wilderness Preservation*. New York: Greenwood Press, 1982.

Anderson, Raymond Kenneth. *Basic Ecological and Recreational Resources Inventory of Sand Island, at Apostle Islands National Lakeshore*. Stevens Point: University of Wisconsin–Stevens Point, 1982.

Anderson, Raymond Kenneth, and C. J. Milfred. *Inventory of Select Stockton Island Resources for Recreational Planning*. Stevens Point: University of Wisconsin–Stevens Point, 1980.

Anderson, Raymond Kenneth, and L. R. Stowell. *Wildlife Management Plan for Select Habitats and Species of the Apostle Islands National Lakeshore*. Stevens Point: University of Wisconsin–Stevens Point, 1985.

Anderson, R. K., C. J. Mildred, W. J. Fraundorf, and G. J. Kraft. *Basic Ecological Study of Outer Island, at Apostle Islands National Lakeshore*. Stevens Point: University of Wisconsin–Stevens Point, 1979.

Aplet, Gregory, Janice Thomson, and Mark Wilbert. "Indicators of Wildness: Using Attributes of the Land to Assess the Context of Wilderness." In *Wilderness Science in a Time of Change Conference*, vol. 2, *Wilderness within the Context of Larger Systems*, compiled by Stephen F. McCool et al., 89–98. Ogden, UT: U.S. Department of Agriculture, Forest Service, Rocky Mountain Research Station, 1999.

The Apostle Islands and Lake Superior. Milwaukee: Cramer, Aikens, and Cramer, 1884. WHS pamphlet collection.

Apostle Islands National Lakeshore, Wisconsin. *Annual Reports*. Bayfield, WI: National Park Service, Apostle Islands National Lakeshore, 1972–85.

———. *General Management Plan*. Washington, D.C.: U.S. Department of the Interior, National Park Service, 1989.

Arnold, David, and Ramachandra Guha, eds. *Nature, Culture, Imperialism: Essays on the Environmental History of South Asia*. Delhi, India: Oxford University Press, 1996.

Aron, Cindy S. *Working at Play: A History of Vacations in the United States*. New York: Oxford University Press, 1999.

Ashland County Board of Supervisors. County Board Proceedings, 1860–1907, 1914–64. NGLVC.

Ashland County Land Use Planning Committee. "Ashland County Intensive Land Use Planning Report." Ashland County [WI] Land Use Planning Committee, May 1, 1941.

Baldwin, Norman S., and Robert W. Saalfield. *Commercial Fish Production in the Great Lakes, 1867–1960*. Ann Arbor, MI: Great Lakes Fishery Commission, 1962.

Beals, E. W., and G. Cottam. "The Forest Vegetation of the Apostle Islands, Wisconsin." *Ecology* 41 (October 1960): 743–51.

Beals, E. W., G. Cottam, and R. J. Vogl. "Influence of Deer on Vegetation of the Apostle Islands, Wisconsin," *Journal of Wildlife Management* 24 (January 1960): 68–80.

Bechtel, William. Interview by Kathleen Lidfors, March 4, 1985. Transcript, Box A, Harold C. Jordahl Papers, AINL Library.

Bederman, Gail. *Manliness and Civilization: A Cultural History of Gender and Race in the United States, 1880–1917.* Chicago: University of Chicago Press, 1995.

Belasco, Warren James. *Americans on the Road: From Autocamp to Motel, 1910–1945.* Cambridge, MA: MIT Press, 1979.

Bell, Mary T. *Cutting across Time: Logging, Rafting, and Milling the Forests of Lake Superior.* Schroeder, MN: Schroeder Area Historical Society, 1999.

Benson, Fred. Interview (interviewer not identified), August 30, 1979, Rocky Island, WI. Tape recording, AINL Library.

Bernstein, Rebecca Sample, and Tricia L. Canaday. "Madeline Island Intensive Architectural and Historical Survey." Report prepared for the Town of La Pointe. 1993. WHS.

Boehme, John. Interview by Phil Peterson, 1983, Bayfield, WI. Transcript, AINL Library.

Bogue, Margaret Beattie. *Fishing the Great Lakes: An Environmental History, 1783–1933.* Madison: University of Wisconsin Press, 2000.

Botkin, Daniel B. *Discordant Harmonies: A New Ecology for the Twenty-first Century.* New York: Oxford University Press, 1990.

Brander, Robert B. "Environmental Assessment: Natural Resources Inventory and Management, Apostle Islands National Lakeshore, Wisconsin." National Park Service, Apostle Islands National Lakeshore, Bayfield, WI, 1981.

Bryant, Keith L., Jr. "Entering the Global Economy." In *The Oxford History of the American West,* edited by Clyde A. Milner II, Carol A. O'Connor, and Martha A. Sandweiss, 195–235. New York: Oxford University Press, 1994.

Budiansky, Stephen. *Nature's Keepers: The New Science of Nature Management.* New York: Free Press, 1995.

Buenker, John D. *The Progressive Era: 1893–1914.* Vol. 4 of *The History of Wisconsin Series,* edited by William Fletcher Thompson. Madison: State Historical Society of Wisconsin Press, 1998.

Bureau of Indian Affairs. Special Cases, 1821–1907. Record Group 75. NA DC.

Burnham, Guy M. *The Lake Superior Country in History and in Story.* Ashland, WI: Ashland Daily Press/R. Browzer Books, 1939.

Burnham, Phillip. *Indian Country, God's Country: Native Americans and the National Parks.* Washington, D.C.: Island Press, 2000.

Callicott, J. Baird. "The Wilderness Idea Revisited: The Sustainable Development Alternative."In *The Great New Wilderness Debate*, edited by Callicott and Nelson, 337–66.

Callicott, J. Baird, and Michael P. Nelson, eds. *The Great New Wilderness Debate: An Expansive Collection of Writings Defining Wilderness from John Muir to Gary Snyder.* Athens: University of Georgia Press, 1998.

Catton, Theodore. *Inhabited Wilderness: Indians, Eskimos, and National Parks in Alaska* Albuquerque: University of New Mexico Press, 1997.

Chicago, St. Paul, Minneapolis, & Omaha Railway. *Health and Pleasure Midst the Pines, Northwest Wisconsin and the Shores of Lake Superior.* St Paul: Pioneer Press, 1885. WHS pamphlet collection.

Churchill, Ward. "The Bloody Wake of Alcatraz: Political Repression of the American Indian Movement during the 1970s." In *American Nations: Encounters in Indian Country, 1850 to the Present*, edited by Frederick E. Hoxie, Peter C. Mancall, and James H. Merrell, 375–409. New York: Routledge, 2001.

Coble, Daniel W., Richard E. Bruesewitz, Thomas W. Fratt, and Jeffrey W. Scheirer. "Lake Trout, Sea Lampreys, and Overfishing in the Upper Great Lakes: A Review and Reanalysis." *Transactions of the American Fisheries Society* 119 (1990): 985–95.

Cole, David N., Stephen F. McCool, William T. Borrie, and Jennifer O'Loughlin, comps. *Wilderness Science in a Time of Change Conference*, vol. 5, *Wilderness Ecosystems, Threats, and Management.* Ogden, UT: U.S. Department of Agriculture, Forest Service, Rocky Mountain Research Station, 2000

Conard, Rebecca. "Applied Environmentalism, or Reconciliation among 'the Bios' and 'the Culturals.' " *Public Historian* 23 (Spring 2001): 9–18.

Cronon, William. *Changes in the Land: Indians, Colonists, and the Ecology of New England.* New York: Hill & Wang, 1983.

———. *Nature's Metropolis: Chicago and the Great West.* New York: W. W. Norton, 1991.

———. "A Place for Stories: Nature, History, and Narrative." *Journal of American History* 78 (March 1992): 1347–76.

———. "The Riddle of the Apostle Islands." *Orion* 22 (May/June 2003): 36–42.

———. "The Trouble with Wilderness, or, Getting Back to the Wrong Nature." In *Uncommon Ground*, edited by William Cronon, 69–90.

Cronon, William, ed. *Uncommon Ground: Rethinking the Human Place in Nature.* New York: W. W. Norton, 1995.

Cullon, Joseph F. "Landscapes of Labor and Leisure: Common Rights, Private Property and Class Relations along the Bois Brule River, 1870–1940." Master's thesis, University of Wisconsin–Madison, 1995.

Curtis, John T. *The Vegetation of Wisconsin: An Ordination of Plant Communities.* 1959. Reprint, Madison: University of Wisconsin Press, 1979.

Dahl, Alma, Carl Dahl, and Bill Noring. Interview by Norma Lien and Jan Moran, February 2, 1981. Transcript, AINL Library.

Dahl, Frederick H., ed. *Diary of a Norwegian Fisherman: The Collected Diaries of Frederick A. Hansen.* Jacksonville, FL: Paramount Press, 1989.

Dahl, Melvin. Interview by Carol Ahlgren, November 12, 1987, Minneapolis. Transcript, AINL Library.

Dahlberg Burton L., and Ralph C. Guettinger. *The White-Tailed Deer in Wisconsin.* Madison: Wisconsin Conservation Department, 1956.

Dalrymple, William F. Papers, 1836–1916. WHS.

Danbom, David B. *Born in the Country: A History of Rural America.* Baltimore, MD: Johns Hopkins University Press, 1995.

Davis, Mark. "Northern Choices: Rural Forest County in the 1920s, Part 1." *Wisconsin Magazine of History* 79 (Autumn 1995): 3–31.

———. "Northern Choices: Rural Forest County in the 1920s, Part 2." *Wisconsin Magazine of History* 79 (Winter 1995–1996): 109–38.

Denevan, William M. "The Pristine Myth: The Landscape of the Americas in 1492." *Annals of the Association of American Geographers* 82 (September 1992): 369–85.

DeVoto, Bernard. "The West: A Plundered Province." *Harper's* (August 1934): 355–64.

Dewey, Scott Hamilton. *Don't Breathe the Air: Air Pollution and U.S. Environmental Politics, 1945–1970.* College Station: Texas A&M University Press, 2000.

Donlan, C. Josh, Joel Berger, Carl E. Bock, Jane H. Bock, David A. Burney, James A. Estes, Dave Foreman, Paul S. Martin, Gary W. Roemer, Felisa A. Smith, Michael E. Soulé, and Harry W. Greene. "Pleistocene Rewilding: An Optimistic Agenda for Twenty-First Century Conservation." *American Naturalist* 168 (November 2006): 660–81.

Drury, William Holland, Jr. *Chance and Change: Ecology for Conservationists.* Berkeley: University of California Press, 1998.

Duncanson, Michael E., and Gilbert Tanner. *A Guide to the Apostle Islands and the Bayfield Peninsula.* Eau Claire, WI: Cartographic Institute, 1976.

Dunn, Durwood. *Cade's Cove: The Life and Death of a Southern Appalachian Community, 1817–1937.* Knoxville: University of Tennessee Press, 1988.

Eckert, Kathryn Bishop. *The Sandstone Architecture of the Lake Superior Region.* Detroit: Wayne State University Press, 2000.

Elder, John. "Inheriting Mt. Tom." *Orion* 16 (Spring 1997): 27–32.

———. *Reading the Mountains of Home.* Cambridge, MA: Harvard University Press, 1998.

Feldman, James, and Robert W. Mackreth. "Wasteland, Wilderness, or Workplace: Perceiving and Preserving the Apostle Islands." In *Protecting Our Diverse Heritage: The Role of Parks, Protected Areas, and Cultural Sites*, edited by David S. Harmon, Bruce M. Kilgore, and Gay E. Vietzke. Hancock, MI: George Wright Society, 2004.

Fiege, Mark. *Irrigated Eden: The Making of An Agricultural Landscape in the American West*. Seattle: University of Washington Press, 1999.

Fifield, Samuel S. "Among the Historic Apostle Islands." *National Magazine* 8 (July 1898): 364–72

———. "The Story of the Apostles." *Picturesque Wisconsin* 1 (July 1899): 67–88.

Fine, I. V. *Apostle Islands: Some of the Economic Implications of the Proposed Apostle Islands National Lakeshore*. Madison: University of Wisconsin, School of Commerce, Bureau of Business Research & Service, and Center for Research on Tourism, 1965.

Fine, I. V., Ralph B. Hovind, and Philip H. Lewis Jr. *The Lake Superior Region Recreational Potential: Preliminary Report*. Madison: Wisconsin Department of Resource Development, 1962.

Fish Commissioners of the State of Wisconsin. *Reports of the Fish Commissioners of the State of Wisconsin*. Madison: Democrat Printing Co., 1883–1918. (E. B. Bolens printed the reports until 1877; David Atwood, until 1882; and Democrat Printing Co., thereafter.)

Flader, Susan A., ed. *The Great Lakes Forest: An Environmental and Social History*. Minneapolis: University of Minnesota Press, 1983.

———. *Thinking Like a Mountain: Aldo Leopold and the Evolution of an Ecological Attitude toward Deer, Wolves, and Forests*. Madison: University of Wisconsin Press, 1974.

Foreman, Dave. "The Pristine Myths." *Wild Earth* 11 (Spring 2001): 1–5.

———. *Rewilding North America: A Vision for Conservation in the 21st Century*. Washington, D.C.: Island Press, 2004.

———. "Wilderness Areas for Real." In *Great New Wilderness Debate*, edited by Callicott and Nelson, 395–407.

Foresta, Ronald A. *America's National Parks and Their Keepers*. Washington, D.C.: Resources for the Future, 1984.

Foster, David R. "Insights from Historical Geography to Ecology and Conservation: Lessons from the New England Landscape." *Journal of Biogeography* 29 (October 2002): 1269–75.

Foster, David R., and John D. Aber, eds. *Forests in Time: The Environmental Consequences of 1000 Years of Change in New England*. New Haven, CT: Yale University Press, 2004.

Foster, D. R., F. Swanson, J. Aber, I. Burke, N. Brokaw, D. Tilman, and A. Knapp. "The Importance of Land-Use Legacies to Ecology and Conservation." *Bioscience* 53 (January 2003): 77–88.

Frängsmyer, Tore, J. L. Heilbron, and Robin E. Rider, eds. *The Quantifying Spirit in the 18th Century*. Berkeley: University of California Press, 1990.

Fraser, Caroline. *Rewilding the World: Dispatches from the Conservation Revolution*. New York: Metropolitan Books, 2009.

Fraundorf, William J. "Forest Vegetation: Inventory and Management Recommendations, Outer Island, Apostle Islands National Lakeshore, Wisconsin." Master's thesis, University of Wisconsin–Stevens Point, 1984.

Frederick, Douglas J., and Lawrence Rakestraw. *A Forest Type Map of Apostle Islands and Pictured Rocks National Lakeshores, from the Original General Land Office Survey Records*. National Park Service, 1976. AINL Library.

Fries, Robert F. *Empire in Pine: The Story of Lumbering in Wisconsin, 1830–1900*. 1951. Rev. ed. Sister Bay, WI: William Caxton Ltd., 1989.

Garrison, Lemuel A. "Practical Experience in Standards, Policies, and Planning." In *First World Conference on National Parks*, edited by Alexander B. Adams, 187–96. Washington, D.C.: Government Printing Office, 1962.

Gerstenberger, Thomas. "Island Hideaway: The West Bay Club." *Lake Superior Magazine* 14 (December/January 1992): 50–53.

Gjerde, Jon. *From Peasants to Farmers: The Migration from Balestrand, Norway, to the Upper Middle West*. New York: Cambridge University Press, 1985.

Glad, Paul W. *War, a New Era, and Depression, 1914–1940*. Vol. 5 of *The History of Wisconsin Series*, edited by William Fletcher Thompson. Madison: State Historical Society of Wisconsin Press, 1990.

Goode, George Brown. *The Fisheries and Fishery Industries of the United States*. Washington, D.C.: Government Printing Office, 1884–87.

Gough, Robert. *Farming the Cutover: A Social History of Northern Wisconsin, 1900–1940*. Lawrence: University Press of Kansas, 1997.

Graf, William L. *Wilderness Preservation and the Sagebrush Rebellions*. Savage, MD: Rowan & Littlefield, 1990.

Grover, Kathryn, ed. *Hard at Play: Leisure in America, 1840–1940*. Amherst: University of Massachusetts Press, 1992.

Guha, Ramachandra. "Radical American Environmentalism and Wilderness Preservation: A Third World Critique." *Environmental Ethics* 11 (Spring 1989): 71–83.

Gulig, Anthony D. "In Whose Interest? Government-Indian Relations in Northern Saskatchewan and Wisconsin, 1900–1940." Ph.D. diss., University of Saskatchewan, Canada, 1997.

Hadland, Cliff, and Harvey Hadland. Interview by author, November 8, 2001, Bayfield, WI. Tape recording.

———. Interview by Martha Neuman, July 25, 1992, Rocky Island, WI. Tape recording, AINL Library.

Hahn, Steven, and Jonathan Prude, eds. *The Countryside in the Age of Capitalist
Transformation*. Chapel Hill: University of North Carolina Press, 1985.

———. "Hunting, Fishing, and Foraging: Common Rights and Class Relations in
the Postbellum South." *Radical History Review* 26 (October 1982): 37–64

Hansen, Michael J., J. W. Peck, R. G. Schorfhaar, J. H. Selgeby, D. R. Schreiner, S. T.
Schram, B. L. Swanson, W. R. MacCallum, M. K. Burnham-Curtis, G. L. Curtis,
J. W. Heinrich, and R. J. Young. "Lake Trout (*Salvelinus namaycush*) Populations
in Lake Superior and Their Restoration in 1959–1993." *Journal of Great Lakes
Research* 21, suppl. 1 (1995): 152–75.

Harmon, Alexandra. *Indians in the Making: Ethnic Relations and Indian Identities
around Puget Sound*. Berkeley: University of California Press, 1998.

Harmon, David. "Cultural Diversity, Human Subsistence, and the National Park
Ideal." *Environmental Ethics* 9 (Summer 1987): 71–83.

Harrington, John. "Shaw Farm Vegetation Survey." 1982. AINL Library.

Hartzog, George, Jr. "The Impact of Recent Legislation on Administrative Agencies."
In *Wilderness in Changing World*, edited by Bruce M. Kilgore. San Francisco:
Sierra Club, 1966.

———. Interview by Kathleen Lidfors, March 7, 1985, Fairfax, VA. Transcript, Box A,
Harold C. Jordahl Papers, AINL Library.

Harvey, Mark W. T. *A Symbol of Wilderness: Echo Park and the American Conservation Movement*. Seattle: University of Washington Press, 1994.

———. *Wilderness Forever: Howard Zahniser and the Path to the Wilderness Act*.
Seattle: University of Washington Press, 2005.

Hays, Samuel P. *Conservation and the Gospel of Efficiency, the Progressive Conservation Movement, 1890–1920*. Cambridge, MA: Harvard University Press, 1959.

Hile, Ralph, Paul H. Eschmeyer, and George F. Lunger. "Status of the Lake Trout
Fishery in Lake Superior." *Transactions of the American Fisheries Society* 80 (1951):
278–312.

Hill, Burt. Account Books. 1914–44. AINL Library.

———. Memoir. Ca. 1941. AINL Library.

Hillstrom, Helen. Interview by Susan Monk, July 1985, Sand Island, WI. Transcript,
AINL Library.

Hokenson, Roy and Irene. Interview by S. L. Fisher, December 9, 1981. Transcript,
AINL Library.

Holbrook, Arthur Tenney. *From the Log of a Trout Fisherman.* Norwood, MA: Plimpton Press, 1949.

Holmer, Katy E. "A Superior Summer: A Landscape History of Rocky Island, an Apostle Islands Fishing Community." Master's thesis, University of Wisconsin–Madison, 2003.

Holzhueter, John O. *Madeline Island and the Chequamegon Region.* Madison: State Historical Society of Wisconsin Press, 1974.

Hotchkiss, George W. *History of the Lumber and Forest Industry of the Northwest.* Chicago: George W. Hotchkiss and Co., 1898.

Hulings, Elizabeth. Interview by Arnold Alanen, October 27, 1988, Bayport, MN. Transcript, AINL Library.

Hurst, James Willard. *Law and Economic Growth: The Legal History of the Lumber Industry in Wisconsin, 1836–1915.* Cambridge, MA: Belknap Press of Harvard University Press, 1964.

Hyde, Anne Farrar. *An American Vision: Far Western Landscape and National Culture, 1820–1920.* New York: New York University Press, 1990.

Island View Hotel Company. *Bayfield Wisconsin: The Most Famous Health and Pleasure Resort in Northern Wisconsin.* Bayfield, WI: Bayfield County Press, 1890. WHS pamphlet collection.

Jacoby, Karl. "Class and Environmental History." *Environmental History* 2 (July 1997): 324–42.

———. *Crimes against Nature: Squatters, Poachers, Thieves, and the Hidden History of American Conservation.* Berkeley: University of California Press, 2001.

Jasen, Patricia. *Wild Things: Nature, Culture, and Tourism in Ontario, 1790–1914.* Toronto: University of Toronto Press, 1995.

Jefferson, Carol A. "Ecology of the Sand Vegetation of the Apostle Islands." In *Proceedings of the First Conference on Scientific Research in the National Parks,* edited by Robert M. Linn, 115–18. New Orleans: Government Printing Office, 1976.

Johnson, Benjamin Heber. "Subsistence, Class, and Conservation at the Birth of Superior National Forest." *Environmental History* 4 (January 1999): 80–99.

Johnson, Ronald W. *The Manitou Island Fish Camp: A Special Study.* Denver: Denver Service Center, National Park Service, 1983. AINL Library.

Jordahl, Harold C. Papers. AINL Library.

Jordahl, Harold C., Jr. *A Unique Collection of Islands: The Influence of History, Politics, Policy and Planning on the Establishment of Apostle Islands National Lakeshore.* Madison: Department of Urban and Regional Planning, University of Wisconsin–Extension, 1994.

Judd, Richard W. *Common Lands, Common People: The Origins of Conservation in Northern New England.* Cambridge, MA: Harvard University Press, 1997.

Judziewicz, Emmet J. "Survey of Non-native (Exotic) Vascular Plant Species of Campgrounds and Developed Areas, at Apostle Islands National Lakeshore." January 9, 2000. AINL Library.

Judziewicz, Emmet J., and Rudy G. Koch. "Flora and Vegetation of the Apostle Islands and Madeline Island, Ashland and Bayfield Counties, Wisconsin." *The Michigan Botanist* 32 (March 1993): 43–189.

Kates, James. *Planning a Wilderness: Regenerating the Great Lakes Cutover Region.* Minneapolis: University of Minnesota Press, 2001.

Keller, Robert H., and Michael F. Turek. *American Indians and National Parks.* Tucson: University of Arizona Press, 1998.

Kinney, J. P. *Indian Forest and Range: A History of the Administration and Conservation of the Redman's Heritage.* Washington, D.C.: Forestry Enterprises, 1950.

Klyza, Christopher McGrory, ed. *Wilderness Comes Home: Rewilding the Northeast.* Middlebury, VT: Middlebury College Press, 2001.

Krech, Shepard, III. *The Ecological Indian: Myth and History.* New York: W. W. Norton, 1999.

Krumenaker, Bob. "New Wilderness Can Be Created: A Personal History of the Gaylord Nelson Wilderness at Apostle Islands National Lakeshore." *George Wright Forum* 22 (October 2005): 35–49.

Kuchenberg, Tom. *Reflections in a Tarnished Mirror: The Use and Abuse of the Great Lakes.* Sturgeon Bay, WI: Golden Glow Publishing, 1978.

Langston, Nancy. *Forest Dreams, Forest Nightmares: The Paradox of Old Growth in the Inland West.* Seattle: University of Washington Press, 1995.

———. *Where Land and Water Meet: A Western Landscape Transformed.* Seattle: University of Washington Press, 2003.

Lash, Jonathan, Katherine Gillman, and David Sheridan, *A Season of Spoils: The Reagan Administration's Attack on the Environment.* New York: Pantheon, 1984.

Lawrie, A. H., and Jerold F. Rahrer. *Lake Superior: A Case History of the Lake and its Fisheries.* Ann Arbor, MI: Great Lakes Fishery Commission, 1973.

Leopold, A. Starker, Stanley A. Cain, Clarence M. Cottam, Ira N. Gabrielson, and Thomas L. Kimball. "Wildlife Management in the National Parks." In *Transactions of the Twenty-Eighth North American Wildlife and Natural Resources Conference*, edited by James B. Trefethen, 29–44. Washington, D.C.: Wildlife Management Institute, 1963.

Leopold, Aldo. "Wilderness as a Form of Land Use." In *Great New Wilderness Debate*, edited by Callicott and Nelson, 75–84.

Lewis, Michael, ed. *American Wilderness: A New History*. New York: Oxford University Press, 2007.

Lidfors, Kate. "Historic Logging Sites in the Apostle Islands National Lakeshore: A Resource Management Plan." 1984. AINL Library.

————. "Sandstone Quarries of the Apostle Islands: A Resource Management Plan." 1983. AINL Library.

Lock, Vickie. "A Summer Place: Elizabeth Hull's Madeline Island Photo Album." *Wisconsin Magazine of History* 85 (Summer 2002): 32–39.

Lockhart, Matthew A. " 'The Trouble with Wilderness' Education in the National Park Service: The Case for the Lost Cattle Mounts of Congaree." *Public Historian* 28 (Spring 2006): 11–30.

Loew, Patty. "Hidden Transcripts in the Chippewa Treaty Rights Struggle: A Twice Told Story of Race, Resistance, and the Politics of Power." *American Indian Quarterly* 21 (Fall 1997): 713–19.

————. "Newspapers and the Lake Superior Chippewa in the 'Unprogressive' Era." Ph.D. diss., University of Wisconsin–Madison, 1998.

Löfgren, Orvar. *On Holiday: A History of Vacationing*. Berkeley: University of California Press, 1999.

Louter, David. *Windshield Wilderness: Cars, Roads, and Nature in Washington's National Parks*. Seattle: University of Washington Press, 2006.

Madeline Island Historical Preservation Association Inc. *On the Rock: The History of Madeline Island Told through Its Families*. Friendship, WI: New Past Press, 1997.

Making the Most of Ashland County Land. Special Circular. Madison: Extension Service of the College of Agriculture, University of Wisconsin, October 1930. WHS pamphlet collection.

Marler, Marilyn. "A Survey of Exotic Plants in Federal Wilderness Areas." In *Wilderness Science in a Time of Change Conference*, vol. 5, *Wilderness Ecosystems, Threats, and Management*, compiled by David N. Cole et al., 318–27.

Marsh, Kevin R. *Drawing Lines in the Forest: Creating Wilderness Areas in the Pacific Northwest*. Seattle: University of Washington Press, 2007.

Marshall, Albert M. *Brule Country*. St. Paul, MN: North Central Publishing Co., 1954.

Martin, Paul S. *Twilight of the Mammoths: Ice Age Extinctions and the Rewilding of America*. Berkeley: University of California Press, 2005.

McCool, Stephen F., David N. Cole, William T. Borrie, and Jennifer O'Laughlin, comps. *Wilderness Science in a Time of Change Conference*, vol. 2, *Wilderness within the Context of Larger Systems*. Ogden, UT: U.S. Department of Agriculture, Forest Service, Rocky Mountain Research Station, 1999.

McEvoy, Arthur F. *The Fisherman's Problem: Ecology and Law in the California Fisheries, 1850–1950*. New York: Cambridge University Press, 1986.

McKibben, Bill. *The End of Nature*. New York: Random House, 1989.

———. *Hope, Human and Wild: True Stories of Living Lightly on the Earth*. Boston: Little, Brown, 1995.

Merchant, Carolyn. "Shades of Darkness: Race and Environmental History." *Environmental History* 8 (July 2003): 380–94.

Merrill, Horace Samuel. *William Freeman Vilas: Doctrinaire Democrat*. Madison: State Historical Society of Wisconsin, 1991.

Meyer, Melissa L. *The White Earth Tragedy: Ethnicity and Dispossession at a Minnesota Anishinaabe Reservation, 1889–1920*. Lincoln: University of Nebraska Press, 1994.

Miller, Char. *Gifford Pinchot and the Making of Modern Environmentalism*. Washington, D.C.: Island Press, 2001.

Miller, Pat. Interview by Kate Lidfors, December 2, 1987. Transcript, AINL Library.

Milner, James W. "Report on the Fisheries of the Great Lakes: The Result of Inquiries Prosecuted in 1871 and 1872." In U.S. Commission of Fish and Fisheries 1872–1873 Report. 42nd Cong., 3d sess., 1872. S. Misc. Doc. 74.

Mitman, Gregg. *Breathing Space: How Allergies Shape our Lives and Landscapes*. New Haven, CT: Yale University Press, 2007.

Mroz, Glenn, and Jeff Martin, eds. *Hemlock Ecology and Management: Proceedings of a Regional Conference on Ecology and Management of Eastern Hemlock*. Madison: Department of Forestry, University of Wisconsin–Madison, 1995.

Nash, Roderick F. *Wilderness and the American Mind*. 3d ed. New Haven, CT: Yale University Press, 1982.

National Park Service. *Apostle Islands National Lakeshore: Statement for Management*. Washington, D.C.: U.S. Department of the Interior, National Park Service, 1977.

———. *Apostle Islands National Lakeshore: Statement for Management*. Washington, D.C.: U.S. Department of the Interior, National Park Service, 1983.

———. *Apostle Islands National Lakeshore, Wisconsin: Draft Wilderness Study/Environmental Impact Statement*. Washington, D.C.: U.S. Department of the Interior, National Park Service, 2003.

———. *Apostle Islands National Lakeshore, Wisconsin: Final Wilderness Study/Environmental Impact Statement*. Washington, D.C.: U.S. Department of the Interior, National Park Service, 2004.

———. *Compilation of the Administrative Policies for the National Recreation Areas, National Seashores, National Parkways, National Scenic Riverways (Recreational Area Category) of the National Park System*. Washington, D.C.: U.S. Department of the Interior, National Park Service, 1968.

———. *Final Fire Management Plan for Apostle Islands National Lakeshore*. Bayfield, WI: U.S. Department of the Interior, National Park Service, 2005.

———. General Classified Files, 1907–32. Proposed National Parks, 0-32. Record Group 79. NA MD.

———. *Management Policies, National Park Service*. Washington, D.C.: U.S. Department of the Interior, 1975.

———. *Management Policies*. Washington, D.C.: U.S. Department of the Interior/ National Park Service, 1978.

———. *National Park Service Management Policies*. Washington, D.C.: U.S. Department of the Interior, National Park Service, 1988.

———. *National Park Service Management Policies*. Washington, D.C.: U.S. Department of the Interior, National Park Service, 2001.

———. *The National Parks: Shaping the System*. Washington, D.C.: U.S. Department of the Interior, 2005.

National Park Service, Apostle Islands National Lakeshore, Wisconsin. *Apostle Islands: Wilderness Study Workbook*. Washington, D.C.: National Park Service, 2002.

National Wilderness Steering Committee. "Guidance 'White Paper' Number 1: Cultural Resources and Wilderness." November 30, 2002. www.wilderness.net/ NWPS/documents/NPS/NWSC_White_Paper_1_Cultural_Resources_final.doc.

Nelson, Gaylord A. Papers, 1954–2005. WHS.

Nelson, Gaylord. Interview by author, May 22, 2002, Washington, D.C. Tape recording.

Nelson, Julian. Interview by author, November 12, 2001, Bayfield, WI. Tape recording.

Nesper, Larry. *The Walleye War: The Struggle for Ojibwe Spearfishing and Treaty Rights*. Lincoln: University of Nebraska Press, 2002.

Neth, Mary. *Preserving the Family Farm: Women, Community and the Foundations of Agribusiness in the Midwest, 1900–1940*. Baltimore, MD: Johns Hopkins University Press, 1985.

Neuman, Martha. *Special History Study: Rocky and South Twin Islands; A History of Commercial Fishing Camps and Resorts*. Bayfield, WI: National Park Service, Apostle Islands National Lakeshore, 1992. Rocky Island File, AINL Library.

———. "What Are Those Cabins Doing There?" Master's thesis, University of Wisconsin, Madison, 1991.

Neumann, Roderick P. *Imposing Wilderness: Struggles over Livelihood and Nature Preservation in Africa*. Berkeley: University of California Press, 1998.

Nevin, James. "Artificial Propagation versus a Close Season for the Great Lakes." *Transactions of the American Fisheries Society* 27 (1898): 17–25.

———. "Fifty Years Experience in Fish Culture." *Wisconsin Conservationist* 2 (November 1920): 6–7.

Noring, Bill. Interview by Norma Lien and Jan Moran, December 16, 1980. Transcript, AINL Library.

———. Interview by William Tishler, September 14, 1981. Tape recording, AINL Library.

Norris, Scott, ed. *Discovered Country: Tourism and Survival in the American West.* Albuquerque, NM: Stone Ladder Press, 1994.

North Central Field Committee. *Apostle Islands National Lakeshore: A Proposal.* Washington, D.C.: U.S. Department of the Interior, 1965.

———. *Proposed Apostle Islands National Lakeshore, Bayfield and Ashland Counties, Wisconsin.* Washington, D.C.: U.S. Department of the Interior, 1965.

Noss, Reed, and Michael Soulé. "Rewilding and Biodiversity: Complimentary Goals for Continental Conservation." *Wild Earth* 3 (Fall 1998): 22–43.

Noss, Reed F., Howard B. Quigley, Maurice G. Hornocker, Troy Merrill, and Paul C. Paquet. "Conservation Biology and Carnivore Conservation in the Rocky Mountains." *Conservation Biology* 10 (August 1996): 949–63.

Notes and Files of the Joint Commission Relative to the Preservation of the Fisheries in Waters Contiguous to Canada and the United States. Record Group 22. NA MD.

Nourse, David. Interview by Greta Swenson, 1981, Bayfield, WI. Tape recording, AINL Library.

Nourse, Grace. Interview by Greta Swenson, 1981, Bayfield, WI. Transcript, AINL Library.

Novak, Barbara. *Nature and Culture: American Landscape Painting, 1825–1875.* New York: Oxford University Press, 1980.

Nute, Grace Lee. "American Fur Company's Fishing Enterprises on Lake Superior." *Mississippi Valley Historical Review* 12 (March 1926): 483–503.

———. *Lake Superior.* Indianapolis, IN: Bobbs-Merrill, 1944.

O'Donnell, D. John. "A Four-Year Creel Census on the Brule River, Douglas County, Wisconsin." *Transactions of the Wisconsin Academy of Sciences, Arts, and Letters* 37 (1945): 279–303.

———. "A History of Fishing in the Brule River." *Transactions of the Wisconsin Academy of Sciences, Arts, and Letters* 36 (1944): 19–31.

Olmanson, Eric D. *The Future City on the Inland Sea: A History of Imaginative Geographies of Lake Superior.* Athens: Ohio University Press, 2007.

Outdoor Recreation Resources Review Commission. *Outdoor Recreation for America.* Washington, D.C.: Government Printing Office, 1962.

Palm, Howard. Interview by Carol Ahlgren, October 17, 1987, White Bear Lake, MN. Transcript, AINL Library.

Peterson, Sheree L. "Camp Stella: Meeting Place of Kindred Souls." Bayfield, WI: Eastern National Park and Monument Association, Apostle Islands National Lakeshore, 1997. AINL Library.

Poff, Ron. *From Milk Can to Ecosystem Management: A Historical Perspective on Wisconsin's Fisheries Management Program, 1830s–1990s*. Madison: Bureau of Fisheries Management and Habitat Protection, Wisconsin Department of Natural Resources, 1996.

Pollan, Michael. "Only Man's Presence Can Save Nature: Beyond the Wilderness." *Harper's Magazine* (April 1990): 37–48.

Prothero, Frank. *The Good Years: A History of the Commercial Fishing Industry on Lake Erie*. Belleville, Ontario: Mika Publishing, 1973.

Prucha, Francis Paul. *The Great Father: The United States Government and the American Indian*. Abr. ed. Lincoln: University of Nebraska Press, 1985.

Pycha, Richard L., and George R. King. *Changes in the Lake Trout Population of Southern Lake Superior in Relation to the Fishery, the Sea Lamprey, and Stocking, 1950–1970*. Ann Arbor, MI: Great Lakes Fishery Commission, 1975.

Rakestraw, Lawrence. "Forest and Cultural History in Apostle Islands and Pictured Rocks National Lakeshores, Lake Superior." Michigan Technological University, Houghton, 1975. AINL Library.

Records of the Great Lakes Agency. Record Group 75. NA GL.

Records of the La Pointe Agency. Record Group 75. NA GL.

Records of the Red Cliff Agency. Record Group 75. NA GL.

Reich, Justin. "Re-Creating the Wilderness: Shaping Narratives and Landscapes in Shenandoah National Park." *Environmental History* 6 (January 2001): 95–117.

Rennicke, Jeff. *Jewels on the Water: Lake Superior's Apostle Islands*. Bayfield, WI: Friends of the Apostle Islands, 2005.

Rettie, Dwight F. *Our National Park System: Caring for America's Greatest Natural and Historic Treasures*. Urbana: University of Illinois Press, 1995.

Reynolds, A. R. *The Daniel Shaw Lumber Company: A Case Study of the Wisconsin Lumbering Frontier*. New York: New York University Press, 1957.

Righter, Robert W. *Crucible for Conservation: The Creation of Grand Teton National Park*. Boulder: Colorado Associated University Press, 1982.

Robbins, William G. *Colony and Empire: The Capitalist Transformation of the American West*. Lawrence: University Press of Kansas, 1994.

———. *Hard Times in Paradise: Coos Bay, Oregon, 1850–1986*. Seattle: University of Washington Press, 1988.

———. "The 'Plundered Province' Thesis and the Recent Historiography of the American West." *Pacific Historical Review* 55 (November 1986): 577–97.

Roberts, Edwards. *Gogebic, Eagle River, Ashland, and the Resorts in Northern Michigan and Wisconsin Reached by the Milwaukee, Lake Shore & Western Railway*. Chicago: Poole Bros., 1886. WHS pamphlet collection.

Ross, Hamilton Nelson. *La Pointe: Village Outpost on Madeline Island*. 1960. Reprint, Madison: State Historical Society of Wisconsin, 2000.

———. Papers, 1874–1969. WHS.

Roth, Filibert. *On the Forestry Conditions of Northern Wisconsin*. Madison: Wisconsin Geological and Natural History Survey, 1898.

Rothman, Hal K. *Devil's Bargains: Tourism in the Twentieth-Century West*. Lawrence: University Press of Kansas, 1998.

Rowlands, Walter A., and Fred B. Trenk. *Rural Zoning Ordinances in Wisconsin*. Circular No. 281. Madison: University of Wisconsin Agricultural Experiment Station, 1936.

Rowlands, Walter, Fred Trenk, and Raymond Penn. *Rural Zoning in Wisconsin*. Bulletin 479. Madison: University of Wisconsin Agricultural Experiment Station, 1948.

Runte, Alfred. *National Parks: The American Experience*. 2d ed. Lincoln: University of Nebraska Press, 1987.

Satz, Ronald N. "Chippewa Treaty Rights: The Reserved Rights of Wisconsin's Chippewa Indians in Historical Perspective." Special issue, *Transactions of the Wisconsin Academy of Sciences, Arts, and Letters* 79, no. 1 (1991): 1–251.

Scott, Douglas W. *The Enduring Wilderness: Protecting Our Natural Heritage through the Wilderness Act*. Golden, CO: Fulcrum, 2004.

———. " 'Untrammeled,' 'Wilderness Character,' and the Challenges of Wilderness Preservation." *Wild Earth* 11 (Fall/Winter 2001–2): 72–79.

———. *A Wilderness-Forever Future: A Short History of the Wilderness Preservation System*. Washington, D.C.: Pew Wilderness Center, 2001.

Scott, James C. *Seeing Like a State: How Certain Schemes to Improve the Human Condition Have Failed*. New Haven, CT: Yale University Press, 1998.

Scott, Walter E., and Thomas Reitz. *The Wisconsin Warden: Wisconsin Conservation Law Enforcement; A Centennial Chronology (1879–1979)*. Madison: Wisconsin Department of Natural Resources, 1979.

Scoyen, Eivind T. "Appendix: National Park Wilderness." In *Wilderness: America's Living Heritage*, edited by David Brower, 185–93. San Francisco: Sierra Club, 1961.

Sears, John F. *Sacred Places: American Tourist Attractions in the Nineteenth Century*. New York: Oxford University Press, 1989.

Sellars, Richard West. *Preserving Nature in the National Parks: A History*. New Haven, CT: Yale University Press, 1997.

Shaffer, Marguerite S. *See America First: Tourism and National Identity, 1880–1940.* Washington, D.C.: Smithsonian Institution Press, 2001.

Shapiro, Aaron. " 'One Crop Worth Cultivating': Tourism in the Upper Great Lakes, 1910–1965." Ph.D. diss., University of Chicago, 2005.

———. "Up North on Vacation." *Wisconsin Magazine of History* 89 (Summer 2006): 2–13.

Short, C. Brant. *Ronald Reagan and the Public Lands: America's Conservation Debate, 1979–1984.* College Station: Texas A&M University Press, 1989.

Silvern, Steven Eric. "Nature, Territory, and Identity in the Wisconsin Ojibwe Treaty Rights Conflict." Ph.D. diss., University of Wisconsin–Madison, 1993.

Smiley, Chas. W. "Changes in the Fisheries of the Great Lakes during the Decade, 1870–1880." *Bulletin of the United States Fish Commission* 1 (1882): 252–58.

Smith, Alice E. *From Exploration to Statehood.* Vol. 1 of *The History of Wisconsin Series*, edited by William Fletcher Thompson. Madison: State Historical Society of Wisconsin Press, 1973.

Smith, Douglas W., and Rolf O. Peterson. "Beaver Ecology in Apostle Islands National Lakeshore." In *Twelfth Research Conference, Apostle Islands National Lakeshore*, edited by Robert B. Brander and Margaret D. Ludwig, 17–18. Omaha, NE: U.S. Department of the Interior, National Park Service, Midwest Regional Office, 1990.

Smith, Hugh M., and Merwin-Marie Snell, comps. "Review of the Fisheries of the Great Lakes in 1885." In U.S. Commission of Fish and Fisheries, *Report of the Commissioner for 1887.* 50th Cong., 2d sess., 1889. H. Misc. Doc. 133.

Snyder, Gary. "Nature As Seen from Kitkitdizze Is No 'Social Construction.' " *Wild Earth* 6 (Winter 1996–97): 8–9.

———. *The Practice of the Wild: Essays.* San Francisco: North Point Press, 1990

Soluri, John. *Banana Cultures: Agriculture, Consumption, and Environmental Change in Honduras and the United States.* Austin: University of Texas Press, 2005.

Soulé, Michael E., and Gary Lease, eds. *Reinventing Nature? Responses to Postmodern Deconstruction.* Washington, D.C.: Island Press, 1995.

Spence, Mark David. *Dispossessing the Wilderness: Indian Removal and the Making of the National Parks.* New York: Oxford University Press, 1999.

Standyk, Lelyn, Richard L. Verch, and Bruce A. Goetz. *Stockton Island Survey: An Ecological Survey and Environmental Impact Study of Stockton Island, Apostle Islands National Lakeshore.* Ashland, WI: Northland College, 1974.

Steen-Adams, Michelle. "Change on a Northern Wisconsin Landscape: Legacies of Human History." Ph.D. diss., University of Wisconsin–Madison, 2005.

Stradling, David. *Making Mountains: New York City and the Catskills.* Seattle: University of Washington Press, 2007.

———. *Smokestacks and Progressives: Environmentalists, Engineers, and Air Quality in America, 1881–1951*. Baltimore, MD: Johns Hopkins University Press, 1999.

Summers, Gregory. *Consuming Nature: Environmentalism in the Fox River Valley, 1850–1950*. Lawrence: University Press of Kansas, 2006.

Sutter, Paul S. " 'A Blank Spot on the Map': Aldo Leopold, Wilderness, and U.S. Forest Service Recreational Policy, 1909–1924." *Western Historical Quarterly* 83 (Summer, 1998): 187–214.

———. *Driven Wild: How the Fight against Automobiles Launched the Modern Wilderness Movement*. Seattle: University of Washington Press, 2002.

Swain, Albert M. "Final Report to the National Park Service on Forest and Disturbance History of the Apostle Islands." Center for Climatic Research, University of Wisconsin–Madison, 1981.

———. "The Role of White Pine and Hemlock in the Forests of the Apostle Islands National Lakeshore: Past, Present, and Future." In *Fifth Annual Research Conference, Apostle Islands National Lakeshore*, edited by Merryll M. Bailey, 13. Omaha, NE: U.S. Department of the Interior, National Park Service, Midwest Regional Office, 1983.

Swain, Albert M., and Marjorie Winkler. "Forest and Disturbance History at Apostle Islands National Lakeshore Park." *Park Science* 3 (Summer 1983): 3–5.

Taylor, Joseph E., III. *Making Salmon: An Environmental History of the Northwest Fisheries Crisis*. Seattle: University of Washington Press, 1999.

Terrie, Philip G. *Forever Wild: A Cultural History of Wilderness in the Adirondacks*. Syracuse, NY: Syracuse University Press, 1994.

Tishler, William H., Arnold R. Alanen, and George Thompson. *Early Agricultural Development on the Apostle Islands*. Madison: Apostle Islands National Lakeshore and Department of Landscape Architecture, University of Wisconsin, 1984. AINL Library.

Toothman, Stephanie S. "Cultural Resource Management in Natural Areas of the National Park System." *Public Historian* 9 (Spring 1987): 65–76.

Turner, Jack. *The Abstract Wild*. Tucson: University of Arizona Press, 1996.

Turner, James Morton. "From Woodcraft to 'Leave No Trace': Wilderness, Consumerism, and Environmentalism in Twentieth-Century America." *Environmental History* 7 (July 2002): 462–84.

———. "The Politics of Modern Wilderness." In *American Wilderness*, edited by Lewis, 243–61.

———. "Wilderness East: Reclaiming History." *Wild Earth* 11 (Spring 2001): 19–26.

Turrittin, Anton H. "Social Change in an Isolated Community: A Study of the Transformation of Madeline Island, Wisconsin." Master's thesis, University of Minnesota, 1960.

Twining, Charles E. "A Brief Look at a Brief Experience: Early Logging on the Apostle Islands." In *Third Annual Research Conference, Apostle Islands National Lakeshore*, edited by Jim Wood, 18–20. Bayfield, WI: U.S. Department of the Interior, National Park Service, Midwest Regional Office, 1981.

———. "Logging on the Apostle Islands: A 19th Century Overview." Northland College Report. 1981. AINL Library.

Tyrrell, Lucy. "An Inventory of Old-Growth Forests on Lands of the National Park Service." Department of Botany, University of Wisconsin–Madison, ca. 1990.

U.S. Bureau of Fisheries. Records Concerning Relations with Canada, International Fisheries Commission. 1908. Record Group 22. NA MD.

U.S. Commission of Fish and Fisheries. *Reports of the Commissioner.* Washington, D.C.: Government Printing Office, 1872–1905.

U.S. Commissioner of Indian Affairs. *Annual Reports of the Commissioner of Indian Affairs.* Washington, D.C.: Government Printing Office, 1850–1905.

U.S. Congress. House. House. Committee on Interior and Insular Affairs. *Apostle Islands National Lakeshore: Hearings before the Subcommittee on National Parks and Recreation.* 91st Cong., 1st sess., August 19, 1969.

———. House. Committee on Interior and Insular Affairs. *Apostle Islands National Lakeshore: Hearings before the Subcommittee on National Parks and Recreation.* 91st Cong., 2d sess., March 23, 24, and June 3, 1970.

———. House. Committee on Interior and Insular Affairs, Subcommittee on Public Lands and National Parks. *Land Acquisition Policy and Program of the National Park Service.* 98th Cong., 2d sess., 1984. Committee Print.

———. House. Committee on Interior and Insular Affairs, Subcommittee on Public Lands and National Parks. *Public Land Management Policy, Part V: Impact of Acquisition Delays on the Lands and Resources of the National Park System.* 98th Cong., 1st sess., 1983.

———. *Message of President on Allotment of Lands in Severalty to Lake Superior Chippewa Indians.* 48th Cong., 1st sess., 1883. H. Exec. Doc. 12.

U.S. Congress. Senate. Committee on Energy and Natural Resources, Subcommittee on Public Lands, Reserved Water and Resource Conservation. *Additions to the Wild and Scenic Rivers System, Boundary Adjustments to Units of the National Park System, and Revision of a Ski Area Permit System on National Forest Lands.* 99th Cong., 2d sess., 1986.

———. Senate. Committee on Interior and Insular Affairs. *Apostle Islands National Lakeshore: Hearings before the Subcommittee on Parks and Recreation.* 90th Cong., 1st sess., May 9, June 1–2, 1967.

———. Senate. Committee on Interior and Insular Affairs. *Apostle Islands National*

Lakeshore: Hearings before the Subcommittee on Parks and Recreation. 91st Cong., 1st sess., March 17, 1969.

————. Senate. Select Committee on Indian Traders. *Chippewa Allotments of Lands and Timber Contracts*. 50th Cong., 2d sess., 1889. S. Rept. 2710.

U.S. Department of the Interior. *Our Fourth Shore: Great Lakes Shoreline Recreation Area Survey*. Washington, D.C.: U.S. Department of the Interior, National Park Service, 1959.

U.S. Department of the Interior, National Park Service. *Family-Managed Commercial Fishing in the Apostle Islands during the 20th Century, with Background Information on Commercial Fishing in Lake Superior*. Bayfield, WI: Apostle Islands National Lakeshore, 1985.

————. *Master Plan: Apostle Islands National Lakeshore, Wisconsin*. Washington, D.C.: U.S. Department of the Interior, 1971.

————. *Record of Decision: Wilderness Study Final Environmental Impact Statement*. 2004. www.nps.gov/apis/finalrod.pdf.

Vilas, William Freeman. Papers, 1827–1959. WHS.

Waller, Donald M. "Wilderness Redux: Can Biodiversity Play a Role?" *Wild Earth* 6 (Winter 1996–97): 36–45.

Wallerstein, Immanuel. *The Modern World-System: Capitalist Agriculture and the Origins of the European World-Economy in the Sixteenth Century*. New York: Academic Press, 1974.

Wallin, Victor C. Papers, 1937–76. NGLVC.

Walsted, Justin. Interview by Roy Tull, 1979, Bayfield, WI. Transcript, AINL Library.

Warren, Louis. *The Hunter's Game: Poachers and Conservationists in Twentieth-Century America*. New Haven, CT: Yale University Press, 1997.

Waskow, Ben F., and George A. Curran. "Deer Hunting on the Apostle Islands." *Wisconsin Conservation Bulletin* 19 (October 1954): 3–7.

Watt, Laura A. "The Trouble with Preservation, or, Getting Back to the Wrong Term for Wilderness Protection: A Case Study at Point Reyes National Seashore." *The Yearbook of the Association of Pacific Coast Geographers* 64 (2002): 55–72.

Webb, Melody. "Cultural Landscapes in the National Park Service." *Public Historian* 9 (Spring 1987): 77–89.

Wehrwein, George S., and Kenneth H. Parsons. *Recreation as Land Use*. Madison: University of Wisconsin Press, 1932.

Wetmore, Clifford M. "Lichens and Air Quality at Apostle Islands National Lakeshore: Final Report." National Park Service, Midwest Region, St. Paul, MN, 1988. AINL Library.

White, Richard. " 'Are You an Environmentalist, or Do You Work for a Living': Work and Nature." In *Uncommon Ground*, edited by Cronon, 171–85.

———. *"It's Your Misfortune and None of My Own": A New History of the American West*. Norman: University of Oklahoma Press, 1991.

———. *Land Use, Environment, and Social Change: The Shaping of Island County, Washington*. Seattle: University of Washington Press, 1980.

———. *The Middle Ground: Indians, Empires, and Republics in the Great Lakes Region, 1650–1815*. New York: Cambridge University Press, 1991.

———. *The Roots of Dependency: Subsistence, Environment, and Social Change among the Choctaws, Pawnees, and Navajos*. Lincoln: University of Nebraska Press, 1983.

Wiebe, Robert H. *The Search for Order, 1877–1920*. New York: Hill & Wang, 1967.

Wilkinson, Charles F. *To Feel the Summer for the Spring: The Treaty Fishing Rights of the Wisconsin Chippewa*. Madison: University of Wisconsin Law School, 1990.

Williams, Michael D. *Americans and Their Forests: A Historical Geography*. New York: Cambridge University Press, 1989.

Williams, Raymond. "Ideas of Nature." In *Problems in Materialism and Culture: Selected Essays*, 67–85. London: Verso, 1980.

Wilson, F. G. "Zoning for Forestry and Recreation: Wisconsin's Pioneer Role." *Wisconsin Magazine of History* 41 (Winter, 1957–58): 102–6.

Wisconsin Board of Commissioners of Public Lands. Surveyors Field Notes, 1832–65. WHS.

Wisconsin Central Railroad Company. *Summer Resorts of the Wisconsin Central Railroad, Lake Superior Line*. Milwaukee: Cramer, Aikens, and Cramer, 1879. WHS pamphlet collection.

Wisconsin Central Railroad. *Famous Resorts of the Northwest, Summer of 1887*. Chicago: Poole Bros., 1887. WHS pamphlet collection.

Wisconsin Conservation Department. Subject Files, 1917–67. WHS.

Wisconsin Department of Justice. Division of Legal Services. Closed Case Files, 1885–1976. WHS.

Wisconsin Department of Natural Resources. *1967–69 Biennial Report*. Madison: Wisconsin Department of Natural Resources, 1969.

Wisconsin Department of Natural Resources. Subject Files, 1967–87. WHS.

Wisconsin Department of Resource Development. *Recreational Potential of the Lake Superior South Shore Area*. Madison: Wisconsin Department of Resource Development, 1964.

Wisconsin Natural Resources Board. Minutes, 1876–2002. WHS.

Worster, Donald. "The Ecology of Order and Chaos." In *The Wealth of Nature: Environmental History and the Ecological Imagination*, 156–70. New York: Oxford University Press, 1993.

———. *Nature's Economy: A History of Ecological Ideas*. 2d ed. New York: Cambridge University Press, 1994.

Young, T. "False, Cheap and Degraded: When History, Economy and Environment Collided at Cade's Cove, Great Smoky Mountains National Park." *Journal of Historical Geography* 32 (2006): 169–89.

Index

Page numbers in italics refer to images and maps.

balsam fir, 4, 25, 27, 54, 144, 146

Barker (boat), 69

Basswood Island: and AINL, 5, 8, 120–23, 198, 204, 221, 227–29; and Apostle Islands State Forest, 168–71; and cut-stone industry, 16, 18–19; and exotic species, 221; and logging industry, 29, 31; rewilding of, 18–19, 120–21, 123; and tourism, 117, 158

Basswood Island quarry, 16, 18, *19*, 204, 216

Bayfield: character of, 5, and commercial fishing, 60, 62–63, 65, 67–72, 75, 77, 79–80, 85–87, 156; and cut-stone industry, 16; and logging industry, 28–29, 55–56, 152; and market relations with Apostle Islands, 129–30, 132–33; and railroads, 67–68, 93, 95; and tanning industry, 40–41; and tourism, 92–93, 95, 99–100, 111, 164, 218

Bayfield Businessmen's Association, 69

Bayfield County Press: and AINL, 153; and Burt Hill, 129–30; and commercial fishing, 67; and community, 128; and logging industry, 56; and tourism, 97, 99, 111, 126, 172

Bayfield Creamery, 129–30

Bayfield Fish Hatchery, 75, *76*, 102, 136

Bayfield Land Company, 28

Bayfield Land Office, 37–38

Bayfield Mercury, 28, 62

Bayfield Peninsula: and AINL, 176–77, 181, 188, 202; and exotic species, 221; and logging industry, 50, 52, 56; and regional economy, 135

Bayfield Trollers Association, 173

Beard, George Miller, 94

Bear Island, 7, 65, 158

Bear Trap Creek, 82

beaver, 23, 25

Benson, Charlie, *103*

BIA. *See* Bureau of Indian Affairs

Bierstadt, Albert, 95, 97

Big Bay State Park, 171–72

Big Bend National Park, 208

black bass, 100

Blackbird, John, 82

black grouse, 167

Blue Ridge Wilderness, 123

Bonde, Edwin, 138

Booth, Alfred, 69

Booth Fisheries Company (post-1909). *See* A. Booth Packing Company

boreal forests, 4, 27

Boutin & Holston, 126

Boutin family, 62–63, 65, 67, 126

Brander, Robert, 26, 44, 209, 220

Bright Angel Trail, 233

brook trout, 97, 100, 102–5

Brule River, 102–5, 135, 137, 176

Brule River State Forest, 172

Budvic Timbers Inc., 195–96

Buffalo, Antoine, 82

Buffalo, John, 31

Bunn, Romanzo, 83

Bureau of Indian Affairs (BIA): and AINL, 177; and allotment, 47–53; and assimilation, 46–48, 53, 55; and forest fires, 51; and forest management, 46–51, 53–55, 245n59; and IRA, 53; and La Pointe Agency, 47–51; and timber scandal, 49–51; and treaty rights, 186; and value of reservation lands, 46–48, 53–54

Bureau of Recreation, 177

Bush, George W., 228

tion, 60–61, 73–74, 76–84, 88–89, 101; and forests, 53–54, 56–57, 114–15; and Progressive conservation movement, 60, 73–74; and quantification, 78, 84; and sport fishing, 82, 90, 100–103, 114; unequal impacts of, 61, 78–84, 89–90, 101

Conservation Commission. *See* Wisconsin Conservation Commission

consumer society: and AINL, 11–12, 151, 206–7, 229; and consumption of nature, 10, 163–64, 206–7; and national wilderness movement, 11, 16, 151, 164, 206–7

Coole Park Manor, 108

Coolidge, Calvin, 102–3, 152

Cooper, James Fennimore, 111

Copper Falls State Park, 172

crash of 1873, 16

crash of 1893, 17

Cronon, William, 122, 147–48

cultural resources, *214, 222*; management of, 17–18, 20–21, 121–23, 227–32, 239n28, 281–82n52; removal of, 14, 20, 120–23, 192, 203, 210–12, 214–16, 220–21, 232

Cultural Zone, 214

Cutler, M. Rupert, 202, 205

cutover: and changing landscapes, 56–57, 166–67; and farming, 106, 113–15; and fire, 23; and land economics, 115–16; and tourism, 138; and zoning, 116–17

cut-stone industry, *17, 19*; as cultural resource, 17–19; and regional economy, 16–17, 38; and shaping of environments, 8, 17–18; significance of, 16, 18–19; and speculation, 38

Dahl family, *174*; Carl, 131, 134, 180; Harold, 180, Melvin, 134

Dahlberg, Burton, 167

Davidge, Ric, 197

Dawes Severalty Act (1887), 51, 83

Death Valley National Park, 123

deciduous forests, 27, 146

deer, *159*; and appearance in Apostle Islands, 158–60; and conservation, 158–61; hunting of, 92, 157–61; population of, 4, 92, 158–61, 167, 220, 267–68n18

DePerry, Michael, 82

Desolation Wilderness, 19

Development Zone, 206

Devils Island, 43, 57

Dinosaur National Monument, 167

DNR. *See* Wisconsin Department of Natural Resources

Duffy, Idile, 187

Durfee, William R., 48–49

East Bay (of Sand Island): and changing environments, 144, 148; and commercial fishing, 65, 125; and Sand Island community, 128, 134, 138, 140–41; and summer homes, 138, 140

East Bay Road, 138

Eastern Wilderness Areas Act (1975), 211

Echo Park, 167–68

Eha, Frank, 137–38, 146, *174*, 195

EIS. *See* Environmental Impact Statement

Elder, John, 20

Ely, Richard T., 114–16

Emerson, Ralph Waldo, 95

eminent domain, 193

Environmental Impact Statement (EIS), 120–22, 226

kayaking, 5, 10, 22, 218, *219*, 226

Kelsey, Harlan, *155*; and evaluation of Apostle Islands, 6–7, 150, 154, 156, 266n9; and exotic species, 221, 223; and failure of first AINL proposal, 7, 150; and recreational parks, 156; and tour of Apostle Islands, 23, 153–54

Kennedy, D. A., 49

Kennedy, John F., 176

King, William, 37

King's Canyon National Park, 208

Knight, John H., *37*; career of, 37; and cut-stone industry, 38; and forest fires, 39–40, 45; and La Pointe Agency, 49–50; and logging industry, 38–41, 135; and scandal, 50, 243n31; and speculation, 36–43; and sport fishing, 102, 104; and Superior Lumber Company, 38, 49–50; and tourism, 99; and Wisconsin's tax system, 39–43, 243n35

Knight, William, 30–31, 216, 263n31

Kolka, Henry, 183

Krumenaker, Bob, 4, 226–27, 229–31

Kruse, Harold, 183

Lac Courte Oreilles Reservation, 46

La Crosse, 29

Lac du Flambeau Reservation, 46, 48

lake herring (*Coregonus artedii* Lesueur): and collapse of whitefish fishery, 85–86; commercial harvest of, 86, 89, 157; and rainbow smelt, 161; and Sand Island's economy, 131; seasonality of, 157

Lake Michigan: and collapse of lake trout fishery, 89, 161; and collapse of whitefish fishery, 60, 62, 68, 73, 77, 79;

and exotic species, 161; and fisheries management, 74–77, 79; and logging industry, 28

Lake Superior: and AINL, 177, 180, 183; and commercial fishing, 59–64, 67–73, 75–79, 85–87, 89–90, 135, 157, 161–62, 173–75; and exotic species, 161–62, 173–74; and fisheries management, 13, 59–61, 73, 75–79, 90, 173–75, 188, 203; and logging industry, 50, 52; and tourism, 10, 52, 92, 95, 98, 164, 172–73; and weather, 22, 28, 129, 180, 191, 218; and wilderness designation, 225–26

Lake Superior Chippewa. *See* Ojibwe

Lake Superior Land and Development Company, 107

lake trout (*Salvelinus namaycush*): and Apostle Islands State Forest, 173; and artificial propagation, 8, 75, 162, 173–74, 217, 251n41; collapse of, 59, 157, 161–62, 173; commercial harvest of, 59–60, 62–63, 85, 89, 135, 157, 162; and impact of sea lamprey, 59, 161–62, 173, 217, 268n20; management of, 59–61, 78, 162, 173–75; recovery of, 157, 173–74; and sport fishing, 97, 173

land economics, 114–16

La Pointe (village), 97–98, 108, 124

La Pointe Agency, 47–51, 66, 246n67

La Pointe Plan, 51

La Pointe Township, 117

Last Chance mine, 233

late goldenrod, 145

Leahy, M. A., 51

"Leave No Trace," 11, 207

Lederle, Louis, 126

legibility: definition of, 12; and fisher-

National Wilderness Preservation System, 11, 183, 205
National Wilderness Steering Committee, 226-27
National Wildlife Foundation, 182
Natural Fire Management Unit, 44, 54-55, 57-58
Nebraska Row, 106-8, *109*
Neegard, H. O., 137
Nelson, Gaylord, *178*; and congressional debates over AINL, 177, 184; and Gaylord Nelson Wilderness, 225; and movement for AINL, 150, 175-76, 181, 184, 189; and national wilderness movement, 165, 181, 203, 205; and Ojibwe, 152, 184, 186-87; and opposition to AINL, 149-50, 186-87; and privatization of land within AINL, 197-98; and wilderness designation, 205-6
Neth, Mary, 135
neurasthenia, 94-95, 97
Nevin, James: and artificial propagation, 75-76, 88; and conservation, 74, 88; and fishing regulation, 61-62, 73, 76, 78, 88; and legibility, 60-61, 73, 78, 85, 88; and Ojibwe, 82; and state authority, 61, 74, 80, 85, 88; and tourism, 114; and whitefish fishery, 60-61, 77, 89
Nixon, Richard, 188
nonconforming conditions, *215*; classification of, 215; definition of, 121; and legibility, 212, 214; and wilderness designation, 121; and wilderness management, 211-12, 214, 227, 229
Noring family: Bergitt, 134, 145, 147-48; Bill, 134; farm of, 119, 129-30, 141, 144-45, 148

Noring farm, *145*; and decline of Sand Island's community, 119, 141, 144-45; and rewilding, 145, 148; and Sand Island's economic patterns, 129-30; and the shaping of environments, 130
Northern Wisconsin Resort Association, 113
North Twin Island, 43
Northwoods, 138, 185
Norway pine, 108
Nourse, Grace and Laurie, 91-92, 157-58, 203
NPS. *See* National Park Service

Oak Island: and AINL, 5, 198, 216-17, 220; and Apostle Islands State Forest, 168-71, 277n16; and commercial fishing, 65; and deer, 160; and exotic species, 221, 223; and fire, 43, 160; and logging industry, 7, 29, 31-32, 41, 43
Oak Island sandspit, 216-17, 220
O'Brien Row, 106
O'Brien, John D., 106
Ohio River valley, 114
Ojibwe: and AINL, 54-55, 176-78, 184, 186-88, 199-201; and allotment, 47-54; assimilation of, 46-48, 53, 55; and BIA, 47-55; and commercial fishing, 61, 66-67, 79-82; and IRA, 53; and logging industry, 31, 47-55, 57, 245n59, 246n67; and Long Island, 6, 188, 199-201; mixed economy of, 61, 66-67, 79-81, 83, 100; and NPS, 54-55, 177-78, 185, 187, 200-201; and speculation, 48-49; and state authority, 13, 81-84, 89, 152; and tourism, 98, 100, 110-13, 152, 258n37; and treaty rights, 46, 54, 59-61, 81-84, 89-90,

163, 165, 172–74, 176–77, 191–92,
201–3, 225–26; and water-based recreation, 22, 175–76; and wilderness
tourism, 10–11, 164, 167–68, 191–92,
207, 218, 233
privatization of land within AINL,
197–98
Progressive Era, 60, 73–74
Public Law 280, 185–86
purple loosestrife, 221, 223

quantification, 78, 84
Quarry Bay, 36, 38, 209, 216
quarrying. *See* cut-stone industry
Quetico-Superior country, 153

Railroads, *33, 42, 94, 155*; and impact
on commercial fishing, 67–70, 128;
and impact on logging industry, 23,
29–30, 32, 41–42, 52; and tourism, 10,
93–95, 97–100, 110–11, 136
rainbow smelt (*Osmerus mordax*
Mitchill), 161–62
rainbow trout, 101, 103, 136
Raspberry Island, 5, 43, 57, 167, 214, 223
RCLC. *See* Red Cliff Lumber Company
Reagan, Ronald, 197–98
Red Cliff Band: and AINL, 54, 177,
184–85, 187–88; and allotment,
47–48, 50–52, 54; and assimilation,
46, 53; and BIA, 47–48, 50–52; and
economic development, 184; and fire,
51; and fishing, 67, 81–83; and IRA, 53;
and logging industry, 47–48, 50–53,
57; and NPS, 54; and railroads, 52;
and treaty rights, 54, 81–83, 187–88;
tribal council of, 177, 187
Red Cliff Bay, 83

Red Cliff Lumber Company (RCLC),
51–52, 188
Red Cliff reservation, 46–48, 50–55, 57,
98, 177, 184
Red Cliff Tribal Council, 177, 187
Red Cliff Unit, 177, 181, *182*, 188
red osier dogwood, 142–43
Rennicke, Jeff, 5
rewilding: definition of, 9; as management dilemma, 14–21, 25–26, 34–35,
44–45, 55, 58, 123, 210, 220–21, 223,
225, 229–30, 239n28; as narrative
for understanding environmental change, 9, 14, 16, 19–21, 23–26,
120–23, 147–48, 189–90, 192–93,
218, 227, 233; other definitions of,
236n7; process of, 9, 18, 140–46, 150,
165–66, 218; and removal of cultural
resources, 120–23, 220–21, 229; and
significance of rewilding landscapes,
148, 223–24, 233; and state authority,
13–14, 17–18, 20–21, 25–26, 34–35,
44–45, 55, 58, 74, 120–22, 165–66, 190,
206–30 passim
roads: and AINL, 153, 181, 202–3; and
tourism, 11, 110–13, 181
Rocky Island, *159*; and AINL, 5, 8, 201,
203–4, 206, 212, 216, 219, 227; and
commercial fishing, 8, 65, 69, 87, 92,
157, 163; and deer, 157–58, 160–61, 167;
and exotic species, 223; and fire, 43,
160; and logging industry, 43; and
tourism, 91–92, 157–58
Rocky Island Air Haven, 91–92, 118, 157,
203, 212
Roosevelt, Theodore, 97
Ross, Hamilton Nelson, 107
Roth, Filibert, 50

Rudd, Charles, 31
rural zoning, *115*, 116–18, 173

S. L. Boutin Fish Company, 131, 138, 140
Salmon, Edward P., 106
Sand Island, *64*, *68*, 119–48 passim, *121*,
   125, *129*, *137*, *144*; and AINL, 5, 8,
   120–23, 149, 178–79, 181, 184, 193–98,
   201–2, 204, 209, 214, 216, 219, 221,
   226–29; and commercial fishing, 65,
   124–26, 128–32, 135; early history of,
   124–27; economic patterns of, 124–41,
   157, 163, 194–95, 262n20; and exotic
   species, 221, 223; and fire, 43; and
   growth of community, 124, 126–30,
   136–38; and landscape change, 126–
   27, 129–31, 134, 142–47; and logging
   industry, 43, 126, 134–35, 146; rewilding of, 120–23, 140–48, 166, 218; and
   stories, 119–20, 122–23, 147–48; and
   summer homes, 126–27, 136–40, 149,
   152, 178; and tourism, 96–97, 126–27,
   136–38; and women's work, 262n18
Sand Island Light, 57, 119, 126, 131,
   141–42, 223
Sand River, 102, 136
Sault Ste. Marie, 92
Schroeder Lumber Company. *See* John
   Schroeder Lumber Company
Scientific Area Preservation Board. *See*
   Wisconsin State Board for Preserva-
   tion of Scientific Areas
Scotch brown trout, 101–5
Scott, James C., 12, 60
Scoyen, Eivind, 208, 279–80n40
sea lamprey (*Petromyzon marinus*
   Linnaeus), 59, 161–62, 173–74, 217,
   268n20

seine nets, 64–65, *66*, 67, 80, 83
Sevona cabin, 216
"Shared Vision," 122, 228
Shaw family, *139*, *143*; Anne Mae (Hill),
   130; economic activities of, 124;
   Frank, 124, 130, 134, 143, 147; Josephine, 124, 143; and Shaw/Hill Farm,
   124, 126, 130, 142–44
Shaw/Hill farm, *139*, *143*; as cultural
   resource, 216, 226; and the Hills,
   129–30, 139–40, 142; and privatization of land within AINL, 197–98;
   and the shaping of environments,
   142–44; and the Shaws, 124, 127, 143;
   and summer homes, 141, 197
sheep sorrel, 223
Shenandoah National Park: and exotic
   species, 221; political advantage of,
   154, 156; problems of, 3; and wilderness management, 20, 208, 212,
   266n9
Sheridan, Charles, 152–53
Sierra Club, 122, 182, 198, 202
Sigurd Olson Environmental Institute,
   200
Sleeping Bear Dunes National Lakeshore, 212
Smiley, Chas W., 71
Smith, James, 71–72
solitude, 5, 219, 232
The Song of Hiawatha, 98
South Bass Trail, 233
South Rim, 233
South Shore Property Owners' Associa-
   tion, 179–80
South Shore Scenic Drive Association,
   181
South Twin Island, *213*; and AINL, 8,

Taff & Dunn, 29

Tanner Trail, 233

tanning industry, 31, 40–41

Tate, Andrew, 29

Thoreau, Henry David, 95

Todd, Kenneth, 169–70, 181

tourism, 91–118 passim, *94, 96,* 115; and
    AINL, 11, 150–53, 175–77, 180–81,
    183–85, 191, 199–204, 206–7, 209–10,
    212, 214, 218, 226, 229, 231; and Apostle
    Islands State Forest, 169–73; automo-
    bile tourism, 110–14, 138, 181, 201–3;
    changing patterns of, 11, 14, 93–98,
    111, 118, 136–38, 170; as industry, 7,
    10–11, 93, 99, 114–16, 152–53, 164–65,
    169–70, 181, 218; and legibility, 92, 114,
    116–17, 172–73, 189, 204, 209–10, 231;
    and lighthouses, 5, 22–23, 96, 126, 214;
    Native American participation in, 98,
    100, 110–13, 152; and outdoor recre-
    ation, 10–11, 13, 22, 92, 97, 100–105, 151,
    160–77 passim, 191–92, 201–3, 207, 218,
    225–26, 233; promotion of, 10, 93–98,
    113–14, 126–27, 136, 138, 160–61, 181;
    railroad tourism, 10, 93–99, 111, 136;
    and relation to other industries, 10, 12,
    91–92, 99–100, 107–8, 116, 140, 154, 157,
    170, 195; and roads, 112–13, 181, 201–3;
    and segregation from other industries,
    10, 12–14, 92, 104, 110, 114, 116, 118, 140,
    151, 173–75, 189, 192, 203; and the shap-
    ing of environments, 10–11, 100, 108,
    114, 126–27, 136, 172, 220, 258n37; and
    summer homes, 102–9, 136–38, 152–53;
    and wilderness, 11, 14, 151, 163–64, 167,
    172–76, 191–92, 196, 201–3, 207, 218,
    231–33

treaty of 1854, 46–47, 50, 81–83

Treaty of La Pointe (1842), 46, 188

treaty rights: and designation of AINL,
    46, 54, 152, 177–78, 184–88; establish-
    ment of, 46; and Indian identity,
    187; and legibility, 84; and resource
    extraction, 59–60, 81–82; restriction
    of, 61, 81, 83–84, 89–90, 101, 185–87

Trollers' Home Resort, 212, *213*

Turner, C. W., 79–80

Two Harbors, Wisconsin, 62

U.S. Court of Appeals, 188

U.S. Department of Commerce, 162

U.S. Department of the Interior: and
    AINL, 176–77, 202; and NPS, 208;
    and Ojibwe, 186; and privatization of
    land within AINL, 197–98; and Wil-
    derness Act, 205

U.S. Forest Service, 210, 259n53

U.S. General Land Office, 28, 124

U.S. Leather Trust, 40

U.S. Lighthouse Board, 22, 25, 57

Udall, Stewart, 176–77, *178,* 184, 208

Upper Peninsula of Michigan, 46

Vanderbilt family, 123

Vilas, William Freeman, *37;* and cut-
    stone industry, 38; estate of, 168,
    170; and forest fires, 39–40, 45; and
    La Pointe Agency, 49–50; and log-
    ging industry, 38–41, 135; political
    career of, 37, 243n30; and scandal, 50,
    243n31; and speculation, 36–43; and
    sport fishing, 102, 104; and Superior
    Lumber Company, 38, 49–50; and
    Wisconsin's tax system, 39–43, 243n35

Voigt, L. P., 172

Voigt decision, 188

Wachsmuth, Henry, 100
Wachsmuth Lumber Company, 55–56
Wakely Mountain Primitive Area, 123
walleyed pike (walleye), 100
Washington, D.C., 48, 152, 180, 197–98
Watt, James G., 197–98
WCD. *See* Wisconsin Conservation
　Department
Wehrwein, George S., 115–16
Wellisch, Gert, 120, *121*, 141, 148
West Bay Club, 137, 141, *174*, 195, 226
Westhagen family, 194–95
Weyerhaeuser, Frederick, 38, 104
WFC. *See* Wisconsin Fisheries Com-
　mission
white pine: and accessibility, 29, 34;
　exhaustion of, 41, 45, 50; and fire,
　40–41, 43–44, 51, 166; and forest
　composition, 7, 27, 33, 43, 146, 166;
　and lighthouse reserves, 146, 166;
　and logging industry, 7, 28–29, 31,
　33–34, 37, 51–52, 105, 126–27, 134; and
　Ojibwe, 46, 48, 50–52; significance to
　Wisconsin, 27
Whitebird, Albert, 185–86
whitefish (*Coregonus clupeaformis*): and
　artificial propagation, 75; collapse of,
　60–61, 68, 70–73, 77, 79–80, 85–86;
　commercial harvesting of, 62, 70–73,
　77, 85, 89, 135, 157, 250n28; manage-
　ment of, 60, 77–78; recovery of, 75,
　89, 157
wilderness: at AINL (*see* Apostle
　Islands National Lakeshore); chang-
　ing definitions of, 11, 15–16, 208,
　210, 279–80n40; and consumer
　society, 11–12, 151, 163–64, 206–7,
　229; debate/critique of, 14–16, 19–20,

123, 210–11, 223, 227; designation
　of, 7, 20, 55, 120, 122–23, 205–6, 211,
　225, 227, 229, 232; eastern vs. west-
　ern, 19–20, 231–32; as experience,
　5, 98–99, 171, 203, 210, 212, 214, 233;
　management of (*see* National Park
　Service: wilderness management;
　Wisconsin Conservation Depart-
　ment: wilderness management);
　and national movement to protect,
　11, 13–16, 120, 122, 151, 164, 167–68,
　182–83, 192, 200, 202–3, 205–7, 211,
　227–29; popular beliefs about, 10,
　39, 93–95, 192; as pristine environ-
　ment, 6–7, 11, 14, 19–21, 92, 109, 122,
　147, 192, 201, 207, 210–12, 214, 223,
　231–32; and "purity" standard, 211;
　and science/ecology, 9, 151, 165–68,
　182–83, 192, 209, 218; and stories,
　6, 9, 14, 19–21, 119–23, 147–48, 225,
　227, 230–33; and suitability studies,
　120, 205–6, 225–27; and tourism, 11,
　14, 151, 163–64, 167, 172–73, 175–76,
　191–92, 196, 201–3, 207, 218, 231–33
Wilderness Act (1964): and AINL, 183,
　205; and cultural resources, 226–27,
　230; and definition of wilderness,
　16, 210–11; and national wilderness
　movement, 168, 183; and National
　Wilderness Preservation System, 183;
　and NPS, 199, 205, 208, 226–27, 230,
　281n48; and WCD, 168
wilderness ideal: and AINL, 201, 204,
　206–7, 209–10, 212, 218; and land
　classification, 204, 206; and national
　wilderness movement, 192, 207;
　and NPS, 13, 192, 201, 204, 206–7,
　209–10, 212, 214, 230–31, 281n48; and

WEYERHAEUSER ENVIRONMENTAL BOOKS

The Natural History of Puget Sound Country
by Arthur R. Kruckeberg

Forest Dreams, Forest Nightmares:
The Paradox of Old Growth in the Inland West
by Nancy Langston

Landscapes of Promise:
The Oregon Story, 1800–1940
by William G. Robbins

The Dawn of Conservation Diplomacy:
U.S.-Canadian Wildlife Protection Treaties in the Progressive Era
by Kurkpatrick Dorsey

Irrigated Eden:
The Making of an Agricultural Landscape in the American West
by Mark Fiege

Making Salmon:
An Environmental History of the Northwest Fisheries Crisis
by Joseph E. Taylor III

George Perkins Marsh, Prophet of Conservation
by David Lowenthal

Driven Wild:
How the Fight against Automobiles Launched
the Modern Wilderness Movement
by Paul S. Sutter

The Rhine:
An Eco-Biography, 1815–2000
by Mark Cioc

Where Land and Water Meet:
A Western Landscape Transformed
by Nancy Langston

The Nature of Gold:
An Environmental History of the Alaska/Yukon Gold Rush
by Kathryn Morse

Faith in Nature:
Environmentalism as Religious Quest
by Thomas R. Dunlap

Landscapes of Conflict:
The Oregon Story, 1940–2000
by William G. Robbins

The Lost Wolves of Japan
by Brett L. Walker

Wilderness Forever:
Howard Zahniser and the Path to the Wilderness Act
by Mark Harvey

On the Road Again:
Montana's Changing Landscape
by William Wyckoff

Public Power, Private Dams:
The Hells Canyon High Dam Controversy
by Karl Boyd Brooks

Windshield Wilderness:
Cars, Roads, and Nature in Washington's National Parks
by David Louter

Native Seattle:
Histories from the Crossing-Over Place
by Coll Thrush

The Country in the City:
The Greening of the San Francisco Bay Area
by Richard A. Walker

Drawing Lines in the Forest:
Creating Wilderness Areas in the Pacific Northwest
by Kevin R. Marsh

Plowed Under:
Agriculture and Environment in the Palouse
by Andrew P. Duffin

Making Mountains:
New York City and the Catskills
by David Stradling

The Fishermen's Frontier:
People and Salmon in Southeast Alaska
by David F. Arnold

Shaping the Shoreline:
Fisheries and Tourism on the Monterey Coast
by Connie Y. Chiang

Dreaming of Sheep in Navajo Country
by Marsha Weisiger

Toxic Archipelago:
A History of Industrial Disease in Japan
by Brett L. Walker

Seeking Refuge:
Birds and Landscapes of the Pacific Flyway
by Robert M. Wilson

Quagmire:
Nation-Building and Nature in the Mekong Delta
by David Biggs

Iceland Imagined:
Nature, Culture, and Storytelling in the North Atlantic
by Karen Oslund

A Storied Wilderness:
The Rewilding of the Apostle Islands
by James W. Feldman

WEYERHAEUSER ENVIRONMENTAL CLASSICS

The Great Columbia Plain:
A Historical Geography, 1805–1910
by D. W. Meinig

Mountain Gloom and Mountain Glory:
The Development of the Aesthetics of the Infinite
by Marjorie Hope Nicolson

Tutira:
The Story of a New Zealand Sheep Station
by Herbert Guthrie-Smith

A Symbol of Wilderness:
Echo Park and the American Conservation Movement
by Mark Harvey

Man and Nature:
Or, Physical Geography
as Modified by Human Action
by George Perkins Marsh;
edited and annotated by David Lowenthal

Conservation in the Progressive Era: Classic Texts
edited by David Stradling

DDT, Silent Spring, *and the Rise of Environmentalism:*
Classic Texts
edited by Thomas R. Dunlap

Cycle of Fire
by Stephen J. Pyne

Fire: A Brief History

World Fire: The Culture of Fire on Earth

Vestal Fire: An Environmental History, Told through Fire,
of Europe and Europe's Encounter with the World

Fire in America: A Cultural History of Wildland and Rural Fire

Burning Bush: A Fire History of Australia

The Ice: A Journey to Antarctica